All You Need Is Love

All You Need Is Love

The Peace Corps and the
Spirit of the 1960s

Elizabeth
Cobbs Hoffman

Harvard University Press

Cambridge, Massachusetts

London, England

Bob Dylan lyrics in Chapter 2 copyright © 1962, 1964 by Warner Bros. Music, copyright renewed 1990 by Special Rider Music. All rights reserved. International copyright secured. Reprinted by permission.

Library of Congress Cataloging-in-Publication Data
Cobbs Hoffman, Elizabeth.
All you need is love : the Peace Corps and the spirit of the 1960s /
Elizabeth Cobbs Hoffman.
p. cm.
Includes bibliographical references and index.
ISBN 0-674-01635-1 (cloth)
ISBN 0-674-00380-2 (pbk.)
1. Peace Corps (U.S.)—History. I. Title.
HC60.5.C626 1998
361.6—DC21 97-42648

For Gregory and Victoria Shelby,
who did not volunteer to be my children,
but who have been truly wonderful at it

Acknowledgments

———————— ✸ ————————

A book is written by one person but shaped by many. For their help I would like to thank the staffs of the many libraries and archives whose holdings I consulted. I am also grateful to the following institutions, whose financial support made it possible to do research on three continents: the Woodrow Wilson International Center for Scholars, the John F. Kennedy Library Foundation, and the Arnold and Lois Graves Fund. I owe a special debt to the University of San Diego College of Arts and Sciences, which generously supported this research for four years and then gave me a sabbatical leave to make it into a book. Patrick Drinan and James Gump, particularly, gave their help at every turn.

This book is based on oral histories as well as on manuscript collections, and I wish to acknowledge the individuals who gave freely of their time in interviews. In the United States I thank Joseph Blatchford, Richard Boone, George Carter, William Delano, Jack Hogan, Harriet Lancaster, Frank Mankiewicz, Bill Moyers, Charles Peters, Sargent Shriver, and Warren Wiggins. In Canada I am grateful to Lyse Blanchard, Ian Smillie, and Keith Spicer. In England I was assisted by Dick Bird, Graham Bray, Alec Dickson, Mora Dickson, Myra Green, and John Nurse. In the Netherlands I am grateful to Bert Barten, W. A. Erath, P. B. M. Knoope, Ton Nijzink, and Yvonne van Vliet. In France I was helped generously by Benôit Chadanet, Lucien Cousin, and Catherine de Loeper, and in Switzerland by Michael von Schenk. In Ghana I wish to thank K. B. Asante, George Ayi-Bonte, Kojo Botsio, Frank Essien, Komla Gbedemah, Kwame Gyeke, and Alex Tettey-Enyo. For their time and assistance I also wish to acknowledge Akira Takahashi of the Japan Overseas Cooperation Volunteers and Volkmar Becker of Deutscher Entwicklungsdienst. Finally, I am deeply appreciative of the Radley and Crozier families for sharing their sons' lives with me.

Many colleagues saved me from errors of fact and interpretation by their willingness to give careful attention to this manuscript in its many guises. I particularly wish to thank Brian Balogh, David Kennedy, Thomas Paterson, Bruce Schulman, William O. Walker III, and Louis Warren for their friendship and help. Joyce Seltzer, my editor at Harvard University Press, gave invaluable advice. Barbara and Alan Finberg and Lois and Cliff Mansfield did much to make my research travels to New York and Washington feasible and fun. To my friend and informal editor of many years, Leon Nower, many thanks are owed. Finally, my husband, Daniel Hoffman, entered into the subject of the Peace Corps as my companion and made the journey a joy. I am deeply grateful for his enthusiasm and support.

Contents

———— ✳ ————

Illustrations follow p. 130.

All You Need Is Love

Prologue

———— ❂ ————

I was present at the creation, when the bright flame
of conviction took hold in the imagination of the
country and the Peace Corps became a promise fulfilled.

BILL MOYERS

At its inception the Peace Corps told Americans what was best about their country and about the 1960s: the promise of youth, the New Frontier envisioned by John F. Kennedy, the humanitarian impulses of the United States, the pioneer spirit reborn, and the persistence of America's democratizing "mission." The Peace Corps reassured a broad cross-section of Americans during a turbulent period that there was at least one aspect of their nation's policy that was indisputably good. It symbolized what America wanted to be, and what much of the world wanted America to be: superhero, protector of the disenfranchised, defender of the democratic faith.

The men and women of the Peace Corps spearheaded a generation that believed deeply in its potency. Their feelings paralleled those of the nation itself, which had attained overwhelming economic, military, and political power in the preceding two decades. As much as Americans enjoyed that power, it sometimes disturbed them as well. Imbedded in the nation's history was a recognition of the corrupting effects of power on political virtue. At its founding, the nation had rejected power politics in principle, if not always in practice. "Honesty is the best policy," George Washington declared in his Farewell Address, and he found this maxim "no less applicable to public than to private affairs." He warned that the United States should refrain from emulating geopolitical intrigues of the Old World type. The United States could guarantee its security and preserve its then-unique republican form of government only by staying as far away as possible from "European ambition, Rivalship, Interest, Humour, or Caprice."[1] But by

1960, two world wars and unparalleled economic productivity had interwoven the destiny of the United States with that of the rest of the globe and delivered into American hands enormous power for good or evil. The cold war that followed convinced U.S. leaders to build that power until it was so preponderant a force that none could best it. Sometimes this meant dealing harshly with opponents both at home and abroad.

Winston Churchill called it *realpolitik*. Having heard one sermon too many from U.S. statesmen on America's selfless intentions, he retorted, "Is having a Navy twice as strong as any other power 'power politics'? Is having an overwhelming Air Force, with bases all over the world, 'power politics'? Is having all the gold in the world buried in a cavern 'power politics?' If not, what is 'power politics'?" Yet Americans were not ready to admit to this characterization—even though their nineteenth-century history was one of expansion at the expense of weaker nations and their twentieth-century history was one of becoming an arsenal for democracy. The nation's statesmen practiced realpolitik, but only to protect a free world in which right, not might, could rule. If the United States could show that power in its hands meant an ability to do good for *all* nations—not just for itself—then it would have moved human history onto a new plateau altogether, in which strength and benevolence were joined: in John Kennedy's words, a New Frontier.[2]

Kennedy served as president at the peak of America's heroic age. Between 1940 and 1968 not only did Americans believe they were entitled to the moral leadership of the globe, but so did much of the noncommunist world. It was a position the nation had pursued since its founding. The Puritan governor John Winthrop had pronounced in 1630, "We shall be as a city upon a hill, the eyes of all people are upon us." In the seventeenth, eighteenth, and nineteenth centuries, American governments exercised their self-appointed function of role model for the world only passively, in what they hoped was an instructive illustration for other peoples. The Monroe Doctrine of 1823 drew a line down the Atlantic to distinguish between the "free and independent" character of the New World and the "essentially different" oppressive systems of the Old World. Several decades later Abraham Lincoln eloquently reinforced the assumption that the United States served as an exemplar—imperiled, but testament to the possibility of "government of the people, by the people, for the people."

It was in the twentieth century, after more than one hundred years of domestic consolidation under a federal government, that the United States undertook as a matter of increasingly broad policy to shape, and not simply sway, the world outside its expanded borders. The foreign policies of both Theodore Roosevelt and Woodrow Wilson evidenced a desire to demonstrate actively the geopolitical power of the United States *and* its power to do good.

Theodore Roosevelt sent the United States Navy on its first grand tour of the world following his negotiation of the Treaty of Portsmouth. (The treaty ended the 1905 Russo-Japanese War and earned him the Nobel Peace Prize.) Woodrow Wilson brought arms to bear to "teach Latin Americans to elect good men." It was the Great War, however, that gave the United States its first opportunity for a central role on the world stage. Yet American participation did not earn it sustained international respect for the simple reason that, having won the battle, it retreated in the peace. Not until World War II, the subsequent economic rebuilding of friend and foe alike, and an unyielding decades-long military commitment to West European security did a consensus of support build for United States leadership of the globe. It took the loss of a guerrilla war in Vietnam to bring the heroic age to an end.

John F. Kennedy was widely perceived as the era's most attractive hero. A hero is not necessarily one who succeeds at his task; like Achilles, he might very well die in the attempt. What matters most is the effort: the courage with which the hero strives to achieve some noble goal. In the words of Joseph Campbell, "The hero is someone who has given his life to something bigger than himself, or other than himself." Events like the Cuban missile crisis of 1962 made the young hero's battle seem apocalyptic. Programs like the Peace Corps hinted at the day that would dawn if he won.[3]

Kennedy articulated the notion that for America to be heroic it needed a higher purpose than simply stopping the Soviet Union or building power for its own sake. Affluence and expansion demanded a counterpoint—something that would show the United States's ultimate intentions. This was especially critical since strategic considerations prompted frequent military intervention around the world in cold war "hot spots" like Vietnam. The Peace Corps sought to demonstrate the other side of American strength: its morality. After Kennedy's death, and as the violence in Vietnam escalated, this characterization of American policy would come under devastating scrutiny.

But the Peace Corps dawned on a sunny day in U.S. history. The new program appeared to represent pure altruism. Indeed, the fact that the Peace Corps ultimately had an evil twin, the Vietnam War, made its purity only that much more important. Because of its deep appeal to the country's imagination, the Peace Corps is perhaps one of our clearest windows onto the abiding tension in the United States between a foreign policy of self-aggrandizement and a foreign policy that promotes the values of democracy and peace. After the sixties, many people, including many Americans, would reject U.S. government pretensions to helping others as nothing but a cynical farce. Yet they would have difficulty explaining the Peace Corps. Even if one could accept that Kennedy and Johnson were callous, scheming men, one still had to account for the tens of thousands of volunteers—who surely were not all CIA agents or naive dupes.

The history of the Peace Corps thus offers clues to larger questions concerning the function of humanitarianism in U.S. foreign policy. Is humanitarianism real or is it a smoke screen for the most basic intent of policy, which is to fulfill the will to power? If it is a smoke screen, whom does it fool, Americans or the rest of the world or both? Why do Americans persist in thinking of their nation's mission—at least to some extent—as a moral one? Why did 150,000 citizens join the Peace Corps? Alexis de Tocqueville commented in 1840 that Americans were "fond of explaining almost all the actions of their lives by the principle of interest rightly understood; they show with complacency how an enlightened regard for themselves constantly prompts them to assist each other, and inclines them willingly to sacrifice a portion of their time and property to the welfare of the State." In other words, Americans defined altruism as self-interest—joining two terms that confound American policy to the present.[4]

As a result, U.S. presidents since George Washington have wrestled with how or if the nation should take responsibility for promoting the general human welfare. Washington debated with Jefferson and Hamilton whether he should come to the aid of the French Republic; Bill Clinton vacillated on sending aid to Bosnia and Rwanda. U.S. leaders have usually rejected altruism for all practical purposes, while continuing to pay it lip service through the notion of "spreading the American dream" or "making the world safe for democracy." But even the fact that these rationalizations are necessary tells us that humanitarian internationalism has a prominent place in American thinking that has been unusual in world experience. This is what one historian calls the "prism" through which Americans have seen their role. At the nation's founding, this prism reinforced a view of power politics as a form of "amoral national selfishness contrary to the principles of republicanism."[5] If and when the United States engaged in power politics, it became necessary to "prove" that it was never for selfish reasons. One might call the frequent resort to republican rhetoric "ideology," a more neutral-sounding term, rather than idealism, but I use the latter word because it conveys the felt values underlying the intellectual stance: the belief that democracy is "good" for all human beings, and that to promote it is virtuous.

Paradoxically, when the United States has been at its most expansionistic, it has been most subject to idealism. The exercise of power calls forth a compensatory impulse. The Peace Corps emerged at the height of U.S. military strength. One conclusion that might be drawn is that humanitarianism is a handy fig leaf for naked ambition. Another conclusion might be that, desirous of but uncomfortable with power, the nation is driven to find ways of convincing itself that its power is beneficial. Exploring this phenomenon might explain why the United States conducted the Vietnam War and founded the Peace Corps at the same time. It might explain why the Peace Corps suffered a relative decline when Americans were most divided on how and where to exercise their power. Although the Peace Corps was perhaps the most explicitly humanitarian means of foreign policy ever undertaken on a long-term basis, one can find glimpses of similar motivations in other policies, from Herbert Hoover's Commission for the Relief of Belgium to the Marshall Plan of the Truman administration to Lyndon Johnson's seemingly unexplainable offer to rebuild the Mekong Delta while he was destroying it. Power begets pretensions to altruism, some of which are never more than pretensions, but some of which express values latent in national culture.

Self-understanding rather than cynicism should lead us to acknowledge that the Peace Corps did at least as much for the United States as it did for any country in which its volunteers served. Nations construct myths about themselves, and whether those myths are embroidered by an elite or arise from everyday experience, they give coherence to the nation state. States, like individuals, operate mostly on self-interest, and internal unity is perhaps the state's highest interest. The Peace Corps, above all else, enabled Americans in the 1960s (despite contradictory evidence during the Vietnam War) to take pride in their country.

The historian Michael Hunt notes that foreign policy has a particularly strong role to play in generating national identity. Domestic policy, because it arbitrates competing interests, tends to divide regions, races, and classes. The ideology of foreign policy, in contrast, has "served to affirm the received definition of nationality, to override divisions at home, and to proclaim American virtue and destiny." From 1961 on, the Peace Corps helped the American people maintain consensus about the nature of their government. It fed what Bill Moyers called "the bright flame of conviction."[6]

Nevertheless, these convictions, especially the belief in America's ability to do good, underwent a severe trial in the 1960s. When Americans look back on what they did to win the cold war and what it cost them, they question whether humanitarianism has any place (in fact, has ever had any place) in foreign policy. If anything, the tension between wanting to do good and wanting to achieve practical political and economic objectives has increased. Many Americans are sorely tempted to discard the notion of mission altogether as self-deluding, not to mention unattainable. Yet Americans may find political consensus ever more elusive if they give up completely on what they see as redeeming aspects of national character. Traditionally, American identity has rested on European political theories of natural rights given a utopian spin. Whether in the Virginia of Jefferson or the wilds of Mormon Utah or the rolling terrain of Amish Pennsylvania, Americans have tended to believe that—as one Kennedy aide said in addressing the Peace Corps—"there is no basic inconsistency between ideals and realistic possibilities."[7]

Peace Corps director Sargent Shriver called it the "point of the lance." He meant that it pierced the armor of injustice and inequality in developing nations. But the Peace Corps also pierced the armor of America itself, going to the heart of the nation's oldest and deepest conflict: how to reconcile its republican idealism with its powerful ambitions.

During the Vietnam War many citizens simply threw up their hands and concluded that if the United States wasn't good, then it was bad.

The women and men of the Peace Corps mostly resisted this dichotomy as false. Such restraint tried their consciences. Many recognized the way in which their activities frequently accorded with the geopolitical self-interest of the United States and their altruism put a positive face on global interventionism. Eager to be morally righteous, they weathered moral ambiguity. A few volunteers ultimately broke with the Peace Corps under the strain, and many more potential volunteers stayed away in droves in the late 1960s and early 1970s.

Americans often have an unsubtle view of the world, in which the spectrum between good and evil is abbreviated. This makes the use of words like idealism, altruism, and humanitarianism problematic, because they are so laden with unrealistically positive connotations. Readers may interpret these words to mean benevolent acts taken with regard to the interests of others without regard for the interests of the United States. Unless "goodness" is unsullied by self-regard, it does not count. But as Bradford Perkins points out, ideals and self-interest are not mutually exclusive categories in foreign policy. "In fact," he says, "mingling is the norm."[8] The policy I examine is one that sought a meeting point for both the crudest and the finest national interests, from military security and the creation of wealth to fulfillment of the philosophical ideas of the Declaration of Independence.

But volunteers in the 1960s instead found themselves on a fault line. One part of national policy, especially concerning domestic matters, moved in the direction of "life, liberty, and the pursuit of happiness." The other side of national policy, most notably foreign policy, moved in the direction of sacrificing others' lives, liberties, and happiness to the pursuit of U.S. global hegemony. Peace Corps volunteers submitted themselves to the discipline of a government institution during a time of cold war. They operated within the limits inevitably imposed by this war. In doing so they stretched the capacity of the nation to accept the view that others' interests had a place in foreign policy, even if a small one, and enabled the humanitarian ideal to persist in difficult times. This ideal, as it turns out, was as important to America as it was to any other nation that chanced to benefit from it.

In addition to what the Peace Corps has to tell us about how Americans coped with their contradictory impulses to altruism and self-aggrandizement, it is also a window onto the spirit of the sixties. The young women and men who came of age early in the decade had

not yet experienced war, but they had been raised by a wartime generation. They knew it was up to them to prevent war in the future. They
had also been raised with a belief in perfectionism: the United States
was "the greatest country in the world." This view fed national and
personal vanity at the same time that it boosted a belief in the possibility
of implementing solutions to grave world problems. Many young
Americans read Rachel Carson's *Silent Spring* and vowed to save the
environment. They read Michael Harrington's *The Other America* and
vowed to help the poor. They witnessed white terrorism in the South
and vowed never to tolerate segregation again.

A parallel spirit was developing in many countries during this time.
Such a global wave of sentiment was not entirely without precedent.
Just as 1848 witnessed revolution and reform throughout Europe, so
1968 saw upheavals and demands for reform in much of the industrialized world. While the United States government actively championed
the Peace Corps as an expression of international altruism, private
groups in Britain, Australia, Canada, and New Zealand quietly pioneered in secular volunteering in the 1950s. And, after the founding of
the Peace Corps, most European governments as well as the Japanese
began volunteer programs modeled on the American program, yet built
upon indigenous foundations. Between 1958 and 1965, nearly every
industrialized nation started volunteer programs to spread the message
of economic development and international goodwill. The Peace Corps
and its contemporaries enabled sponsoring governments to shape world
opinion toward their nations. But these organizations also heralded the
emergence of a global grass-roots movement that directed its arrows at
racial inequality, poverty, and the rule of "experts" who had created a
war machine capable of ruining the planet.

The Peace Corps is thus perhaps the quintessential social reform
institution of its unusual decade. Indeed, what could be more "sixties"
than the Peace Corps, started by the man who was to many the hero
who began it all? Looking closely at the Peace Corps raises the question
anew of why the sixties happened. If we accept that this outburst of
reform was a global phenomenon, then we should seek its sources both
in the history of the nation itself and in that of the world.

Americans were neither the first nor the only ones to express altruism
through the act of volunteering. The United States was the first nation,
however, to incorporate volunteering into its foreign policy in an at-

tempt to demonstrate one alternative to power politics. The Peace Corps enjoyed the most generous government financing, as an expression of the United States' leadership in the cold war and the nation's willingness in the 1960s to use federal power to promote innovation. The sheer size of the Peace Corps distinguished it, pointing to what may be an American characteristic worthy of note: the preference for bigness, the impulse to create programs on a large scale in order to demonstrate that the activity they represent is important.

The story of the 1960s, one of the great waves of reform in U.S. history, has up to now been told primarily in the spirit of bemoaning its good intentions gone awry. William O'Neill noted about liberals in 1971, "Having failed to transform the human condition in a decade, they felt guilty and ashamed."[9] Much of what has been said about the Peace Corps since the sixties reflects the disdain felt on both the far right and the far left toward liberal reformers of that era. Some have criticized the Peace Corps' patronizing naiveté and the unintentional damage it caused when it tried to "wreak some good on the natives."[10] Domestic reformers in the United States were also notably attempting to wreak good on the natives through the Great Society, and these reformers had counterparts in most industrialized countries.

The Western volunteer movement had roots in a rebellion against mass society and in the widely popular existentialist emphasis on individual choice—coupled in the American case with a desire to recapture the rigors of the old frontier. The Peace Corps emphasized emotion and personal commitment as keys to social change, as did the civil rights and peace movements. "The Peace Corps is about love," said its second director, Jack Vaughn. But love operated within political limits. Emotional social activism sometimes did more for the helpers than for the helped.

This book takes its title from the Beatles' song "All You Need Is Love" in part because of the song's enormous popularity in the sixties and the way in which it captured the most tender hopes of the decade. But the title also evokes a fundamental tension within the Peace Corps and its counterparts abroad that exists even today. Volunteers recognized that "love" was not sufficient to change the harsh conditions of poverty, yet only an emotional willingness to share in that suffering persuaded many volunteers to keep getting up for work every day. And in some cases, the resistance of cultures to change meant that "love"—

moral support—was all that volunteers fundamentally could give. Some other volunteers, however, ultimately rejected the "love" or "solidarity" aspects of their institutions as subtly self-serving, and sought to hone harder-edged development tools.

The Peace Corps was an institution rife with the contradictions, creativity, hubris, self-delusions, and hopes of the 1960s, some of which were unique to the United States, and some of which were not. We should expect that much of the early history of the Peace Corps demonstrates the naiveté of the period. It threw young volunteers at the third world in the way the United States Army threw draftees at the Vietnam War—with approximately the same effectiveness at times, and with some of the same assumptions: namely, that American will was enough to enable the nation to prevail. But the hopes of the 1960s look less unfounded when one realizes the extent to which they were shared around the world, just as America's love affair with John F. Kennedy looks less foolish when one realizes that many other peoples had the same response to him. Only by carefully comparing the U.S. Peace Corps with those of other nations can we understand the relative effectiveness of the American organization, the broad historical currents that swept volunteers along, and John Kennedy's global effect.

This does not mean, of course, that our mental picture of Kennedy need reassume heroic proportions. Historians have whittled the man down to manageable size over the last few decades, documenting the frailties of his character, the timidity of his civil rights policy, and the sometimes aggressive character of his foreign policy. But we are still left with an enigma. The Peace Corps illuminates the Kennedy popularity that continues to mystify historians who know the shortcomings of the man in office so briefly.[11] At the same time we should remember when evaluating the Peace Corps that Kennedy did not create it alone. It grew out of popular demand.

The 1960s have prompted roughly three decades of denunciation or self-criticism by conservatives, neoconservatives, liberals, and radicals alike. More objective, and more global, understandings of this period are still needed. One outcome may be a better understanding of the ways in which the United States can appropriately express the humanitarian ideas emblematic of its culture, neither exaggerating the nation's adherence to them nor denying that they matter very much. Looking at the Peace Corps is a way to begin.

1

Love and Youth
in a Brave
New World

———— ❋ ————

One saw him immediately. He had the deep orange-brown
suntan of a ski instructor, and when he smiled at the crowd
his teeth were amazingly white and clearly visible at a
distance of fifty yards.

NORMAN MAILER ON JFK

At the pitch-black, frosty hour of 2:00 in the morning on October 14, 1960, John Kennedy arrived at the University of Michigan at Ann Arbor. He had just flown from New York, where he had debated his fellow-candidate Richard Nixon for the last time on television. It was impossibly late. The candidate had no prepared remarks. Ten thousand students, nearly half of those enrolled in the university, waited in the cold darkness. When the parade of convertibles finally pulled up, directly into the throng, impatient fans climbed over the hoods of parked cars to get a better look. They chanted Kennedy's name as he went up the steps of the student union building.[1]

Pleased at this reception, John Kennedy extemporaneously challenged the students to undertake the adventure of a lifetime. "How many of you are willing to spend ten years in Africa or Latin America or Asia working for the United States and working for freedom? How many of you who are going to be doctors are willing to spend your days in Ghana; technicians or engineers, how many of you are willing to work in the foreign service and spend your lives traveling around the world? On your willingness to contribute part of your life to this country will depend the answer whether we as a free country can compete."[2]

The Michigan students took up the gauntlet, and a few weeks later presented the candidate during a short airport stopover with a petition signed by eight hundred young people. Alan Guskins, a student organizer, threw the challenge back to the attentive Kennedy: "Are you really serious about the Peace Corps?"[3]

John F. Kennedy won the election three days later by the slimmest margin in twentieth-century presidential elections: the votes of 116,550 people, barely enough for a middling town. Few college students could help Kennedy directly since the voting age was then twenty-one, but their enthusiasm lent excitement to the senator's campaign. Among adult voters Kennedy's choice of a Texan as running mate undoubtedly helped in the South; his adroit defusing of anti-Catholic sentiment moderated one of the chief obstacles to his election; and his October phone call to Coretta Scott King in support of her jailed husband swung critical black votes to the Democratic ticket. The candidate's frequent mentions of Africa during the campaign had not hurt either. Adlai Stevenson had been the liberals' first choice, not the more conservative Kennedy. Kennedy's talk of a Peace Corps and his repeated references to countries like Ghana helped strengthen his image as a liberal on foreign policy and race.[4]

But Kennedy also had something more. On the eve of the election, the novelist Norman Mailer framed the choice between Vice President Richard Nixon and Senator John Kennedy as a contest between the "psychic security" of the mass man and "the mystery of uncharted possibilities." Mailer questioned, "would the nation be brave enough to enlist the romantic dream of itself?"[5] Many voters decided not to make what was undoubtedly Mailer's personal choice. But an ever so slightly greater number chose Kennedy. At least some of them must have been swayed by Kennedy's ability to project the American myth "that every man was potentially extraordinary." This made him a hero, according to Mailer, "because only a hero can capture the secret imagination of a people."[6] Kennedy put it more bluntly after the first wildly enthusiastic response to the Peace Corps in Ann Arbor. He told an aide on his way to bed that night that he felt he had "hit a winning number."[7] It was the only new proposal to emerge from the close race.

The Peace Corps idea preceded Kennedy's interest in it, however, and volunteer work by private organizations in both the United States and British Commonwealth preceded the Peace Corps idea. Still, coming from Kennedy the notion seemed newer and better. The Canadian historian of that nation's own youth volunteer program later commented that "the idea seemed to spring forth—like Excalibur, shining resplendently in the hand of the youthful, would-be President."[8] In Britain and Australia, private individuals had already started programs to send volunteers to the third world, but they struggled for recognition. United States proposals to do the same floated about the halls of Congress, but attracted only a few adherents. It took Kennedy to launch what seemed a new voyage of discovery. The fervency of his language and his vibrant looks helped. So did Kennedy's willingness to place himself squarely in favor of international issues like decolonization that seemed morally right. But above all he was able to capture the imagination of the entire world because, after 1945, the world had more in common than ever before.

The historian Akira Iriye has noted that "nations like individuals sometimes use force to protect themselves and engage in selfish pursuits to enrich themselves, but . . . they also develop visions, dreams, and prejudices about themselves and the world that shape their interactions." These perceptions sometimes constitute a "shared consciousness across nations."[9] Between 1960 and 1965, nearly every nation with pretensions to international influence sent young volunteers to the third world. All of these programs aspired to harness the idealism of young people. Since these nations acted in highly similar ways, we must assume that they were affected by common cross-currents of belief. These beliefs flowed from shared experiences of war and revolution.

Missionaries, like the poor, have always been with us. Even before the Crusades, Christians went off to foreign continents to convert, uplift, or if necessary beat into submission native peoples. But in the middle of the twentieth century there appeared the secular volunteer. The secular volunteer movement had its roots in the decade following World War II and the decolonization of India. The first of these events, the war, profoundly shaped the character of the international movement, while the second, decolonization, provided its raison d'être. In the United States, domestic issues that had particular salience in the 1950s also laid the basis for volunteering by young people and shaped the character of its only state-run foreign volunteer program, the Peace Corps.

World War II shocked humankind. The physical devastation of large regions, the genocide and the concentration camps, the millions of civilian deaths, and the blinding atomic explosions that finally silenced the fighting—combined with the cold war that followed—all forced a reexamination of basic questions such as the purpose of nation states and the place of the individual in a mass society capable of mass destruction. Philosophies that emphasized individual moral choice and the struggle to create meaning out of meaninglessness gained new strength, as did efforts to reverse the world's destructive trends.

The movements to decolonize Asia and Africa, promote peace through international service, and legitimize conscientious objection began together at the onset of the century. Each phenomena spurred on the others. For Americans the conquest of the Philippines in 1901 saw the flowering of a small but influential anti-imperialist movement. One of its spokesmen, the philosopher William James, later made the first recorded appeal for a national service program as the "moral equivalent of war." Youth would be enlisted to fight the arbitrary injustices of "Nature" rather than other peoples. Not only would the world become a better place, but "unmanly ease" would be eliminated and "our gilded youths [would] . . . get the childishness knocked out of them, and . . . come back into society with healthier sympathies and soberer ideas."[10] World War I sparked additional anti-imperialist appeals. At Versailles, Woodrow Wilson campaigned for his Fourteen Points, five of which argued against the colonization of white Europeans by one another. Ho Chi Minh, who attended parallel peace meetings, argued for an end to the colonization of brown peoples.[11] His day, and that of Gandhi, would come after the next great war.

World War I also brought new attention to the problem of conscientious objection and to proposals for alternative service. Of the major belligerents, only the Anglo-American nations recognized a right of conscientious objection. The recognition was grudging, though, and granted only on religious grounds. In Britain, 6,200 men who objected on political grounds were arrested, and many spent two years in solitary confinement. Toward the end of the war, the Netherlands and the Scandinavian countries adopted provisions for conscientious objection.[12] Switzerland's most famous objector, Pierre Ceresole, suffered repeated imprisonment and was inspired by William James to pioneer the first international service camp to promote peace. He began in a ruined village near the bloody battlefields of Verdun. In the severe cold of November 1920, volunteers came from England, Switzerland, Hungary, and Germany to build shelters for the homeless. They were commonly assumed, like Peace Corps volunteers decades later, to be spies.[13]

World War II and the cold war spurred the decriminalization of conscientious objection throughout continental Europe and increasingly placed it in moral rather than religious terms. West Germany, which executed objectors during World War II, legally recognized in 1949 that citizens must be granted the right to "an inner moral conviction of what is right and wrong and the resulting obligation to act or not act in a certain way."[14] France decriminalized conscientious objection in 1963. President Charles de Gaulle explained, "It is absurd and undignified to let conscientious objectors be treated as delinquents." Under Lenin the Soviet Union had had the most liberal conscientious objection statutes in Europe, but Stalin eliminated them in 1939. All East Bloc countries harshly suppressed conscientious objectors, although by the late 1960s some allowed unarmed military service in "shovel brigades."[15]

The rise of secular conscientious objection paralleled the rise of secular volunteering overseas. In the European countries that exercised ongoing universal conscription, overseas development work commonly became a legal form of alternative service. Solidarity with "underdeveloped," decolonized nations also grew out of Europe's own experiences with cross-cultural work camps for postwar reconstruction. In the British Commonwealth countries, which drafted citizens only during war, and in America, where the thirteen colonies began legalizing conscientious objection in the seventeenth century, the ideas of peaceful service, individual moral choice, and opposition to war were just as strongly intertwined. During the cold war, this would lead to volunteer programs that sought to inculcate the martial virtues of self-sacrifice and self-discipline while promoting international goodwill.

Although influenced by the broad trends of war and decolonization and by a long history of voluntary association, the U.S. Peace Corps owed the timing of its creation to events of the 1950s. The political innovations of the 1960s, including the Peace Corps, expressed discontents that arose in the prior decade, some of which were limited to the United States and some of which had currency throughout the West. The United States' new status as a superpower manifested itself in an unprecedented level of affluence and influence. This wealth and power laid the basis for ongoing debates over national purpose, world unity, race, and the role of the individual in the modern world.

In the 1950s social scientists, novelists, theologians, politicians, and just about anyone in a position to ponder the state of the national soul feared that it was in danger. The crisis of McCarthyism had done much to exacerbate this sense. Book burnings, the purging of libraries, the hauling of respected citizens before the House Un-American Activities Committee, the besmirching of General George C. Marshall, and the eagerness of union officials, movie moguls, professors, and others to tear one another down in order to court McCarthy's approval all caused intellectuals to wonder where America had gone wrong. How had a nation whose first principle was freedom of speech come to be, in William Lederer's words, "a nation of people who are afraid to speak up on unpopular issues?"[16]

Some saw McCarthyism as a reflection of America's love of the demagogue. The sociologist Daniel Bell called for an "end to ideology" in the belief that ideology was the basis of fanaticism. The historian Richard Hofstadter saw McCarthyism as an example of the "paranoid style" of American politics, which he argued was as evident in nineteenth-century populism as in twentieth-century red-baiting. This paranoia about conspiracies against the "American way of life," and the demand for conformity it bred, arose partly out of the "status anxieties" that were felt most acutely by old Anglo-Saxon families on their way down the social scale and by immigrants on their way up.[17] Louis Hartz, another political theorist, explained America's "conformitarian ethos" as deriving from its early avoidance of a class-based revolution. Not having had to overthrow an upper class or root out its ideology of aristocratic rule, America was sublimely unaware that the truths it considered self-evident and universal were actually specific to its circumstances and even disputable. The United States, said Hartz, "refused to pay its critics the compliment of an argument," never realizing there was one.[18]

But as Hartz's broad speculations suggest, criticisms of America went much deeper than simply the question, "Why McCarthy?" There were many writers who traced both McCarthyism and America's diminished moral fiber to events much more recent than the Revolution. In a sense, the historian Frederick Jackson Turner had earlier set the stage. In his famous "frontier thesis," Turner defined the prototypical nineteenth-century American as a pioneer, self-sufficient to the point of being antisocial and democratic to the point of being unruly. The hardiness of frontier life, the demands of nature itself, had created a people for whom democratic "institutions" were the agreements they made daily among themselves. They acted according to their own inner values and best instincts, and took the consequences. Their isolation from Europe and increasing distance from the Atlantic Ocean made them carve their own paths and united them as a people. And in 1890, Turner asserted, the frontier had gone and with its going had "closed the first period of American history."[19]

It was not simply for the sake of colorful expression that John F. Kennedy called his program the New Frontier. Throughout the 1950s, social critics elaborated on the end of the frontier, even when they did not mention it by name. The frontier became a subliminal metaphor for all that America had lost. An untamed wilderness produced one kind of person. A mass, industrial society produced another. David Riesman, David Potter, William Allen Whyte, Paul Goodman, and many other popular writers captured this sense of loss and contributed to a compelling, unflattering portrait of the mid-twentieth-century American.

David Riesman saw Americans as "other-directed" individuals lost in the "lonely crowd." In the nineteenth century, scarcity and the obstacles of nature had produced inner-directed individuals capable of enterprise and self-reliance. But the successes of capitalism, more striking in the United States than anywhere else, had eliminated the need to strive against nature. According to Riesman, who became an advisor for the Peace Corps, "in a centralized and bureaucratized society and a world shrunken and agitated by the contact . . . of races, nations, and cultures . . . *other people* are the problem, not the material environment."[20] The need to get along and go along in the neighborhood, in the university, and in the corporation took increasing precedence over other skills. Reading clues about others' preferences, and modeling himself on them, were the preeminent characteristics of the other-directed man. Echoing Willy Loman in Arthur Miller's 1951 *Death of a Salesman,* whose highest praise of his alienated son Bif was that he was always "well liked," Riesman saw parents in mid-twentieth-century America as concerned not so much about their children's possible "violation of inner standards as about [their] failure to be popular."[21]

In 1954 the historian David Potter asserted that the central fact of twentieth-century life in America was abundance on a scale never before seen in history. This abundance produced individuals pampered by their surroundings, cut off from nature, reared by nursery schools in which all values were granted relative merit, and educated by Madison Avenue. Potter argued that America's one indisputably unique contribution to the world was advertising, the spawn of redundant productivity. Although it is not clear whether or not Potter realized what a low blow this was, his argument put a wicked twist on the notion of American exceptionalism. Winthrop's "City on a Hill" became the "Billboard on the Hill."

In its own more benign way, Potter's America was vaguely reminiscent of Aldous Huxley's nightmarish *Brave New World* (1932). The English writer foresaw a scientific dictatorship in which "the problem of happiness" was solved by breeding individuals who "love their servitude."[22] For Potter, advertising was one of the primary engines of social control. "If the economic effect is to make the purchaser like what he buys," said Potter, "the social effect is, in a parallel but broader sense, to make the individual like what he gets."[23] When Kennedy said in 1960 that the old pioneers were not "the prisoners of their own price tags," he echoed the sense that the dreams of modern man had been reduced to the search for dollar discounts.[24]

William Allen Whyte borrowed from Huxley's nightmare even more directly in *The Organization Man,* published in 1956. According to Whyte, Americans had essentially succumbed to the "social ethic" of collectivization. The premise of this collectivization was:

> Man exists as a unit of society. Of himself, he is isolated, meaningless; only as he collaborates with others does he become worth while, for by sublimating himself in the group, he helps produce a whole that is greater than the sum of its parts . . . By applying the methods of science to human relations we can eliminate . . . obstacles to consensus and create an equilibrium in which society's needs and the needs of the individual are one and the same.[25]

The only choice, Whyte asserted, was to "*fight* The Organization" and its "constant and powerful" demands for surrender to meaningless work, to a reverence for form over content, and to the idea that the interests of the individual and "those of society can be wholly compatible."[26] Whyte's appendix told readers "How to Cheat on Personality Tests." It foreshadowed the guerrilla tactics of the next decade.

The irony of this vision, of course, was that it mirrored U.S. fears about the nature of communism. In *Red Nightmare,* a 1953 Warner Brothers film produced for the Department of Defense, the gravelly voiced narrator punishes the protagonist Jack Kelly with a communist nightmare for his failure to participate in the voluntary organizations that supposedly guarantee American liberty—the Boy Scouts, his union, the Army Reserve, the parent-teacher association, and so on. In the nightmare, family members lose all allegiance to one another and identify instead with the state. When Kelly protests because a church is turned into a propagandistic museum, the jury of a show trial condemns him to death for his "deviationism." Kelly "wakes up," declaring that he will never again allow the lure of an evening in front of the television to turn him into a fair weather citizen. Although the dream world is communist, the film imparts the message that only the active expression of voluntarism and personal initiative can arrest the easy slide into a statism that tempts even the West.

The notion that the trend of modernity was toward the obliteration of individuality was not limited to the United States by any means, as the writings of Huxley, H. G. Wells, and George Orwell attest. The Western world as a whole had come a long way since the nineteenth century's faith in progress had culminated in technophilic novels like Edward Bellamy's *Looking Backward,* published in 1888. The finest minds had produced the greatest horrors. In Nazi Germany seven of the fifteen men who met in 1942 to plan the logistics of the "Final Solution" had Ph.Ds. The Hollerith data-processing machines with which they counted their victims were produced by a German subsidiary of IBM.[27]

In the United States, though, misgivings about science, bureaucracy, and luxury raised questions not just about the meaning of life and progress but about the meaning of America. Louis Hartz and David Potter both doubted whether America could fulfill the goal at the core of its identity as a nation: to be, as prophesied by the Puritans, a beacon guiding the rest of the world toward the fulfillment of its potential. By the city lights of the United States in the mid-twentieth century, that meant capitalist economic growth and democratic political structures. But, Hartz and Potter argued, the United States' historical experience and contemporary reality were far too exceptional for Americans even to understand other peoples, much less guide them. "Born equal" (according to Hartz) under conditions of "abundance" (said Potter), Americans had no way of appreciating the bitter struggles of the rest of the world. Blind to democracy as an outcome of economic well-being, Potter stated, Americans "condemn, quite unjustly, the countries which fail to establish a democracy like our own, as if it were plain obstinacy or even outright iniquity which explains their behavior."[28] For Hartz, the United States' "difficulty of communication with the rest of the world" lay in its inability to understand "nonpolitical definitions of 'freedom.'"[29] Americans had simply been too lucky to appreciate misfortune.

Historians of this era came to be known as the Consensus School of American history, and were later criticized for not acknowledging the deep faults of race and class that ran under the landscape of America the beautiful. But irony weighted their writings. Their doubts about the American experience were expressed in two parallel arguments. First, the transition from a frontier economy of scarcity to an industrial economy of abundance had resulted in a flabby, materialistic American imprisoned in a conformity he did not even perceive. Second, the United States could not act as a model for other nations because it did not share their experiences. These propositions placed the essential mission of the nation, as well as its ability to fight the cold war, in question.[30] They converged into a persuasive social analysis. Combine the need for challenging experiences where Americans could taste freedom and hardship anew with the need to understand the real lives of less fortunate peoples and one arrives at a powerful argument for the Peace Corps. As the agency announced to its first candidates, "The Volunteer must be prepared to lead a pioneer life."[31]

In 1958 William Lederer and Eugene Burdick wrote a novel that explicitly wove together anxiety over the national character with the perception that America could no longer communicate with less privileged peoples and was thus losing the cold war. *The Ugly American,* a

Book-of-the-Month Club selection that went through fifty-five print-
ings in two years, became a direct motivation for the Peace Corps. John
F. Kennedy, along with a group of leading politicians, sent a copy to
every member of the Senate in January 1959, and nearly every leader of
the Peace Corps would later call it the inspiration for his efforts.

Lederer and Burdick scathingly condemned American foreign policy
in the third world. They argued that every post of the foreign service
was filled with time-serving, self-promoting, luxury-loving bureaucrats.
These so-called representatives of America transplanted the abundance
they knew back home into "golden ghettos" in foreign lands where
they could live without experiencing even the smallest privations. They
viewed local peoples as "strange little monkeys" whose language was
beneath them. Local governments, for their part, viewed American
foreign service officers as "stupid men" easily flattered. Honest, progressive foreign leaders found the Americans maddeningly thick-
headed; Communists found them delightfully easy to trick.[32]

The heroes of *The Ugly American*, with the exception of one career
diplomat who is demoted for breaking rank with the State Department
"organization," are private citizens. They learn the local language, eat
the local foods, and initiate small, hands-on projects based on their own
homespun expertise. They reject racism, refusing to play the superior
white man. "It is not for me to say," Father John Finian responds when
local men ask him what to do about Communist infiltration. "It is your
country, your souls, your lives." The character of Homer Atkins, the
"ugly American" himself, has the ugliness of the mechanic—hands that
bear the "tiny nicks and scars of a lifetime of practical engineering." But
he is content not to be one of the manicured bureaucrats, and he
immediately finds his counterpart, with whom he shares labor and
profits equally, in a mechanic from the fictitious country of "Sarkhan"
whose "fingernails were as dirty as Atkins'." When the local mechanic
improves upon an idea of Atkins the ugly American and the ugly Asian
conclude the first "binding legal document between a white man and a
Sarkhanese." Race and culture supposedly do not divide "men that
work with their hands and muscles."[33]

The Ugly American portrays an America that can save itself, and in
the process the world, by rediscovering its frontier character under
frontier conditions. Lederer and Burdick's damning analysis was at base
amazingly optimistic. It reflected the conviction, still easy to maintain

in the 1950s, that American exceptionalism was essentially positive. "Just be yourselves" was the authors' prescription. Lederer and Burdick asserted that Americans were at base marvelous people whom the rest of the world could not "fail to trust and respect" if they only knew U.S. citizens as they really were in the heartland. Again and again in the *Ugly American,* the Asian characters claimed that if Americans abroad would only act like *real* Americans, as they were "in their natural state," the sheer force of American personality and sincere goodwill would be enough to "drive the Communists out of Asia in a few years." All the Americans had to do, according to these characters, was to "live life out here on our level." As one character said, "average Americans . . . are the best ambassadors a country can have."[34] It was a prescription for the Peace Corps, and for a war for "hearts and minds" in Vietnam.

In the debate over national identity, the Peace Corps became the preeminent response of the Kennedy administration because it seemed to give expression to the key attributes that supposedly characterized the real American, whose qualities were essentially those of the mythical frontier man described by Turner in 1893 and, even earlier, by Tocqueville. The real American labored hard, worked for the common good without sentimentality, and exercised his autonomy through private, voluntary initiatives.

But by the 1950s there was not enough "man's work" left to shape real men. Paul Goodman wrote in *Growing Up Absurd* that "organization" work was not real work—an assertion underscored by Riesman and Whyte.[35] Devoid of social merit or content, the organization relied on appearances. The "slots" that young men filled drained them of honest emotion. The work could never call forth "love, style, and excitement," because so little of it concerned tasks undertaken for their own merit. Americans would "get back" their country, Goodman argued, by giving young people jobs that met real human needs, by appealing to their idealism, and by respecting their rebellion against authority.[36] If the nation did not, the price would be high.

From the level of popular writing to the inner musings of the nation's elite, the question in the United States became how to save the materialistic man, who seemed more typical of rich America than of any other part of the Western world. Friendly foreigners perceived the problem, too. The British historian Arnold Toynbee, in an article that Sargent Shriver clipped and sent John Kennedy, stated that "America's present affluence has sidetracked America from the main line of the world revolution, and it has insulated her from the rest of the human race . . . Any effort to break down the insulating barrier is a service to the human race as a whole; and this is the ultimate significance of the Peace Corps."[37]

The notion that the Peace Corps could re-create America at its best would find expression in the way that the organization was structured and in the way that its founders and volunteers spoke of it. John F. Kennedy expressed this in remarks to Peace Corps staff when he said: "The Peace Corps, it seems to me, gives us the opportunity to empha- size a very different part of our American character . . . and that is the idealistic sense of purpose . . . which is very important and a real part of American character, and has motivated a good deal of our international policy."[38] The Peace Corps gave Americans the chance "to dedicate themselves to meaningful work worthy of free men," as Shriver wrote to the *New York Times*.[39]

The Peace Corps proved the existence of deep reservoirs of goodness in the American polis, its founders thought. "It is a part of the real 'other America' that exists somewhere beneath the tinsel, the neon signs, the racial hatred, and the poverty," Sargent Shriver wrote in *Point of the Lance*. "It is the America we are often embarrassed to talk about unless we hide it in the lyrics of songs."[40] In other words, it was the America that believed in its ideals and in the power of "love, style, and excitement" to accomplish them. There was, of course, an element of circular reasoning in all this: the "best" parts of America were the most "real," because at its most real, America was a good (perhaps even the best) country.

Also underlying the Peace Corps' immediate popularity was its appeal to a generational belief in the absolute necessity of universal values respecting the dignity of all peoples. In the words of two student founders of Canadian University Service Overseas—begun in the same year as the Peace Corps—"Our generation, born into war and its aftermath, has seen an increased awareness of . . . and concern for the concept of the international community."[41] The young and youngish people who started the volunteer movement were highly conscious of themselves as part of a postwar generation. Modern means of destruc- tion made isolation a thing of the past; world unity was the only alternative. Franklin Roosevelt's Four Freedoms—freedom from fear,

freedom from want, freedom of speech, and freedom of worship—
which he announced in 1941 as the founding principles of the "united
nations," heralded a policy commitment to universalism. This policy
expressed the increasingly popular postwar belief that all humans were
alike, wanting and deserving the same rights. The rise of universalism,
like the debate over national character, contributed profoundly to the
creation of the Peace Corps.

Universalism in American thought dated back to the Revolution and
to the European Enlightenment that inspired it. In the mid-twentieth
century universalism came to have practical existence. Reinhold Niebuhr, the influential writer and professor at New York's Union Theo-
logical Seminary, divided the adherents of universalism ("idealists") and
the adherents of national advantage ("realists") into the "children of
light and the children of darkness." In this century, Niebuhr argued,
technology had shrunk the global community, making universalism a
"technical-natural fact." The ancient origins of universalism, he said,
arose from monotheistic religions that proclaimed, along with one god,
the existence of absolute, universal moral laws, such as the Ten Com-
mandments. "The convergence of two forces of universality," said Niebuhr, "one moral and the other technical, creates such a powerful
impetus toward the establishment of a world community that the children of light regard it as a practically inevitable achievement. As always," he warned, "they underestimate the power of particular [self-in-
terested] forces in history."[42]

Niebuhr went on to claim that "the preservation of a democratic
civilization requires the wisdom of the serpent and the harmlessness of
the dove. The children of light must be armed with the wisdom of the
children of darkness, but remain free from their malice."[43] In other
words, they must possess the martial virtues of strategy and persever-
ance, but use them in the service of international peace. Niebuhr used
his pulpit to stir students to "protest injustice in the name of God and
human decency." He warned them to enter the ministry only if they
"lost the battle to stay out," with the result that by the end of an hour,
as William Sloane Coffin (a Peace Corps advisor) later recalled, "I'm
sure mine wasn't the only soul crying out, 'Take me!'"[44]

The 1940s and 1950s in America saw an increasingly explicit rejection of nationalism or even regionalism in favor of universalism, from
the person on the street to the highest levels of the government.

Roosevelt tried to combine "realism" with "idealism" by giving the United Nations a Security Council. The council became the practical realization of Roosevelt's "Four Policemen" concept in which the great powers would have enforcement responsibilities in their regions. He also steered the way to maintaining a regional sphere of influence (an updated Monroe Doctrine) in Latin America.

But Roosevelt's overall vision of the United Nations was nonetheless strongly universalist, and in the U.S. State Department, the universalist faction largely triumphed over forces that argued for a more regional emphasis. In the Grand Alliance, Roosevelt led the fight for the United Nations, negotiating for a universalist order against the unapologetic realpolitik of Stalin and even Churchill.[45] Nor did universalism attract only a partisan, Democratic following in the United States. Wendell Wilkie, Roosevelt's opponent in the election of 1940, published *One World* three years later, a passionate exposition of universalism. Dwight D. Eisenhower defended U.S. participation in the United Nations against conservative Republican Party members like Robert Taft who argued for a "Fortress America" isolationism. Each president in this period kept alive the ideal of equality among nations, even as he resorted to manipulations designed to make the United States first among equals.

On the popular level, universalism expressed the general revulsion toward the extreme nationalism and racism that had fueled the Nazi assault on Jews and Slavs. Universalism was also helped along in the United States by the widespread belief that American norms represented the pinnacle of progress and were self-evidently good, and that to encourage their replication around the world was not imperialistic, but in fact just the opposite. The historian David Hollinger notes that many Americans demonstrated an "extravagant universalism" based on Enlightenment notions that themselves were the product of particular Western cultures and that expressed a "covert ethnocentrism." But the demonstration was largely sincere and indeed more benign than the capitulation to national rapacity witnessed in Europe in World War II.[46]

Universalism played a central role in all the efforts to establish secular volunteer programs in the West. In the European context, this took the form of "solidarity." Beginning with the pacifist Pierre Ceresole after World War I, solidarity meant the active expression of the common humanity of Europeans against their own volatile nationalisms. Of his first reconstruction brigade, Ceresole wrote, "Let this work bear witness to the fact that there are constructive forces strong enough to wipe out the destructive forces. Especially that Germans and Frenchmen may be able to build together. To be brothers rather than enemies."[47]

For the British solidarity meant expressing universalism within the Commonwealth, which after 1947 had a multiracial membership represented by five white prime ministers (Canada, Australia, South Africa, New Zealand, and the United Kingdom) and three brown ones (India, Pakistan, and Ceylon). The original British and Canadian programs for secular volunteering were based largely on the idea of strengthening ties between the poorer and richer members of the Commonwealth. Most volunteers went to British colonies or Commonwealth nations.

Around the world as well as in the United States, much of John F. Kennedy's popularity sprang from his eloquent insistence on solidarity and universalism. The Peace Corps made tangible his assertion—contrary to those who believed that good fortune had made Americans too exceptional to understand others—that Americans were one with the rest of the world, partners in humanity's common struggle. "Ich bin ein Berliner" ("I am a Berliner"), Kennedy told the grateful crowds in West Berlin. "They think you're on their side," the president of Colombia explained to Kennedy when thousands of workers and *campesinos* thronged into Bogotá to catch sight of the young, Catholic world leader. Kennedy challenged American youth to throw their lot in with the developing countries of the world. "There is certainly a greater purpose," Kennedy asserted, than seeking "economic advantage in the life struggle."[48] Fighting for universal values and progress was that greater purpose.

Sargent Shriver spoke of "the indivisibility of the human community" and the "universality of men's aspirations."[49] Noting that Thomas Jefferson was only thirty-three years old at the time he wrote the Declaration of Independence, Shriver frequently made a connection between the youthful, Enlightenment generation that fought the Revolution of 1776 and the volunteers of the Peace Corps. Both, he wrote in *Foreign Affairs* in 1963, represented a "declaration of the irresistible strength of a universal idea connected with human dignity, hope, compassion and freedom."[50]

But fear for the American character and hope in the possibility of universal values or world unity were not the only motivators of the

Peace Corps and its counterparts. As W. E. B. Du Bois had presciently declared in 1903, "the problem of the twentieth century is the problem of the color-line."[51] For Kennedy, Shriver, and most of the other people directly involved in founding the Peace Corps, the distance between universalism and a critique of American race relations was very small, as was the distance between the Nuremberg laws requiring Jews to wear yellow stars and the Jim Crow laws of the American South. Race intruded persistently on the world's conscience after World War II. By 1960, according to the British historian Trevor Lloyd, "Racial discrimination had acquired the same status as a uniquely evil institution as slavery had done in the nineteenth century."[52]

For the British Commonwealth, the problems were largely foreign rather than domestic. For the United States they were both. Domestic racial injustices impinged on the nation's position as leader of the "free world."[53] The Peace Corps responded directly to the challenge of the third world that the democratic nations take the hand, literally as well as figuratively, of the black and brown peoples whom they professed to lead.

For the United States, the racial prejudice that World War II made seem immoral and that decolonization made outdated did not exist only "out there." Although black activists like Rosa Parks, Martin Luther King, Jr., Ralph Abernathy, and Thurgood Marshall initiated and sustained the civil rights movement, white liberals increasingly helped to magnify their efforts for public view. From well-known figures like Eleanor Roosevelt, Earl Warren, and Reinhold Niebuhr to anonymous white undergraduates who undertook the role of "witnesses" in Southern protests, non–African Americans in greater and greater numbers grew incensed over the unceasing violation of the law and "universal truths" on which the nation had been founded. Of all the black leaders, Malcolm X drew most directly on the Enlightenment tradition, citing the Bill of Rights and quoting Patrick Henry, "Give me liberty or give me death." World War II metaphors also surfaced in the struggle, especially for the significant numbers of Jewish participants. One college student told her worried mother, "If someone in Nazi Germany had done what we're doing then your brother would still be alive."[54] John F. Kennedy, when president, remarked to one of his aides that the television images of German shepherds attacking protesters reminded him of the Nazis.

The election of 1960 further heightened consciousness of race when Kennedy brought the subject of "Negro children" into the first-ever televised presidential debates and made the telephone call to Coretta Scott King that swung the African-American vote. Domestic race issues remained at the forefront of Kennedy's years in office.

Race issues also became part of Kennedy's foreign policy agenda. International criticisms of American domestic policies strongly influenced the emergence of the Peace Corps, which sought to show that America was not at base a racist nation. Peace Corps volunteers, unlike the bureaucrats depicted in *The Ugly American*, were the "real" Americans who could live alongside black and brown people in an atmosphere of harmony and justice.[55]

This view contrasted directly with the evidence before the eyes of the world, however. Americans would discover when they went abroad or when they listened to visitors to their shores that most of the decolonizing world believed that the United States was on the wrong side of the color line and making little attempt to reach across. William Sloane Coffin, who helped design the first Peace Corps training program, found when he traveled to Africa in 1960 that "Little Rock seemed to be the best-known town in America." Later that fall, when he invited a student from Ghana to speak to his Yale congregation, the audience received a friendly lecture on how "African and Asian diplomats are daily offended here in your country. Landlords refuse to rent to them, beaches ban their families, schools their children. Stores won't let them try on clothes." The speaker noted that African diplomats to the United Nations in New York had had such trouble finding suitable housing that the Soviet Mission had announced that it would provide lodging for them.[56]

The geopolitical result was to make desegregation "a Cold War imperative."[57] Within the first week of Kennedy's presidency, racial discrimination against diplomatic personnel made headlines in the *Washington Post*, as had occurred several times since the preceding summer. Secretary of State Dean Rusk wrote Attorney General Robert Kennedy that the problem was "deep-rooted" and involved racial barriers not only to housing but to "the easy and full enjoyment of the entire range of public and personal services such as restaurants, hotels, barber shops, and similar [segregated] facilities." Compounding the problem, one State Department memo said, was that "eighteen countries, sixteen of which are in Africa . . . attained their independence in 1960 . . . [and] are either in the process of setting up their diplomatic establishments in Washington or plan to do so in the near future."[58]

John Kennedy's immediate response was to create a New Nations Division within the State Department Office of Protocol. From 1961 to 1963 it was headed by Pedro Sanjuan, who lobbied realtors and restaurateurs. Harris Wofford, Kennedy's special assistant on civil rights, wrote the president following a trip to Africa that "Sanjuan is practically an American folk hero because of the word which has gone back about his help to African diplomats." Still, Wofford noted, many diplomats believed that they would be attacked by whites upon arrival and one diplomat from Togo even begged his president "not to send him to . . . the U.S. but to send him to Germany so that he would not have to risk losing his life."[59]

At the top of the Peace Corps' list of implicit goals was to show skeptical observers from the new nations that Americans were not monsters. Peace Corps director Sargent Shriver took his cue from John Kennedy's Cow Palace address at which, shortly after the speech in Ann Arbor, he had pledged himself to start the Peace Corps. That night in November 1960 Kennedy delivered a stinging critique of the State Department. Seventy percent of its new foreign service officers had no foreign language training whatsoever; it had neglected the newly independent nations of the world; less than 1 percent of all its officers were black. The Peace Corps, in contrast, would recruit volunteers from "every race and walk of life," train them to speak the languages of the people, and concentrate them in the third world where they would build goodwill.[60]

"The Communists are against the white man . . . [and] the white man has not always been just," an Asian character explained in *The Ugly American*.[61] The Peace Corps owed its existence and popularity partly to the fact that the Kennedy administration promoted it as an ideal way to give Asians, Africans, and Latin Americans personal experiences of Americans who were not like the typical "white man."

In addition to its appeal to issues of national purpose, world unity, and race, the Peace Corps idea fit with contemporary fears about assaults on individualism. The belief that individualism had declined with the end of the frontier helped to fuel the debate over American identity. But this concern was by no means confined to the United

States. The works of European existentialists like Jean Paul Sartre and
Albert Camus and moralists like Martin Buber, Paul Tillich, and Dietrich Bonhoeffer were widely read on college campuses throughout the
Western world. Christian existentialism, in particular, deeply influenced
the perceptions and choices of young activists in the American South,
some of whom became leaders of national protest movements.[62] The
Peace Corps appealed to Americans, just as their own volunteer programs appealed to Canadians, Australians, Germans, the Dutch, the
English, the French, and others because, in addition to everything else,
it gave rise to what these philosophers called the "existential act." This
act enabled the individual to create meaning through rebellion against
the forces of impersonality and to create morality through an act of
idealism. The outcome of the act was, in a sense, irrelevant. The moment of bravery and uncynical commitment counted above all else. Or,
as Camus said through the character of Dr. Rieux in *The Plague*, "All I
maintain is that on this earth there are pestilences and there are victims,
and it's up to us, so far as possible, not to join forces with the pestilences."[63]

The notion of the existential act was implicit in the Peace Corps,
from the Kennedy and Shriver emphasis on the act of going ("you will
be the personification of a special group of young Americans," Kennedy
told volunteers) to the organizational unwillingness to plan the volunteer assignment in detail lest such plans hamper the moment of epiph-
any in which individual meaning was realized.[64] Existentialism demanded that people should be treated as ends, not means, and that
individual responsibility and creativity be defended. The voluntary heroic act, undertaken with love and honesty, was the only salvation for
modern man and woman.

In *I and Thou*, first published in English in 1937, Martin Buber had
described the majority of human relationships as based on an "I-It"
dichotomy in which the only fully realized and recognized human
worth lies in the "I." The challenge of modern relations was to transcend the propensity to relate to others as "it" and instead to grant that
each human is a "thou," and "not a thing among things."[65] Tellingly,
when a group of students at Princeton in late 1960 asked a Kennedy
spokeswoman what the incoming administration was "going to do"
about the Peace Corps, she paraphrased Martin Buber. "I refuse to
accept the I-You dichotomy," she responded. Students must accept

responsibility for making the Peace Corps happen and not just leave it to government officials.[66]

Paul Tillich underscored the ways in which all human beings, even to themselves, became "things" in the context of twentieth-century life. "The safety which is guaranteed by well-functioning mechanisms for the control of nature, by the refined psychological control of the person, by the rapidly increasing organizational control of society—this safety is bought at a high price: man, for whom all this was invented as a means, becomes a means himself in the service of means."[67] Sargent Shriver, writing in *Foreign Affairs* in 1962, quoted world-renowned cellist Pablo Casals saying much the same thing and commending the Peace Corps for freeing Americans from the "tyranny of the enormous" and bringing them "back to a realization that the beginning and the end are man."[68] For the founders of the Peace Corps, the emphasis on humans as ends, not means, would be expressed partly in the organization's rebellion against attempts to define it primarily as a cold war tool rather than as an end in itself.

Existentialism increased a commitment to individual responsibility among young Americans. To deny a person responsibility (as in denying students their responsibility for the Peace Corps) could be equated with denying them their full personhood. For Americans, and perhaps especially for males of the period, existentialism resonated as well with the notion of proving oneself. Since the frontier was gone and since weapons of mass destruction seemed to make war unthinkable, other opportunities for acting manfully had to be manufactured. The historian William Chafe notes that many of postwar America's cultural themes "derived from the broader, philosophical underpinnings of existentialist philosophers and their followers. People as diverse as Humphrey Bogart, Jackson Pollack, James Dean, and Camus shared in common the image of trying to understand chaos . . . and find a niche for individuals who wanted to create their own freedom in a world increasingly controlled by structures beyond human influence."[69] One could add that those he mentions were not only diverse, but famous as well for their macho personas.

In the 1956 Warner Brothers' film *Rebel without a Cause,* James Dean was the quintessence of adolescent individualism and male yearning for serious purpose. But his attempts to find meaning in the world and to escape the emasculation suffered by his character's father (who appears in a whole scene wearing the mother's frilly apron) is perverted by the lack of anything to stand up for, except perhaps the class weakling played by doe-eyed Sal Mineo. The character of Jimmy in the 1957 British play *Look Back in Anger* similarly asserted with great bitterness that there were no "good, brave causes left."[70] Men without causes could not be men.

Albert Camus gave voice to the latent rebelliousness of the Silent Generation (as the youth of the late 1950s were called) in his 1956 essay *The Rebel*. Camus defined rebellion as the most authentic expression of humanity and individuality: "Its purest outburst, on each occasion, gives birth to existence." But for Camus, rebellion had to have honor, and he set a standard of high idealism to which many would aspire. The genuine act of rebellion reflected "insane generosity . . . which unhesitatingly gives the strength of its love and without a moment's delay refuses injustice. Its merit lies in making no calculations."[71] For Keith Spicer, a founder of the Canadian volunteer program, this meant giving young people the chance to do things "gratuitously worthwhile."[72] For young Americans in the late 1950s looking for causes they could define as their own, Camus provided courage. The Christian Faith-and-Life Community in Texas, which sent many followers to the civil rights movement, devoted weekend seminars to close study of the writer.[73]

Camus emphasized that the act counted more than the outcome, especially because it was all that the individual could control. We must "do what good [lies] in our power," says the priest in *The Plague*, in which Camus used bubonic plague as a metaphor for Nazism and by extension modern evil. Dr. Rieux, the central character, muses that there is no "final victory," only the story of what has to be done by all who "while unable to be saints . . . strive their utmost to be healers."[74]

Camus tempered the rationalism underlying Enlightenment ethics with the passion of the nineteenth-century Romantics. The Enlightenment philosopher Immanuel Kant had written that the moral act arose from the cognition of "duty." But for Camus, a Frenchman writing in the aftermath of occupation and collaboration, morality flourished in spite of duty. The duty of the soldier was to obey. The responsibility of the human was to rebel. The wellspring of that rebellion was emotion, not reason. "Rebellion," he asserted, "cannot exist without a strange form of love."[75] In *The Rebel* and *The Plague,* Camus managed to make love manly, idealism a form of survival, and social responsibility an expression of individualism. Similarly, the Peace Corps made it possible to be idealistic without seeming foolish.

"Words like purpose and commitment are used without apology . . . idealism is back in style," Norman Cousins wrote in a *Saturday Review* editorial for which John Kennedy sent the author a note of thanks. "The reason for it goes by the name of the American Peace Corps," Cousins told his readers. "Instead of dreary conversation about the meaninglessness of existence, students are now earnestly exchanging ideas about the different needs of communities in Asia and Africa."[76]

Creating opportunities for the exercise of individualism reverberated through the literature of volunteering. In a book on Canadian University Service Overseas written by volunteers, the reverberation became an echo: "CUSO has always felt that the key to success of the programme is the *individual* and that the organization should always serve to reinforce the role of the *individual,* rather than be seen as an overpowering and all-embracing benefactor. The strength of CUSO derives from its voluntary character as well as from its personal and *individualistic* approach in support of *individual* volunteers."[77] What the individual actually did was important, too, of course, and this gave a political overtone to the idea of the existential act.

World War II had helped to glorify the individual rebel. Throughout Europe, the United States, and the Commonwealth, stories of resistance became the morality plays of this period. In the two postwar Germanys, the one symbol of resistance to Nazism they could agree upon was that of the so-called White Rose movement of 1942, led by Munich students Hans and Sophie Scholl. Anne Frank, Dietrich Bonhoeffer, the Swedish ambassador Raoul Wallenberg, and the Polish orphanage director Janusz Korczak all seemed to represent what was best in humanity under extreme conditions. A generation later, the director of the first Peace Corps program in the Philippines emphasized about the young people he knew, "The single strongest unifying motivation of volunteers appears to have been the desire to improve the world as *individuals on their own.*"[78] Bill Moyers, who became Sargent Shriver's deputy director, noted that in his own early development as a seminary student the biography of Dietrich Bonhoeffer, "who had stood up to the Nazis," was "very important" in shaping his ideas.[79]

The sense of individual resistance as an existential act can be seen again and again in the literature of foreign volunteering. From an earlier era Pierre Ceresole, the first to give concrete expression to peaceful, nonmilitary service, was later characterized by his biographers as one who undertook "an existential act" and as "not the least of the great cloud of witnesses who . . . challenge us to run worthily the race which is set before us."[80] The Danish peace corps, Mellimfolkelight Samvirke, began as a resistance group to the German occupation and evolved into the country's foreign volunteer organization in 1963.[81] The German peace corps, Deutscher Entwicklungsdienst (DED), chose as its first director one of the few surviving members of the German resistance to Hitler. Canadian volunteers, quoting Camus in the first book written about CUSO, pleaded for the inherent value of "millions of solitary individuals whose deeds and works every day negate frontiers and the crudest implications of history."[82]

The Peace Corps and its equivalents around the industrialized world were remarkable for the way in which they revealed a nearly global matrix of ideas, sentiments, and perceptions, giving insight into how ideology was shaped by experiences in common. Governments had their own reasons for encouraging this movement, of course, and the United States adopted it as entirely consistent with both its cold war strategy and its domestic political needs. But the youth volunteer movement also had deep roots in everyday culture, as reflected in its borrowings from two other important elements of popular ideology: the themes of love and youth.

The most popular slogans of the 1960s, a decade that glorified slogans in the form of bumper stickers and banners, contained the word love: "Make Love, Not War," "Peace and Love," "Love, Not Hate," and so on. Hippies and antiwar protesters alike would attend "love-ins." Some thought to overcome racial discord through the power of love. "We were an army of love," wrote one white activist about the "Freedom Summer" of 1964, "and if we integrated Mississippi we would conquer hate's capital."[83] The novelist James Baldwin, in the letter to his nephew that preceded the prophetic essay *The Fire Next Time,* counseled the boy that the only and "terrible" solution to race hatred was love. "And if the word *integration* means anything," Baldwin wrote, "this is what it means: that we, with love, shall force our brothers . . . to cease fleeing from reality and begin to change it."[84]

Later in the decade female antiwar protesters would put flowers in the barrels of soldiers' guns and kiss their cheeks. When Jack Hood Vaughn took over the Peace Corps from Sargent Shriver he told *Look* magazine, "I equate love with commitment."[85] Two otherwise rather cynical Peace Corps veterans later wrote, "It never sounded trite when Vaughn said the Peace Corps meant love."[86] Che Guevara, the young Argentine doctor who fought in the mountains of Cuba with Fidel Castro, said much the same thing: "The true revolutionary is moved by strong feelings of love."[87] The sixties saw a resurgence of classical Romanticism, with its emphasis on feeling as a guide to moral right, which crossed all borders in the decade and mingled simultaneously with a renewed belief in natural rights as defined by the Enlightenment.

One expression of the power of love to triumph over evil came in the form of a popular children's book. Written by an American in 1962, it won three prizes for children's literature, made the *New York Times* best-seller list, and led to a series by the same author. Madeleine L'Engle's *A Wrinkle in Time* took universalism literally. The plot revolved around the efforts of children to save the universe from "IT," a giant brain that enveloped planets in darkness, transforming societies into brave new worlds. On these planets children skipped and bounced balls in unison, and if they did not they were painfully retrained out of their "aberration" by "Central Intelligence." Everyone was "perfectly channeled" and war was eliminated because people were no longer "confused and unhappy" trying to "live their own, separate, individual lives."[88]

L'Engle's young protagonists learned they were part of a cosmos-wide "grand and exciting battle" against the powers of darkness in which Jesus and "Schweitzer and Gandhi and Buddha and Beethoven and Rembrandt and St. Francis" had all been resistance fighters. When the brightest child of all is subsumed by IT, his sister is told that there is only one thing that can save the boy and that she alone possesses it. On the verge of losing the battle, she suddenly realizes: "Love. That was what she had that IT did not have."[89] Through the power of love, the universe is saved.

As a modern fable, *A Wrinkle in Time* worked to show that evil was not historically limited to particular political systems. It also tapped into the popular theme that young people would lead the way to a better world. The Peace Corps and its counterparts in other countries, without exception, began with youth as volunteers. Of course there were precedents. Among the most emotional images of the civil rights movement were those of young girls in starched dresses and shiny Mary Jane shoes clutching their books, terrified but facing down crowds of adults to enter white-only schools. In 1960, the year that Kennedy promised to found the Peace Corps, African-American college students in Greensboro, North Carolina, upstaged the adult leadership of the movement in "sit-ins" at segregated lunch counters. Colleges soon became the center of white support for civil rights, free speech, an end to the war in Vietnam, and other reforms.

John F. Kennedy was a generation older than the baby boomers, but he was young and stylish enough to become their hero. As a senator he drove a red convertible and married a beautiful photojournalist. As a candidate he attracted large crowds of young women who jumped up and down at his approach, swooning over him as if he embodied what one Southern senator characterized as "the best qualities of Elvis Presley and Franklin D. Roosevelt."[90] The youngest man ever elected president, Kennedy surrounded himself with aides and appointees mostly in their early and mid-thirties, including his brother Robert. Kennedy's victory and his emphasis on young people—to whom he spoke directly in his inaugural speech—promised to give youth a substantial role in solving the country's and the world's problems.

The presence of a relatively large number of young Americans contributed to popular perceptions. The baby boom that began in 1945 coincided with increased prosperity, laws preventing child labor, and federal funding of higher education to produce a greater distinction between adults and adolescents than ever before in the nation's history. While on the one hand this was supposed to give young people a chance to indulge in carefree fun, on the other hand it deprived youth of the opportunity to make the moral choices and undertake the serious work that gave meaning to existence.

Not coincidentally, juvenile delinquency emerged as a subject of fascination and concern. In the United States, films like *Rebel without a Cause* and *West Side Story* suggested that the lack of a meaningful role did youth no favors. Paul Goodman said that "growing up absurd" meant a choice: cynically resigning oneself to the depersonalizing "system" or turning to drugs and dropping out altogether.[95] Alec Dickson of the British Voluntary Service Overseas bluntly asserted that "with the prolongation of adolescence—through earlier biological maturing, and the extension of education to an increasingly later age—comes a postponement of adult responsibility that brings its own problems of frustration and cynicism."[92] Lacking a sense of serious accomplishment, youth veered out of control.

At the same time young people were portrayed as having the honesty to name what everyone else denied. Goodman claimed that "Beat, Angry, and delinquent behavior" had an "existential reality" much admired by young people who were not "phony." In words that showed intellectual borrowing from across the Atlantic, Goodman wrote: "The English Angry Young Men have specialized in piercing the fraudulent speech of public spokesmen . . . When a million Americans—and not only young men—can learn to do this, we shall have a most salutary change."[93]

The mystique of the youth culture paved the way for arrogant putdowns of those over thirty, but it sprang in part from the older generation's hopeful expectation that a "new generation" would emerge from the world so painstakingly patched back together after 1945. Mora Dickson, who with her husband Alec cofounded the British Voluntary Service Overseas, later recalled her own assumption that the postwar generation possessed an inherent internationalism and a distinctiveness that made it "easier for young people to communicate with other young people even across cultures and national boundaries than with their parents."[94] Similarly, Peace Corps staff members David Hapgood and Meridan Bennett speculated that "agents of change" under the age of thirty had a greater ability to intuit "the process of development, when their elders . . . find difficulty grasping it."[95] Last, as a practical matter, ventures like the Peace Corps had to rely on individuals who had the freedom to give themselves over to idealism and adventure, and this meant drawing mostly upon unattached, middle-class youth.

The Peace Corps appealed deeply to the imagination of America and the world because, like all powerful symbols, it was rich in meaning and because the charismatic Kennedy had elevated it for all to see. In-house critics of American society could latch onto it as an answer to the problem of flabby national character. Others could see in it an opportunity for expressing interracial solidarity. Still others might view it as an expression of global unity, or as an opportunity to take a stand as an individual against the "pestilences" of the world. Americans supported or joined the Peace Corps for many reasons, undoubtedly some (like the classic mountaineer) simply because it was there or because it was a way to get out of the house. Similarly, the Peace Corps and its counterparts abroad had meanings for the governments that funded them, and these meanings could coexist comfortably with popular ones because volunteer programs portrayed themselves as a collection of individual aspirations and efforts. Just as liberalism defined itself broadly in the 1960s, so did the Peace Corps. That was part of its charm and, ultimately, the key to the chameleon-like adaptability that allowed Sargent Shriver to sell the Peace Corps to both Democrats and Republicans. Appealing to the nation's oldest ideals and to its newest fears, the Peace Corps could credibly claim that its mission was America's own.

2

Shriver Hits
the Ground
Running

What most people, young or old, want is not
merely security or comfort or luxury . . .
They want meaning in their lives.

ROCKEFELLER BROTHERS FUND, 1961

In the early 1960s the generation whose parents had fought World War II appeared to crave a historical task of equivalent stature. The peeling away of colonialism from one-quarter of the world's surface seemed to provide such an opportunity. New countries more than doubled the size of the United Nations in just two decades. Most were small, poor, and stripped of resources as colonizers withdrew—but struggling to be free. "What FDR said to the American people in the 1930s, I say to you now," John Kennedy told them. "This generation of Americans, your generation, has a rendezvous with destiny."[1] The belief in humanity's inherent need for great meanings infused the Peace Corps from the start.

In all eras Americans have experienced conflict between their financial ambitions and their political convictions, between being the strongest and richest and being equal. The result has been a multitude of contradictions in both domestic and foreign policy. Idealism has helped Americans to live with these warring tendencies. Unwilling to part with either their prophets or their profits, citizens and politicians have long justified what are seen as necessary policies by reference to high ideals. Involvement in international power politics, especially, has traditionally called forth lofty idealism. The United States, lacking a place on the ideological spectrum that might countenance self-serving policies (accepted by many other nations as realpolitik), unable to justify its quest for power as anything but the fulfillment of the democratic dream (which it sometimes has been), has historically relied on its good intentions to purify deeds at odds with its liberal principles.

Some generations have needed great meanings more than others. After World War II, when the United States undertook to guarantee the security of every noncommunist nation on the globe even if it meant implementing the nuclear policy of Mutual Assured Destruction (appropriately abbreviated as "MAD"), idealism had its day. America would show that it could build as well as destroy. The Peace Corps promised that in spite of whatever the nation had to do to win the cold war, the "real" America, the America of its own intentions, would live on.

From his first speech as nominee, John Fitzgerald Kennedy had warned that he intended to ask a lot of the American people. The thrill that Kennedy sparked around the world came in part from his promise to take anyone who would come with him beyond the safe, the comfortable, the known—to high adventure in the line of highest duty. "The pioneers of old gave up their safety, their comfort and sometimes their lives to build a new world here in the West," Kennedy told the Democratic nominating convention. "They were not the captives of their own doubts . . . the New Frontier of which I speak is not a set of promises— it is a set of challenges. It sums up not what I intend to *offer* the American people, but what I intend to *ask* of them."[2]

Turning the rhetoric of campaign promises on its head, Kennedy evoked the paternal image of a man who expected the American people to live up to his ideals for them, rather than the reverse. (He was the strong father that "rebel" James Dean craved.) It was an effective campaign strategy that placed the voter rather than the candidate in the position of proving himself. Implicit in Kennedy's challenge was confidence in American greatness and benevolence. With rhetoric to match Winston Churchill's "I have nothing to offer but blood, toil, tears and sweat," Kennedy made the notion of self-sacrifice compelling. The theme awaited only a means of practical expression.

On November 2, 1960, roughly two weeks after his speech at Ann Arbor, Kennedy addressed a surging crowd in San Francisco's cavernous Cow Palace. Kennedy chastised the diplomatic service for its "ill-chosen, ill-equipped, and ill-briefed" ambassadors. The Russians, in contrast, sent out hundreds of well-trained technicians, doctors, and teachers, all of whom worked at the grass-roots level. "I therefore propose . . . a Peace Corps," Kennedy announced, using the future program name for the first time.[3]

In the few short months before Kennedy's inauguration, over 25,000 Americans sent letters to Washington inquiring how to join. A Gallup poll found that 71 percent of Americans favored a Peace Corps; only 18 percent opposed it. More people wrote to the president-elect's transition team offering to work for the nonexistent Peace Corps than for all the existing agencies of the government put together.[4] Reflecting the yearning for heroism, thousands more sent letters following the inauguration. "We are only as great as our ideas," one young woman wrote to Kennedy from Ohio. "Please don't let my desire to serve my country in a depressed area of the world be cast aside like a seed upon barren rock." A railroad switchman from Oklahoma pleaded, "Sir . . . let me help you fight communism as a National Peace Committeeman, or as anything." A Pennsylvania real estate broker predicted that millions of "men and women could and would endure considerable sacrifice to aid this world undertaking if only they were shown HOW."[5]

The "how" had actually been under consideration some time before Kennedy made his proposal. The Peace Corps idea in the United States had multiple parents, foremost of whom were Congressman Henry Reuss and Senator Hubert Humphrey. From 1957 on, these two had made speeches in Congress and on college campuses about starting a national service program to send young people abroad. Then, in 1960, both Humphrey and Reuss introduced legislation: Humphrey to start a "Peace Corps" and Reuss to fund a feasibility study for a "Point Four Youth Corps." (Point Four was the name of the foreign aid program begun under President Harry Truman.) Humphrey's bill never made it through the Senate, but the House of Representatives approved $10,000 for a study of the Point Four Youth Corps. The Colorado State University Research Foundation got the contract. It released its final report in May 1961, three months after Kennedy created the Peace Corps by executive order. Although the Kennedy staff borrowed from the Humphrey and Reuss plans, from the preliminary findings of the Colorado group, and from suggestions sent in by academics and admirers around the world, it was Kennedy's brother-in-law, R. Sargent Shriver, who gave the Peace Corps its shape.

The day after the inaugural, Kennedy called Shriver to ask him to head a presidential task force that would recommend how to fashion the new program. Shriver, who had grown up in segregated Maryland, earned a law degree at Yale, and worked as a businessman in Chicago, was familiar with America's many moods. Like his Kennedy brothers-in-law, his style was buoyant, self-deprecating, and hard-driving. With shrewd political instincts, Shriver had become a key assistant to the president on sensitive matters. During the campaign, he had advised Kennedy to call Coretta Scott King when her husband Martin was jailed. Immediately after the election Kennedy placed Shriver in charge of assembling a Cabinet. Shriver's success in recruiting some of "the best and the brightest" in the country (Robert McNamara, McGeorge Bundy, and Dean Rusk, among others) further increased Kennedy's reliance on his sister Eunice's husband. Kennedy's selection of Shriver to head the Peace Corps task force reflected the president's intuition that Shriver was the best man for a sensitive job.

Shriver in turn chose Harris Wofford, Kennedy's campaign advisor on civil rights, to help start the task force, which quickly drew on both men's backgrounds in cross-cultural ventures. Shriver had headed the Catholic Interracial Council of Chicago and had been to Europe three times with the Experiment in International Living, a student exchange program. Wofford had helped initiate a small volunteer program in the 1950s. Soliciting advice from the widest possible array of sources, Shriver and Wofford were soon inundated with a variety of plans, often in contradiction with one another. The economist Max Millikin of MIT, who prepared the earliest report at Kennedy's request, recommended that the Peace Corps start slowly "on a limited pilot basis" with a few hundred volunteers. Other experts seconded his cautious approach, adding that the program should be supervised by established agencies. These suggestions had little appeal to Shriver and Wofford, who kept testing the waters for a bolder plan.

It came in an unsolicited memorandum from two young foreign service officers, Warren Wiggins and William Josephson. They titled it "A Towering Task," borrowing a phrase from Kennedy's 1961 State of the Union message in which he had said that the response to the towering challenges of the noncommunist world "must be towering and unprecedented as well." Wiggins and Josephson realized that there were many small volunteer programs lending a hand overseas, including the numerous American voluntary agencies ranging from the American Friends Service Committee to CARE to the Heifer Project (which crated up and sent cows to developing countries). To merit recognition as a genuine departure in foreign policy, the Peace Corps would have to operate on an entirely different scale from that of its predecessors. Having promised a new dawn of idealism and self-sacrifice, Kennedy would look foolish, Wiggins and Josephson suggested, sending in a few young people led by the official foreign aid staff.

"If you want to succeed with an idea that may fail," Wiggins later philosophized, "you have to do something big enough and bold enough to overcome the critics." A small Peace Corps would never attract the political talent, legislative attention, and public sympathy necessary to its success. It would not have sufficient clout to solve the inevitable problems. Drawing on the analogy of the Marshall Plan (for which Wiggins had worked), Wiggins and Josephson pointed out that "history might have recorded the European Recovery Program as a failure [if it hadn't been] . . . started on a scale sufficiently large to enable the United States and the European countries to 'handle it right.'" The Peace Corps should field 5,000 to 10,000 volunteers the first year. Wiggins, who did most of the writing, tried to make the proposal "sing."[6]

"A Towering Task" was music indeed to Sargent Shriver's ears. Shriver opened the first meeting of the presidential task force on February 6, 1961, by asking everyone in attendance to take a moment to read the proposal. Wiggins and Josephson, previously unknown to anyone else present, became central to the organization in that moment. They captured in their statement the insight also noted at the time by Samuel Hayes of the University of Michigan, speaking of the Kennedy plan. "While the idea [is] . . . not wholly new, there is novelty in lifting to a much higher level and to a much broader scope a type of activity which has so far been carried on mainly by a few voluntary agencies, with relatively modest financing. The prospect of a major new governmental program, undertaken as a matter of national policy, is different enough . . . to account for the wide enthusiasm it has engendered."[7]

Sargent Shriver warmed immediately to the idea that the Peace Corps should do nothing in a small way. Top to bottom, the organization would reflect everything valued by Americans and their government: size, speed, change, individual initiative, and political point-scoring. To meet his goals, Shriver and staff had to accomplish many extraordinary tasks simultaneously. They had to devise a program while recruiting volunteers for it, convincing third world nations to embrace it, and making sure it met its own goals while helping to win the cold war. They also had to secure bipartisan political support while paving the way for future electoral triumphs of the Kennedy administration. Where to start?

Kennedy gave Shriver the month of February to develop a plan he could announce in response to the mail, polls, and editorials that continued to pour in. In the two weeks following its first meeting, the task force drafted, debated, and redrafted the report. The president called Shriver twice to see how it was coming. Twenty-six-year-old William Josephson, who was also an attorney, worked out the legal questions. He suggested to Shriver that the only way to start the new program immediately would be by Executive Order. Passing new legislation would take a minimum of six months, costing the Peace Corps all of the college graduates completing school in June who would turn elsewhere if Kennedy had nothing in place. The president should start the program with contingency funds ($12 million) from the Mutual Security Act, avoiding the necessity for special authorization.[8]

Warren Wiggins meanwhile fought for giving the Peace Corps as much autonomy as possible from its potential competitors in government and the private sector. Gordon Boyce, a member of the task force and the head of the Experiment in International Living, took the opposite tack. The Peace Corps, he asserted, should fund universities and private organizations (like his) to run the projects that were contemplated. The Peace Corps would funnel volunteers to them. Wiggins countered that this would rob the Kennedy program of the chance to exert a unique vision. Shriver led the way to a compromise by focusing the task force on practical questions. Where would the volunteers come from and where would they go? The final report to the president proposed a combination of types of placements, beginning with private sector organizations already in place overseas and ending with Peace Corps–supervised projects.

Shriver gave this solution an ideological justification that echoed the debate over national character: "The [entire] American genius for voluntary action and private organization must come into full play . . . This must be a cooperative venture of the whole American people—not the program of some alphabetical agency in Washington." Not to mention that it would be quicker to place volunteers in existing projects run by nonprofit organizations. But while Warren Wiggins did not win the battle he won the war. Within a couple of years, nearly all volunteers would work in jobs devised by the Peace Corps.

Shriver's final report to the president recommended semiautonomy for the Peace Corps, warning that otherwise "an opportunity for the American people to think anew and start afresh" would be jeopardized. "The establishment of the Peace Corps as a subdivision in ICA [International Cooperation Agency] would inevitably identify the Peace Corps with the public, political and bureaucratic disabilities which grew up in recent years," the report stated. The Peace Corps needed its own identity and power. Shriver, Kennedy, and most liberal politicians of their era assumed that power in the right hands (theirs) was good. Just as maximum power had enabled the United States to prevail in World War II, so would it in the cold war. Alec Dickson of the British Voluntary Service Overseas remarked of the Peace Corps mindset that it was "as though Standard Oil had moved in on the Quakers."[9]

Shriver further recommended that the organization be called by the name Kennedy had given it at the Cow Palace: the Peace Corps. The State Department warned that "corps" sounded militaristic and "peace" sounded like the Soviets, who had appropriated the word as their own. In what the German chancellor Willy Brandt later called "unparalleled propagandist effrontery," the Russians named the barrier built across Berlin that same summer the "Peace Wall." But Shriver could come up with no alternative as catchy as the president's first phrase. It was a name that "the public at large could grasp emotionally as well as intellectually."[10]

To get the report out, the Shriver team worked nights and weekends. Josephson later recalled, "The final draft of the Report was done with Charles Nelson sitting in one room writing basic copy, me sitting in another room rewriting it, Wofford sitting in yet another room doing the final rewrite, and Wiggins running back and forth between the three rooms delivering pieces of paper along the chain."[11] Scrutinizing the assembly line, of course, was Shriver, whose name would go at the top.

On Friday morning, February 24, 1961, Shriver delivered his recommendations. "Having studied at your request the problems of establishing a Peace Corps, I recommend its *immediate* establishment," the first line read. The report further promised that if Kennedy approved the program, "we can be in business Monday morning." Sargent Shriver's proposal was an urgent one: with energy, with passion, with commitment, practical idealists could change the world now. "For a moment," presidential assistant Richard Goodwin later wrote, "it seemed as if the entire country, the whole spinning globe, rested, malleable and receptive, in our beneficent hands."[12]

The president took hardly more than a day to consider the matter. On March 1, following Shriver's advice, John Kennedy signed Executive Order 10924 creating the Peace Corps on a "temporary pilot basis" until Congress could consider legislation. It was a political risk well understood by top Kennedy assistants like special counsel Theodore Sorensen and congressional liaison Lawrence O'Brien. Executive orders placed the president's prestige on the line, as they had since Franklin D. Roosevelt used one to sell destroyers to Great Britain at the start of World War II. The president had better be right when he infringed on the prerogatives of Congress.

John Kennedy took the additional risk of selecting Sargent Shriver to run the agency. Kennedy had previously braved charges of nepotism by appointing Robert Kennedy as the nation's youngest-ever attorney general. Time quickly vindicated the choice when Robert Kennedy led his agency into effective attacks on the Mafia and on segregationists. John Kennedy's choice of Shriver also proved astute. First, the president announced that his brother-in-law would work for a dollar a year, as a volunteer. Then Shriver himself insisted on Senate confirmation, which was not required since the agency had been established by executive authority, thereby demonstrating that he wished to be accountable to the American public and not just to his brother-in-law. With deference to political etiquette, Shriver helped pave the way for congressional approval. Shriver also had the very qualities that the Peace Corps would seek in its volunteers. At age forty-four, he was intense, creative, and still relatively young—a talented amateur. Consistent with the imagery of the Old Frontier, he had no special degree to qualify him for the monumental tasks ahead. But he had what the Kennedys liked to call "vigor." Central casting could not have found a truer type.

Executive Order 10924 gave the Peace Corps $1.5 million from the president's discretionary funds, along with sixth-floor space in the Maiatico Office Building across Lafayette Park from the White House. Sargent Shriver began assembling a staff on March 2, turning to the task with the single-mindedness he had shown in assembling the president's Cabinet. Stories abounded of talented individuals he tracked down in remote vacation hideaways or stole from other government agencies or talked off planes heading west, away from Washington and the Peace Corps. He became known as the capitol's most ardent suitor.[13]

Within a month Shriver put together a team from whom he exacted enthusiastic effort from morning to night. Shriver turned to the Ivy League for experts like the psychologist Nicholas Hobbs of Harvard, who helped organize the recruitment of volunteers; to the press for men like the prize-winning journalist William Haddad, who headed the planning division; and to politics for men like Charles Peters, a veteran of Kennedy's West Virginia campaign, who headed evaluation, and Franklin Williams, California's first black assistant attorney general, who became the Peace Corps liaison to the United Nations.

Other top staff sought out Shriver. Twenty-six-year-old Bill Moyers had pestered Lyndon Johnson since the campaign to release him from his obligations to go to work for the Peace Corps. Not only was the vice president reluctant, but so was the president. "He's the only one on Johnson's staff we trust," presidential assistant Kenneth O'Donnell told Harris Wofford. "The president's going to tell him to stay here, and you can tell Sarge to keep his cotton-picking hands off Moyers." Shriver, ever alive to competition with other Kennedy advisors, pressed for Moyers to be allowed his own choice. He was delighted when the president told Moyers to follow his heart.[14]

To Moyers, a Texan trained as a Baptist preacher, the Peace Corps moved in the deep stream of American idealism that had always flowed parallel to the stream of American opportunism. "In my Baptist church there was a continuing emphasis upon the importance of service, upon the value of commitment, upon expressing your faith in practical, realistic ways," Moyers later commented. For him the Peace Corps grew out of this religious experience as well as out of "the barn building myth . . . [the idea of] America as a social enterprise . . . of caring and cooperative people."[15] It was the definition of America of which Moyers wanted passionately to be a part.

Harris Wofford insisted on working with the Peace Corps, too, even though the president had asked Wofford in February to remain his special assistant for civil rights. Wofford was known for being perhaps the first person to suggest publicly that Gandhi's techniques of nonviolent resistance might be applied effectively to the civil rights struggle. "A young white lawyer of great vision," as Wofford was later described in the *University of Virginia Law Review,* he had made the suggestion in a speech at Hampton Institute shortly before the onset of the Montgomery bus boycott of 1955. In 1961, however, Wofford wanted to be more than Kennedy's liaison. He accepted the president's job offer on the condition that he be able to devote half his time to the fledgling Peace Corps.[16]

Shriver immediately organized a Peace Corps Advisory Board, drawing on a variety of Democratic luminaries including Eleanor Roosevelt and David Lilienthal. Reflecting the informal but strong Peace Corps connections to the civil rights movement, the board had a significant number of prominent blacks, too. The singer Harry Belafonte, Benjamin Mays, president of Morehouse College, and James Robinson, director of Crossroads Africa (one of the first American programs to send young teachers abroad) all joined the Peace Corps Advisory Board. Vice President Lyndon Johnson, whom Kennedy had asked Shriver to include, came on as chairman. Shriver initially wanted to invite the elderly Herbert Hoover, who first trumpeted "voluntarism" as the American way after World War I. But Shriver soon had good reason to be glad for Lyndon Johnson's larger-than-life presence.

Shriver needed all the talent he could get to organize a program that promised to field hundreds of young Americans within a matter of months in jobs that had not been created in countries that not yet been consulted. But even before this could be done, the Peace Corps had to face its first great hurdle.

In April Shriver traveled to Africa and Asia. His goal was to obtain the foreign invitations for volunteers that had failed to materialize by themselves through the good offices of the U.S. embassies abroad. While he was away, the president called a meeting to decide on where ultimate authority for the Peace Corps would reside. Shriver had argued strongly from the start that the Peace Corps not be made a division of the International Cooperation Agency largely because he did not want it to be identified with the very people criticized in *The Ugly American.*[17] The question was under consideration by a presidential committee when Shriver left, with no final resolution but with Peace Corps staff confident that as usual their charmed leader would have his way. The president, however, appeared not to have strong feelings about Peace Corps autonomy. Kennedy was also coping with the aftermath of the disastrous Bay of Pigs invasion of April 17, and had far weightier matters on his mind. At the last minute he left the final decision to special assistant Ralph Dungan, whom Kennedy asked to chair the meeting of April 26 in his absence.

Warren Wiggins was left to defend Shriver's position against the persuasive counterarguments of Henry Labouisse, retiring head of ICA, David Bell, the director-designate of the new Agency for International Development (AID), and a representative of the all-important Bureau of the Budget. Upon hearing them out, Dungan decided that the Peace Corps should be subsumed under AID. "Many if not most Peace Corps projects will supplement and enrich other government financed programs and projects and be dependent upon them for related technical assistance," the committee concluded in the oily language of takeover. Thus it should not be a separate agency with its own legislation. The Peace Corps would be a project of AID.[18]

Shriver was stricken when he heard. Pacing up and down in the 110-degree heat of New Delhi with a telegram from Wiggins, Shriver consulted with Wofford and his other companions. He recalled a conversation he and Bill Moyers had had with the vice president shortly before leaving the States. "Boys," the fatherly Johnson told Moyers and Shriver, "this town is full of folks who believe the only way to do something is their way. That's especially true in diplomacy and things like that, because they work with foreign governments and protocol is oh-so-mighty-important to them, with guidebooks and rulebooks and dos and don'ts to keep you from offending someone. You put the Peace Corps into the Foreign Service and they'll put striped pants on your people."

"This boy here," said Johnson, nodding at Moyers, "cajoled and begged and pleaded and connived and threatened and politicked to leave me to go to work for the Peace Corps. For the life of me I can't

imagine him doing that to go to work for the foreign aid program . . .
If you want the Peace Corps to work, friends, you'll keep it away from
the folks downtown who want it to be just another box in an organizational chart."[19]

The Agency for International Development, like the Peace Corps,
was fighting for its future. Kennedy had undertaken to reorganize the
foreign aid system, and the agency he created would outlast its predecessors (the Mutual Security Agency and the International Cooperation
Agency) by many decades. But in addition to a new name and a cleaner
organizational chart, AID had to show its many critics in Congress an
improved program. The Peace Corps, along with Kennedy's soon-to-
be-proposed Alliance for Progress, would be useful for giving foreign
aid a new face. David Bell wanted it.

With the committee process exhausted, Shriver hit on a last-ditch
maneuver for getting to the president, without seeming to appeal personally to his brother-in-law over the head of Ralph Dungan. Shriver
called Moyers from India. Harris Wofford remembered hearing Shriver
tell Moyers that before he "hung crepe out the windows," he should
ask Vice President Johnson to make one last personal plea to the
president. Johnson called Kennedy and asked for a private meeting.

The Kennedy-Johnson relationship was as complex as the men themselves. As a legislator, the Senate majority leader from Texas was by far
the more successful. As a person, the New England aristocrat-*cum*-war
hero was by far the more popular. It was not fair, perhaps, but it was
fact. As vice president, the ebullient Johnson became nearly self-effac-
ing. The Kennedy staff did not particularly respect LBJ's accomplishments and asked little of him in the way of legislative help. Johnson,
normally aggressive but in this context insecure, retreated further. The
president himself tried to be generous and even magnanimous toward
LBJ in public forums, giving the senior senator his due without giving
him the idea that they were sharing power. It may be, then, that the
Peace Corps was an ideal favor for Kennedy to grant: something
Johnson wanted, but nothing terribly important. Sargent Shriver returned to the United States to find that Lyndon Johnson had carried
the day. In that moment Shriver developed an appreciation for the
southern vice president unusual among the New England Kennedy
clan. Johnson, he declared, was "a founding father of the Peace
Corps."[20]

Autonomy had its price, though, and the euphoria of Peace Corps leaders about their victory turned swiftly into concern over getting the Peace Corps Act through Congress without the help of presidential assistants who were busy fighting for the AID bill. Eunice Shriver reported to her husband following a family conversation at Hyannis Port, "Jack feels that you and Lyndon Johnson demanded that the Peace Corps be separate and that therefore the two of you ought to get your damn bill through Congress by yourselves." A separate appropriation for the Peace Corps meant a separate fight. The president was not going to lay his prestige on the line twice. If the Peace Corps wanted its own appropriation it would have to go and get it.[21]

Bill Moyers went back to Johnson for advice. Shrewdly, Johnson told Moyers to have Shriver sell the bill "retail," approaching each member of Congress one by one. "You've got a great asset in Shriver," Johnson told his protégé, "No member of Congress will turn you down because it is the president's brother-in-law and they will know that that will give them cachet as well as access [to the White House]." Moyers and Shriver followed the master politician's advice to the letter.[22]

Over the next few months, Shriver and Moyers visited every member of Congress. "Sarge and I called on 535 members of Congress," Moyers later said, except for one who "was dead and we didn't call on him."[23] Shriver reported to the president that he often visited five congressmen before lunch. One ranking member of the House Rules Committee recalled, "One night I was leaving about seven-thirty and there was Shriver walking up and down the halls, looking into the doors. He came in and talked to me. I still didn't like the program but I was sold on Shriver—I voted for him."[24]

Shriver's personal enthusiasm, combined with his command of the materials that Moyers carefully prepared for the legislative assault, won converts for the Peace Corps in great numbers. Wisely, Shriver spent as much effort courting Republicans as Democrats, insisting at every step that "the philosophy of the Peace Corps really is the philosophy of America."[25] In addition to his in-person calls, Shriver frequently sent notes to representatives about volunteers who had joined the program. He made sure that there was at least one volunteer from each state and invited members of Congress to visit training sites in their districts. Bill Moyers set deadlines for replies to congressional mail, and staff who failed to meet them got the full effect of his Baptist preacher's indignation. The entire top staff closely planned Peace Corps responses to questions like "To what extent will or should PCVs [Peace Corps volunteers] be salesmen for the American way of life" and, "Does America really have enough altruism today to furnish PCVs in the numbers needed?"[26]

Shriver and his colleagues knew they labored under certain handicaps and took great care as a consequence. Foreign aid was unpopular with Congress, and the administration fought a losing battle for larger budgets. Ralph Dungan and others who had been outmaneuvered during the debate over Peace Corps autonomy turned rather cool. Gerard Rice notes, "Deploying Vice-President Johnson was considered particularly sharp practice." The embarrassment of White House aides deepened when stories of the disagreement reached the press.[27] The agency struggled along on its own with Congress.

At the same time that it was resented by some White House staffers, the Peace Corps also had to soothe the jealousies of Congress, which had not taken lightly the president's unilateral decision. In July Shriver wrote to Johnson asking for the help that he was not getting from the president or his aides. Congress was threatening to postpone a decision on the Peace Corps out of annoyance over the Executive Order. This would "seriously damage" the Peace Corps and "embarrass the president and the Administration politically," Shriver told Johnson. Johnson stepped in immediately and lobbied personally with Senators William Fulbright, Bourke Hickenlooper, John Sparkman, Mike Mansfield, and Hubert Humphrey. A relieved Sargent Shriver slipped Johnson a handwritten note expressing his "deep thanks and gratitude."[28]

The fight was not yet over, though, and only a few days later, on August 2, 1961, the *New York Times* quoted Senator William Fulbright, chairman of the Foreign Relations Committee, as advocating a smaller Peace Corps. Shriver wrote in desperation to Kennedy, telling him in effect that the time had come for their most powerful weapon—the prestige of the president himself. "Bill Moyers and I have been living on the Hill," Shriver informed his brother-in-law. "At this point, the Peace Corps itself has done all it can." A week later, shortly before the debates in Congress were to start, Kennedy reiterated to the Washington press corps his continuing strong support for the Peace Corps and pulled the agency back from the legislative brink. "I am hopeful that the Congress will support this effort," the president told the newsmen, sending a message to his former Senate colleagues.[29]

When it finally came time to testify before the Senate and House, Shriver had many supporters in the audience. In spite of opposition from a few leading Republicans like Bourke Hickenlooper of Iowa and continuing but muted skepticism from Southern Democrats like Otto Passman of Louisiana and William Fulbright of Arkansas, the Peace Corps passed. The Senate cleared it with a voice vote on August 25, 1961, and the House approved it by a margin of 288 to 97 on September 14. The fledgling program's efforts had been a model of how to get a bill through Congress.

The Peace Corps Act established three goals for the organization: first, to help interested countries meet their needs for trained men and women; second, to promote a better understanding of Americans on the part of the peoples served; and third, to promote a better understanding of other peoples on the part of Americans. Officially, these became known as the Three Goals.

The proposal that had come to life as a campaign issue, and had been dismissed accordingly by the party out of power, ended up being recognized for exactly what Shriver called it: the bipartisan image of America itself. President Eisenhower had initially said, "If you want to send Peace Corps Volunteers to an under-developed area, send them to the moon." (The New Frontier ultimately went both places.) But within a year many members of the Republican establishment had moved well beyond lampooning the agency to being some of its genuine admirers. Senator Barry Goldwater, the rising but unpredictable star of the Republican Party, told a group of Ivy League alumni in early 1962 that "the Peace Corps is beginning to remove the doubts from the doubters' minds . . . I'll back it all the way." Although the Daughters of the American Revolution passed a resolution at their 1961 Seventieth Continental Congress (by a vote of 2,600 to a very brave 1) opposing the Peace Corps because it would make "socialists" of American youth and remove them "from the moral and disciplinary influences of their homeland," the DAR's isolationist form of patriotism fell on increasingly deaf ears in the early sixties.[30] Pulled by the magnetism of world power, idealism swelled to high tide.

The Peace Corps patted itself on the back for its appeal to Americans of all political persuasions, but its cause was also helped by the donated services of Madison Avenue companies that executed the Peace Corps media campaign at the request of the National Advertising Council. Relying heavily on free public service announcements, agencies like Young & Rubicam gave the Peace Corps a name recognition that vied with that of Smokey the Bear. Free ad copy was sent to all national print media, all television stations, 1,000 radio stations, all college newspapers, and all major municipal transit authorities—which posted over 80,000 signs in buses, trains, and subways during the first year. The news commentator Eric Sevareid characterized the effort as "pure intentions backed by pure publicity." The result, Warren Wiggins recalled with satisfaction, was that 50 percent of Americans could correctly answer the question, What is the Peace Corps?[31]

Peace Corps organizers managed to override the trenchant regional divisions within the Democratic Party, whose fractures over race and states rights deepened almost daily. Senator Russell Long of Louisiana publicly defended the Peace Corps, chastising those who would ridicule it and calling their cynicism "shameful." In their sophisticated campaigns, the Young & Rubicam advertising agency, together with Shriver and Company, had done much to establish the Peace Corps as a cultural icon and a beacon for the American consensus.[32] It would be a decade before the Peace Corps had to fight for its basic appropriation again.

Meanwhile, the internal structure and organizational culture of the Peace Corps blossomed like time-lapse photography. The organization had many elements, not the least of which was glamour. But three emphases emerged immediately: democracy, individualism, and reform. These characteristics typified not just the Peace Corps but the whole generation.

With an authority that grew more from personality than from position, Sargent Shriver set out to create an organization that leveled hierarchical distinctions and honed democratic instincts. He encouraged intimacy. Staff and volunteers called him "Sarge." He phoned people at their homes and on occasion whisked them away to his. He posted mottoes on his office door, notes that suggested humor and an informal dialogue with everyone from secretaries to presidential aides. "Nice guys finish last" and "good guys don't win ballgames," they warned—the "Standard Oil" side of the Peace Corps personality teasing the "Quaker" side. Himself a novice at government, Shriver gloried in what amateurs could do and he respected the right of everyone to have a say.

The civil rights movement, with which Shriver was well acquainted and which set the standards for reform activity, had gotten its impetus from the bottom up. Ordinary people were restructuring America. And even the civil rights movement would be restructured in the course of time as younger, nonclergy members demanded consensus decision making and refused to defer to the church and to adults. The college and high school students who took to the front lines of social change created an authority for themselves that grew out of their bravery and willingness to take risks. Perhaps one of Martin Luther King's most unusual pastoral attributes was his willingness, like Shriver, to grant the young their due when many others of his own generation would not.[33]

Springing from the "same seed" as the civil rights movement, as Shriver put it, the Peace Corps created specific structures that challenged authority.[34] Shriver encouraged his staff to rebut one another's points of view. Most specifically, he created an Evaluation Division headed by the journalist Charles Peters that was infamous for its scathing critiques. Peters brought journalists, academics, and social scientists from outside government to visit each Peace Corps country and program annually for two to three weeks. To a person, they were unhesitating in their willingness to be hypercritical of the young agency. When returned volunteers were recruited by the Evaluation Division after 1963, at Shriver's suggestion, they were especially eager to perfect the program and lambaste former bosses.

Evaluators quickly honed in on a problem that Peters called "phony jobs." Sargent Shriver wanted the program to start out on as large a scale as possible and to grow quickly from there. Before the Peace Corps was a month old, Shriver gave his staff the amazing directive to have volunteers ready to begin training for Tanganyika within two weeks, the Philippines within three weeks, and Nigeria within four weeks. In the case of Tanganyika this meant finding, interviewing, testing, selecting, and setting up a training program for thirty-five men in ten working days. Although spurred by the president, Shriver also acted on his own hunch that size and speed would earn admiration for the spunk of the Peace Corps. In the logic of booming government, an agency could not be important without being big. Shriver set in motion plans to put over 650 volunteers in the field by January 1962.[35]

As a result, the Peace Corps gave some countries far more volunteers than they could absorb. Staff members Kevin Lowther and Payne Lucas later lamented, "The Brazil program quadrupled to 545 volunteers within one year; India grew by almost 1,000 in a year's time; the Philippines reached 620 in its first year; nearly 600 were scattered among the Micronesian Islands in a period of months; and 350 poured into Bolivia in 1964, where an evaluator warned prophetically that 'there is a real limit to the number of volunteers a poor country with a relatively small administration can use.'"[36]

In some cases neither the receiving countries nor the Peace Corps could readily figure out ways to channel the volunteers' contribution. Nations whose needs were clear to themselves, and who wanted the kinds of skills the Peace Corps could offer, made good use of the young Americans. Malaysia and Ghana had the best programs initially, Charles Peters found. But in a country like Pakistan, where Peters estimated that only sixteen out of sixty-one volunteers had serious jobs, the Peace Corps seemed a cruel joke—especially to the young people who had committed two years of their life to it. In the Philippines, where there was an oversupply of qualified local teachers, hundreds of volunteers were sent as teachers' aides and ended up doing petty instructional tasks, much of it make-work. A staff member of the Canadian volunteer program who visited Jamaica in 1964 reported that the PCVs he met "indicated that as far as they were concerned their only job description was to inflate volleyballs at 9 o'clock in the morning, and deflate them at 5:30."[37]

Angry volunteers and staff called it the "numbers game," bigness for its own sake and to impress Congress, with little thought given to the consequences of overexpansion. Shriver read closely Peters's controversial reports, which were circulated throughout the Washington staff, and he fired the entire overseas staff for Pakistan. Peters himself, whose biting evaluations between 1962 and 1967 frequently provoked fury from those he criticized (who felt they were doing their best under difficult circumstances), came more than once "within an inch of being fired."[38] Shriver certainly wanted the kinds of reports that a man with Peters's temperament generated, but they were not always easy to take.

Nor was Shriver himself immune from criticism. The director mingled socially with volunteers in the early days, communicating to them and everyone else that he wanted to hear their candid opinions. "The officials sponsored a beer party the first night here," one Peace Corps recruit wrote home from his training site at Rutgers University, "and Shriver, Reuter, and all the officials got drunk as hell or so they acted." The swinging ethos of the Kennedy era helped to create an esprit de (peace) corps that valued playing hard as well as working hard. Informality reigned at the level of bureaucratic procedure, too. Gerard Rice notes, "Every Peace Corps policy directive was entitled 'interim,' denoting that it could be changed if necessary," and in the five years that Shriver directed the Peace Corps he never printed a policy manual.[39]

"We have a great deal to do with shaping the program and policies," a volunteer to Colombia wrote his family, adding, "we extended the training course one week."[40] Although such an extension may not have meant a great deal, what is remarkable is the extent to which this volunteer was made to feel he had power. When Shriver reviewed the first draft of the new agency's organizational chart, he noted that it had not included a box for volunteers. Taking a pencil Shriver drew a large box in the center, labeled it volunteers, and connected every other box to it. It was this attitude that endeared the director to most recruits.[41]

In a multitude of ways Shriver and his colleagues sought to infuse the new agency with a democratic ethos that freed volunteers' critical instincts. Sometimes bedlam was the result. "I've rarely found so much general disagreement on everything . . . Everybody in the Peace Corps feels at liberty to attack the Director of the Peace Corps at any moment of the night or day . . . I'll bet you Secretary [of State Dean] Rusk has never been told off that way about his Department," Shriver once said to a group of returned volunteers in a mock complaint that suggested more pride than displeasure in his antiauthoritarian offspring.[42]

This leveling of social distinctions and encouragement of creative dissent involved a fine balance. The volunteers' fondness for Shriver generally tempered their assessments, as did the hopeful atmosphere of the Kennedy presidency. But when Shriver later took this style into Lyndon Johnson's War on Poverty, he was little shielded from the stinging assaults of community organizers who felt he did not do enough and conservative critics who felt he had done too much. Rancor touched the Peace Corps far less than it did many government activities, but the agency was part of a national spirit that sowed the seeds of rebellion far and wide, making followers into leaders and leaders into targets.

Harris Wofford noted in a 1965 speech that the Peace Corps attempted to be "an organization for those who don't want to become organization men." Its crowning achievement was the "Five Year Rule." Franklin Williams first proposed what he called an "in-up-and-out" plan that would limit all Peace Corps personnel to a tenure of five years. Sargent Shriver quickly approved the proposal to prevent a "bureaucratic hardening of the arteries" and asked Bill Moyers to shepherd the proposal through Congress. Against the opposition of the Civil Service Commission, and in the face of congressional befuddlement over why anyone would want a term limit, the Peace Corps had its way. On August 24, 1965, Congress enacted a limit on staff tenure in the Peace Corps for all personnel above grade GS-9 (which excluded secretaries). Sargent Shriver himself resigned from the Peace Corps on March 1, 1966, five years to the day after John Kennedy had appointed him. The "five-year flush," as staff irreverently nicknamed the rule, stayed with the Peace Corps as it approached the year 2000, making it the only federal agency with such a mandate.[43]

The youth-centered organizational chart, the structure that encouraged criticism, and the transient positions of power all gave substance to the Peace Corps promise that as part of the New Frontier it would rejuvenate democracy in America. The founders of the Peace Corps shared in a broad national concern about making American democracy real, or at least "participatory," that was reflected in the civil rights movement (culminating in the Voting Rights Act of 1965) and in groups like Students for a Democratic Society. But Shriver and his colleagues also wanted to do more than this. Like the founders of similar programs in the British Commonwealth, they sought to create a niche for the expression of individualism in a mass society. This interconnected goal was built into the Peace Corps in myriad ways, but especially in the organization's ambivalent attitude toward planning.

From the beginning, the founders of the American, Australian, British, and Canadian programs all emphasized that the "spirit" of the volunteers was vitally important, and at times even more important than anything they specifically did. The leaders' refrains expressed a point of view that may have seemed national or personal but was, in fact, international. "The spirit in which our Peace Corps Volunteers go forth is just as important as the skill they carry with them," Sargent Shriver told America. "The spirit that has taken you overseas is what you have to give," Mora Dickson told Britain's eighteen-year-old volunteers.[44] What leaders of the international volunteer movement thought this spirit would do varied. Sometimes the Peace Corps spirit was described as incendiary, sometimes as calming, always as creating a bridge of human empathy. Nevertheless this emphasis on the spirit of the individual led to considerable tension within the young Peace Corps and its European counterparts, hampering efforts to give a specific structure to many volunteer assignments.

One reason for "phony jobs" was simply the rapidity with which the Peace Corps expanded. But perhaps the most important reason was the Corps' ideological commitment to a rugged individualism which called on volunteers to figure out, along with the peasants of a country, what they should do. As a consequence, even after evaluators began pointing out that the volunteers needed more guidance, it took years for this message to change substantially the way the Peace Corps operated. The expectation that volunteers would create their own jobs took two forms. First, those placed in highly specific vocations like teaching or nursing were also expected to develop ad hoc activities outside their assigned routines. On their weekends, for example, they might help build a road or plant a community garden or organize a girls' sewing circle. The second form that this expectation took was the job category labeled Community Development. Of all volunteer positions, those in community development resulted in by far the highest proportion of jobs whose outlines were so vague, and which required such intense personal initiative to launch, that it was only the rare volunteer who could make anything of them. But the Peace Corps enshrined this type of volunteer for the reason that he or she exemplified the qualities of character that were supposed to typify the ideal American: hardy, inventive, and persistent.

The classic story of this mythic type volunteer was recounted by Kennedy himself to a group of volunteers in 1962:

Recently I heard a story of a young Peace Corpsman named Tom Scanlon, who is working in Chile. He works in a village about forty miles from an Indian village which prides itself on being Communist. The village is up a long, winding road which Scanlon has taken on many occasions to see the chief. Each time the chief avoided seeing him. Finally he saw him and said, "You are not going to talk us out of being Communists." Scanlon said, "I am not trying to do that, only to talk to you about how I can help." The chief looked at him and replied, "In a few weeks the snow will come. Then you will have to park your jeep twenty miles from here and come through five feet of snow on foot. The Communists are willing to do that. Are you?" When a friend saw Scanlon recently and asked him what he was doing, he said, "I am waiting for the snow."[45]

The public taste for such "Paul Bunyan in the Cold War" stories reflected the American hunger for reassurance that it still had the rugged individualists necessary to fight the important fights. The Peace Corps defined itself in contradiction to all that reeked of the complacency of mass society, especially the foreign aid administration caricatured by *The Ugly American*. AID used planners; Peace Corps used people. AID went by the book; Peace Corps flew by the seat of its pants. AID had experts who lived in golden ghettos; the Peace Corps had creative amateurs who lived in peasant shacks—and were willing to walk twenty miles in the snow.

The Peace Corps was quietly smug about these differences. One staff member reporting to Shriver on difficulties in convincing government lending institutions to give money to Latin American colleges told a story guaranteed to get laughs at a Peace Corps staff meeting. He recounted that one of the banks "laid down nine conditions for financial aid to universities abroad." When the comment was made that these nine conditions could be fulfilled only in utopia, "The answer came back that 'Utopia is not a member of the bank.'" His listeners, of course, proud citizens of utopia, firmly believed that too many conditions spoiled the pudding. To evaluators in 1965 who criticized the Brazil program for placing volunteers in empty assignments, the staff retorted that "all of the Peace Corps is an act of faith anyway" and that "if you let the programming process dominate, you run the danger of becoming like AID."[46]

This attitude went straight to the top of the Peace Corps. According to Harris Wofford, Sargent Shriver personally resisted the development of a more professional approach. On the top of another critical report suggesting greater use of programmers, Shriver jotted sarcastically:

They will be "experts." They will issue forth from a program "office" . . . huge "program documents" . . . prepared in the field at huge expense in time and money. Secretaries will type them with copies for five different Washington offices, all of whom will have to "sign off." The Peace Corps will receive an award for clean-cut, hard administrative efficiency from Forbes Magazine and the director of the Peace Corps will move from his post to an exec V-P post in a large industrial concern in Dayton.[47]

Like many others in the sixties who believed that "the movement" itself was the most important engine for change—whether it was the civil rights, antiwar, peace and love, or women's movement—the Peace Corps leadership tended to place more faith in the idealism of its volunteers than in the content of specific projects. To some extent these movement leaders were right: a sea change in national beliefs brought about by passionate individuals ended legal segregation and the Vietnam War. Sargent Shriver and most of his colleagues, deeply committed to the idea that every American was a potential pioneer, felt it a betrayal to develop programs on the assumption that most people are not extraordinary—or at least need a great deal of direction. In doing so, the Peace Corps director echoed the refrain of John Kennedy's presidency: that all Americans had not only the responsibility but the capability to make the world better. Shriver, himself, though a year older than the president, felt a slight wonder at his brother-in-law's bold practice of this notion: "He placed such confidence in us."[48]

Shriver in turn placed his highest confidence in the volunteers. "In a very real sense he idolized them," staff members Kevin Lowther and Payne Lucas noted, "and they in turn regarded him with awe and respect."[49] Volunteers typically repaid Shriver's belief in them by giving their all to the Peace Corps. But while most felt fired up, some eventually felt set up. The ideologues at the top of the Peace Corps could accept with a fair degree of comfort the idea that community development was a messy business that had to be conducted with "a certain freedom from past authoritarian methods."[50] They were not the ones stuck on a mountaintop or in a swamp for two years without clear objectives. Community development placed far too many neophyte organizers in positions where they could hardly help but fail. Yet the Peace Corps did so because of the very historical impulses that had set it in motion—to find new frontiers on which young American men and women could prove themselves.

A less romantic reason for the emphasis on individual initiative to the detriment of organizational planning was the widespread ignorance of what actually produced development. Experts from Harvard, MIT, and Berkeley could not even agree among themselves which came first, modern industry or modern attitudes. Did advanced capitalism spring from Karl Marx's "material conditions" or from Max Weber's "Protestant work ethic"? In the late 1950s and early 1960s, modernization theory suggested that a combination of the two was necessary, with an emphasis on the need for entrepreneurial aspirations. Applied to the Peace Corps, modernization theory reinforced the notion that "the spirit that has taken you overseas is what you have to give." Gary Bergthold and David McClelland, two sociologists who studied the Peace Corps program in Ethiopia in 1968, arrived at much the same conclusion: "Research shows that a few key attitudinal variables like an achievement orientation are key reasons for economic growth . . . Peace Corps Volunteer teachers now tend to foster these essential attitudes, even without explicitly being trained to do so . . . This evidence suggests that even if Peace Corps programs volunteers in rural transformation, it should train them primarily as teachers of attitudes rather than as experts."[51]

Promoting democracy and fostering individualism were tightly interwoven with another defining element of Peace Corps organizational culture: the commitment to reform. In the early 1960s, "making the world a better place" appeared to define America's national purpose. The commitment to this project had been building since Franklin D. Roosevelt first pledged the United States to the defense of the Four Freedoms. This heroic age saw the United States gradually evolve an ever more powerful consensus that the Four Freedoms must be put into practice at home and abroad, regardless of cost. Some of those costs were two wars in Asia, foreign aid to most of the third world *and* most of the developed world, desegregation of the South by means peaceful and violent, race riots in the North, East, and West, and a commitment to personal liberty that by century's end seemed to compromise the commonwealth for the individual. What the nation bought with these expenditures were formal desegregation, a world ultimately free of Soviet influence, and a global marketplace more competitive than anyone ever dreamed possible. Uncertain that the gains equaled the losses, most Americans modified these aspirations in the middle 1970s.

But in 1961, the generational belief in the perfectibility of the world had not yet peaked. As Shriver and his staff rushed to get the Peace Corps off the ground before the arrival of the first volunteers in Africa on August 30, they brushed in broad strokes some of the ways in which the Corps would reform America and the world. It would demonstrate in every conceivable way its own commitment to desegregation. In the region of the world where the United States had most control (Latin America), the Peace Corps would declare war on class warfare. And the Peace Corps would raise a new generation of "change agents" who would endear the world to America and America to the world.

On racial issues, the director directly implemented Kennedy's pledge that the Peace Corps would recruit from "every race and walk of life." Like the Office of the Attorney General under Robert Kennedy, the Peace Corps actively sought to hire as many qualified African Americans as would apply, and to convince many who might never have considered applying to do so. It did so as much for the sake of young white Americans as for young black Americans: experiencing one another as equals was prerequisite to accepting the essential equality of all humankind and proving that America could live up to its ideals.

Before the first groups of volunteers went to Ghana and Nigeria, Peace Corps recruitment staff fanned out across black colleges. The commitment to racial diversity was self-imposed but reinforced by Africans. One field representative reported that in the initial contingent sent to Sierra Leone, white volunteers were often asked "why there was no more than one Negro Volunteer in the group and if this was Peace Corps or U.S. Government policy." Intense recruitment efforts that had yielded a few more black volunteers were encouraging "because of the continuing desire of Sierra Leonians to meet American Negroes." Once overseas, volunteers were expected to display careful respect for people of all races at all class levels. "We should always call people by their names abroad," Shriver told his staff, "never using such phrases as 'boy' for servants or other helpers."[52]

Black American leaders reinforced the Peace Corps commitment to desegregation. Early in the process of developing training sites, the director had told his staff that "in no case" would the Peace Corps give contracts to segregated institutions. It would also not bring minority volunteers to institutions where "off-campus racial attitudes" would force them to limit their activities. A few days later a meeting of black newspaper editors and college presidents urged the Peace Corps to go further, advising Shriver against establishing a training program anywhere in the South. One unintentional result of Shriver's decision to boycott all segregated institutions—and that meant virtually all colleges between Georgia and Texas—was that, at the ground level of the volunteer, many African-American recruits found themselves in highly unfamiliar environments, surrounded by northern whites and far from the communities where they had grown up.[53]

Still, when a Maryland tavern close to Washington headquarters refused service a few months later to a group that included Ethiopian trainers, Shriver must have felt justified in the policy. "The Ethiopian project was endangered last night," it was reported the next day. The insulted staff and volunteers "withheld action" only at the Peace Corps' request.[54] The director himself issued a dignified protest to the newspapers. Like other Kennedy administration officials—and Shriver was in the camp most dedicated to a faster pace on civil rights—he sought to put forth a new ideal of American race relations without tempting opponents or supporters to volatile confrontations that might shatter the Democratic administration and the Peace Corps along with it. The moral high ground was not easy to hold onto, as Americans of all colors would discover.

The Peace Corps also sought white volunteers who would present the desired image of America. "A Peace Corps Volunteer must have *no prejudice* against men and women of races, religions, nationalities or economic or social classes different from his own," the Colorado State University feasibility study emphasized in its ten-point list of volunteer qualities.[55] Conversely, another study urged in April 1961 that training should weed out "those psychologically unsuited to intimate contact with persons of other races."[56] Overall, the Peace Corps met its goal. "We have struck gold," Harris Wofford reported to Kennedy following a trip to Africa. "They are the kind of vigorous, intelligent and good-humored Americans we needed to send and Africans needed to see."[57]

The effort was not simply public relations, however. Retraining humanity lay at the heart of the Peace Corps mission. "We have sent black Americans to white men's countries, white Americans to black men's countries," Shriver boasted in *The Point of the Lance* in 1964. "We were told that we couldn't send Protestants to certain parts of Catholic countries in Latin America, but we sent them. We were told that we couldn't send Jews to Arab countries, but we sent them." Frequently Peace Corps actions had just the effect Shriver hoped. One of the first attempts to novelize the Peace Corps experience, *The Zinzin Road* by Fletcher Knebel, captured the experience attested to by many volunteers. "Working day in and day out with Negro volunteers and staff members of the Peace Corps . . . he began to forget completely about the difference in skin pigmentation . . . he began to feel a pride in the Peace Corps for leading him to his new understanding."[58]

Issues of race and class came together in another Peace Corps reform effort: reshaping Latin America. Ironically, only a proprietary sense as old as the Monroe Doctrine could have led a U.S. agency to think it had this capacity.

The Peace Corps was not Kennedy's largest initiative in Latin America. Months before the president commissioned Sargent Shriver to begin the Peace Corps, he asked a wide range of experts to design a $20 billion aid program that would transform the hemisphere into "a vast crucible of revolutionary ideas and efforts." Essential to the plan was the assumption that, as Kennedy said to a top aide, "Latin America's not like Asia or Africa. We can really accomplish something there."[59] Among other things, the Alliance for Progress held out the carrot of loans and gifts to nations that would undertake land reform, brought together presidents of democracies in a Kennedy-sponsored "club," used fiery rhetoric to legitimize "peaceful" class upheaval, and even created a forum for public debate with Che Guevara at the 1961 Punta del Este conference where the alliance was founded. President Kennedy himself led the way along the path of revolutionary rhetoric that was well trod during the first years of the Peace Corps presence in Latin America. "Those who make peaceful revolution impossible will make violent revolution inevitable," Kennedy warned.[60]

Because of more pressing responsibilities and Shriver's competence, John Kennedy rarely looked into the business of the Peace Corps. But when he did, it was to steer Shriver in directions he thought the director ought to go. "I note that you have plans of increasing the number of Peace Corps volunteers in various parts of the world, such as North Borneo," Kennedy jotted in 1962. "I would like for you to keep in mind the importance of Latin America, which I think should be the primary area. At the present time do we not have as many in the Philippines as we have in all of the Latin American countries?"[61]

The point of the lance was designed to fight old injustices in a new way, many of which had been wrought by the "colossus of the North" itself. Although the historian Glenn Sheffield doubts that the Peace Corps leadership genuinely wanted to do anything more than find clever ways of enhancing American control, Shriver and his staff at least told one another something different. They were flattered that leftists in Latin America saw their efforts as the one aspect of American policy that merited trust. "The new government is considered to be to the Left and has . . . been sitting on [the proposed] ICA/AID program for months," a field representative reported to the director. The Peace Corps, by contrast, "had a complete program prepared under the signature of Minister of Education" in one day.[62]

At the same time, the Peace Corps was prepared to respect that some Latin Americans would change their perceptions of the United States only very slowly. When the Mexican government refused to yield to Peace Corps blandishments, the director restated his policy: "The Peace Corps will *not* inveigle its way into any country but will go only where it is clearly invited by the host government." The invitation for more gringos never arrived. (Mexico did, much later, invite Japanese volunteers.) Still, other Latin Americans were impressed. One Chilean official told the Peace Corps that "these young people have brought to us the reality of the generosity of the United States in a way which could not have been done by 15 ambassadors in Santiago."[63]

The Peace Corps assignment in Latin America was to further peaceful social change through community development. In Africa 80 percent of volunteers worked in education. In Latin America close to that same percentage worked in community development, which most officials thought had greater potential for stimulating rapid class organizing. In fact, in the early sixties the majority of community development done worldwide by the Peace Corps (69 percent) was directed at Latin America.[64] Volunteers were supposed to synthesize villagers into "juntas" (groups) which would meet regularly to discuss local problems and identify community needs. Once these "felt needs" were identified, volunteers would help villagers devise creative ways to meet them, whether by building roads, latrines, and schools or by petitioning their municipalities for a greater share of government resources.

Frank Mankiewicz, first director of the Peace Corps program for Peru, forged the emphasis on community development. Community development had practical appeal because it could absorb "B.A. generalists" (college graduates with liberal arts backgrounds who were the majority of applicants). In addition, because the job was vague, a nation could not know how many community developers it might need and therefore could be persuaded to take more volunteers. Community development helped in the numbers game.

But the origins of community development were far from cynical. A lawyer with a flair for dramatic rhetoric, Frank Mankiewicz exemplified the ways in which domestic reform influenced international reform, which in turn reinforced domestic reform. Son of the Hollywood screenwriter who had penned "Citizen Kane" and nephew of the man who had directed Elizabeth Taylor in "Cleopatra," Mankiewicz came to the Peace Corps through his friendship with Franklin Williams. Mankiewicz and Williams had worked together in the Anti-Defamation League and the NAACP, of which Williams was the regional director.

In the West, as in the South, racial segregation drew lines through neighborhoods, but in California the distinctions were largely between Mexicans and "Anglos." Williams and Mankiewicz traveled together to El Centro, California, where they helped Ernesto Galarza organize farmworkers from the green, irrigated fields that stretched as far as the eye could see around the dusty border town. They also protested segregation in the school system, for which they were arrested. In Los Angeles Mankiewicz worked with organizers using the methods of the Chicago community organizer Saul Alinsky ("rubbing the sores of discontent," as Mankiewicz recalled) to help poor people in East Los Angeles start services for themselves.[65]

When he was recruited for the Peace Corps, Mankiewicz was immediately impressed by the mentions of community development as a potential technique. He was also intrigued by a lecture that the economist John Kenneth Galbraith gave one spring morning to the fledgling staff. Underdevelopment, Galbraith said, had different causes and cures in different places. A nation like India needed capital. Africa needed schools. Latin America, he said, had both teachers and money, but it had a feudal social system that prevented the majority from rising above a peasant existence. White teachers would tell Peruvian children, a consulting anthropologist reported, that they spoke an "ugly animal dialect" (Quechua) which they should replace with Spanish as soon as possible. "It made me think of East Los Angeles," Mankiewicz later said, "a rigid, class-ridden, racially tinged social structure."[66]

With Shriver's approval, Mankiewicz concluded that Latin Americans could benefit from Alinsky's subversive techniques. Volunteers, fired by ideals and educated about Latin American class prejudices (if ignorant of American ones), could revolutionize the continent by "going around the government" to help local people make war on feudalism. What the volunteers would *do* from day to day was not intrinsically important. "Structure" would be a hindrance to creativity. A Peace Corps evaluator, David Hapgood, later noted that Mankiewicz "trusted American youth to such an extent that he scarcely questioned the ability of an average volunteer to transmit a feeling of self-reliance to Peruvian Indians."[67] With a fine disregard for national sovereignty—fed by a belief in the universality of human rights and ambitions—Mankiewicz encouraged volunteers to think of themselves as revolutionaries. "Our specific objective," one ironic volunteer in Ecuador recalled, was "to win the affection of Jorge Rodriguez, our department's chief, so that we could overthrow him later on."[68]

The Peace Corps never even remotely intended to (and never did) destabilize governments. But "revolution" was a popular word in the sixties when so many countries attained independence, and individuals like Mankiewicz used it to symbolize the spectrum of social change from *campesinos* building schoolhouses to elected assemblies restructuring land ownership. One Peace Corps representative in Colombia wrote in 1962 that ideas like community responsibility, initiative, and self-reliance were "so commonplace in the United States that it is hard to realize how revolutionary it is in Latin America." Thus a revolutionized Latin America might look more like Toledo, Ohio, than Havana, Cuba.[69]

Paraphrasing officials like Mankiewicz, with whom he deeply disagreed, Charles Peters later wrote that through community development "volunteers could empower the powerless and array the heretofore helpless campesino against the oligarchs who were oppressing him. The catch was that actually accomplishing all this required a volunteer who was a combination of Jesus Christ and John Kennedy, with a bit of Tip O'Neill thrown in. So the community development volunteers, with a few heroic exceptions, accomplished little."[70]

But, some Peace Corps officials must have reasoned, even peaceful revolution was a tricky thing. Those who could pull it off were supposed to be exceptional. Frank Mankiewicz and Richard Goodwin (Goodwin acted as Kennedy's special liaison to the Alliance for Progress and subsequently quit the State Department to join the Peace Corps) later admitted a certain admiration for revolutionaries like Fidel Castro and Che Guevara—even though they hoped to put them out of business. They respected the young Cubans' seeming willingness to risk all to change the world. "'More brave than me' . . . Che Guevara was also a child of the sixties," Goodwin wrote.[71]

In Africa and Asia, in contrast, where governments and cultures were thought to be utterly different from those of America, the Peace Corps took a position of studied neutrality on everything from authoritarian rule to polygamy. But in the Americas, which the United States government had insisted since the Monroe Doctrine on defining as one family under its patriarchal sway, "otherness" was reduced to "sameness," in the words of Eldon Kenworthy.[72] The American republics, which had thrown off European rule within decades of one another, were presumed to have a unity of democratic aspirations. In this context, Frank Mankiewicz's assumption that Americans barely out of their teens could relate politically to Peruvian Indians, and vice versa, was at least comprehensible.

The Alliance for Progress and the Peace Corps both failed to prevent violence, although the United States did manage to contain leftist revolutions. Military dictatorships gradually took over in the sixties. Conservatives both below and above the border constrained the Alliance. Large landowners did not want land reform, Congress refused to pay for it, and American presidents were prepared to land Marines wherever necessary to maintain U.S. power in the hemisphere. Nine national armies overthrew civilian governments in the first five years of the Alliance. Yet the Peace Corps took seriously the hope of promoting reform, and often staged its own mini-rebellions against the Monroe Doctrine. When the Johnson administration sent the Marines to the Dominican Republic in 1965 to abort attempts to overthrow a military regime and reinstate exiled President Juan Bosch, Peace Corps volunteers helped suture, bandage, and even carry to the morgue civilians wounded or killed by the invading Americans.

Ironically, Bosch had been elected in 1962 when the Kennedy administration pressured the heirs of Rafael Trujillo to quit their dynastic dictatorship. But Bosch subsequently proved to be too far to the left for Johnson's comfort. Nearly 3,000 Dominicans would die in the four months that volunteers dodged bullets to help doctors in hospitals that had no electricity. One volunteer later recalled that she came to understand the expression the "smell of blood" from the experience. They also wrote a letter of protest to Lyndon Johnson, care of Frank Mankiewicz. Flying down to Santo Domingo, Mankiewicz told the volunteers that if they released their letter, the president would pull them out of the country. From the start, LBJ had warned Shriver against allowing the "three C's" into the Peace Corps: "The communists, the consumptives, and the cocksuckers." He would brook no opposition from "doves." Mankiewicz left the decision to the volunteers. They chose to make their stand by staying, rather than protesting. It was a difficult but typical choice for Peace Corps volunteers. It was the style in which the Peace Corps, overall, served the cause of reform in the sixties.[73]

In a sense, the Dominican volunteers' choice was an existential one. Volunteers saw themselves as "change agents." Like Dr. Rieux in Camus's *The Plague,* they had to decide whether they would flee "pestilences" or whether they would, as individuals, stay to see every last patient saved or buried. Borrowing the Christian rhetoric of the early civil rights movement, Frank Mankiewicz wrote in an article for all Peace Corps volunteers that it was "the task of the Volunteer to call attention to his fragmented community . . . to ease the sense of alienation, to function, in short, in the best Christian sense of the word, as a 'witness' to the existence of the majority of the nation's citizens."[74]

In this world view what the volunteer achieved in the way of economic development was not highly important. Young Americans in Latin America functioned like white students in the freedom rides of the civil rights movement: they "witnessed" injustice. The process was supposed to change both the witness and the community being witnessed. Bob Dylan, who along with a generation of folksingers stirred the American conscience, expressed a similar belief in the power of seeing (and the crime of not doing so) when he asked: "Yes, 'n how many years can some people exist, Before they're allowed to be free? Yes, 'n how many times can a man turn his head, Pretending he just doesn't see?" In the Peace Corps of Frank Mankiewicz, the volunteer brought change to the community by witnessing its inequalities and demonstrating his or her own lack of subservience.

Of course volunteers did not accomplish what Charles Peters, or perhaps even they, thought they should accomplish. By Peters's standards, being a witness was not enough. The gap between identifying needs and devising precise solutions was usually too great for young volunteers to bridge. But the Peace Corps was a microcosm of a national and even an international dispute over what drove change: technical expertise expressed in clearly planned projects or the sheer human will that things should be different. This struggle would be expressed again and again in ways that confounded easy conclusions, such as when "primitive" Vietnam held out against the United States. Students all over the world in the sixties expressed their concurrence with the human will side of the equation through incessant "manifestos"—as if making a problem manifest was nearly equivalent to solving it.

One such declaration came from Mexican youth after the October 2, 1968, army attack on protesters prior to the Olympic Games in Mexico City. North American students picked up copies of the manifesto, one of which eventually came to rest in the Canadian National Archives. "The Students' Movement of 1968 is the most evident and clear expression of . . . the accumulation of problems with a wide social meaning," the authors wrote, reflecting their conviction that students held a mirror up to society. "The Mexican student who participated in the movement," the manifesto continued, was thus the "most important change agent."[75] Official development programs, it concluded, had little to offer society.

The Peace Corps, however, was an official development program, regardless of its informal style. Shriver's involvement in all the shenanigans of the American political process—intense lobbying, skillful public relations, bureaucratic in-fighting—attested to the extent that the Peace Corps would inevitably be captive to the system. It had to satisfy its sponsors. To do so it would make political compromises. This fact was hardly surprising, but did not fully accord with the rhetoric of idealism. The Peace Corps was also part of American foreign policy. In the 1960s this policy jumbled idealistic features, such as the Peace Corps and the early Alliance for Progress, with coldly manipulative, militaristic features such as the Green Berets, the plots to assassinate Fidel Castro, and a growing commitment to the corrupt government of South Vietnam. The combination made for a schizophrenia that was more dramatic than in many other eras, but certainly not atypical. The American conscience had always struggled to reconcile the practice of realpolitik with the principle of humanitarian internationalism, usually with little success. The Peace Corps lent its weight to the weaker half of the equation. Similar organizations in other parts of the English-speaking world lent their weight also.

3

Peace Corps
Cousins

———— ✹ ————

Canada is in a sense "a city set on a hill whose actions
cannot be hid"; whose actions indeed are watched by
countless millions of people all over the world.

LEWIS PERINBAM, 1961

The Peace Corps and its volunteers, searching for great meanings and
determined to live out an idealism as potent as their nation's power,
reinforced many of their society's aspirations at the beginning of the
1960s. These aspirations represented an uneasy blending of the desire
to be preeminent in the world with the desire to help it. American
volunteers' efforts also reinforced those of other young volunteers from
the British Commonwealth, some of whom had begun nearly a decade
earlier. The similarity of their ideas on race, the cold war, and world
peace makes it clear that Shriver and his followers were more a part of a
global wave of sentiment than they realized. The similarity of volunteers' experiences once they arrived in the third world further suggests
that problems such as ill-defined jobs and unrealistic expectations were
by no means confined to the Peace Corps. The Peace Corps and its
Anglo-world counterparts shared a cultural kinship that made for a
certain alikeness, including the sense of a special mission. Australians
had made the first forays, followed by the British and then the Canadians and Americans.

The egalitarian structure of the Commonwealth itself had opened the
door. Created in 1930 to express a parity of power between the former
white dominions and the United Kingdom, the Commonwealth disas-
sociated the colonies from the British Parliament while uniting them
under the Crown. In doing so, it placed the British government in a
position quite unlike that of the United States, whose president had no

peers. This was especially significant once the membership ceased to be all white. The Commonwealth structure not only precluded Britain from exercising authority over former dominions like Australia, but it prevented the white dominions from claiming pride of place over the brown. The 1953 coronation of Queen Elizabeth II featured the sight of the Commonwealth prime ministers attending the court of their monarch with the representative of South Africa standing uncomfortably near to Jawaharlal Nehru of India and the prime ministers of Ceylon and Pakistan.[1] (South Africa was forced out of the Commonwealth in 1961 over its policy of apartheid.) But, uncomfortable though a multiracial Commonwealth was to some, to others an association based on the equality of peoples contained exhilarating possibilities for reshaping human destiny.

In 1950 events combined to spur the development of interracial Commonwealth links. In January, the Commonwealth nations along with representatives of other British territories in South and Southeast Asia met in Colombo, Ceylon, to forge a program of bilateral aid between richer and poorer nations. The result was the Colombo Plan, in which participating Commonwealth nations undertook to respond to the specific requests of countries in the region for aid with economic development. For the British, the Colombo Plan informally extended its influence as the Commonwealth's leading member. Countries like Canada also felt it gave them a special role. "Canada, a non-colonial power," Canadian volunteers later wrote, "can perhaps make a unique contribution, offering honest service with tact, discretion and sensitivity."[2] The spirit of brotherhood across racial lines heightened the sense of the Colombo Conference as historic. "For the first time representatives of the South and Southeast Asian nations sat down with those of Anglo-Saxon origin, not as inferior colonials but as equals on Asian soil, to exchange views on world problems," one participant recalled, in a book that inspired the start of Canada's volunteer program.[3]

But an Indonesian student visiting Bombay actually had the idea first. Over a cup of tea, or perhaps on a street corner (no one could quite remember later), an Indonesian delegate to the 1950 World University Service Assembly in India argued to an Australian student that technical experts could best help people in the third world by entering "into the whole life of the society in which they worked." Another student delegate declared, "We don't want boxes of boots. Teach us how to make them for ourselves." John Bayly, an architecture student, took both statements to heart. Upon his arrival back in Australia, Bayly contacted friends at the University of Melbourne.[4]

The National Union of Australian University Students sponsored a committee to investigate Bayly's idea of a corps of university graduates who would go to Indonesia to work at the level of the average citizen. They began with an indictment of current foreign policy. Like the authors of *The Ugly American,* they found that foreigners in Indonesia demanded special privileges and pay rates, and made little attempt to appreciate the country. A recognition of racism permeated the students' consciousness. Australians and Europeans generally did not fraternize with Asians. "One might fondle an animal, but must never brush shoulders with an Asian," an Australian observer wrote.[5]

One member of the committee, Herb Feith, had earlier met through the mail an Australian woman married to an Indonesian revolutionary. She arranged for Feith to become the first Australian volunteer.

The son of Austrian Jewish refugees who had fled prewar Nazi Europe, Feith and some of his future colleagues in the Volunteer Scheme had run a canned food and old clothes drive for Europe in 1946 while still in secondary school.[6] With a strong sense of international responsibility, Feith was impatient to begin in Indonesia and heedless of his parents' anxieties. Only twenty years old when he boarded an Italian ship for Jakarta in June 1951, he wore a suit, tie, and shirt with a starched collar for the start of the tropical voyage. A picture taken on the gangplank showed a pale, dark-haired young man with high cheekbones, an earnest gaze, and a gentle smile. When the crowded boat anchored in the reputedly dangerous port of revolutionary Jakarta, he was the only one to disembark.[7]

Herb Feith paid his own way, as did the two volunteers who followed him. One, a woman, was a bacteriologist. The other, a man, was a radio and aeronautical engineer. The three worked at the "invitation" (wrangled by the Australian students) of the Indonesian government and by 1954 had ironed out an agreement between the two countries. Under the provisions of the Colombo Plan, Australia would give each volunteer boat fare, a bicycle, and £50 for clothes and other miscellania. Indonesia would pay salaries at the local rate.

Feith operated as chief optimist, confident that Indonesia could use as many volunteers as Australia could provide. Although skeptical of competitive European nationalisms, Feith made allowances for revolutionary nationalism. Just as the creation of Israel in 1948 guaranteed a homeland to the Jews for the first time in almost two thousand years, the decolonization of India, Indonesia, and the Philippines shortly after World War II confirmed the right of all peoples to exist as peoples. Working on a master's degree in political science, Herb Feith was exhilarated by the newness of self-government for the historically dispossessed. "Will democracy prove transplantable? Will the social servility bred of feudalism and colonialism be broken?" he wrote home in an open letter to other students in 1951. "Will the emancipatory nationalism become aggressive and chauvinistic or will internationally conscious elements gain the ascendancy?" Feith identified with the "internationally conscious elements." Like later Peace Corps volunteers, he and other young Australians proselytized intercultural understanding as the best hope for peace on earth.[8]

The fundamental prerequisite for building this understanding was a thorough-going acceptance of racial equality. Feith wrote potential recruits, "You'd have to be free from any colour superiority notions." Ollie McMichael, one of the two graduates who followed Feith, wrote home in 1953, "It is senseless coming up here unless you are free from colour barriers or race prejudices." In its pamphlets, the student union reiterated that "these young people assert by the way they live, that racial equality is real."[9] It was a novel idea, in need of emphasis.

Letters from Ollie McMichael also conveyed a sense of the perilous alternatives to social and economic equality, and revealed a patriotic sense of Australian exceptionalism and a cold war anxiety remarkably similar to that of the founders of the Peace Corps. The Indonesian revolutionary spirit, if broken by intransigent poverty, would be followed by a loss of hope. "They'll turn to the Communists—like China," McMichael warned. Australia, he believed, was uniquely positioned to win over the revolutionaries to the way of the West. "No country matters more to Indonesia than we do," he asserted. "Britain and Holland—NO—colonial countries. America—NO—imperialist. Russia—NO—imperialist. If Australia fails—they'll turn to China." Quoting an Australian chargé d'affaires, McMichael added: "If Indonesia fails, Australia is sunk!"[10]

By the mid-1950s, the Australian concept of national security had begun to evolve from rejecting ties with Asians to cultivating them. From the first days of nationhood, Australians had insisted on a whites-only immigration policy. Indeed, anger over the British failure to help keep Asians out of Australia fueled the movement for national independence. The first time the independent Parliament met (1901), it passed a White Australia Policy that kept Asians out of Australia for most of the twentieth century by requiring literacy in a European language.[11] In 1919 the Australian prime minister William Hughes insulted the Japanese by blocking their proposed clause on racial equality in the League of Nations Covenant.

After World War II, government officials as well as students like Herb Feith increasingly recognized that the White Australia Policy gravely impeded friendship with the Asian Pacific islands to the north that could screen the nation from Communist China and expansionist Japan. The Colombo Plan, according to the historian John Rickard, made the first "symbolic dent" in the White Australia Policy. Student volunteers kicked it in further. By 1960 nearly forty young Australians had worked in Indonesia. Upon their return, many joined immigration reform groups.[12]

As in the Peace Corps, some volunteers felt they had worked hard in Indonesia, but others found themselves in empty assignments with no accomplishments to offset the sacrifice of two years away from home and career. Yet volunteers resisted making public that their assignments were not always effective. President Sukarno himself once took off time to greet new volunteers. Cabinet ministers spoke at length with newly arrived Australian students. The Indonesian ambassador to Australia, addressing the University of Melbourne in 1956, said that the spirit of racial equality in which the volunteers undertook their tasks was "worth immeasurably more to us than the rupiahs it saves our treasury." For the first time, he told the students, "white people have been ready and eager to live among us on our own standards of salary and living . . . It is a demonstration of goodwill and understanding which has moved our hearts greatly."[13] The students struggled to live up not only to their own ideals but to the faith the Indonesians had placed in them.

Alec and Mora Dickson, who founded British Voluntary Service Overseas seven years after Herb Feith left for Jakarta, shared the Australians' desire to help the third world as well as the belief that not to do so would present important problems for their own country. In a serendipitous borrowing of ideas, the Dicksons found their thinking prompted by an American with a rubber raft. Alec and Mora Dickson had picked up a mobile canteen in Edinborough from the British Council of Churches, taken it by ferry across the Channel, and driven through the night in late October 1956 to help Hungarians escape Soviet oppression. They hid in the trees, assisting students from Western universities who were operating a freelance rescue mission across the border canal. Fearful that the demands of their reform government for withdrawal from the Warsaw Pact might trigger a reaction, those Hungarians who could fled the country. Two weeks later Soviet troops crushed the rebellion, sealed the border, and executed the premier, Imre Nagy. Although embarked on a dangerous task, the Western students enjoyed the adventure and bantered in the darkness with Alec and Mora Dickson. When the flowing water grew too cold to enter, an American student went to a Vienna sports shop and purchased an inflatable boat. The students hid it in the reeds during the day and ferried refugees at night. The Britishers marveled at the ingenuity and spirit of the "kids."[14]

Hungary gave Alec Dickson an idea. Dickson, in his early forties, had already lived an adventurous life. As a schoolboy he had adored Rupert Brooke, English poet of World War I. Dickson worried that he had missed the last chance for real adventure and so entered journalism in pursuit of great events. Serving as a correspondent, Dickson was asked by the British War Office in 1938 to help monitor the peace treaty of Munich. Dickson and other British officers watched as Hitler's troops invaded Prague. During World War II itself, Dickson served in Northeast Africa, organizing a mobile propaganda unit of Africans designed to convince British colonials to support the Union Jack. After the war he worked with the "displaced persons directorate" in Berlin, and then organized a leadership training program for young Africans.

In Hungary in 1956, Dickson saw the answer to the problem that World War II had solved for him but that a new generation now faced: how to give young people, especially males, a chance to develop qualities of character normally called upon only under conditions of war. He sought what William James had described as the "moral equivalent of war." Dickson admired the Civilian Conservation Corps that President Roosevelt had developed in response to the Depression. But the postwar world was a different place. In the "affluent society . . . [and] highly industrialized Welfare State that is Britain today," Dickson wrote in 1958, conditions deprived young people of the challenge of responding to circumstances of genuine urgency and need.

"Nothing like enough imagination has been shown in working out the implications of adventurous service and what it should mean today," Alec Dickson argued. "Our young people . . . are expected to be satisfied with chores, under the title of social service, scarcely more stimulating than the collection of library books for old age pensioners." Like John Kennedy, Dickson harked back to harder, more primitive times, saying, "The Spartans exposed their young on hillsides, so that only the strong might be saved. If *our* young are to be saved, then we should be exposing them . . . to situations of social need, where a sense of compassionate service may be aroused."[15]

In 1957 the British playwright John Osborne wrote *Look Back in Anger*, the play that brought into popular consciousness the phrase "angry young men." Its leading character "Jimmy" lamented that without any causes left to die for, there was nothing to live for. "Let's pretend that we're human beings, and that we're actually alive," he chided his male buddy.[16] Featuring superstar Richard Burton in a film version, the play opened shortly before the elimination of the "call-up," British military conscription. It was in this cultural context that the intrepid student with the raft sparked Dickson's fertile imagination. Here was the soul of adventure, a youth who had found something to live for and die for.

The next year Alec and Mora Dickson traveled to Sarawak (Borneo) in the South Pacific. They came away with vivid impressions of the indigenous people and especially the young, who seemed to have "a sense of their own place in the framework of living and of the duties and importance of that place."[17] Alec Dickson noted that, in contrast, local young people who had had the "privilege" of Western educations seemed less enterprising. "It has emasculated their sense of manhood," he wrote, using words that echoed American fears of the loss of manliness in technologically advanced societies. Sarawak made Dickson think of the lost generation back home. Returning to England, Dickson proposed in the journal of Her Majesty's Overseas Service that new opportunities for "adventurous service" might be found not "in this

overdeveloped island of ours" but in "the underdeveloped areas overseas . . . [where] young people might be enabled to give a period of
service, under sacrificial conditions."[18]

Sending young people to serve would solve another problem as well:
how to help countries truly in need without condescension. Dickson's
observations abroad had led him to conclude that at "a certain stage of
development the comfortable cause deeper resentment than the cruel—
and smugness is less easy to forgive or to forget than severity." Dickson
argued that being supplicants of aid always wounded human pride. "We
ourselves know well enough how difficult a sentiment is gratitude
toward America," he noted in reference to World War II and postwar
reconstruction.[19] With no pretensions to expertise, young volunteers
were best placed to express British solidarity with the developing world.

In arguments for what became Voluntary Service Overseas (VSO),
Alec Dickson hit on the idea of using the youngest possible age group:
high school graduates during the year before college who previously
would have gone to military service. Most colleges in Britain, basing
their enrollments on incoming veterans who had delayed school to
serve their stints, were not even prepared to admit the extra high school
classes that would be freed up when conscription stopped. Dickson
found an ally in Launcelot Fleming, the bishop of Portsmouth, a
former explorer who had slaked his own thirst for adventure in the
Arctic and now had a pastor's interest in the young men cut adrift in
what was called "the year between." Dickson and Fleming wrote a
letter to the *Sunday Times* in March 1958 calling for volunteers to serve
in Sarawak and West Africa, and sent a letter marked "urgent" to
Britain's public schools.[20]

Alec and Mora Dickson spent the next six months sorting out the
400 responses that poured into their home until the living room was
knee deep in applications. They chose eight high school graduates to
start—five for West Africa and three for Sarawak. The Dicksons served
the teenagers tea and fruitcake; the Colonial Office gave them a reception; a BBC interviewer introduced them to the nation on "In Town
Tonight"; a clergyman cautioned them not to drink spirits before 6:00
P.M. in the bush. ("We lose all our best men that way," he confided.)
Martin Garner, one of the first teenagers to go, crossed in an airplane
the South China Sea that his grandfather had traversed in a tea clipper,
preyed on by pirates. Others came from families that had never ven-

tured off their island nation. Within twelve months, twenty volunteers were serving abroad. All found adventure.[21]

Like the Australians and the later Americans, VSO's founders showed a strong concern that their volunteers exhibit the right "attitude of mind," as a 1959 recruiting letter described it. "Africa, Asia, and the Caribbean have outlived the Great White Master epoch," the pamphlet lectured. Only people who could set aside cultural and race prejudice were wanted. Local sponsors ("understandably," Dickson emphasized) would spurn "any hint of condescension or superiority."[22]

Britain had its own long-standing internal critique of the colonial mentality predating *The Ugly American*. Writers like E. M. Forster and George Orwell had well portrayed the moral bankruptcy of colonialism. Lederer and Burdick could have cribbed from the novelist Arthur Koestler, who wrote of the British in 1946, "At home they are different . . . Why could they never show themselves [abroad] as they really were?"[23]

White volunteers taking up the banner of equality in the postcolonial world knew that both ignorance and conceit compromised their convictions. John Seely, who volunteered at age seventeen, wrote to Alec Dickson, "As for Africans, my opinions of them [before going] varied between admiration for them as a race savagely persecuted, as in South Africa, and suspicion of them as a race of primitives." British recruits felt keenly their responsibility to a new world order and the need for having correct attitudes to go with it.[24]

Lewis Perinbam, a founder of the Canadian volunteer program, reported to his comrades from Southeast Asia: "Throughout my tour, I was constantly aware of the enviable and respected position that Canada holds in the world today." The nation, he asserted, had a unique role to play as "a city set on a hill." To citizens of the United States raised consciously or not on John Winthrop's claim, the notion that *Canada* was actually the model for the West, watched in 1961 "by countless millions," might be unexpected.[25] Yet the sense of special destiny to which Winthrop gave voice radiated outward from England to all the Anglo-settled nations. Since the Glorious Revolution of 1688, Britons had celebrated their exceptionalism (embodied in representative government and the rule of law) as a model for the unruly, more fractious areas of the world (beginning, of course, with France). Alec Dickson believed deeply in the special place of Britain in the world and its "responsibility" to its former colonies. Australians, similarly, believed that they had a special destiny in Asia. And, Canadians, too, accorded themselves a unique role as a leading member of the Commonwealth without Britain's sins of imperialism or their pushy southern neighbor's sins of self-promotion.

The Canadian University Service Overseas, like the Peace Corps, had a number of fathers. Lewis Perinbam, Keith Spicer, and Guy Arnold each wrote proposals for a Canadian volunteer youth service within the same year and a half. Perinbam submitted his to World University Service of Canada and to the Canadian government. Spicer, a Ph.D. candidate in political science, gave his plan to Prime Minister John Diefenbaker. Guy Arnold, an English immigrant, circulated his ideas to whoever would read them. Although the resulting disputes over paternity would briefly trouble Canadian University Service Overseas, the organizers settled the matter in a typically Canadian spirit of compromise. (One founder later joked, "Why do Canadians cross the road? To get to the middle.") Besides, the idea to which they were all attracted clearly had a life of its own.

Lewis Perinbam borrowed the concept from the Australians. As a staff member of World University Service, Perinbam had seen what harm innocent cultural misunderstandings could wreak. Chaperoning a high-spirited group of students at a seminar in India, Perinbam found himself in 1953 explaining to the maharaja of Mysore why students might mimic the maharaja on "skit night" and why he should not deport all Canadians. Perinbam felt strongly that only a stint of living abroad would cure sheltered Canadians of the provincialism that handicapped them in a multicultural Commonwealth.

Perinbam first talked with the Canadian embassy in Indonesia about starting a program similar to the Australian one. The embassy staff told Perinbam that, while they admired the "plucky" Aussies, they did not think the idea would appeal to soft Canadian youth. Undaunted, Lewis Perinbam presented a full proposal in 1959 to the Canadian Colombo Plan officials for a "Canadian Volunteer Graduate Program." Canada had a "growing stature," Perinbam wrote, which imposed "fresh and increasing demands for Canadian leadership" throughout the world. Young people who had had a period of service abroad would ultimately contribute to such a personnel pool. Their service would also be "a practical demonstration of racial equality, goodwill, and technical assistance."[26] Canadian officials still did not share Perinbam's enthusiasm. The proposal collected dust on a shelf in Ottawa.

Guy Arnold, meanwhile, was working on his own idea for building cross-cultural solidarity. An immigrant to Canada, Arnold traveled to British Guiana with two eighteen-year-old Canadian students in 1960. There they met a youth from British Voluntary Service Overseas who gave them an inspirational account of his experience.[27] They also met the first Englishman in the colony to have given, not long before, a desegregated tea party. The Canadians stayed in guest quarters on a sugar plantation where "house boys" older than themselves attended exquisitely to their every need. The students in turn felt exquisitely uncomfortable, thinking that much remained to be done if the egalitarian structure of the Commonwealth was to achieve real life.[28] It was the same year that fourteen black African countries became independent. The news appeared to have traveled slowly to the outer fringes of the Empire.

Guy Arnold came back to Canada in early 1961 with a proposal for a Canadian Voluntary Commonwealth Service (CVCS) whose goals were to give help where it was "urgently needed," to build Commonwealth understanding, and to break down "racial barriers" among students who would "form the opinion of the future."[29] Arnold distributed his proposal to students, parents, and faculty at the University of Toronto. In the summer of 1961, as the first Peace Corps recruits for Ghana were learning Twi at Berkeley, Guy Arnold's group sent six undergraduate students to Jamaica for four months. They went with few instructions, other than to make themselves somehow useful in the fields of community development, leadership training, youth activities, or agriculture. "The main contribution that volunteers will be able to make is in the field of ideas," Arnold prophesied grandly, though he cautioned that it would also be helpful to know a few basic skills. For example, since the jobs would be on tropical islands, it would be good to know how to swim.

Arnold's emphasis on spirit over expertise came out in his casual suggestions that "rugger players should re-orientate themselves to soccer and learn about refereeing; girls should know a few simple recipes and something about sewing."[30] Although Arnold sketched his vision in more simple colors than did the founders of the Peace Corps, his portrait of a world movement for peace and development led by camp counselors had much in common with their belief in the power of innocence and youth.

Keith Spicer, befitting a Ph.D. candidate, placed his 1960 proposal in geopolitical terms. Spicer argued that Canada had the opportunity to develop a pilot program that "would be available for rapid adoption by other Commonwealth nations, the United States and Japan [and] . . . [e]ventually, the entire Western world"—reflecting an optimism about his nation's power to influence other countries that nearly equaled Sargent Shriver's. Still, Spicer's initial inspiration was anything but hard-bitten realpolitik. Spicer had read the book of the Canadian missionary Donald Faris, *To Plow with Hope,* which placed development aid in a Christian context, arguing that "life's fullest expression is found in serving others." Faris suggested that instead of sending "balding experts" to the world's neediest villages, government aid agencies send a hundred thousand young people "equipped with humility and courage, with sincerity and wisdom."[31]

Spicer sought to transform the Canadian missionary tradition into a real foreign aid program. In the summer of 1959, well before the Kennedy campaign promises regarding the Peace Corps, Spicer talked his way into the prime minister's office. There he explained to John Diefenbaker that he wanted to start a volunteer program and intended to research its feasibility while traveling in the Middle East and Asia for his doctoral research. Diefenbaker cabled Canada's ambassadors and high commissioners overseas and told them to welcome the young graduate student.[32]

Upon his return to Canada in mid-1960, Spicer began writing a proposal for the prime minister. By the time he finished it, Kennedy's Peace Corps proposal had hit the airwaves. Spicer incorporated it into his formal "Submission to the Government of Canada." If the Canadian government moved quickly, Spicer wrote, the program could be launched in a matter of weeks, with the first volunteers arriving by the autumn of 1961. Implicit was a hope that they would beat the United States to the punch. In a *Toronto Daily Star* article the next month, Spicer said that India and Ceylon had already promised to find jobs for Canadian volunteers, and that President Kennedy's proposed scheme would "likely be a year behind" the Canadian one.[33] Spicer was without doubt acting on his own ideas, but being out in front of the charismatic young American president must have added zip to the enterprise for Canadians unaccustomed to first place in the hemisphere.

Prime Minister Diefenbaker promised his moral support for a program of "voluntary egalitarian service."[34] Spicer used this vague endorsement to garner support wherever he could find it. On campus, he roped in prominent professors such as Paul Martin, who later became head of the Canadian International Development Agency (CIDA). He also convinced Member of Parliament Fred Stinson to back the cause. Stinson had the political skills that the brash graduate student lacked, and he brought the aura of legitimacy that came from political office.

Fred Stinson got the plan incorporated as Canadian Overseas Volunteers (COV). He then approached newspaper editors when he and Keith Spicer finally decided that the only way to obtain the needed funds was to "sell" volunteers to individual sponsors. "It was a kind of a slave market," Spicer later recalled. He and Stinson convinced editors, businessmen, service clubs, and churches to pay $2,000 each for their "own" volunteer in exchange for monthly letters back home. Using Diefenbaker's name, the duo raised enough to send fifteen volunteers.[35] The first contingent was set to go ahead of schedule, in front of the Peace Corps by a month.

Guy Arnold and Keith Spicer learned of each other's efforts through the *Toronto Daily Star*. On the opposite coast of Canada, students who had met Spicer convinced the University of British Columbia to sponsor the first two Canadian volunteers, who went to Ghana in 1961. Lewis Perinbam, meanwhile, decided to approach the dean at the University of Saskatchewan. Dean Francis Leddy was unaware of Guy Arnold, Keith Spicer, and the others, but he had known of the Australian and British programs for years.

After consulting with some of Canada's key university heads, Leddy decided with Perinbam to call a meeting of all university presidents, to which they also invited Fred Stinson, Guy Arnold, Keith Spicer, and representatives from a total of twenty-one organizations. They placed only one item on the agenda: the creation of "Canadian University Service Overseas" (CUSO), an organization for groups that sponsored volunteers. Leddy and Perinbam tried to come up with a name as exciting as the Peace Corps, but in the end they settled for a more denotative title that staked out both the new group's Canadian identity and its university affiliation.

To Keith Spicer and Fred Stinson, the meeting on June 6, 1961, at McGill University, was little more than a Canadian-style coup d'état: a polite way of taking over the movement to which they had given every waking moment. Leddy and Perinbam, convinced that Spicer was only a talented amateur (he was a student, after all), believed that their CUSO was the only way of placing the volunteer movement on a national level, as Kennedy was doing in the States. Keith Spicer found them arrogant. "We had thought through the idea," he later said, "convinced everybody who needed to be convinced, from the Prime Minister on down, raised the money, got the people. Then all of a sudden we had a lateral move by a couple of bureaucrats—there is no other word—who said that this thing had to be put on a solid footing."[36]

The June meeting at McGill saw clashes between age and youth, between advocates of national coordination and believers in local control, and between students and college administrators. Chaired by Leddy, the meeting began with Fred Stinson reading a list of strong objections to the proposed CUSO constitution. The constitution would "stifle local autonomy and initiative," he warned. It would place administrators and faculty at the helm, another participant pointed out. "The movement must be a student one with the inspiration and control in student hands," he insisted, voicing demands for student power that would soon grow stronger on college campuses around the world. Guy Arnold argued against government financing. "Government-sponsored bodies may be suspect abroad, while private financing leads to the greater personal involvement of Canadians." Volunteer idealism should not be tarred with the brush of great power politics.[37]

The denouement came when a young woman stood to speak. She recounted her solitary experience in Afghanistan, where she had volunteered on her own for two years. If she had gotten seriously ill, there would have been no one to take care of her. Placements needed to be coordinated for the sake of the volunteers and to avoid confusion in host countries. When she sat down, the president of the University of Alberta moved that CUSO be formally established. The motion carried 21 to 7, with Fred Stinson among the dissenters. COV and CVCS joined on the proviso that the organization act only as a coordinating body and not directly compete for volunteers or funds.[38]

The imminent departure of COV's first volunteers distracted Stinson and Spicer from worrying further about CUSO's intentions. On August 16, fifteen volunteers boarded a British flight to London, from which point they traveled by ship through the Mediterranean and Red

Sea to India, Ceylon, and Sarawak. Their first lessons concerned how to change the world *and* survive on salaries of 280 rupees a month ($56), which was about one-third the subsistence wage paid to Peace Corps workers.

Lewis Perinbam meanwhile was doing his best to see CUSO launched. Canada's External Aid Office funded an assessment trip by Perinbam in July and August 1961 to England to consult the founders of VSO, but then made it clear that not much more could be expected. Prime Minister John Diefenbaker disliked Kennedy intensely, and now resisted anything that smacked of the Peace Corps. Perinbam turned to a friend in the United States. Alan Pifer, president of the Carnegie Corporation of New York, gave Perinbam $10,000 to send CUSO's first seven volunteers to Nigeria in 1962.[39]

Financial challenges led to the formal merger of most volunteer groups into a single "CUSO" by 1964. Members of Guy Arnold's organization fretted about what would happen to the spirit of "idealism and sacrifice" when their volunteers were paid the higher subsistence rates of CUSO recruits. Stinson and Spicer's group worried about the organization's becoming an impersonal part of the establishment.[40]

Time softened the conflicts, however, and necessity drew the groups together. A unified CUSO reapproached the Canadian government in 1965, and this time obtained half a million dollars to field 250 volunteers. The secret to their success: CUSO's emergence as the single national volunteer-sending agency; the incoming Liberal administration which replaced Diefenbaker; and the siren call of Kennedy's legacy and the Peace Corps, then leading more and more Western governments to send volunteers to foreign shores. Duncan Edmonds, the government official who finally obtained public financing for CUSO, later described Kennedy as "perhaps the most inspiring and uplifting figure of contemporary history, who did more to re-awaken our faith in ourselves and in the future than any man for a long time."[41]

Kennedy sparked the idealism of many peoples. He was "quite unbelievable," in the words of one Dutchman who would go on to become a volunteer and administrator in that nation's equivalent of the Peace Corps. The American president's confidence in the future was catching, and his youthfulness inspired a new European generation that "wanted to pack its bags and hitchhike to Paris."[42]

But Kennedy was appealing because he spoke about things that young people already wanted to do, quite on their own. For young Australians, Britishers, and Canadians as well as Americans, that meant addressing the great issues of the day: creating a world of racial justice, seizing opportunities for individual heroism, and surviving the cold war. It also meant seeing the world. In his community study of the student movement in Austin, Douglas Rossinow notes that it was a generation that "seemed hungry for knowledge of the world distant from Texas." They were graduates and undergraduates who had "studied the political movements that were sweeping the world at this time" and found them exhilarating, in part "because of the role played by other students in these movements." These young people thought third world nationalism "inevitable and healthy."[43]

As the fifties moved into the sixties, young people in the West demanded more and more strenuously that their perspectives on the third world be taken seriously. They found Kennedy's leadership meaningful because he suggested that the United States (and through him the older generation in power) would now lend a friendlier ear to third world insurgencies. In Australia, Britain, and Canada this enabled volunteer leaders to cultivate stronger domestic financing because Kennedy also attracted the attention of Western governments. Kennedy helped these governments conceive of a marriage of altruism and realpolitik. Volunteers could serve both national interests and higher interests. The two were not necessarily incompatible, as Americans had long maintained. Such a marriage was especially convenient for leaders coping with perhaps the most enduring international problem of the twentieth century: decolonization.

4

The Cold War
versus
Decolonization

We are in the middle of a world revolution—and I don't mean
Communism. The Communists are . . . just moving in on the
crest of a wave. The revolution I'm talking about is that of
the little people all over the world. They're beginning to learn
what there is in life, and to learn what they are missing.

GEORGE C. MARSHALL

In July 1947 India proclaimed its independence from Great Britain.
"When India becomes free," Gandhi had prophesied to Franklin D.
Roosevelt, "the rest will follow." That same month, George Kennan
published his famous "Mr. X" article in *Foreign Affairs* advocating
vigilant containment of the Soviet Union. It was an enemy, he had
argued to fellow members of the State Department, that was "committed fanatically to the belief . . . that it is desirable and necessary that the
internal harmony of our society be disrupted, our traditional way of life
be destroyed, the international authority of our state be broken." The
United States spent the next forty-two years, and much of its wealth,
meeting the threat.[1]

In mid-1947, on the heels of global war, the United States thus
confronted new developments that promised to rewrite the maps of the
world once again. The decolonization of the third world and the cold
war ran on parallel tracks for much of the twentieth century. Although
logically these events were separable, in fact they intersected constantly.
Decolonizing and developing countries used the threat of communism
to gain political and financial support from the West. Yet they also
resented the superpowers for making their aspirations into a sideshow
of the cold war. The U.S. government recognized decolonization as an

important event in its own right. But most of the officials, politicians, and military men responsible for U.S. security were nevertheless drawn to read almost all phenomena by the light of the Soviet threat.

The Peace Corps was born of this tension. It owed its political existence to the cold war and to Kennedy's belief that Washington needed to compete more effectively with Moscow for the allegiance of newly independent countries. At the same time, the Peace Corps embodied Kennedy's genuine determination to respond to the needs of these nations.

Kennedy had shown more interest than most leaders of his generation in the decolonization of the third world. In 1951 he traveled to Asia to assess for himself the French struggle in Indochina. He came back convinced that the French had erred gravely in not granting independence to the Vietnamese and that they would never win the war. Kennedy also met Jawaharlal Nehru, whose arguments persuaded the young congressman that the United States had to concede greater autonomy to the nonaligned nations. Throughout the 1950s Kennedy spoke disparagingly and publicly of U.S. policy toward third world independence efforts. In 1957 he became famous for it.[2]

On July 2 Kennedy gave a speech in the Senate that aroused fury in France, joy in Africa, scorn from conservative colleagues, admiration from liberals, and a complaint from President Eisenhower about "young men getting up and shouting about things." Kennedy told the Senate in withering rhetoric that France should let Algeria go free and that the United States should stop its "cautious neutrality on all the real issues." As chairman of the Senate Subcommittee on African Affairs (and as a child of the colonized Irish, perhaps), Kennedy warned his colleagues: "Call it nationalism, call it anti-colonialism, call it what you will, the word is out and spreading like wildfire in nearly a thousand languages and dialects—that it is no longer necessary to remain forever in bondage."[3]

In 1959 John Kennedy told his campaign aide Harris Wofford that he wanted to initiate a "new relationship" between the United States and the developing world.[4] Walter Hixson notes that between 1945 and 1961 the U.S. government had come to recognize that cultural diplomacy could "transcend governments and reach the masses of people," but that the militarization of the cold war "dwarfed efforts to devise an effective cultural strategy."[5] Kennedy wished to appeal to other peoples directly (rather than to their governments), and viewed with impatience Eisenhower's reluctance to support decolonization openly. When Kennedy told Wofford that he sought a new relationship, these words condensed a decade of unsuccessful lobbying as both a congressman and a senator. Because Kennedy came to the idea of the Peace Corps at the end of his 1960 campaign and spent relatively few hours on it as president, some critics have concluded that it was not important to him. This is incorrect, however.[6]

Through the Peace Corps the Kennedy administration wrestled with the competing trends of history, never escaping the pull of the cold war but managing to rise sufficiently above it to earn the respect of many third world leaders and peoples. A major foreign policy initiative toward minor states, the Peace Corps used culture-to-culture diplomacy to make friends in nations that had little inherent power but that could without warning become theaters of the cold war. Kennan himself had argued that the United States should be prepared to intervene "at a series of constantly shifting geographical and political points." At the same time, the Peace Corps struggled to transcend these important but narrow, strategic considerations. In doing so it earned for John F. Kennedy in countries like Nigeria and Ethiopia, Guatemala and Gabon, a reputation among the populace as "the great one," "the good man," and "the friend of the colored man everywhere."[7] The Peace Corps was the basis for Kennedy's renown in the world's most impoverished and isolated regions.

Yet the agency had more than one or even two targets. Through it, Kennedy looked east, south, and west. The Peace Corps was a countermove against the Soviets and a gesture of friendship toward the third world. It was also a rallying point for the West. Alliances are the sine qua non of victory in war. The Peace Corps, among its many uses, strengthened the Western alliance by serving as a symbol of the free world's moral solidarity.

Peace Corps organizers began by encouraging as many nations as possible in the Western bloc to adopt volunteer programs. This goal reflected the persistent, inescapable duality of policy. On the one hand, Sargent Shriver told Kennedy, inviting other countries to start their own volunteer programs would dispel "an appearance of arrogance in

assuming that young Americans automatically can teach anybody else."
All nations would be invited to become teachers and to contribute to
the world community. "Underdeveloped" countries would benefit
most. On the other hand, the Peace Corps leadership needed to charac-
terize its efforts as part of a worldwide movement "before the Soviets
beat us to the punch."[8] Both cold war preoccupations and a desire to
respond compassionately to decolonization motivated the Kennedy administration.

From the start Shriver emphasized that the United States had to
show the international community that the Peace Corps was not intended as an arm of the cold war, lest it be dismissed as another
example of self-serving realpolitik. Shriver suggested that the United
States relinquish any claim to exclusive ownership of the Peace Corps
idea. "In presenting it to other governments and to the United Nations," Shriver recommended, "we could propose that every nation
consider the formation of its own peace corps and that the United
Nations sponsor the idea." Kennedy latched onto Shriver's suggestion,
telling Congress, "Let us hope that other nations will mobilize the
spirit and energies and skill of their people in some form of Peace
Corps—making our own effort only one step in a major international
effort to increase the welfare of all men."[9]

Within a month Shriver persuaded the assistant secretary of state
Harlan Cleveland to arrange a meeting for him with Adlai Stevenson,
U.S. ambassador to the United Nations. At the meeting in early April
1961, Stevenson agreed to push a two-part initiative in the United
Nations. First, the Peace Corps proposed to appoint volunteers directly
to UN programs, such as UNESCO. Second, the Peace Corps proposed that the United Nations give "comparable opportunities" to
volunteers from other member countries.[10] To achieve this second objective, Stevenson agreed to place a motion on the agenda of the 32nd
session of the UN Economic and Social Council, meeting in July and
August 1961.

The move to place some volunteers under international control had
support in the United States among the liberal constituency on which
Kennedy increasingly relied. In June 1961 hearings before the Senate
Committee on Foreign Relations, a Quaker spokesman advocated that
the Peace Corps "increasingly work through international organiza-

tions like the United Nations" and noted with approval Adlai Stevenson's efforts. This would "assure doubting neutrals that Peace Corps members are serving the broad interests of mankind." A representative of the Women's International League for Peace and Freedom argued that "the league would like to see this type of project done eventually through the United Nations, so that qualified people from a wide range of countries wishing to serve could have the opportunity to do so."[11]

The U.S. resolution to "use volunteer workers in the operational programmes of the United Nations" passed the 32nd session of the UN council despite the opposition of the Soviet Union. The harmlessness of the proposal stymied its effort. "The Soviets completely overplayed their hands with an hour-long attack on the Peace Corps . . . hint[ing] that all the US sought was to place spies and CIA agents throughout the underdeveloped world," the chair of the U.S. delegation noted afterward with satisfaction. Still, he cautioned, Peace Corps cooperation with the UN would be "watched" very carefully. "By the time that the next [Economic and Social Council] . . . session rolls around we should be able to demonstrate that this was a sorely needed program and that it was being executed effectively."[12]

Peace Corps staff recognized the need to keep the CIA and other spy agencies out of their operations. They knew they were being "watched." Frivolous accusations of spying were a nuisance. Founded accusations would be deadly. Shriver and his staff designed a stringent protocol in September 1961 to keep spies out. Every volunteer was required to obtain a national security clearance, first to make sure that he or she was not a spy for the other side, and then to make sure he or she was not a spy for the United States. Any person who had previously worked for the Central Intelligence Agency, or who was married to someone who had, was automatically disqualified. (In a 1978 agreement between the Peace Corps and CIA, the disqualification was conditionally extended to anyone who had had any family member in the CIA.) Volunteers, following their duty in the Peace Corps, were then prohibited from joining the intelligence service for a "cooling off" period of five years, and if they did so later they were prohibited from being assigned to any nation in which they had been trained by or served with the Peace Corps.[13] On February 28, 1962, the CIA's assistant director, Stanley Grogan, assured the White House that the

"CIA has nothing whatever to do and wants nothing whatever to do with the Peace Corps." He added, "Nothing could be more fatal to the Peace Corps than to have a CIA connection."[14]

Shriver also sought specific assurances from the president and the secretary of state that the CIA, regardless of its protestations of innocence, would be kept at bay. In April 1963, acting on vague rumors, Shriver telephoned the president. "I'm getting rather suspicious over here that . . . despite your instructions . . . some of our friends over in the Central Intelligence Agency might think that they're smarter than anybody else and that they're trying to stick fellows in the Peace Corps," he told his brother-in-law. The president, who had had his own share of disasters with the rogue CIA in Cuba and the Congo, agreed that "we don't want to discredit this whole idea." He instructed Shriver to call Richard Helms, the CIA's deputy director, and tell him "that I don't want anybody in there . . . And if they are there, let's get them out now."[15]

Dean Rusk also sent a warning to ambassadors in countries where the Peace Corps operated. "The Peace Corps is an opportunity for the nations of the world to learn what America is all about . . . To involve the Peace Corps, by accident or design, in any activity which is not within the purview of this statement would be to compromise the role of the Volunteer and jeopardize the Peace Corps and its purpose," Rusk wrote. "I wish each Chief of Mission to . . . comply with the letter and spirit of these instructions."[16]

William Delano, responsible for trying to screen out possible undercover agents, did so by looking for the "gaps" in an applicant's resume. He later admitted that if the CIA had recruited someone as early as high school, it was possible that he or she could have slipped through the Peace Corps' elaborate checks. Even the KGB and the CIA were not immune to unfriendly infiltration. Still, between 1961 and 1997 the Peace Corps never uncovered any CIA "plants," nor did any of its frequently suspicious host governments. Fidel Castro of Cuba, who would have had much to gain from proving such a connection, later volunteered to Senator Christopher Dodd, a PCV in the 1960s, "In all the years I have been in office, despite rumors that have flowed from all sources, we never once have had one piece of specific information to link any Peace Corps volunteer . . . with any foreign intelligence operation."[17]

Perhaps the CIA took John Kennedy's injunction seriously. It is likely that no one will ever know for certain, since the CIA has never opened its personnel records, in part to protect the lives of its agents. Yet, as a later Peace Corps official noted, it is probable that "after thirty-five years, someone somewhere would have uncovered the evidence of such a connection if it existed." On the other hand, if someday a volunteer with CIA links is discovered, it certainly will say more about the intent of the CIA than the intent of the Peace Corps. In any case, Shriver could maintain with confidence that "in an era of sabotage and espionage . . . the Peace Corps and its volunteers have earned a priceless yet simple renown: they are trustworthy."[18]

The Peace Corps did what it could to foil spurious accusations of spying as well. When Sargent Shriver heard that Colorado State University had asked volunteer trainees to keep diaries, he quashed the idea. Even if it was "a loss to the research program," the director emphasized, volunteers should be strongly discouraged from recording their impressions in this way. Ed Smith, a volunteer to Ghana, later noted that he was told upon arrival that there were always "'those on the prowl for evidence of the Peace Corps' commitment to a subversive ideology,' and a diary was all they needed to confirm their distrust."[19] He refrained for five months and then, like many volunteers, capitulated to the desire to keep himself company. Paranoia was oppressive.

Franklin Williams, deputy director of the Peace Corps and the point man to the United Nations, visited Paris a week after the end of the UN conference at which the Peace Corps had first deflected accusations of spying. Meeting with senior officials of the UNESCO Secretariat, Williams spread the idea of an eventual UN volunteer program. A member of the U.S. embassy in Paris called Williams's visit "very successful in engendering interest and enthusiasm in the peace corps and in stimulating serious thought by the secretariat on possible U.S. Peace Corps-UNESCO cooperation."[20]

The initiatives in the UN arena fit within a larger pattern of monitoring international responses to the Peace Corps. On March 1, 1961, the same day that President Kennedy signed his executive order, Dean Rusk sent a memo to U.S. embassies worldwide ordering that "local reaction to [the] idea [in] all countries should be canvassed and reported." Within a week, U.S. embassies in Austria, Britain, Cyprus, Denmark, Egypt, Ethiopia, the Netherlands, and Sweden sent word of enthusiastic newspaper and government commentary. Positive reports came even from the Communist countries. The first editorial in Yugoslavia called the Peace Corps an attempt to reinvent the "petrified policy" of the United States toward the third world, but also acknowledged that it recalled "much of the old forgotten spirit of idealism and renaissance dating from the days of the American pioneer." Privately, junior Soviet officials evidenced "admiration tinged with envy."[21] Eleven months later the Peace Corps received reports that small contingents of Chinese, Czech, and East German Communists were passing themselves off in Afghanistan as "their country's equivalent of the Peace Corps."[22] To his own staff, Shriver crowed victory.

The United States Information Agency joined in the effort to assess both world reaction and the possibility of transferring "some of America's aid burden to Western Europe." In 1961 the agency contracted confidentially with local, private pollsters in Great Britain, France, Germany, and Italy to gauge popular responses within the allied nations without biasing responses through "knowledge of U.S. sponsorship." The survey responses revealed the perceived moral leadership of the United States in the post–World War II, pre-Vietnam era. Although each European group tended to have a high opinion of its own contributions to world aid needs and a low opinion of the contributions of other European nations, the nationalities polled evinced a consistently high regard for the efforts of the United States. Nearly half (48 percent) believed that the United States was either "doing more than [its] fair share" or "doing about its fair share" (37 percent had no opinion or did not believe in giving aid). The British (60 percent) and the Germans (53 percent) assessed the U.S. performance the most favorably, the French the least. But even the doubting French, only 34 percent of whom thought the United States was doing its fair share or more in the world, ranked it nearly twice as high as they ranked any of their neighbors.[23]

The survey showed that an average of 15 percent of the populace in the four countries had heard of the Peace Corps by the end of Kennedy's first year in office, and that 10 percent could correctly identify it as sponsored by the United States. While this hardly compared to the 50 percent of Americans who could identify the new organization, the fact that one in six Europeans knew of the Peace Corps was nonetheless remarkable. Although the survey indicated that Europeans were evenly divided on how much they thought the Peace Corps could accomplish, three times more people thought it was designed "to help" the third world than thought it part of some U.S. scheme "to dominate."[24]

Despite the UN resolution to encourage the use of volunteers in development, Peace Corps staff nonetheless found that opportunities with the United Nations were not readily forthcoming. They also found they did not need the UN. After Sargent Shriver's first eight-country tour of Africa and Asia in 1961, when he met Kwame Nkrumah of Ghana and Jawaharlal Nehru of India, the Peace Corps received requests for volunteers from over two dozen third world countries. Gradually the agency dropped its ambition to place significant numbers of volunteers with the United Nations and instead focused on developing bilateral relationships with "Peace Corps countries" in Africa, Asia, and Latin America.

But the Peace Corps did not cease its efforts to persuade other industrialized nations to adopt its model. It hardly needed to convert the other English-speaking nations to the idea, of course, although in the words of one Australian, Kennedy's initiative "softened up" his government to appeals for funds. In 1965 the Australian government finally found significant monies for Australian Volunteers Abroad, which expanded to nine countries beyond Indonesia. It took John Kennedy in America to popularize the notion in Australia.[25] Alec Dickson, too, found new avenues to the British government opened up by the Peace Corps, which for the first time began to take VSO seriously.

But the Peace Corps also stimulated competition among the British Commonwealth programs, whose organizers were stunned by the scope of the Kennedy initiative and its place of prominence in the New Frontier. Indeed, the most obviously unique characteristics of the American program were its immense scale (2,816 Americans the first full year compared with 100 Canadians and 85 British around the same time) and its status as a government initiative.[26] Unlike its predecessors, the Peace Corps was bankrolled by a wealthy government as an expression of its foreign policy.

Alec Dickson of VSO feared that the British were "getting hopelessly left behind in comparison" and urged his government to commit significant resources to the program. A more sanguine civil servant observed that the size of the U.S. initiative was simply a reflection of "the realities of wealth and power." The Peace Corps, he noted, was "only one of a hundred fields in which we can have no hope of keeping up with the United States." Still, Dickson and others continued to lobby for a more vigorous British response to the swelling of American influence in the former imperial colonies.[27]

The organizers of CUSO also found themselves racing the clock of the Kennedy administration. CUSO's volunteers reached Africa first, but the rapid-fire diffusion of the Peace Corps around the globe "created difficulties," Lewis Perinbam noted, because in many countries "they got there first and offered a completely free service." Still, Prime Minister John Diefenbaker remained determined not to appear that he was copying Kennedy.[28]

As it turned out, copying was exactly what the Kennedy administration had in mind. In early 1962 Peace Corps staff began organizing an "International Conference on Middle-Level Manpower," to be held in Puerto Rico in October. Vice President Lyndon Johnson signed on to head the U.S. delegation.

State Department officials expressed "serious objections" from the start. Much that the Peace Corps had done over the preceding year had been greeted with incredulity by department members. "We feel confident that it is not the intention that Americans should have no special privileges . . . and should live on African standards," one diplomat wrote to Dean Rusk, before being apprised that that was exactly what the Peace Corps intended. Other officials expressed the sentiment that Shriver needed "a gentle straightening out" to bring him more into line with classic cold war thinking—that is, to convince him to place volunteers in hot spots such as Algeria and Vietnam, which Shriver refused to do. Department of State condescension was perhaps best epitomized by the career diplomat Elliot Briggs's description of the Peace Corps as a naive agency "wrapped in a pinafore of publicity, whose team cry is 'Yoo-hoo, yoo-hoo. Let's go out and wreak some good on some natives.'" The disdain was entirely mutual. "Many of the volunteers say there was an anti-AID tone to their training," one evaluator reported in 1963, and "were told in so many words to stay away from AID and missionaries."[29]

The State Department's concerns about the proposed middle-level manpower conference reflected a desire to keep a tighter rein on spin-offs of the Peace Corps, which the department could hardly contain as it was. Officials particularly objected to the Peace Corps proposal that the conference end by creating an international organization to encourage other national volunteer programs. Department members instead advised a passive approach. The president had already invited other industrialized nations to undertake similar ventures. That was enough.

"We hesitate to take any risks to internationalize it," one policy memo stated, especially since "Soviet participation in such international machinery would be contrary to our foreign policy objectives and . . . make it difficult for less developed countries to refuse to accept Soviet volunteers." Department members also urged that as few American volunteers as possible be placed in UN agencies, lest the Soviets demand a quid pro quo arrangement that would allow them to plant significant numbers of youth "controlled from the Kremlin."[30]

Dean Rusk overrode his staff's objections to the conference. Rusk, whom Shriver had recruited for Kennedy's Cabinet, consistently demonstrated support for the Peace Corps over the objections of the career foreign service staff. Rusk's own view reflected an implicit recognition of one of the many paradoxes of the cold war. "The Peace Corps is not an instrument *of* foreign policy because to make it so would rob it of its contribution *to* foreign policy," he cabled the ambassadors in all countries with volunteers. Rusk called it a policy of friendly disassociation. Unlike other offices of the U.S. government abroad (such as those of AID and USIA), local Peace Corps offices were not even housed in the embassies and were often located miles away.[31]

Rusk's position and the Peace Corps' high political profile mostly insulated the agency from State Department efforts to keep it small and out of the way of the cold war, or to integrate it more fully with specific foreign policy objectives. "The State Department knew we were anointed by the president," observed Warren Wiggins, himself a former foreign service officer. "If you're in the State Department and you're dealing with somebody that's anointed by the president you treat them nice."[32]

Rusk spared no effort to make the manpower conference a success. With Kennedy sending his vice president, the department considered it imperative that other countries respond in kind, lest Johnson and the nation suffer an embarrassment. It was "vital that other participants also have high level representation," Dean Rusk cabled the embassies.

"The success of this conference is of personal concern to the President and Secretary." He also provided ambassadors with arguments to help persuade foreign decision makers.

"Our experience . . . has demonstrated that overseas volunteers can have a substantial impact on the attitudes of the people and government of the recipient country toward the donor government. This is of special interest to the French, Belgians, and British who are concerned with their relations with former colonial territories," Rusk noted, fully aware that all of these countries hoped to enjoy a special relationship with their former possessions. Playing to the allies' competitive instincts, Rusk added, "You might make [the] point that thousands of young Americans will soon be working as volunteers [in] these countries." The American secretary of state also showed his awareness of the Peace Corps' domestic role. "In addition volunteer programs have substantial political impact within [the] donor country," Rusk advised his colleagues to say. "Our own Peace Corps has created great enthusiasm among American youth and generated much good will." A political appointee, Rusk was undoubtedly aware of how the Peace Corps had burnished Kennedy's popular image. He concluded that volunteering thus had "political ramifications far beyond [the] important contribution it can make to development."[33]

Attended by the vice presidents or foreign ministers of forty-three nations, the International Conference on Middle-Level Manpower met in Puerto Rico in October 1962 with Lyndon Johnson presiding. The gathering voted to create an International Peace Corps Secretariat (later renamed the International Secretariat for Volunteer Service to diminish the perception of U.S. sponsorship). What the secretariat was actually to *do* was undefined, leaving much to the imagination of its organizers. The French and Swiss governments later bridled at the activist approach that the American-run secretariat immediately adopted under Shriver's appointee, Richard Goodwin. The authority that the Secretariat had been granted in Puerto Rico, the French said, was simply "to assemble the documents of the Conference."[34]

Goodwin went into high gear, nonetheless, spending much of the next year soliciting funds and staff support from the United States' major allies. Israel gave funds and staff first, with the Dutch and Germans contributing paid staff support. The Philippines, the only former colony of the United States and its major ally in the Pacific, contributed the fourth international staff person. Goodwin and his staff traveled around the world meeting with potential organizers of national youth volunteer programs.

Nowhere did they meet with significant resistance. A number of countries immediately took up the idea, which had the advantage of being both popular and "noncontroversial," in the words of an Italian observer. At the Puerto Rico meeting, twelve countries announced plans for their own overseas or domestic Peace Corps. In 1963 the Netherlands, Germany, Denmark, France, and Norway all started new programs. Japanese youth groups pressured their government to establish an equivalent. In May the secretariat hosted representatives from thirteen countries at a two-week "Workshop for Peace Corps Development" in Washington.[35] The participants had their picture taken with President Kennedy. The *International Volunteer* newsletter that the secretariat began publishing monthly in March 1963, with expensive glossy photos on every page, highlighted these developments.

The State Department continued its support for the Peace Corps initiative, which now included both domestic and foreign volunteer programs. The logic behind encouraging domestic volunteering derived from the recognition that youth predominated in developing countries with high birthrates. Just as literature and films in the United States explored themes of youthful rebellion in the 1950s and early 1960s, so did policymakers. In 1961 one influential report noted with reference to revolutionary Algeria, "In a comparatively youthful population, impatience to realize rising expectations is likely to be pronounced. Extreme nationalism has often been the result."[36] From 1946 onward, the State Department and the Central Intelligence Agency competed with the Soviet Union in their support of student groups claiming to represent the youth of the world. Although there is no evidence that the CIA penetrated the Peace Corps, its secret funding of the National Student Association from 1952 to 1967 at a cost of more than half a million dollars a year demonstrated the conviction that youth per se constituted a theater of the cold war.[37]

Dean Rusk conveyed a sense of urgency about the task of reaching youthful populations in a February 1963 memo to American embassies in Latin America. "A domestic Peace Corps in a Latin American country is essentially an effort to mobilize the youth of that country . . . in the cause of their own national development." Local volunteer opportunities, he stated, could "exert profound social and psychological influence on the thinking of youth who are frustrated in their desires to realize national goals, unable to find useful employment and who are thus easy prey for extremism or apathy."[38] National service programs, the secretary of state implied, could channel these emotions in ways acceptable to the United States and to local governments eager for social control.

Rusk urged embassies to make every effort to further the cause. He also instructed embassy officers to inquire whether the country would accept foreign advisors from the International Peace Corps Secretariat. "If not an American, would they accept a German or Israeli or other?" Rusk queried, aware of the value of a multinational staff that could be deployed strategically according to national prejudices. Such a staff could also, of course, be a liability. The embassy in Khartoum, Sudan, warned that the Israeli staff member of the secretariat would "raise a red flag in the eyes of Arab countries." Yehuda Benron was instead sent to sub-Saharan countries like Tanganyika, where he spent six weeks helping set up a domestic volunteer program.[39]

By the end of 1963 a number of countries in Asia, Africa, and Latin America had announced plans for volunteer programs. One of the first was the Philippines, whose volunteers in the organization "Work a Year with the People" labored alongside an enormous Peace Corps contingent. Argentina, traditionally competitive with the United States, did not accept Peace Corps volunteers but in July 1963 announced that it was starting its own "Maestros Para America" (Teachers for America) and would send fifty volunteers to work elsewhere in Latin America.

The programs most closely modeled on the Peace Corps, however, were those of the northern industrialized countries. Between 1961 and 1965 nearly every government friendly to the United States initiated or expanded its own youth corps. Kennedy's Peace Corps started as an off-the-cuff campaign promise. By 1965 the United States had 13,248 volunteers in the field and important allies were emulating it worldwide. The Peace Corps idea proliferated because it fit, neatly and readily, into the foreign policies of many nations. Although critics at the time questioned what possible significance these "kiddie corps" could have for third world development, sponsoring governments staged them as high drama.

President Kennedy bid Peace Corps recruits good luck in the Rose

Garden. Queen Juliana of the Netherlands received the first Dutch volunteers at her palace and then saw them off at the airport. President Heinrich Luebke and Chancellor Konrad Adenauer invited the U.S. president to speak at the inauguration of the German volunteer program. Israel's foreign minister, Golda Meir, personally attended the Puerto Rico conference to shake hands with America's vice president. Each nation pushed its volunteers into the limelight. Just as the volunteer movement reflected popular culture, so it reflected key dimensions of government policy. The cold war, the Western alliance system, decolonization, and the need of governments to build domestic consensus came together to inspire an eagerness in officials of many countries after 1962 to begin their own "peace corps."

The cold war was one backdrop. In material ways, the North American experience of the 1950s differed dramatically from the experience of Europe and Japan, in which individuals and families still suffered postwar privations. While Americans enjoyed big cars and new televisions, the rest of the industrialized world struggled to rebuild. "The fifties in Holland were gray," one Dutch volunteer later commented. "The Cold War was severely felt . . . [There was] not much space for things that were outside the most immediate necessities of life."[40] Western Europeans also felt the chill and fear of the cold war with special immediacy as they watched Soviet tanks roll down the streets of their near neighbors in Czechoslovakia, Hungary, and Poland.

In the United States the cold war helped to end a crumbling two-hundred-year-old tradition of no large standing army in peacetime. In 1950, the year after the Soviets' detonation of their first atom bomb, President Harry Truman approved NSC-68. The plan "meant doubling or tripling the budget, increasing taxes heavily, and imposing various kinds of economic controls," Truman later wrote. "It meant a great change in our normal peacetime way of doing things."[41] NSC-68 assumed that the United States would be on a wartime footing as long as the Soviet system endured. This required attention to preparedness in all its dimensions.

From its experience in World Wars I and II, the U.S. government had learned the importance of psychological warfare. Wars had to be sold to the citizenry; the advantages of alliance had to be sold to neutral countries; the enemy had to be convinced of the futility of struggle and the mercy to be expected upon surrender. In World War I, the Com-

mittee on Public Information churned out movies, posters, advertisements, and pamphlets designed to keep patriotism high. Woodrow
Wilson used his famous Fourteen Points to define the war terms of the
United States, establish a bargaining position with the Allies, convince
Germany that the war could end in "peace without victory," and
counter Bolshevik peace propaganda with his own version of the "new
diplomacy."[42]

In the next war, the Office of the Coordinator of Inter-American
Relations under Nelson Rockefeller began the first propaganda efforts
in 1940 to convince wavering Latin Americans of the benefits of alliance. Rockefeller added a new dimension to the war of words,
though—the lure of practical assistance with economic development.
He not only persuaded Walt Disney to create new cartoon characters
(as in *The Three Caballeros*) and commissioned flattering busts of Latin
American presidents, but sent breeding chickens, garden hoes, medi-
cines, and an array of advisors to Latin America. To General George C.
Marshall, Rockefeller described his overall mission as "psychological
warfare in the Hemisphere." His agency subsequently became the
model for the Office of War Information once the United States
officially entered the conflict on December 8, 1941.[43]

Alec Dickson also had responsibilities for foreign propaganda during
the war. The Japanese had conquered Hong Kong, Singapore, and the
Dutch East Indies. India, Burma, and Ceylon were threatened. Dickson
worried about the response of African colonials if a Japanese fleet
appeared off the coast of Africa. He proposed and then took responsibility for running a so-called Mobile Propaganda Unit. African soldiers
drawn from twenty different tribes serving in the British forces used
drama and music to reach villagers who had no radios and were largely
illiterate. The soldiers explained the purpose of the war and that there
were "different kinds" of colonizers.[44]

After World War II the United States developed the Marshall Plan
and Point Four, using economic aid to extend American political
influence. For the most part these plans were eagerly accepted by
countries desperate for funds. In a further, unpublicized innovation,
Truman broadened the mandate of the new Central Intelligence
Agency to include covert political warfare. The Voice of America radio
network became the advance guard for overt propaganda efforts. But
the Russians jammed the American broadcasts and the continuing esca-

lation of the cold war led Truman to approve several efforts to diversify the nation's psychological warfare program.

One of these efforts was Project TROY—named for the donated wooden horse that proved deadly to the Trojans. Project TROY brought together scientists, social scientists, and historians in a top-secret study group to develop new ways of waging "political warfare" and countering anti-American propaganda. Publicly, Truman told U.S. newspaper editors "we must make ourselves known as we really are."[45]

Project TROY was the first committee to float the idea of a government peace corps. The group developed plans for propaganda in both Western and Eastern Europe, but when it came to areas of the world with only rudimentary technology, project members recognized the need for unusual methods. In an annex to the final report, Robert Morison of the Rockefeller Foundation suggested that "face to face contact on a wide scale" might be the only way to reach people in areas like China and Southeast Asia, which lacked modern communications systems. Morison proposed "the recruiting of a group of American youth willing and able to spend two or four years of their lives in intimate personal contact with the village people of Asia. Their primary task would be the demonstration of suitably modified western techniques of public health and agriculture. If they were the right sort of representative Americans they would also make use of their position to transmit almost automatically American ideas of cooperation in the common job, respect for individual dignity, and the free play of individual initiative."[46]

As director of the Rockefeller Foundation's medical sciences program, Morison spoke from long experience. The foundation had been bringing Americans into face-to-face contact with Asians for decades through the Peking Union Medical College. Cold war necessities led people like Morison to think of the ways in which the proselytizing strategies with which they were familiar might be applied to psychological warfare.

Throughout the 1950s a number of prominent public figures alluded to or directly advocated the idea of a peace corps to supplement the expanding U.S. war corps. Nelson Rockefeller, special assistant for foreign affairs to President Dwight D. Eisenhower, emphasized that the United States had to make a convincing case of what it was for, not just what it was against. His efforts culminated in the book *Prospect for*

America. One contributor was Max Millikin, a member of Project TROY and the author of the first policy report that John F. Kennedy solicited for the Peace Corps.

New moves by the Soviets to strengthen their ties with the third world undoubtedly fed Rockefeller's worries and those of many other government officials in the middle and late 1950s. Following the death of Stalin in 1953, the Soviet leadership attempted to develop a more sophisticated approach to the conflict with the West. In 1955 the Soviets expanded trade with Latin America by 34 percent, and in January 1956 their premier, Nikolai Bulganin, announced a program of technical assistance to the impoverished countries in America's traditional "backyard." Soviet officials also toured the newly independent countries of Egypt, Indonesia, and India, promising lavish economic assistance programs. President Eisenhower reflected that "the new Communist line of sweetness and light was perhaps more dangerous than their propaganda in Stalin's time."[47]

Vague ideas for a youth corps to counter growing Soviet influence coalesced into a concerted push for new policy in 1960. In January, Congressman Henry Reuss introduced his bill to fund a feasibility study and six months later Senator Hubert Humphrey proposed his bill to establish a "Peace Corps." In his early November campaign promise, Kennedy said "Our young men and women, dedicated to freedom, are fully capable of overcoming the efforts of Mr. Khrushchev's missionaries who are dedicated to undermining that freedom." William Lederer, author of *The Ugly American,* advocated shortly thereafter the formation of a "United States Strategic Service Corps" to counter the Soviets, again fitting it into the paradigm of psychological warfare.[48]

Once the Peace Corps got under way, Shriver evidenced a keen awareness of the duality of the organization's purpose. Although he hammered the point again and again—to staff, to volunteers, to members of the State Department, Congress, and United Nations—that the Peace Corps was not an "arm" or "tool" of the cold war, Shriver nevertheless deeply believed that the Peace Corps would help the United States win it. Volunteers should have been in Colombia for the "last ten years," he told Kennedy in reference to local communists and their Soviet mentors. "Best of all," he wrote gleefully to his wife while on a trip to Asia, "we have received word that Indonesia wants the Peace Corps—500 strong—and that Sukarno wants me to come to

Jakarta to discuss starting a program with him. Sukarno has been very pro-Soviet, as you know, and this is the first time since Jack has been president that Sukarno has invited any operating agency of the U.S. Government to start work in his country." The nonaligned nations were "lining up behind PC," Shriver triumphantly cabled to his staff member George Carter in Ghana, despite "loud-mouthed, extreme public opposition" by local communists.[49]

Shriver and many others thus sincerely believed that the Peace Corps was both a means to an end and an end in itself. Later critics of the Peace Corps would argue that "its foreign policy role was carefully crafted, diligently obscured, and consistently denied."[50] But from his first speech at Ann Arbor, Kennedy had claimed that the future of the "free world" depended on American youth. In publications like *Foreign Affairs,* Shriver openly acknowledged the Peace Corps' foreign policy role, while asserting that it was a subtle one. Dean Rusk also said explicitly on several occasions that the Peace Corps made a contribution to foreign policy. None of these men soft-pedaled their position on the cold war. Yet, in a simultaneous spirit of neutrality, the Peace Corps did not reward only allies with volunteers, nor did it withdraw volunteers from countries hostile to the United States unless asked. It was a hybrid—an agency struggling to be several things at once. Perhaps the closest analogy one could find for Kennedy's and Shriver's view of the role of the Peace Corps in the cold war would be that of favorable weather in a battle. The Peace Corps might not be a kind of matériel, but it established conditions—built relationships—undeniably useful to the United States, that might even be the sine qua non of victory.

American government officials were not the only ones concerned about the cold war. Keith Spicer of CUSO later freely acknowledged that the cold war increased his sense of urgency even though he feared that "politicians would corrupt what I thought was a good, humanitarian cause by bringing in these sordid political considerations." Francis Leddy praised CUSO volunteers for "the luster which they have quietly given to the reputation of Canada throughout the World." The Australian volunteer Ollie McMichael worried from the first that without significant attempts by the West to establish goodwill, the third world would go communist and his country would be threatened.[51]

The cold war provided one framework in which policymakers and even the public could readily understand the need for something like the Peace Corps. For the governments that had allied with the United States in this war, starting their own "peace corps" fit into another framework as well: supporting the United States as leader of the Western alliance.

Private individuals had organized the first volunteer groups. In the apt phrasing of the Peace Corps veterans David Hapgood and Meridan Bennett, "it was left to the United States to make the idea into official policy and to back that policy with the power of the national treasury." This policy might have remained unique to the United States had it not been for the post–World War II alliance system. Within this system the U.S. government strove continuously for coherence between its own domestic and foreign policies and those of its allies. Similarly the allies, to greater and lesser extents, attempted when expedient to conform their policies to those of the acknowledged leader of the system. Cooperation with U.S. hegemony produced many benefits.[52] European security and economic prosperity depended heavily on these benefits throughout the 1950s and into the 1960s.

In the first and second years of the Peace Corps, the message went out, loud and clear, that the United States wanted its allies to emulate the American effort. Their doing so would show the moral unity of the free world and the allies' approbation of the United States. In the cold war, such rituals of solidarity and strength played a critical role, much as the pageantry of a court in medieval times told other states to think twice. The Soviets enacted their own rituals—massive tank and troop processions through Red Square and unanimous votes in the Warsaw Pact. Of course, the United States did not have (or want) the same means that the Soviets had at their disposal for ensuring the appearance of unity. Economic and strategic matters frequently divided the Western allies. But the Peace Corps was something to which no one could object and which touched core beliefs in many countries.

The speed with which the allies responded to Kennedy's appeal matched the friendliness of their relationships with his administration. The sentiment in Holland, for example, corresponded to the reminder often given to Dutch youth: "They won the war for us." The West Germans themselves sought ritual reassurances of unity with the United States in this period—including parades of American presidents and vice presidents. (Robert Kennedy, visiting Berlin in 1962, gently chided the encircled citizens that they "must wean themselves from the suspicion that the United States had written off its solemn obligations if a senior American official failed to visit Berlin once a month to reaffirm them.") The Federal Republic started its volunteer program in mid-1963.[53]

The French and Canadian governments responded more testily to the U.S. initiative but soon joined in. The bandwagon effect was mutually reinforcing: each new forum for the peace corps idea created additional ones. The announcement of the American Peace Corps, for example, gave supporters of the British VSO an opportunity to initiate a debate in the House of Lords, which prompted a Stockholm newspaper to ask when there would be a "Swedish initiative in the same direction." The "Peace Corps has had a marked impact," one British official wrote in early 1962, creating a "climate of opinion in other countries and in international organizations [that] is further stimulating interest in Britain."[54]

The founding of peace corps look-alikes by nearly all the countries of the free world within four years testified both to the perceived inherent merit of the idea and to the prestige of the United States in the Western alliance system during the early 1960s. Creating a national volunteer program was a way to keep abreast of the United States that cost little in treasure or national pride. Demonstrating solidarity with the alliance was the responsibility of each allied nation, and they all undertook to fulfill it when they could. Fortunately, the volunteer scheme also fit conveniently with the array of solutions to the thorny problems of decolonization then being considered.

Allard Lowenstein, the prominent American liberal who acted as a bridge between the Establishment and the radical youth movement of the 1960s, recounted the gallows humor attending the struggle of black Africans to reclaim their continent. "Fashionable Johannesburg has tried for years to laugh at the story of the kindly housewife who asked her devoted black cook if in a 'show-down' she would really kill the family of which she was virtually a part," Lowenstein reported in his 1962 book *Brutal Mandate*. "'Oh, no, Missie,'" the cook is supposed to have replied, "'I kill the family next door, cook next door kill you.'"[55]

One of the main events of the twentieth century—rivaling the world wars and the cold war in its consequences for human populations—was the decolonization of major parts of Africa, Asia, and the Middle East. The dominant nations of the northern hemisphere did not uniformly oppose this process. In fact, because of their conflicts with one another, the more powerful countries often abetted it. In World War I, Woodrow Wilson raised the hopes of submerged nationalities from Estonia to Indochina when he attempted to impose an American peace on the contenders in the great conflict. His Fourteen Points went directly to the principle of national self-determination.

In the interwar period, Britain in Africa and the United States in Latin America took unprecedented steps to ensure loyalty in the face of Hitler's challenge, promising greater freedoms and benefits to regions under their sway. President Roosevelt promised to be a "good neighbor" and respect territorial sovereignty. Sumner Welles, assistant secretary of state, began efforts to boost Latin American economies, including the first loan for competitive industrialization ($20 million to Brazil for the tropics' first steel plant). The British colonial secretary Malcolm MacDonald stated in Parliament in 1938 that the ultimate, if distant, aim of policy was evolution toward self-government. He also forged the proposal that resulted in Cabinet passage of a Colonial Development and Welfare Bill in 1940 at the height of the wartime emergency, when only measures of extreme national priority obtained funding. The bill's sponsors took pains to refute the notion that it was "a bribe or a reward for the Colonies' support in this supreme crisis," which was probably the best evidence of its being so.[56]

Japan's conquest of European and American colonies in Asia further shook the colonial system. Nationalists in Indonesia, Vietnam, and even the Philippines gained heart (and ammunition) from the easy collapse of the Caucasians under Japanese attack. In part to secure the assistance of guerrilla fighters like Ho Chi Minh during World War II, the United States took an officially anti-imperialist stance toward postwar arrangements. So did the Soviet Union. This heightened the expectations and political leverage of many nations attempting to overthrow a legacy of external domination, even though later policy was sometimes completely at odds with official rhetoric.

In the United States, the policy of anti-imperialism was constrained by the Monroe Doctrine and the alliance system with Europe. On the one hand, the U.S. government refused to see any parallels between its own sphere of influence and the spheres maintained by European imperial powers. Although the United States gave up its only Asian colony before the other allies gave up theirs (the Philippines in 1946), Latin

America remained a special case for the United States. The hemisphere added twenty votes to that of the United States in the sixty-member United Nations. Secretary of state Henry Stimson commented during the UN charter debate, "I think it's not asking too much to have our little region over here which has never bothered anybody."[57] Not only did the Monroe Doctrine represent an obvious contradiction not lost on America's imperialist allies, but it gave an opening to America's enemies. The Soviets later used the Organization of American States to justify the Warsaw Pact.

On the other hand, the U.S. policy of self-determination also remained largely rhetorical because of the need to court European allies. France wanted to keep Indochina; Churchill vowed not to preside over the dismantling of the British Empire; the Netherlands, Belgium, and Portugal all had a stake in Africa and Asia. During World War II, Roosevelt refused to risk antagonizing Churchill over the question of India's independence. Instead, Roosevelt asked Gandhi to unite in the "common cause against a common enemy." Later, obtaining French consent to critical strategies of the cold war such as the rearming of Germany became far more important to the United States than granting the principle of self-determination to Vietnam or to any other of a bunch of ragtag, would-be nations.[58]

But U.S. policy began to change as these would-be states came closer to real sovereignty. When it became clear that the Dutch could not regain control of the East Indies and that Indonesian nationalists might side with communism after their impending triumph, the United States pressured the Dutch to withdraw. Indonesia became independent in 1949. The most telling break with the past came when the United States sided with Egypt, which had gained independence in 1954, against the French and the British during the Suez Canal invasion of 1956. When Gamal Abdel Nasser nationalized the canal, prompting retaliatory strikes by the two European powers, President Eisenhower furiously demanded that they withdraw lest Nasser seek military support from the Soviets. U.S. officials threatened to cut off Britain's oil supply if it refused. The episode "badly split the western alliance . . . and marked the true end of the British empire."[59] It also hurt the French war effort in Algeria, where Nasser was supplying the revolutionaries.

Successful independence movements forced the United States to reorder its priorities. Just as independent Vietnam had been sacrificed in 1946 to placate France, ten years later French interests had to be sacrificed to placate Egypt. In both cases the overarching goal remained the same: outmaneuvering the Soviet Union. Vice President Richard Nixon attended the ceremonies marking Ghana's independence in 1957, and in travels to eleven other African nations he recommended steep increases in aid to the continent.[60]

Senator John F. Kennedy nevertheless criticized the Eisenhower administration's policy toward Africa as inadequate. There had been a tendency, he stated, "to allow U.S. policy toward Africa to be formulated in the capitals of Europe." Kennedy's 1957 speech on Algeria brought numerous delegations of African nationalists to his Senate door. The result, according to one historian of Africa, was ultimately to make Kennedy the most "revered" of all American leaders.[61]

Just as decolonization forced the United States to reorder its priorities, the imperialist nations of Europe found that they, too, had to reorder their thinking about the world. For Britain and France especially, whatever remaining claims they had to being world powers after 1945 were attached to their old empires. Flanked by the friendly but overbearing United States and the hostile Soviet Union, the European nations at first resisted the trend of decolonization. They also worked to develop other means for talking on equal terms with the superpowers, such as creating the European Community and exploding their own nuclear weapons.[62]

The Dutch and the French both fought bloody wars to keep their colonies, which they ultimately lost. In 1958 the French returned Charles de Gaulle to the presidency, and he began the slow process of ending the Algerian war. He also began to look for new ways of responding to the cry for decolonization, a search that would culminate in France's decision to relinquish power in all of its thirteen sub-Saharan colonies in 1960, two years before Algerian independence. At the same time, de Gaulle sought ways of keeping the former colonies in the French orbit. Not only did their continuing allegiance enhance the "grandeur of France," but it also meant thirteen countries voting along with France in the United Nations. "We are more important than our own single country," one French foreign aid official later observed, "because we have the African countries with us."[63]

French economic assistance in the transition to independence helped to sustain African allegiance. Aid that went exclusively to Francophone countries also sustained cultural ties. French continued to be taught in African schools in part because the French helped run the schools. A country that rejected the continued affiliation could expect harsh treatment. When Guinea in 1958 replied "non" to de Gaulle's offer to join the allied French Community, colonial officials took all records and every stick of furniture in government offices, including phones off the walls.[64]

The idea of using young volunteers to deliver aid and help sustain cultural ties, coming one year after the watershed of 1960, slipped easily into the overarching policy. The French Ministry of Cooperation, housed in the old colonial offices in Paris, organized the Volontaires du Progrès in 1963. The first volunteers went to Francophone Africa in January 1964 as agricultural workers who were instructed to "build their own dwellings, African style." The emphasis in volunteer selection was on recruiting peasants who could work with their hands. "The idea," according to a later Volontaires du Progrès recruiter, "was that peasant-to-peasant communication would be effective."[65]

British imperial policy had had a subtle history, evolving from outright rule in the nineteenth century to "indirect rule" at the start of the twentieth century to Commonwealth participation by the mid-twentieth century. At each step, for the most part, the British had held tightly to what they could, while yielding with greater grace than the French what they could not. They withdrew from India without a fight in 1947 when it became clear they could hold on no longer, and from Ghana ten years later. Still, in the 1940s and 1950s the ruling British Labour Party continued to seek new ways of persuading colonies to remain in the fold. The most prominent of these attempts was the Colombo Plan, which was also Britain's answer to the Marshall Plan.[66]

Economic and cultural ties to the former colonies were essential not only to Britain's growth and its identity as "Britannia" but also to its credibility as one of the five permanent "great power" members of the UN Security Council. Eventually, after the 1956 Suez crisis, the Conservative Party under Harold Macmillan led the way to accelerated decolonization as a means of avoiding the risks of both enormous bloodshed and the loss of nationalist movements to communism. The Commonwealth model for decolonization remained important, however, because it held out hope for an enduring relationship. This was particularly true in 1962, when Britain found itself betwixt "Empire" and "Europe": denuded of its colonies and denied membership in the European Economic Community by France.[67]

The idealistic founders of VSO and CUSO argued to anyone who would listen that their organizations gave real, personal meaning to postcolonial ties. The earliest Canadian groups used "Commonwealth" in their names. In Britain, the Commonwealth Relations Office characterized the work of VSO as "excellent." Dickson's efforts fit well with the larger national policy of emphasizing the Commonwealth. In 1958 the British Cabinet redesignated Empire Day as Commonwealth Day, converted the Imperial Institute into the Commonwealth Institute, and began sponsoring "Commonwealth weeks" across the country. VSO and CUSO promised to ease the transition to Commonwealth "brotherhood"; they would help create an environment in which the cook next door would not kill the family in a final showdown.[68]

There was one final attribute that made the Peace Corps and its international counterparts such policy naturals in the early 1960s: their role in generating national consensus. Since at least the time of Machiavelli, "princes" have self-consciously used foreign policy to facilitate domestic unity. Although other governments did not take up the banner of volunteering until the United States did, when they did so it fit well with the larger project of nation-building at home.

For Britain and France, which experienced significant internal dissension over decolonization, volunteering could garner support simultaneously from those opposed to colonialism and from those who sought to retain political and economic ties. Mora Dickson of VSO said of the British colonial experience, "We were a total reaction against all that." Yet Prime Minister Harold Macmillan told the headmaster of Eton in 1963 that he was "taking a close interest in the matter" of expanding Britain's voluntary service and wanted a plan for an increased campaign. As demonstrated by widespread editorial approval in Britain at the time, volunteer programs could be a cheap, popular way of generating domestic consensus on a normally divisive subject.[69] In France, Cabinet members told Richard Goodwin explicitly that they saw the Peace Corps idea "as a way to alleviate the disillusionment of French youth over failure in Algeria."[70]

For Canada and the Netherlands, countries not in contention for great power status yet desirous of playing a role on the world stage, volunteering fit with the quest for a sense of national identity and importance. Keith Spicer of CUSO argued later that amid the disintegrating forces of "too much geography," American cultural dominance, and Québécois-Anglo antagonisms, Canadians had found that "helping out abroad unites us at home." Canada made its presence felt to itself and other nations as a broker between the great powers and the third world after 1945. Participation in the United Nations and the Colombo Plan gave Canada more weight in world councils. It also brought recognition. Canada's prime minister Lester Pearson won the Nobel Peace Prize in 1956 for his leadership in the UN peace-keeping force at Suez.[71] Inspired by Pearson, young people like Spicer saw volunteering as a way to expand Canada's new role.

Dutch identity and foreign policy also resonated well with the Peace Corps idea. Following the virtual end of Dutch colonialism in 1949, underscored when Indonesia seized the small remains of Holland's Asian empire (Western New Guinea) in 1962, the Netherlands had to consider what to do with its former colonial administrators and with a new generation that would not have the same socializing experiences that had reinforced Dutch nationalism in the past. Both would be funneled into the Jongeren Vrijwilligers Programma (JVP).

For the former colonial administrators, who became the first staff of JVP, later renamed SNV, developing youth placements fit neatly with their previous field experience. For youth, volunteering allowed them to step into the shoes of generations of Dutch traders. "People were used to going abroad; in every family there were people who had been abroad," one of the early Dutch volunteers said in retrospect. "We're traders," an official of SNV later commented, "and those people who sailed around Africa to Indonesia came back as heroes. In the 1960s and seventies, you could still be a hero by working for SNV." The volunteer program also confirmed Dutch influence in superpower affairs. The Netherlands quickly joined the International Peace Corps Secretariat. One Dutch political cartoon joked: "Coming soon: The Peace Corps from the Netherlands." The caption read "Holland speaks its little words."[72] The irony was not to be missed: though it was little, Holland still had a say.

For Israel, constantly fighting for its survival in the 1950s and 1960s, domestic identity was not a problem in any usual sense. Jews had always been conscious of themselves—and when they weren't the world made them so. But the Peace Corps idea fit extremely well within the larger geopolitical strategy of the tiny country. Nearly encircled by hostile nations, Israel under David Ben-Gurion and Golda Meir looked to build bridges to other countries beyond the Arab world. Harris Wofford, visiting Israel in 1963 after traveling through sub-Saharan Africa, wrote that it had "leaped the Arab noose." Israel's volunteer program was the most effective Wofford had seen. "Because Israel is so small and so unique," he noted, "it is easier for African countries to accept advice and aid from her." Arab leaders discovered at an important gathering of African heads of state "how much other Africans appreciate what Israel is doing."[73]

In the United States, the Peace Corps idea proved its usefulness many times over in promoting national consensus. At a very practical level, Kennedy found in 1960 that it helped him win more of the vote. But perhaps the greatest perceived contribution of the Peace Corps to domestic nation building was that it helped ensure, to borrow Seymour Martin Lipset's phrase, "the continued vitality of antistatist individualism."[74]

The assaults of the cold war—the "Red threat" both at home and abroad—stimulated an unusually high degree of consciousness about what was, and was not, "American." A common view was that only the continued health of private, voluntary associations could stave off the perils of either welfare statism or communism. According to Grant McConnell, the threat of totalitarian mass movements consolidated the position after 1945 of a "body of doctrine" that exalted "the private association as an essential feature of American democracy, perhaps of any genuine democracy."[75]

While government support for private association seemed a contradiction in terms, there was nonetheless significant evidence of it in the postwar era, from tax laws that encouraged corporate philanthropy to the formation of the Peace Corps as a kind of private diplomacy. One early exposition on the Peace Corps in 1961 captured this sentiment when it noted that the "new theorists" of foreign aid operated on the understanding that Alexis de Tocqueville was right "to see a connection between the stability of the American system and our national habit of voluntary association." Sargent Shriver stated the problem more apocalyptically: "The character of American society itself is at stake."[76]

The first director of the Peace Corps in the Philippines, Lawrence

Fuchs, reflected that the Peace Corps responded to "the need of Americans to live out the ideals of their culture." Some of Kennedy's unique popularity at home and abroad derived from his ability to recognize and weave together the many needs of the nation (psychological and material), including the need to respond *as* Americans to the cold war. George Kennan, in his famous long telegram, had urged that "every courageous and incisive measure to . . . improve self-confidence, discipline, morale and community spirit of our own people, is a diplomatic victory over Moscow worth a thousand diplomatic notes and joint communiqués." Through the Peace Corps, Kennedy did just that.[77]

More specifically, Kennedy saw the Peace Corps as a chance to reform the Department of State. Although a Democrat, Kennedy was undoubtedly influenced in his view of the State Department by his fellow Irish Catholic Joseph McCarthy (R-Wisconsin), whom Kennedy declined to join his Senate colleagues in censuring at the end of 1954. Many Americans accepted as accurate McCarthy's famous denunciations of the department as a collection of effete, anglophilic, fancy-dressed, traitorous men "born with silver spoons in their mouths." These accusations and the purges of the State Department that followed them, along with the publication of *The Ugly American,* had created an extremely bad image for the department by the end of the 1950s. The department reacted in a number of ways, one of which was to drop the foreign language part of the Foreign Service exam. The goal, recalled a State Department historian, was to create "a more diverse set of new officers, not ones who came out of only the best schools or families." In self-defense, the department sought "a massive infusion of main street."[78]

In his two and a half years in office, Kennedy repeatedly emphasized that the Peace Corps would revitalize the department. "My own hope is that the Peace Corps men and women will . . . come and serve in the Foreign Service," Kennedy said in June 1962, on the anniversary of the selection of the first group of volunteers. "They are exactly the kind of people whom we want to get into the Foreign Service, the kind we need," he added. Privately, Kennedy raised the question again as the first contingent of volunteers prepared to return home in 1963, telling Shriver, "Let me know if there's anything we can do, because these are the guys I'd like to get into the Foreign Service." Shriver assured his brother-in-law shortly thereafter that special efforts were being made to fulfill his wishes. The U.S. Information Agency, for example, had given a special test for returned volunteers and nearly one-third of those would be offered jobs, well above the 8 percent normally inducted.[79] The Peace Corps also attempted to influence the foreign policy establishment through its display of competency in all foreign languages (not just official ones), from Tagalog to Turkish to Twi.

In many, if not most, cases during the period 1947 to 1989, decolonization and development were held hostage to the cold war. United States officials frequently found it difficult to distinguish between nationalism and communism, and not all even cared to entertain the distinction. Policy was often openly, though not rhetorically, opportunistic. Through CIA-engineered coups d'état in Guatemala, Iran, and Chile, the United States struck hard at "Communist-influenced" forces. In Egypt and Indonesia, "Communist-influenced" forces were treated with greater circumspection, to sustain their nominal neutrality.

Through the Peace Corps Kennedy attempted to project a nonopportunistic image and reinforce the perception of other nations that the primary objective of the United States toward the third world was not "to dominate" but "to help," in the words of the 1961 USIA poll. Its success in doing this was indicated by the speed with which other Western nations adopted the same technique and applied it in their own former colonies and spheres of influence. In 1967 approximately 30 percent of foreign youth volunteers in the third world came from France, Britain, Germany, and Canada, 10 percent came from other countries, and 60 percent came from the United States. The success of the Peace Corps mission was further indicated by the enthusiastic reception given to most U.S. contingents. Of the forty-three countries that requested American volunteers between 1961 and 1965, twenty-nine nations still wanted them nearly two decades later. The Peace Corps effectively signaled that—quite separate from the exigencies of the cold war—Kennedy had "less patience with countries which still have colonial aspirations than had the Eisenhower administration."[80]

The newly independent nations also used the Peace Corps. On a practical level, the agency provided skills and extra hands. Welcoming volunteers also allowed weaker nations to express approval of the United States and thereby obtain benefits that could accrue from cooperation with the world's wealthiest and most powerful nation. At other times, in rejecting such assistance, these nations were able to express disapproval in a way that did not create a threat to national security. The volatility of nationalist politics and of world opinion toward the United States during the Vietnam War, for example, led to a rash of rejections of the Peace Corps in the late 1960s. By 1971 eleven countries had thrown out the American organization, scorning U.S. policies in the process without necessarily creating a diplomatic rupture or endangering more important economic relations. Turning down the Peace Corps was a safe outlet for national pride, made intentionally so by Peace Corps officials who refused to criticize these decisions.

In 1966 Sekou Touré of Guinea became the first to expel volunteers. Touré had accused the United States of prompting the government of Ghana to mistreat some Guinean officials who passed through that neighboring country in October 1966. He ordered the Peace Corps out in retaliation. Indonesia, Ceylon, Libya, Mauritania, Gabon, Somalia, Turkey, Tanzania, Bolivia, and Malawi followed within five years for varying reasons. Mauritania, for example, disapproved of the United States' support of Israel in the 1967 war. Ceylon became upset when its nationalization of American businesses brought about the cessation of AID grants and loans. Tanzania opposed U.S. policies in Vietnam. In Bolivia the government objected to Peace Corps support for family planning, but also hoped to upstage its domestic opponents among the anti-American left. Once the point had been made, countries often invited the Peace Corps to return. Of these eleven, seven eventually asked the Peace Corps back.[81]

The Peace Corps was one way in which the United States creatively shaped the global history of the decade. The organization could not compensate, of course, for other policies that sacrificed third world development to the cold war. But it attempted within the context of East-West enmity to recognize that the greatest division "cutting across the world," as Shriver noted, was that "between the economically developed northern countries and the newly developing southern continents; . . . between the white minority and the colored majority of the human race." And, to the extent that the Peace Corps sustained this focus on North-South (as opposed to East-West) issues, it was appreciated.

One volunteer in Latin America wrote home after the Kennedy assassination that "many have told us how they wept when they heard of his death and many have pictures of him. It's so hard to explain."[82]

John Kennedy's Peace Corps policy, undoubtedly, is a significant part of the explanation. In the 1960s, at least in part owing to the revolution in telecommunications, symbols took on a more explosive importance in politics than ever before. In foreign policy, phenomena like the Berlin Wall, Sputnik, the Bay of Pigs, the Gulf of Tonkin Resolution, and the Peace Corps all became symbols, with broadly accepted meanings. Like "Munich," one had only to say the phrase to know what it implied. "Peace Corps" was Kennedy's way of saying: "Know that our ultimate intent is social justice, even if we make mistakes getting there." Such a message was an important one to convey as the United States and its allies vied for the allegiance of the skeptical third world.

The volunteers themselves, however, actually made the program work. When they were successful, their efforts gave substance to a foreign policy of humanitarianism. The Peace Corps called volunteers "change agents." They strove to live up to this ideal.

5

The Hero's Adventure

Chicago seems so small and far off.

LARRY RADLEY, AGE 22

His parents had worried that he was afraid of mice. "So far tonight, I have caught 13," Larry Radley wrote home confidently. Mice were nothing when you had fallen into a pre-Columbian burial mound earlier in the day and the week before been stampeded in the center of town by a crazed bull. "Town" was Armenia, a hardscrabble hamlet perched ("or possibly glued," he wrote) on the top of a narrow ridge in the Andes. From his back porch, Radley could drop a stone 3,000 feet to the river gorge below. From the church facing him on the other side of the street, he could drop a stone 2,500 feet to the fertile valley owned by rich coffee planters.

For Larry Radley, age twenty-two, life in the Peace Corps was an adventure. It was also a life of extremes—from sharing a pallet with bedbugs and rats in a campesino's hut to drifting to sleep in the soft bed at the home of the president of the university. Like the Peace Corps placements of most volunteers, Radley's was rife with contradictions. Try as one might to find a pure ideal to live for, to give selfless service to one's country and the world, ambiguous realities always elbowed their way in. The peasantry whose hardships you had intended to share treated you like visiting royalty. The culture you had determined to appreciate, come what may, refused to return the favor and considered you odd. You meant to give and then found there was so much to take. And the job you had come to do often could not be done. But like the majority of volunteers, Radley found a way to live with the contradictions of life in the Peace Corps in Colombia. He also died there. On

April 22, 1962, Larry Radley and David Crozier became the first volunteers to lose their lives.[1]

A year before, Radley had been in the first group selected to answer Kennedy's challenge, "Ask not what your country can do for you, but what you can do for your country." Poised to graduate in journalism and sociology from the University of Illinois, Larry Radley eagerly signed up. Merle Radley, Larry's mother, was not surprised by her first-born's desire to join the untested Peace Corps. At age sixteen, when he had broken his leg, Radley spent the night in a Chicago hospital. When his family came to pick him up the next day, they found him shaving all the old men in the ward. "Larry loved people," his mother said.[2]

Larry Radley also loved adventure. The forty letters he wrote home carried with them a trove of heroic images drawn from American popular culture—each one a mental picture of a carnival strong man placard with a hole cut out for the face, for *your* face. Many volunteers wrote letters to family and friends which placed them in the spotlight of exotic adventures with exclamations like "Well, I got it—malaria!" or "Killed a little cobra last night!"[3] In the imagery suggested by his actions, Radley was no different. He was Humphrey Bogart in *The Treasure of Sierra Madre,* pitching down a treacherous mountain on horseback, "riders with flowing ruanas and sombreros—all in the moonlight." He was James Bond, carrying an illegal microphone in his breast pocket when he met John Kennedy. ("I got it all on tape," he excitedly told his parents about his White House conversation.) He was a GI in Paris, passing out nylon stockings to beautiful Colombianas who wanted to go home with him to America. He was a Texas Ranger in the Old West, riding "into a strange town on horseback . . . looking for someone." He was a nameless medic, carrying a child from a remote village into town to have the doctor operate on a crushed foot ("Have you ever tried to convince a little boy that he doesn't really need his little toe?").[4] The photos Radley sent home showed nothing of the slight, urban adolescent who had left Chicago. Leaning against the door of a Colombian house with a blanket slung over his shoulder—or in another picture, taken in the jungle, with a large knife hanging from a fringed belt—he could have been John Wayne or Che Guevara.

The imagery of adventure drew many volunteers into the Peace Corps. In this and other ways, Larry Radley's service contained many of the elements common to that of all Peace Corps volunteers. "Adventure" was a frame around the experience. Different volunteers might choose different frames, but whether they saw themselves as Albert Schweitzers or "great white hunters" or Latin Lotharios or school marms in the jungle, they had a sense of being *in* a picture, and this sense lent a feeling of momentousness to their tour of duty. But just as volunteers placed a frame around the life of the villagers whom they met, the villagers also placed a frame around each volunteer carved out of their own cultural preconceptions. The result was a "Through the Looking Glass" experience; volunteers hardly recognized the persons whom the villagers took them to be. The volunteer also had a job to do, but the job frequently could not be done in a way that conformed with initial expectations. Still, in the end, most volunteers came away with a sense of having "made it," of having endured a test that defined them as men and women, and perhaps as Americans.

It began with recruitment. In the initial press to do everything at once, Shriver had hoped that recruitment would take care of itself. But in May 1961 Warren Wiggins alerted the director that the Peace Corps would have to do more than wait for the mail if they wanted sufficient volunteers. Shriver approved a series of recruitment campaigns, and with help from the National Advertising Council, the Peace Corps flooded the country with recruitment information. It also targeted individual faculty members to become the Peace Corps contact persons on campus. Then the agency sent its most engaging staff members to speak at over two thousand colleges, passing out literature in bulk and exhorting seniors to sign up. The applications poured in: 13,000 in 1961, 20,000 in 1962, 35,000 in 1963, 46,000 in 1964.[5]

Peace Corps staff struggled over what their message should be. Like the volunteers, they had to frame the experience to make it understandable, but the frames did not always fit and could even be at odds with the deeper intent of the program. Some early ads adopted a travel brochure tone: Nepal was advertised as "The Land of Yeti and Everest." Gerard Rice notes that recruiters sometimes told applicants for programs in tropical areas to "bring your bathing suit, the swimming is great." One volunteer warned Shriver that some of his more serious friends resisted joining the Peace Corps because it seemed "too superficial an organization." Travelogue language implied that the third world was an amusement park for gilded youth—an image that warred with Shriver's desire to create an atmosphere of respect for the "colored majority's" struggle. Existentialist victories were not won on Disneyland's "Jungle Ride."

The Peace Corps began to modify its techniques. Alternating between "informing" people about the Peace Corps and "selling" it to them, Shriver's staff gradually came to emphasize the "toughness" of the assignment. One advertisement from 1963 featured a blow-up of a shovel with the blurb, "The Peace Corps brings idealists down to earth." Another pamphlet showed one inch on a ruler with the slogan, "This is how the Peace Corps measures success." A *New York Times* ad from 1964 told prospective volunteers, "The Peace Corps works in 46 countries—not changing the world dramatically, but not leaving it the same either. It's tough to get into the Peace Corps. But we'll be glad to check you out." A later poster showed two identical photographs of a Peruvian shantytown, one labeled "Chimbote, Peru," the other labeled "Chimbote, Peru, two years after the Peace Corps." Perhaps the most famous Peace Corps slogan, which became the title of a recruitment movie made in 1978, was "The toughest job you'll ever love."[6]

"Toughness" fit the Peace Corps picture more snugly than "fun" or even "success." From an existentialist point of view, the attempt mattered more than the outcome, and it was something over which the individual had more control. Volunteers knew they could "try" to create a better world, and Shriver knew that this was the best that most of them would achieve. They thought it a worthy victory. John Kennedy himself struck this philosophical stance in his inaugural address, declaring "a good conscience our only sure reward."

To many potential volunteers, the idea of rigorous adventure was especially intriguing. Julius Amin, who studied the Peace Corps in Cameroon, notes that adventure ranked high on the list of reasons volunteers gave for going. In fact, for most volunteers, "desire to live and travel in another culture" probably preceded the desire to respond to Kennedy's challenge. William Leuchtenburg notes that higher incomes and the rapid postwar expansion of commercial aviation led many middle-class Americans to exotic places that had previously "seemed the destinations only of the well-heeled." In the 1950s Americans increasingly defined adventure as foreign travel. Here the superficial allure of the Peace Corps coincided with its deeper purpose. The president made heroic something that was already attractive.[7]

Others, of course, were drawn by the New Frontier itself. Paul

Tsongas, who volunteered in 1962 and went on to become a Massachusetts senator, recalled Kennedy's influence as the major factor that led him to volunteer, in spite of his Republican father's objections. The Peace Corps received its greatest number of applications in one week (2,550) in the seven days following John Kennedy's assassination. For many, it was a tribute. Still other volunteers found that the Peace Corps fit with preexisting plans. One volunteer recruited for Ghana had already decided he wanted to spend a period teaching in Africa when Shriver gave him the opportunity.[8]

A missionary impulse influenced some volunteers, although they were not likely to announce that sentiment to the carefully secular Peace Corps. The organization did not compile religious data on early volunteers, but Charles Peters later reported that he was often impressed by the spiritual beliefs of volunteers. "I think the hidden secret of the Peace Corps was that it was about forty-five percent Catholic," Peters guessed. Although Catholic volunteers did not join in order to proselytize, the missionary model provided their frame of reference, including the notion of adventure through personal sacrifice. Canada's CUSO, whose volunteers closely resembled those of the Peace Corps, also found that for most Catholic volunteers "it is a plan which has matured for several years."[9] The religious traditions of Jewish volunteers like Larry Radley and Southern Baptists like David Crozier also provided a framework of meaning. During the vigil that David Crozier's mother kept after his plane disappeared she told newspapers, "I feel our mission on earth is to help others . . . We're Christian people with deep feelings for the Lord, and it's sustaining us now."[10]

The women and men who signed up were overwhelmingly B.A. generalists who had recently graduated and had not yet made a final career commitment. The Peace Corps soon found that most professionally or technically oriented students had immediate postgraduate plans that precluded taking two years off to discover themselves or the world. Applicants were also overwhelmingly middle class and white. Ardent attempts to recruit nonwhite or blue-collar Americans generally fell flat. In 1964, Gerard Rice notes, 40,000 applications were mailed off to Michigan automotive workers in the hope of getting skilled mechanics for Latin America. The effort generated twenty-five volunteers. In the 1960s, young skilled industrial workers could make ready money at home.

The Peace Corps also failed to recruit ethnic minority volunteers to the extent that Shriver had hoped for. Although he was able to boast in *Foreign Affairs* that "today 7.4 percent of our higher echelon positions are filled by Negroes as compared to .8 percent for other government agencies," at the field level the picture was different. Minority groups generally chose ways other than the Peace Corps to serve their country in the 1960s. Black volunteers, for example, represented somewhere between 1 and 5 percent of all volunteers in the 1960s, when African Americans constituted roughly 11 percent of the overall population. Still, the agency persisted. The Peace Corps became perhaps the first American institution to seek endorsements from professional black athletes.[11]

Peace Corps officials did not blame minorities for their failure to join, however. The president himself told one audience that many talented minority youth felt such a keen sense of responsibility for their own people "that they really feel that they cannot afford in a sense the diversion of going across the ocean." Many African Americans probably also felt, in the words of one black volunteer, that it was "incredible that a Negro would want to sacrifice two more years of a life that had been molded out of nothing *but* sacrifice." It may also be true that other such youths simply could not find cultural referents that enabled them to picture themselves in the heroic roles imagined by Larry Radley. The images of "great white hunters," or John Wayne, or Victorian missionaries were not an easy fit. Historic black heroes were then largely unknown or they had fought for civil rights in America.[12]

The Peace Corps did, however, recruit enough African Americans to be noticeable. Alec Dickson of Britain's VSO publicly praised the Peace Corps in January 1962 for its inclusion of blacks and Asian Americans, including in leadership positions. Shriver placed his people strategically. The Peace Corps liaison to the United Nations, Franklin Williams, was black, as were George Carter and Samuel Proctor, the first Peace Corps country directors in Ghana and Nigeria. Julius Amin, in studying the agency operations in Cameroon, found that the "integrated" Peace Corps helped convince many people that President Kennedy "had declared war against 'apartheid' in the United States."[13]

The Peace Corps public relations emphasis on the toughness of its mission carried over into testing and training. After completing a detailed questionnaire and submitting six personal references, each applicant took a six-hour exam with lengthy sections on biology, ecology, parasitology, and language aptitude. Of those who applied, the Peace Corps invited roughly 20 percent to begin training. The volunteers then had to undergo thorough medical testing and either provide certified reports of vaccines or be revaccinated. "I began the series of fifteen innoculative shots," Larry Radley wrote home from his training site at Rutgers; "my arms are killing me." David Crozier wrote his parents that he was afraid of being disqualified because of asthma—a fear that did not materialize when he was able to convince doctors that he had hay fever instead.[14]

Volunteers underwent repeated psychological testing, which for many constituted the most stressful aspect of training. In the Peace Corps, psychiatry was king. Psychological testing had gradually come into its own over the twentieth century, but it became more accepted after its use by the military during World War II. Nicholas Hobbs, the psychologist whom Shriver made the first chief of selection, had himself helped design U.S. Air Force selection methods during the war. Where previous generations had left such judgments to the clergy, by the 1960s many Americans accepted the authority of psychiatrists to assess the frailties and strengths of human character.

From the start, the Peace Corps acted on the premise that "the personality characteristics of greatest interest . . . were the non-intellective aspects," and specifically the volunteers' motivations for serving. Hobbs gave psychiatrists and psychologists assigned to the training programs responsibility for "selecting out" trainees whom they considered unfit. Perhaps because of Shriver's particular concern that the program be perceived as expertly run, only the U.S. Peace Corps relied on psychiatry in this way. Canada's CUSO, for example, explicitly rejected this aspect of the Peace Corps model as an American peculiarity, even though the Canadians closely observed and even copied other aspects of U.S. training.[15]

The American psychiatrists' techniques heightened the volunteers' anxieties. Trick questions like "Have you ever talked to God?" and "Do you think your private parts are beautiful?" were common, and implied that neither sexual nor religious "obsessions" would be tolerated. The interviewers kept the pressure on the volunteers intentionally, visiting each week and periodically disqualifying those not deemed fit, for reasons they would not reveal. "Today I saw the psychiatrist. Yesterday was the psychologist," Larry Radley wrote his parents. Moritz Thomsen, another volunteer in the 1960s, later reflected that training was "a period of structured tension, of subtle and purposive torture in which it was calculated that the individual trainee would be forced to reveal himself."[16]

Even the language of the psychiatrists and psychologists was ambiguous. Whether a volunteer was "selected in" or "selected out," he or she was "selected," which normally connotes a positive outcome, even though it might not. Volunteers frequently thought they detected Orwellian double-speak. One self-described Peace Corps "reject" recounted how he and others were deselected by a stranger from Washington. "In a slow, tired voice, greeted with a modicum of big-brother benevolence, he told us the Board had decided after a considerable amount of painstaking deliberation that we were not suited." When asked why, "he only repeated, 'the Board felt,' 'the Board decided,' 'the Board carefully considered,' the Board this, the Board that." "The Board" may sometimes have had good reasons. This particular volunteer had originally written to Kennedy asking to be taken into the Peace Corps because he had been unemployed nineteen months and acceptance into the Peace Corps would "improve my economic status."[17]

Roy Fairfield, who headed the 1962 training program for Cameroon at Ohio State University and saw ten of his fifty-six volunteers deselected by psychiatrists, later said that the psychiatrists "operated from the standpoint that the volunteers were sick to begin with." Overall, the psychological staff may have detracted from the volunteers' mental health. "Having two psychiatrists, plus psychologists, involved in evaluation certainly created an atmosphere which was paranoid to say the very least," Fairfield believed. The final contingent sent to Cameroon was seventeen people short of the number promised.[18]

Adele Davidson, in contrast, who coordinated the training program at UCLA from 1963 to 1965, thought that the psychologists who worked with her program were "fantastic." The local psychologists rarely if ever selected-out a volunteer against his or her will. According to Theodore McEvoy, one of the UCLA staff, he saw himself "as an advocate for the candidate," and carefully explained the evaluation with the volunteer before handing it to the Washington-based psychologists. The most frequent reason for deselection in his experience was volunteer ambivalence over whether or not to go. For women the question of marriage frequently intervened. At the time, as Betty Friedan noted, life for many women consisted of the "frenzied, desperate search for a man." More than 70 percent of all women in the early 1960s married before age twenty-four. One volunteer, McEvoy recalled, faced an agonizing choice when "her boyfriend proposed marriage on the way to the airport."

Men had their problems, too. McEvoy recalled another young volunteer, male, who sought to join the Peace Corps as a desperate act following a failed love affair (à la the French Foreign Legion). These were the kinds of candidates whose long-term stability in the Peace Corps UCLA psychologists questioned. The success of the whole mission, the UCLA training manual told volunteers, depended on each volunteer's willingness to "select himself out of the program" if he or she was unable "to make freely, a profound and binding commitment to the goals of the Peace Corps, to the ideals of universal brotherhood, to service and to humility."[19]

The skill and tact of the individual staff psychologists could do much to compensate for the inherent discomfort in being evaluated psychologically, especially in the group observation format commonly used. Nevertheless, stories abounded of psychologists less sensitive than the ones at UCLA, and more prone to place great confidence in their professional ability to spot "abnormal" types. "We don't want to inflict you on the poor people of the world," one assessment officer told a woman who asked, crying, why she was considered unfit. The same University of New Mexico assessment officer made trainees line up alphabetically to receive sealed envelopes that contained the news, for better or worse, of their fate. "A psychiatrist should not play so central a role," Roy Fairfield of Ohio State complained to Washington headquarters.[20]

At the same time, Shriver gave every indication that he wanted the program kept as rigorous as possible. "We are not going to lower standards at all," he told his staff in 1962, "and are not going to be edgy or worried if some of the projects don't end up full." Shriver, Kennedy, and their cohorts prided themselves on their mental toughness. One of the great fears of the cold war, beginning with the treatment of American prisoners of war in North Korea, concerned Communist "brain-washing." This fear had special relevance to Peace Corps volunteers in neutral countries where Communist propaganda might be widespread. Recruits like Larry Radley, who could endure what he called the "psycho tests" and then irreverently dismiss them as "Mickey Mouse," probably appealed most to Peace Corps administrators.[21]

The overall structure of training was based on a boot camp model, even though administrators proclaimed that what they wanted recruits to learn was not military discipline but "inner discipline." Recruits typically began their days with physical training at 7:00 A.M., followed by eight hour-long classes in area studies, languages, job training, U.S. history, current events, and basic first aid and disease prevention. Trainees worked six days a week, usually until 10:00 at night. Larry Radley and David Crozier drilled on horseback in 103-degree heat; Ohio volunteers hiked ten miles over the Buckeye Trail; volunteers at the training camp in Puerto Rico swung through trees on ropes, scaled sheer cliffs, and were thrown into rivers tied hand and foot. William Sloane Coffin, who helped set up the camp based on the British Outward Bound model, argued that such physical challenges measured "a man's stamina, courage and resourcefulness."[22] Implicit in his wording was that such tests also measured his masculinity. What they did for females was less clear, although many women must have benefited from programs that demanded physical confidence of them, perhaps for the first time in their lives.

The Peace Corps awarded most of its training contracts to universities, which had the few language and area experts who could train volunteers in obscure African and Asian cultures as well as prepare them for more familiar locations in South America. Universities, of course, could also easily house, feed, and give examinations to large groups of students, and they gave academic credibility to the Peace Corps. Names like Berkeley, Rutgers, UCLA, and Ohio State showed that Kennedy and Shriver were putting America's best thinking behind the Peace Corps. The choice was also expedient. The universities could start programs as early as summer vacation 1961.

By involving the universities the Peace Corps further extended its political reach. Training contracts brought money and prestige to seventy academic institutions strung out across the United States. Shriver could show congressmen the Peace Corps sites in their own districts. Barry Goldwater himself was convinced of the validity of the Peace Corps when the president of Arizona State University told the senator that the volunteers trained there were a credit to the nation.

Beyond the language, physical education, and psychiatric dimensions

THE HUMAN CARE PACKAGE

There is a man somewhere who has nothing.
Maybe you'd like to give him something.
Here are some suggestions.

Send him patience. He'll appreciate it for
the rest of his life.

Send him understanding. It's something he can use.

Send him kindness. That's something
that'll never go out of style.

Send him the one thing only you can
give him. Send him you.

The Peace Corps, Washington, D.C.

Young & Rubicam, a Madison Avenue advertising firm working for free, created most Peace Corps publicity in the 1960s. They sought to show an America that cared. In the process they gave the Peace Corps a name recognition that vied with Smokey the Bear. *(Young & Rubicam, Inc.)*

Above: John F. Kennedy told a campaign aide that he intended to initiate a new relationship with the third world once he became president. The African national-ist Kwame Nkrumah, president of Ghana, became one of Kennedy's first official state visitors on March 8, 1961. *(John F. Kennedy Library)*

Below: A buoyant Sargent Shriver leads eighty Ghana and Tanganyika volunteers to the Rose Garden for a personal send-off from President Kennedy in August 1961. *(John F. Kennedy Library)*

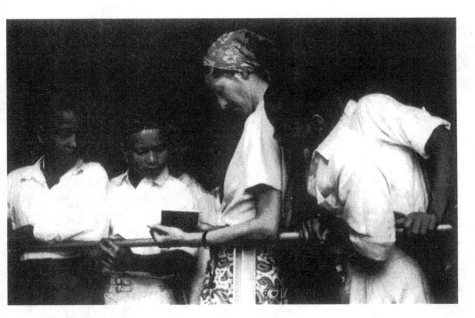

Above: Mora Dickson, along with Alec Dickson, her husband and co-founder of British Voluntary Service Overseas, found themselves deeply impressed on a trip to Sarawak (Borneo) in 1957 by the maturity of local young people given significant responsibilities in the life of their nation. Together the Dicksons began Voluntary Service Overseas, two years ahead of Kennedy's campaign pledge to create a "peace corps." *(Courtesy of Mora Dickson)*

Below: Peter Nolan, a British youth who was one of the first Western volunteers, teaches carpentry in Nairobi in 1960 through Voluntary Service Overseas. *(Courtesy of Mora Dickson)*

Above: Canadian volunteers vowed to ship out ahead of the Americans. Here they pose proudly with the prime minister of India, Jawaharlal Nehru. *(Courtesy of CUSO)*

Below: In October 1962 Vice President Lyndon B. Johnson led the U.S. delegation to the Puerto Rico Conference on Middle-Level Manpower, urging American allies to start their own youth volunteer programs to the third world. Here he greets the Israeli foreign minister, Golda Meir, and the Italian under secretary of the foreign ministry, Guiseppe Lupis. *(Reprinted from the* International Volunteer*)*

Left: Oblivious to all but each other's smile, Peace Corps volunteer Elaine Willoughby (1972–1974) and her young charge in Jamaica came to symbolize the Peace Corps' goal of a color-blind world. *(Peace Corps)*

Below: The Peace Corps posted African-American volunteer Jerry Page, twenty-seven, to develop recreational programs in the slums of Caracas not far from where mobs had attacked Vice President Richard Nixon in 1958. Page and the children walk past anti-American graffiti that says "Kennedy get out." *(John F. Kennedy Library)*

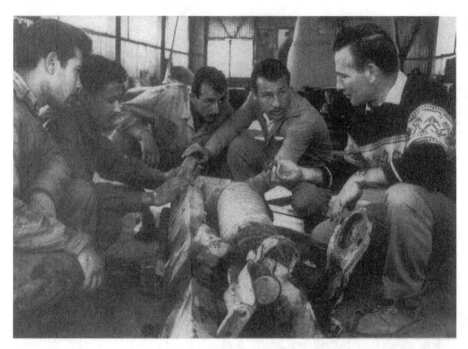

Above: Peace Corps volunteer Alfred Carpano, thirty-seven, of Massachusetts was one of the few blue-collar workers in the early Peace Corps. A one-time aircraft mechanic, he gave instruction in the heavy equipment repair shop of the Turkish soil conservation department in the port town of Mersin. Like many volunteers, he gardened and helped farmers after hours. *(John F. Kennedy Library)*

Above: Volunteer James Fischer, a classic "B.A. generalist" at age twenty-two, teaches English at Katmandu's only teacher training college. He makes a shy student giggle with his unusual American methods—including class outside on the grass. *(John F. Kennedy Library)*

Left: Hands open wide for touching and counting, Barbara Wylie runs an after-school program that she started for children of "untouchable" servants. Older than the average volunteer at age thirty-three, Wylie's formal assignment was to teach English in Katmandu. Peace Corps administrators—sometimes embarrassed by the tame image of teachers—often commended volunteers more for such "secondary" projects than for their primary jobs. *(John F. Kennedy Library)*

Above: Joe Grant of the Bronx teaches physical education in Chimbote, Peru. Like Grant's hometown in the United States, Chimbote's struggle to overcome poverty registered gains very slowly. The Peace Corps stressed the modesty of its goals, though, in contrast to Lyndon Johnson's domestic War on Poverty.
(John F. Kennedy Library)

Right: Seeing the life of her hosts as normal and everyday represented one of the greatest personal achievements for any Peace Corps volunteer. Here, twenty-one-year-old Beverly Heegaard, as usual, gets her feet wet fording the river to work.
(John F. Kennedy Library)

Above and left: The life of Larry Radley's family changed forever in 1962 when they lost their twenty-two-year-old son on a remote Colombian mountainside. The first volunteer to lose his life, along with PCV David Crozier, Radley had struggled to implement the innovative concepts of community organizing. Like all volunteers suffering from culture shock he also sought a mental frame for his experience: American *caballero* or capitalist jungle revolutionary? *(Courtesy of Merle Radley Katz)*

"Let's see -- four years prep school . . . Princeton, Magna Cum Laude . . . three years Harvard Law School . . . two years Peace Corps . . . "

Above: Volunteers often saw themselves as having been shaped more by the Peace Corps than by any other preceding experiences. *Saturday Evening Post,* poking fun in 1963, concurred. *(Used with permission of the Saturday Evening Post © 1963)*

Right: Young & Rubicam's 1968 campaign to staunch the damage to the Peace Corps brought on by the Vietnam War ultimately could do little to lessen the organization's losses. But it did ask Americans to choose between two perspectives: "The whole idea of a Peace Corps is hypocritical while we are at war," or "The Peace Corps is not hypocrisy. Peace is bigger than war and the waging of peace cannot be stopped, even by war. If the Peace Corps idea doesn't work, nothing will." *(Young & Rubicam, Inc.)*

The Peace Corps is bad.

1. Who needs a Peace Corps when we have enough trouble right here. You don't need to go halfway around the world to find problems.
2. The whole idea of a Peace Corps is hypocritical while we are at war. We've got to make up our minds which way it's going to be.
3. The Peace Corps is part of the establishment.

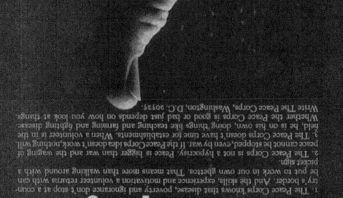

Whether the Peace Corps is good or bad just depends on how you look at things.
Write The Peace Corps, Washington, D.C. 20525.

3. The Peace Corps doesn't have time for establishments. When a volunteer is in the field, he is on his own, doing things like teaching and farming and fighting disease.

2. The Peace Corps is not a hypocrisy. Peace is bigger than war and the waging of peace cannot be stopped, even by war. If the Peace Corps idea doesn't work, nothing will be put to work in our own ghettos. That means more than walking around with a picket sign.

1. The Peace Corps knows that disease, poverty and ignorance don't stop at a country's border. And the skills, experience and motivation a volunteer returns with can

The Peace Corps is good.

MAKE AMERICA A BETTER PLACE.

LEAVE THE COUNTRY.

Of all the ways America can grow, one way is by learning from others.

There are things you can learn in the Peace Corps you can't learn anywhere else.

You could start an irrigation program. And find that crabgrass and front lawns look a little ridiculous. When there isn't enough wheat to go around in Nepal.

You could be the outsider who helps bring a Jamaican fishing village to life, for the first time in three hundred years. And you could wonder if your country has outsiders enough. In Watts. In Detroit. In Appalachia. On its Indian reservations.

Last year, for the first time, Peace Corps alumni outnumbered Volunteers who are now out at work overseas.

By 1980, 200,000 Peace Corps alumni will be living their lives in every part of America.

There are those who think you can't change the world in the Peace Corps.

On the other hand, maybe it's not just what you do in the Peace Corps that counts.

But what you do when you get back.

The Peace Corps, Washington, D.C. 20525.

Above: Young & Rubicam 1968 campaign poster. Playing on the popular conservative slogan, "America—Love it or leave it," the Peace Corps suggested that one could love America, *and* leave it, and come back and change it after "learning from others." *(Young & Rubicam, Inc.)*

Right: The existentialist credo continued to echo gently in Peace Corps posters: life's meaning came from meaningful work and moral commitment. *(Young & Rubicam, Inc.)*

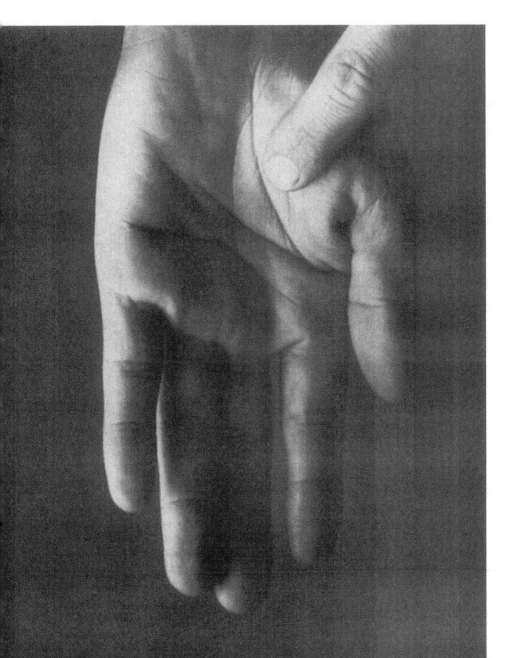

This is your life line. If you're not doing something with your life, it doesn't matter how long it is.
The Peace Corps.

Above: Nixon Peace Corps director Joseph Blatchford, assailed frequently by both the political right and the left, enjoyed a rare peaceful moment in 1971 when he presented a check to UN Secretary General U Thant and American representative George Bush to help launch the United Nations Volunteers. *(Courtesy of Joseph Blatchford)*

Right: The age of volunteers crept upward in the 1970s and 1980s, but individuals like Odi Long remained the heroic exceptions. At age seventy-nine he was the oldest serving volunteer in 1981, helping with school construction in Sierra Leone. *(Peace Corps)*

In the 1990s the Peace Corps found itself where John Kennedy could never have dreamed: the Soviet bloc. In his early sixties, Robert Matt volunteered for two years in Poland. Formerly the owner of two Ethan Allen furniture stores, Matt worked exclusively with small- and medium-sized business owners and developed a local chamber of commerce. *(Peace Corps photo from 1994)*

of the early program, the Peace Corps emphasized preparing volunteers for what they would encounter politically, as Americans. Trainees heard lectures about American political traditions and problems, especially civil rights, along with lectures on Marxist-Leninism and Soviet policy toward the developing world. The Peace Corps initially had little choice but to concern itself with these questions. Unlike the programs from other parts of the former British Empire, the Peace Corps was immediately attacked as an outfit of spies, part and parcel of the cold war. Trainees needed to be prepared to counter these assumptions.

Such training derived as well from early congressional insistence that volunteers understand the "history and menace of communism." Early in his campaign to pass the Peace Corps Act, Shriver had withstood the blasts of Congressman Bourke Hickenlooper, who demanded that the director disqualify a volunteer who had shown insufficient respect for anticommunism. The preceding year the Rotary Club had forcibly ejected Charles Kamen when he burst out laughing at a U.S. propaganda film called *Operation Abolition*. A volunteer in training at the University of Pennsylvania during the summer of 1961, the twenty-two-year-old Kamen came under intense scrutiny. Newspapers revealed that "until recently he was bearded," a fact that some took as proof of un-American traits. Shriver resisted congressional demands that Kamen be summarily dismissed, but at the end of training he quietly let Kamen go for undisclosed reasons. Congress added a loyalty oath requirement to Peace Corps training, and the first groups of volunteers were given a pamphlet entitled "What You Must Know about Communism." Charles Kamen was not the only young American skeptical of the older generation's Red Scare mentality, however. Volunteer rejection of anticommunist hyperbole soon led to the substitution of more objective texts and the lessening of the time devoted to them.[23]

Attention was also paid to the United States' glaring civil rights problem. The Peace Corps coached trainees going to Africa on civil rights issues, and gave them articles from African newspapers on incidents across the ocean in America. "Events in Alabama . . . have come as a surprise to only those who had erroneously regarded the United States as a free nation," one Cameroon newspaper commented.[24] But even students going to Asia and South America were alerted to civil rights problems and the importance of avoiding "Ugly American" types of behavior. Course materials varied widely because universities turned over to individual faculty the responsibility for designing classes, but common fare included the reports of the Civil Rights Commission and books like *The Negro Revolution in America* and *The Negro Revolt*.

The Peace Corps did not want volunteers to adopt a "shaky apparatus of slogans," however, as stated in each UCLA training manual. Rather, it hoped "to give the trainees a cram course in political sophistication, so that they will better understand and therefore better represent this nation." In language reminiscent of "teach-ins" that antiwar groups would sponsor during the late 1960s, the UCLA manuals added that their goal was to "quicken the trainees' comprehension of the key issues" and encourage "a sense of the political."[25] Shriver and other Peace Corps officials repeatedly emphasized that Peace Corps volunteers should be prudent, but they should also feel free to express their own views.

Still, underlying the emphasis on Jeffersonian freedom of thought was the unspoken conviction that the Peace Corps had the right to give moral instruction. Like all activist groups, the Peace Corps was neither neutral nor relativistic in its core political values. A training manual put together by the University of Chicago in 1966 contained selections from George Orwell's anticolonial writings, Joseph Conrad's *Heart of Darkness,* and Rudyard Kipling's satirical "White Man's Burden." Staff taught recruits that racial discrimination was un-American, that imperialism was bad, and that every citizen had a personal responsibility to promote democracy in the third world. They were not values on which all Americans would agree, but the Peace Corps took them as gospel.

Volunteers also received training (though not enough, many would complain) in the specific jobs they were to perform abroad. Rural construction units received instructions on how to build latrines, schools, and wells; health teams heard lectures on hospital organization and public hygiene; teachers received information on pedagogy; and community developers memorized lessons on how to organize. Training typically lasted ten to fourteen weeks at a university in the United States (which might include two to four weeks at one of four outdoor Peace Corps training camps in the tropics), followed by a brief one-to-two week training session "in country." In following decades, the ratio of U.S.-based training to in-country training would be nearly reversed, but until the late 1960s the structure of the Peace Corps relationship with host countries was still too weak to attempt this level of cooperation.

Then, after three months of intense togetherness, volunteers went their separate ways. For all of them, the hardest test in the Peace Corps was not during the "finals boards" of training when they were selected in or selected out. The real challenge began, not surprisingly, with the volunteer's actual assignment: the simple day-to-day attempt to fit in, hang on to one's own sense of self, do a job well, and last the full two years.

The diversity of Peace Corps jobs was, and still is, great. Generally, the Peace Corps placed highest priority on work that brought volunteers into contact with a broad segment of society, rather than on jobs that required narrow technical expertise but did not meet the goal of promoting "a better understanding" between Americans and the rest of the world. Volunteers working off by themselves in laboratories would not fulfill the broadest intent of the Peace Corps. Even the first Peace Corps project to Tanganyika (soon renamed Tanzania), which sent thirty-five highly sought-after surveyors to design roads, was judged to fall short of the ideal placement. The transiency of the job kept the volunteers from establishing close ties with African communities, and an unexpected government budget cut meant that the highly technical assistance went to waste. Better to find jobs closer to the people whose success depended only upon their own small resources.[26]

Between 1961 and 1965 more than half of the volunteers worked as teachers. Another thirty percent worked in community development, and the remaining 20 percent went to agriculture, health care, public works, and public administration. These figures did not change much over the next few decades. In 1996 nearly 40 percent of volunteers still worked in education, with the rest spread out over health (16 percent) and other fields that were extensions of what would earlier have been done under the rubric of "community development" (environment, small business development, and agriculture).[27] The experience of volunteers also did not change in some significant ways. Although the Peace Corps became smaller and somewhat more technically focused over time, enabling it to develop more "real jobs" and curb the number of "phony jobs," certain challenges remained.

"Things are finally beginning to get me down and I now have what is categorically called 'culture shock,'" Larry Radley wrote home at the end of his first three months in Colombia. "I have these deep feelings of inadequacy and inferiority. Don't worry [though], no matter how hard things are I will stick them out for the two years." The Peace Corps brought into the American lexicon a new term—culture shock— which it did not invent but certainly helped to popularize. Trainers told volunteers like Radley that within months of their arrival they would likely experience an overwhelming revulsion at the conditions of their placement. Calling this reaction "culture shock" gave volunteers a way of understanding the experience that helped them toughen their sensibilities rather than reject the nation they hoped to help. Culture shock was another way of promoting cultural relativism and thus the ideal of universal respect. Gerard Rice notes that a volunteer in Ethiopia called it "a baptism by fire . . . a collision of different values and different expectations, of values that are never wholly transferable, of expectations that are never fully realized." A female volunteer in the Far East admitted that when faced with "rotten teeth, foul breath, smells, sores, filth, rags, I couldn't take it. I was astonished to find that my reactions were so diametrically opposed to my ideals . . . I simply and truthfully hated it and wanted to go home."[28]

Culture shock resulted partly from the experience of seeing extreme poverty from so close a vantage point. But perhaps the greatest sense of dislocation came from being unable to find the right "frame" through which to view one's own experience. When volunteers experienced disgust with their hosts, they were suddenly unable to see themselves as heroes either. Paul Cowan, numbed by the daily pleas of deformed beggars in Ecuador, said the experience made "you wonder what kind of beast you've become that you can listen so impassively."[29] Larry Radley, like many volunteers, found his compassion eroded by not being able to do his job. The padre of the local church, the only authority for miles around, appeared jealous of outsiders and stymied all Radley's efforts. Radley built a small road to a mountain school, taught English classes, dug latrines, helped out the itinerant doctor on his day in town, set up a dining cooperative, held meetings with villagers to help them identify what the Peace Corps called "felt needs," and developed detailed plans for making a film on community organization to show to peasants.

But when the priest refused to lend his horses and repeatedly "forgot" to announce community meetings in church, Radley found time hanging heavily on his hands. Peace Corps policies also caused conflict. When a community gathering indicated that its "felt need" was a new church building, the Peace Corps representative told Radley and his partner that they had to stay away from anything promoting religion "because of potential repercussions in the States" for Kennedy's Catholic administration. Later, a villager got hold of a book supplied to Larry Radley by CARE called *Eres Libre* (You Are Free) which said, among other things, "You have the right to the religion you choose."[30] When Radley was away from the village the priest announced that there were "two forces in the world—Catholicism and Communism." Radley discovered upon return that the Peace Corps along with its Colombian government co-workers from Acción Comunal had become "poison in this town," and that the word was spreading throughout the near countryside. Six months of work were at an end. "I just want to get away from the Catholics," Larry Radley wrote bitterly to his parents, admitting, "sometimes I just hide in my room so I don't have to go out in the street and say hello to everyone." Unable to love his community because of its rejection of his liberal values and his Jewishness ("I am sick and tired of apologizing for my nonbelief in the 'virgen,'"), unable as a result to finish the projects he started, Radley felt himself a failure.

To the Peace Corps he kept up a brave front ("I would like to say that the PC has made many friends in Armenia"), and was consoled by the assurances that "Armenia is considered a really tough site because of the padre." But to his parents he admitted that he counted on frequent escapes to the lively town of Medellín and friends there to see him through "the remaining 17 months." The Peace Corps and Acción Comunal both decided to pull their workers out of Armenia. Larry Radley ultimately was unable to see himself as a hero there, and the frame that its people had placed around him created a portrait he did not recognize. In the view of the local people "there is . . . [even] something wrong with you, my parents," he wrote home, "because you only had three kids." And yet Radley, like most volunteers, gradually came to a more realistic understanding of the obstacles to changing the world all at once. His example had encouraged other friends to join the Peace Corps, and he had built a "small but beautiful road leading . . . to the school." He looked forward to his reassignment in another town.[31]

Most other volunteers overcame culture shock as well, indicated by the fact that 94 percent of all volunteers from the agency's first three years said after completing their assignment that they would do it all again. Not included, of course, were those who did not complete the two years or who were deselected in training. Still, the "cultural adjustment" was harder for most people than the physical adjustment, according to one country director. Paul Cowan, bedeviled by the contradictions of life in Ecuador, wrote to his brother that "the distance between our lives and thoughts and our neighbors' might exhaust anyone who really tried to cross it." Quoting T. E. Lawrence, Cowan added, "I believe that madness would be near the man who could see things through the veils at once of two customs, two educations, two environments."[32]

Most volunteers struggled with being accepted. They found that their hosts saw them as the mirror opposites of what they were considered by their own culture in the United States. Slim coeds found that African men took them for "skinny, sickly" spinsters who volunteered because they could not attract a husband. Pacific Islanders saw female scrawniness as the "worst physical defect a body could have." Young African children ran screaming from the "white ghosts" with their beakish noses and "falling down" hair. Black volunteers in the Far East had parents point them out to their gawking children as if to say (in the words of one volunteer so treated), "Son, they are members of a black-skinned, woolly haired, flat-nosed and thick-lipped African race. Try to remember what they look like."[33]

In Africa, in contrast, black volunteers found that they were "accepted," but as something they never would have guessed. The natives often thought they were white. "They said I was the first *European* they'd seen to wear an African hair-style," one black volunteer wrote home to her mother, reporting that one student described her as "tall, of white colour, well-built." At the other extreme, another volunteer found himself repeatedly mistaken for a member of an enemy tribe. To get by one threatening soldier at a roadblock who would not accept that a black man could be an American, the volunteer claimed (successfully) to be Japanese.[34]

Other volunteers from non-Anglo backgrounds had similar problems. In South America, an Asian-American volunteer could not "enter a bus without having people whisper *'Mire al Chino'* (Look at the Chinaman)" and a Hispanic-American volunteer could hardly convince locals that she came from the United States, where they believed every-one was blond. "When will a *gringo* Peace Corps volunteer come?" they asked, plaintively explaining, "You're a Mexican and Mexicans don't know as much as *gringos*."[35]

Caucasian volunteers, many of whom had joined the Peace Corps in the hope of contributing to a color-blind world, also found their pig-ment the source of constant, unremitting comment, especially in Africa. Volunteers found the word "white" chasing them wherever they went. George Packer described an experience noted repeatedly by many. "Nothing was more unnerving than the children," Packer said of his time in Togo. "They were all yelling *'Yovo!'* at you. Sometimes it came in a kind of child's verse, chanted the way American kids chant 'nanny nanny nanny goat': *'Yovo, yovo, bonsoir!'"* Adults were more subtle. "Each time I caught an old woman's eye she said simply, *'Yovo,'* as if she were pointing out something interesting and faintly comical." *Yovo*, of course, meant white.[36]

Many volunteers also found, sometimes to their surprise, that they were seen as highly desirable despite (or because) of their exoticism. Young women in Colombia treated Larry Radley like a movie star. George Packer in Togo found that the standard repartee of market women was, "No wife? Then let's get married." Paul Theroux novelized his experience, but the similar accounts of other volunteers would lead one to conclude that there was much truth in his happy description of "unlimited and guiltless sex." One volunteer wrote to a Peace Corps staffer in 1962 that the Africans "tend to worry about us . . . They see a man alone and, if they like him, they will try to match him up with some local girl." When a volunteer declined an offer of the companionship of one man's sister, the African replied, "Don't you like my sister?"[37]

For North American women the attention (more intense if they were not too slender) could be disconcerting. "Sex in Ghana is extremely casual," Marian Zeitlin wrote. "This is so different from our way of thinking that an American girl may be told it without really realizing or believing it is true . . . The only thing that is considered abnormal is for a person to live alone." Recently married, Zeitlin kept her head. She recommended that the Peace Corps give female volunteers advice on how to turn men down politely, in ways that could be explained as cultural differences rather than misconstrued as racial preferences. But

Jeanna Baty, a CUSO volunteer in Trinidad, admitted that "being a white, single, Canadian female, not to mention plump . . . and barraged by requests for dates, gave me an inflated feeling of myself."[38]

Sometimes the attention was unwelcome, however. Worldwide patriarchal traditions, including the aggressive use of women as sexual objects by men, placed female volunteers in a far more challenging situation than male volunteers who could easily brush off flirtations they did not desire. Susan Rich, a later volunteer in Niger, saw her role as an English teacher to be that of "a visionary, a transformer." Teachers raise children and children make the world. But occasionally she wondered if these were children or a "mafia gang." Adolescent males in the former French colony would slink into class "wearing sun glasses and shirts with plunging necklines to the navel." They practiced their English with questions such as "Are you enamored with African men?" and "How old are you?" In a volunteer newsletter from Sierra Leone, "Ma Manners" counseled "Blushing in Bombali" who reported that "recently a dark-skinned gentleman approached me on the street and . . . announced that he 'wanted me for love.' How does one turn down such a request in a graceful and culturally sensitive way?" Ma Manners suggested "assuming an expression of delighted amusement at such a proposition, followed by a sustained chuckling that the gentleman could suggest such a patently absurd scenario." The suggestion was good, and mostly worked. But in the course of three decades a few Peace Corps workers were raped. Courageously, a woman in Sierra Leone returned after a painful eight-week compassion leave to give two more "very happy" though occasionally "traumatic" years to her adopted country. Another conquered her anguish to return to St. Kitts in the West Indies.[39]

Host nationals also sometimes sought out the friendship of both male and female volunteers for the social status such a link might convey, or for the monetary gifts they hoped they might receive. As with consensual sex, such exchanges were fraught with the likelihood of misunderstanding.

And yet, at some point, the great majority of volunteers found a way to overcome the cultural gulf without either exploiting it or feeling victimized by it. Even if they could achieve this with only one or two people, attaining an understanding—a point at which the frames came together and the volunteer and host could see the picture of a common human experience—meant a personal triumph. "It was always miraculous when it happened," the agricultural volunteer Moritz Thomsen recalled, writing the story of how one night a young fisherman friend said, "I think you're a good man; let's be brothers." He said it so naturally, so sweetly, Thomsen remembered, "that for a second the room actually blazed with light."[40]

Achieving such understanding required movement on both sides. For the volunteer this meant setting aside preconceptions and finding a way to see the normal life of their hosts as indeed normal. "After years of pausing before museum dioramas and dreaming of this day, Africa surrounded my curious eyes, animated, real . . . I burst with the thrill of it all," Kinney Thiele wrote of her first day in Sierra Leone, where she learned to take an "African bath" in an open-air stall with a bucket and cup. To her hosts, she recognized, the procedure was trivial, routine, and far from exotic. Yet another volunteer wrote that what seemed unbelievable was "to arrive here in this city which I could never really believe existed and to find that it looks just like all the pictures we have seen. It really is a city, too, where people live; not the inferno . . . where the only human activity is to suffer and decay."[41]

For the hosts, most of whom acted with generosity and grace, seeing these "rich Americans" as real became easier when the volunteers inadvertently revealed their youth or inexperience. In Africa this was easy because men and women in their twenties who had yet to have children were themselves considered children. Even the volunteers recognized their prolonged youth. Contemplating the not-too-distant marriage of a sunny ten-year-old African friend, a neighbor's baby strapped to her back, one twenty-year-old volunteer realized that her young friend was "far more ready to assume the roles of motherhood than I. She would be ready to relinquish childhood."[42]

To host nationals, seeing the young volunteers stumble stirred humor and compassion. A volunteer in Peru in 1963 recounted how his "showcase project" was to start a cattle-breeding center with two government-loaned Brown Swiss bulls. On opening day, surrounded by a throng of curious farmers and their families, the bulls were put to work in a pen of local cows. "But the young bull wanted to suck udders, while his older partner was only interested in mounting him," Ron Arias later wrote. Peace Corps luck: one bull with gender confusion, another who wanted only mama. "It was a small lesson in laughter,"

Arias noted, but one that brought him together with people he wanted to know. In Nepal a female volunteer had a similar experience in trial and error. "PCV woman veterinarian wants seven inches rectal thermometer for buffaloes," a State Department telegram read. "Five inches too short."[43]

Laughter, indeed, was one of the best cures for culture shock, and volunteers and staff often sent back stories of cultural differences that struck them as more funny than lamentable. Harris Wofford wrote home in an open letter which reached Bill Moyers that volunteers who got sued for inadvertent damage to other people's property in Somalia were ordered to pay their fines in camels. One particularly stern judge ordered a volunteer to deliver eighty of the four-footed ships of the desert. Another volunteer, Wofford reported, was convicted of sexually assaulting a horse. "The volunteer's stallion did the dirty work to the mare," he reassured his readers, "but the court docket read: 'John Jones—for Raping a Horse.'"[44]

Volunteers in Sierra Leone kept up one another's spirits through their irreverent newsletter, which grew to such a length that Peace Corps staff had to ration the volunteers' use of paper. Tips for volunteers soon to return home included the reminder that in the States, "When searching for a house or apartment do ask for three rooms and a bath, not three rooms and a path." Each issue carried detailed news on every conceivable American sport, from the results of basketball's NCAA "Sweet Sixteen" to scores for baseball, football, soccer, tennis, ice hockey, and even boxing. News was precious. Tim Wilkinson wrote his parents from Zaire in 1983 that he had heard a rumor of a car bombing in Beirut. What was that about? He had no idea that 241 U.S. Marines had perished. Volunteers also used the newsletter to gripe about the living allowance that never lasted the month and the diet that sometimes sent their intestines into their own form of culture shock. Tom Johnson reported that during a bout of "runny belly," he discovered that an unfortunate chicken had chosen his latrine for her roost. "I tell you, I didn't come to this country to shit on some poor defenseless chicken every two hours!" he protested. Another volunteer commented that "American dogs don't even know what a dog's life is."[45]

Volunteers also occasionally poked fun at staff insistence on being the holier-than-possible type of American praised by Lederer and Burdick and avoiding all the sins of the Golden Ghetto. One anonymous postcard sent to the Peace Corps central office in Manila read: "Urgent—dozens of volunteers sighted at happy hour, refusing to report to assignments . . . hobnobbing with tourists and fat cat Americans and generally just not taking cues from the culture. Please airdrop fifty copies of *Doctor to the Barrios* . . . Urgent, send fast. Can't talk now, hostesses closing in."[46]

Beyond the humor that helped volunteers let off steam, PCVs occasionally experienced the joy of discovering a real hero, and not just one from a celluloid dream. Sometimes the discovery derived from a simple gesture. For Larry Radley, his hero was the occasional privileged Colombian who drank tea with the maid or cleaned up the dishes. (Radley reserved his sharpest comments not for the priest but for the socialites who looked past poorer Colombians as "nobodies.") For Mike Tidwell, a volunteer in Zaire in 1985, it was the chief who placed his bare foot on a hot metal shovel 100,000 times to dig a fishery. The man looked like a "museum piece," Tidwell first thought, a hunter with a spear in a grassland where the clock ran a "thousand years slow." But in time Tidwell came to know him as a man whose extraordinary patience and strength would bring something new into his village. "I had a hero," Tidwell said.[47]

Sometimes even the volunteer got to be a real hero. "Pide Lynch is a local heroine since she saved the life of a premature baby with a cardboard-box incubator she learned about in training," a Peace Corps evaluator reported to Washington in 1965. "The parents asked for a picture of Pide 'so we can show it to our baby when he grows up and tell him he wouldn't be alive if these Americans hadn't come to Brazil.'" Another volunteer, bitten in Nigeria by a venomous green mamba, killed the snake and then, demonstrating on his own bloody thigh, calmly showed his awed students how to use a snakebite kit.[48]

Diana Louise Stahl, a volunteer in the Philippines, a decade later recalled experiences that reflected a more subtle heroism growing out of an unusual ability to perceive local needs and opportunities. A B.A. generalist, Stahl recounted that she "took up the crusade of rabbits as a protein source mainly because they breed faster than people and could keep up with the population explosion." She taught herself all the phases of rabbitry, building her own hutch and reading all the materials she could find on the temperate-zone raising of rabbits. She then made adjustments for the tropical climate on an experimental basis. When she felt she had learned all she could, she approached a local pastor who shared her interest in rabbits and suggested they write a book together. Stahl took all the photographs, carefully showing how to select, breed, house, kill, and skin the rabbits, and how to incorporate the meat into native Philippine dishes. She put Reverend Juan Sicwater's name ahead of hers on the book, which they titled "For the Health of the Nation Go into Rabbit Production." Stahl then made a home movie on rabbit production, with which she toured the country. At the end of her assignment she petitioned to stay another year so that she could help a leper colony develop its own rabbit production. "Labor saving designs were necessary," Stahl explained matter-of-factly, "because some lepers do not have the use of their hands or legs." Stahl and her leper assistants designed a unique ecosystem. Using a hose, workers washed manure from under the cages down a trough into a compost pit that then provided fertilizer to grow grass for the rabbits to eat. Stahl left the Philippines, after three years and ten months, "reluctantly."[49]

Even more rarely, volunteers and their hosts discovered they had heroes in common. Tom Hebert found African chiefs who shared his love of Shakespeare. John Coyne, in the 1962–63 contingent to Ethiopia, gave a ride to an old man on a dirt road. When asked if he had ever met the slain U.S. president, Coyne "told him how I had once shaken his hand on the White House lawn." After a moment, the Ethiopian seized Coyne's hand, shouting "Messenger of Peace" (the Amharic translation of Peace Corps) over the roar of the Land Rover. "He was shaking the hand that had shaken the hand of John F. Kennedy." A world away from the world of Washington, "we shared a moment, were connected by the death of a martyred president," the volunteer reflected. Most volunteers, of course, had few such experiences of heroism, either their own or anyone else's. But the Peace Corps gave them the possibility. It was a precious gift that enriched both the individual and the nation.[50]

For Larry Radley and David Crozier, the chance to be heroes came unexpectedly and at great cost. "Should it come to it, I would rather give my life trying to help someone than to have to give my life looking down a gun barrel at them," David Crozier wrote his parents from Jardín, Colombia. As it was, neither Crozier's life nor his death was so dramatic. He and Larry Radley were part of the enormous wave of community developers whom the Peace Corps sent south in the 1960s.

They died, like almost all of the 227 volunteers who lost their lives between 1961 and 1997, as a result of a simple accident. (Of all Peace Corps fatalities, approximately 74 percent were caused by accidents, most involving moving vehicles. Roughly 15 percent were caused by illness, and 13 percent resulted from "intentional injuries," meaning homicide or suicide.)[51]

Volunteers to Latin America were given the most daunting task in all of the Peace Corps, to bring "democratic cooperation" to the peasantry, with the least specific directions on how to do it. Many fledgling national development agencies accepted volunteers before they had figured out how best to deploy their own people, much less large numbers of foreigners. Larry Radley, left largely to his own devices in a town that was a speck on the map of Colombia, alternated between throwing himself into ad hoc service activities in Armenia and escaping its rigid mores and intractable poverty in colorful Medellín. As Armenia's rigidity and intractability became ever more apparent to him, his escapes became more frequent.

Until the community development programs were made more specific at the end of the 1960s and volunteers were recruited for identifiable skills to use in fairly well defined jobs, volunteers obtained little direction from staff. Radley did not blame his supervisors, however, for not giving him more specific strategies for approaching the priest, and like many volunteers in the rural areas he kept himself busy doing this and that. But two years was a long time for busywork, and he longed for a major, substantive activity to which he could commit his full energy. His predicament had parallels all over Latin America. "I will be losing my partner, John, very soon," Betsy Long Bucks wrote her parents from Colombia in 1966, "Peace Corps has advised him to get out as long as the Padre stays . . . since he impedes all and any kind of community action work."[52]

Volunteers in urban community development had perhaps an even harder task. Poverty along with corruption and cynicism became even more overwhelming in dense urban areas. One group of twenty volunteers assigned in 1966 to work for the municipal government of Guayaquil, Ecuador, found government bureaucrats to be as disillusioned as they were powerless. Unable to accomplish much themselves, local functionaries could give no direction to volunteers on what might be meaningful tasks. Peace Corps field representatives were equally useless. Dedicated to the premise that a "good" volunteer could use his personality and organizing techniques to ignite the people, the staff ignored volunteers' problems and urged them to push ahead. "I sort of gave up," one volunteer to Latin American said. "My rep told me to keep trying; he said I was making progress; but when I asked him how, he didn't say."[53]

American volunteers were not the only ones to feel abandoned. Ian Smillie notes that by 1968 CUSO had also overextended itself in Latin America. "In the rush to develop programs," he writes in a passage that could easily describe the Peace Corps, "staff was not always able to check requests [from host countries] very closely, and some volunteers . . . found that there was little for them to do in their postings."[54]

In the *municipio* of Guayaquil, fifteen of the twenty volunteers dropped out of their putative urban assignments after a few months. They found their attempts to develop ancillary projects in the surrounding *barrios* even more discouraging. "Our neighbors," Paul Cowan later wrote, "were dismally certain that they would never progress." They were also certain that the Peace Corps was hostile to their religion. "All the people there think that your organization has come to Ecuador to spread your religion and make it triumph over Catholicism," a woman told Cowan one morning. For him it was an ironic misunderstanding typical of the Peace Corps: here he was, a Jewish volunteer sent by a Catholic president being accused of trying to spread Protestantism.[55]

Two of the Guayaquil volunteers eventually worked their way into the heart of the community enough to develop roles that they and others could see as useful, but they were the exceptions. Excuses of "culture shock" did little to ease the alienation of the others. Many became deeply depressed. Even a PCV mechanic assigned to a garage found the workers resistant to his presence. After a year and a half of frustration he observed to friends, "You know, I think the most lucid piece of political theory in the whole twentieth century is '*Yanqui*, go home.'"[56]

The organization's problems in Latin America did not end overnight. Through the 1960s the Latin American region had the highest rate of attrition in the Peace Corps. Charles Peters's evaluation division regularly raked the regional staff over the coals, excoriating them for absurdly unrealistic expectations. But the Latin American staff was not only hampered by its grandiose ideology; two other simple facts also intervened. On average, volunteers in Latin American countries worked with people who were more deeply impoverished than did volunteers in many areas of Africa, the Near East, and Asia (excluding India). Volunteers in Africa, for example, saw mainly the children of peasants self-sufficient enough to allow their offspring to attend government boarding schools. Latin American volunteers also faced the handicap of being *gringos.*

Paul Cowan found the Guayaquil *municipio* awash with anti-American rumors. Betsy Long Bucks wrote her parents about having "missed the excitement of seeing students from the Colombian University burn the American flag and stomp on it . . . shouting Castro *sí*, Yanqui *nó.*" She added, "am sure it would have made me furious." Many volunteers to Latin America suffered a dual guilt. They could not be part of the solution, and they suspected or believed their own country to be part of the problem. In the 1960s, Latin America was a difficult place to be if one was from the United States. At least in countries like Ghana and India, one could blame the nation's ills on the British.[57]

Gradually the Peace Corps came to recognize that good intentions were not enough. Two critical American staff members later recounted, "A Peace Corps official once likened the agency's efforts in community development to a memorable scene from the 'Peanuts' comic strip. 'Good grief,' says Charlie Brown, looking perplexed and dejected on the pitching mound, '184 to nothing. I don't understand it. How can we lose when we're so sincere?'"[58] Volunteers, Peace Corps programmers came to realize, had to have not only the right attitude but also the right job.

Larry Radley and David Crozier did not live to see these changes. The peasant who brought news of the boys walked two and a half days through the jungle to Quibdo, Colombia. The plane had hit the mountainside early in the morning. Manuel Salvador Moreno, alone, had seen it go down on the jagged peak. He decided he should find someone to tell. In Chicago, a Colombian friend of Larry's at their side, the frightened Radley family awaited word of their son. In West Plains, Missouri, the Crozier family prayed for good news, refusing to give up hope. The governments of the United States and Colombia sent eight planes to scout the range in which the plane had gone down without a trace on Easter morning. Their search came to an end when

Manuel Moreno reached his destination and reported what he had seen.

Larry Radley, along with David Crozier and two other Peace Corps friends, had decided to celebrate his transfer to Venecia with a short vacation to see the orchids on the coast at Bahia Solano. His last letter home suggested that he had made peace with the idea of small accomplishments. "It is better to live humbly for a cause than to die nobly for one," he resolved. Photographs from the outing showed the young men with their sunglasses and rolled-up pants posing happily in jungle clearings, machetes and cameras at the ready. David and Larry said good-bye to their comrades at the airport, boarded a thirty-seven-passenger flight over the Baudó mountain range, and were never seen again. They died along with the Colombian passengers and crew, their plane obliterated on a mountaintop too steep to allow any of their bodies to be recovered.[59]

"I render homage with admiration, gratitude and love to the members of the Peace Corps who died in the terrible airplane crash," the president of Colombia said afterward. They came, he told his countrymen, "to understand us, to help us . . . to suffer our misfortunes and dangers." Their sacrifice, he concluded "with profound respect and deep emotion," had made "the common grave of the Baudó . . . one of the cornerstones of a new American understanding."[60]

One year later Larry's mother stood in her kitchen holding a telegram from the Peace Corps addressed to her daughter. The message congratulated Elena Radley on her acceptance into the program for Colombia. "I thought I would die," Merle Radley later recalled. "She felt she had to finish what Larry had started. It was very difficult for me to send her . . . but I wasn't asked." Gordon Radley, her youngest son, joined five years later. David Crozier's parents, whose only other child was already safely married and herself had young children, wrote Shriver after the accident thanking him for giving David the opportunity to serve through the Peace Corps. "We are not sorry he went to Colombia," they said. It had made David happy. The Croziers sent $1,700 to complete the school that David had begun building in Jardín. The Croziers, Southern Baptists from Missouri, and the Radleys, Jews from Chicago, spent Christmas 1962 together, remembering their children and endeavoring to understand the common ideals that had bonded two such different young men.

They were the same ideals that bonded most volunteers and that gave them the feeling, upon return, of being veterans of a common struggle. Paul Cowan, a radical, complained that they were the middle-class children of "the Ford dealer from Phoenix or the hardware-store owner from Waukeegan," whose parents believed in the American dream of success. Cowan was right that most did not seek radical political change, but wrong that freedom meant to them "the sacred right to buy a second car." Peace Corps volunteers like Radley and Crozier (whose parents, respectively, sold *World Book* encyclopedias and ran a small-town pharmacy) represented precisely the reform mood of the mainstream in the 1960s. They were not without delusions and foibles, and if David Crozier had lived he might indeed have found himself "looking down a gun barrel" in Vietnam. But they were optimistic and idealistic. They thought that power brought opportunities for benevolence. They believed deeply that it was possible for Americans to do better and be better. And, like the 150,000 volunteers who followed them, they were at least willing to try.

6

Ghana

— ❀ —

It is a morale booster when you have volunteers from the
greatest power on earth coming here helping you—
not what they are doing, but to give you hope. You feel
that you are *part*, you belong to a world, you are not
unimportant or neglected.

K. B. ASANTE, 1995

The surf pounds the rocks at the base of Cape Coast Castle, shooting glittering plumes of water into the bright blue sky. The imposing white ramparts, dotted with black cannons, tower above the misty spectacle, looking out on the far waves where slave ships once dipped and bobbed, awaiting the dories that brought them new cargo. Large, separate dungeons for men and women, built deep into the fastnesses of the castle, admit none of the light that bathes every surface, none of the salty spray. Bats now haunt the dank cells, to which the first American volunteers were taken on their orientation to Ghana.[1]

The slave trade fueled the growth of Europe and North America for nearly three hundred years. It also brought treasure to warrior tribes like the Ashanti of Ghana, who displayed riches from the slave trade in gold furniture and regal kente cloth, in which they wove silk from the Orient together with native cotton. Adinkra cloth, also made by the Ashanti and decorated with their ancient symbols, even had a special marking for the lucrative traffic in captives: two interlocking squares meaning "You are the slave of him whose handcuffs you wear."[2] In the hierarchy of historical evil, however, conquerors generally outrank collaborators. And though the two may share the same motives, it is the conquerors who generally get to keep their booty. Brought to heel by the British after a series of wars ending in 1900, the Ashanti and other tribes of Ghana served to build British wealth until independence in 1957.

The Peace Corps sent its first volunteers to Ghana. Shriver selected Ghana because it was one of the first colonies to achieve independence and because of its role as the leader of the anti-imperial movement on the continent. But, like the German voluntary group Aktion Süh-nezeichen which sought in 1959 to send its first volunteers to Poland, Russia, and Israel ("whose people we have hurt the most"), the United States could have chosen no more fitting spot to declare its commitment to a world of greater racial and economic equality than Ghana, with its fourteen stone slave-trade castles spaced along a coast barely 150 miles long.[3]

Yet it was equally true that the government and people of Ghana chose the volunteers. Beginning in 1958, Ghanaians requested help with a national commitment of their own: to make better use of their own human resources and to diminish through a national system of education the kinds of tribal rivalries that in the past had fed the slave trade and that thirty years later would make Rwanda a symbol of genocide. In the four decades since independence this commitment has been imperfectly realized, but the extent to which it has been is due in important part to the convergence of the free world and African goals that brought Kwame Nkrumah together with the Peace Corps.

The minister of education was panicked. Jumping out of bed after an illness of eight days, he hurried to the meeting he had called to address the principals of Ghana's handful of teacher training colleges. He stressed the urgency of the situation. More teachers had to be trained immediately. The headmasters should begin by installing double and triple bunk beds in all the dorms; more teachers must be processed to meet the emergency. The president, the Osagyefo ("Savior"), had placed the responsibility for this critical national task in their hands: to achieve in one year what had been planned for four.[4]

President Kwame Nkrumah, charismatic, American-educated leader of the decolonization movement, had had this idea while on his way to give a speech in the remote rural town of Sunyani, eighty miles north of the old Ashanti capital of Kumasi. He announced to the surprised dignitaries, "I have decided that as from next year, there will be free and compulsory education throughout the country." The date was December 12, 1960. The next year was two weeks away. The president's secretary sent a memo to the Ministry of Education a few days later. "I should explain," he began, "that there has been no prior consultation with your Ministry on this matter, because it was not until the Osagyefo reached Sunyani that it was decided to make this policy declaration."[5] The Ministry of Education received another memo from the Ministry of Justice the same day. "Is it [even] known," the first Principal Secretary inquired of the other, "whether teachers will be available to staff the increased number of schools?"[6]

This question reverberated through the halls of the Ministry of Education from the first day of 1961 to the last. The ministry, in a long series of emergency reports and meetings, estimated that to find a place for every child over the age of five would require a thousand new schools before the academic year began in September. Trained teachers were already in short supply, and it was almost impossible to convince those with degrees to take jobs in the untamed countryside, where few people had running water or electricity and where one could still spot elephants, baboons, hyenas, and crocodiles. Village youth pursued education to escape primitive conditions, not to return to them. The ministry would have to draft anyone who could read. Three days after John F. Kennedy signed the executive order that would eventually bring Peace Corps teachers to Ghana, the unsuspecting education officer for the inland northern region of the country wrote to the Ministry of Education that he knew of no reason "to hope that by a miracle the position [the lack of teachers] can be changed overnight."[7]

Kennedy desired a small miracle, too. He had opened himself to charges of usurping the power of Congress by establishing the Peace Corps under executive order. Such a usurpation could be justified only by an urgent need. In its first month, however, the Peace Corps had not received one invitation to send volunteers abroad. The sense of alarm drifted downward. Warren Wiggins was equally in need of a miracle. He came into the Peace Corps leadership as a former foreign service officer, and thus as something of an outsider. He was the polished expert in an organization that glorified the amateur. Sargent Shriver had given him the task of obtaining overseas job slots, and Wiggins had failed. "Everybody's careers and jobs and reputation were on the line," Wiggins later recalled. Shriver "got very irritated with me . . . I was doing my best . . . but the programs weren't coming in."[8]

In fact it appeared that the Peace Corps might be rejected. National pride and suspicion of American motives made third world responses "unpredictable," in the words of more than one ambassador. In Brazil, considered a possible pilot country because of its role as the leading ally in South America, the embassy said it could not forecast how the Peace Corps would be treated "as a political issue." Volunteers might be invited if the United States could avoid creating the impression that it had made a unilateral decision to "send the Peace Corps to Brazil."[9] In Africa, favorable press reactions in Egypt and Ethiopia were offset by hostile reactions expressed at the All African Peoples Conference held that spring in Cairo. In Ghana, the press harped on American neocolonialism.[10]

Kennedy suggested to Sargent Shriver that he travel to some of the key developing countries to meet with heads of state to convince them of the Corps' seriousness and good intent. Meanwhile, through the personal intervention of Undersecretary of State Chester Bowles, the Peace Corps made contact with Julius Nyerere of Tanganyika, who indicated that road engineers might be welcome. Another break came when a cousin of Jawaharlal Nehru arranged for a meeting between the Indian prime minister and Shriver.[11] With these first tentative indications of interest, the new head of the Peace Corps left on April 22, 1961, for a twenty-six-day journey that would take him to eight key states in Africa and Asia: Ghana, Nigeria, Pakistan, India, Burma, Malaysia, Thailand, and the Philippines.

As the first stop, Ghana was risky. Since winning its independence peacefully in 1957, the government of the former Gold Coast had promoted the slogan it used against the British, "Self Government Now," throughout colonial Africa. More than a dozen new nations emerged in the following three years, and they looked admiringly to Ghana as a model. Recognized by the United States as "the then leading spokesman for African nationalism," President Kwame Nkrumah also headed the continental movement for African unity, conferring regularly with other independence leaders such as Sekou Touré of Guinea, Julius Nyerere of Tanganyika, and Patrice Lumumba of the Congo.[12] His support, or denunciation, of the Peace Corps would be critical.

The ten years he had spent as a student in the United States, from 1935 to 1945, gave Nkrumah a unique perspective. His first-hand experience of American segregation encouraged a race-consciousness (including exposure to the ideas of Marcus Garvey and W. E. B. Du Bois) he might otherwise not have attained. But while certain experiences rankled (such as being shown to the garden hose when he asked for a drink in a restaurant), others inspired him. Nkrumah, like many other Ghanaians, admired what the United States had made of itself since independence from Britain. "Forget about slavery," one early education officer later said; "we knew that Americans had struggled to achieve."[13] Ghanaians also recognized America's historic resistance to Britain. For most Americans the stories of their own rebellion had faded, but to Africans like Nkrumah they were vivid and in the early 1950s had immediate relevance.

Nkrumah also admired the American schooling system, in which he had studied for his bachelor's and doctoral degrees in education. Nkrumah was unusual in this respect, since at the time most Ghanaians considered the British school system far superior to the American. His close companion Kojo Botsio later attested that Nkrumah believed that when it came to practical training, "You couldn't beat America."[14] Nkrumah himself wrote in an article for the Penn State University journal of education in 1943 that "the colonial school program of Africa . . . should give way to a new process of training and educating in life and current social, political, technical, and economic ideals now in vogue in progressive schools in America, China, and Russia."[15]

This reference to the trio of "America, China, and Russia," then allies in World War II, foreshadowed the most important source of conflict between Ghana and the United States following independence. From the start, when Nkrumah with British approval invited China to attend Ghana's independence day celebrations instead of Taiwan, the United States objected to the sympathies of his government, which formally adopted socialism in 1962. Nkrumah, however, wanted to be free to pick and choose what he thought best in each system: for example, American education and technology and Russian economic planning. In the context of the cold war, however, that meant playing the Americans against the Russians and vice versa to obtain aid from both.

In the same year that Nkrumah traveled to the Soviet Union for the first time, he completed negotiations with Kaiser Aluminum for the American company to build an aluminum smelter. The smelter's guaranteed electricity purchases would enable Ghana to negotiate American, British, and World Bank loans to build Akosombo Dam and a hydroelectricity plant within it. With Kaiser Aluminum as a steady customer, Ghana would have the income necessary to repay the loans. The first home-rule government of Gold Coast had originally tried to convince the British in the early 1950s to build the dam, but had been turned down repeatedly by the Colonial Office. Finally, with the critical intervention of Edgar Kaiser and the signature of John Kennedy on the master agreement, Ghana built the dam. With it came enough excess energy to power much of the country.[16]

Alternately wooing American support and damning Western imperialism and capitalism, Nkrumah related to Kennedy as "a real friend" at the same time that he sent Ghanaians to Russia for military training. A wily fish, Nkrumah swam back and forth between the Russian and American hooks, confident that neither side would cut bait. From the United States, according to K. B. Asante, a diplomat who headed the African Affairs Secretariat, "he wanted assistance and understanding— assistance to develop Ghana as a modern state, and later when he turned strongly to socialism . . . understanding of the reasons why he turned that way, and for the assistance to continue still."[17] The hope that the United States would "understand" was mostly naive and certainly self-serving, but because of the Peace Corps it was not entirely misplaced. The Corps was Kennedy's olive branch to nonaligned nations like Ghana, India, and Indonesia—softening the otherwise harsh American disapproval of their contacts with the Soviet Union and building American understanding through the volunteers themselves.

Still, when Sargent Shriver and his contingent landed at Accra Airport in late April, they had little idea if their olive branch would be accepted. The day that Shriver boarded his plane in Washington en route to Africa, the *Ghanaian Times* published a scathing editorial about the "surprise and hardly welcome visitor." The newspaper denounced the Peace Corps as an "agency of neo-colonialism, [and a] clever move in [the] vicious game of teleguide diplomacy." The editors scoffed at the idea that the Peace Corps was in any way humanitarian, even though "few organizations could have been presented to the world in more grandiose terms."[18]

Luckily for the Peace Corps, however, the newspaper had misstepped in the game of revolutionary one-upmanship. Normally, condemning the West for its "neo-imperialism" would have elicited nods of approval from Nkrumah. What the editors could not know, however, was how serious the president was about increasing Ghana's educational capacity.[19] Many top officials, including the president himself, had been trained to be teachers. In Gold Coast secondary schools, Kojo Botsio had formerly taught geography and English, K. B. Asante had taught high school mathematics, and Finance Minister Komla Gbedemah had taught botany. Right after independence, in 1958, Nkrumah created the "Ghana Educational Trust," which almost immediately doubled the size of the secondary school system. Still, under the new plan, as Education Minister Kojo Botsio wrote at the time, "perhaps the most important problem . . . was . . . the strictly limited numbers of trained teachers available."[20]

The Nkrumah regime's determination to educate the populace grew out of a tradition in which the British had simultaneously stimulated and thwarted the hope for progress. On the one hand, following the defeat of the Ashanti in 1900, the British had decided to make Gold Coast a showcase of enlightened imperialism. The Royal African Company had brought in the Society for the Propagation of the Gospel to build Gold Coast's first schools in the 1750s, but after 1900 the British undertook to educate native administrators in a serious way, even founding a university at Cape Coast. By independence, Gold Coast had the best schools and the best civil service in Africa.[21]

At the same time the British were concerned not to spend too much of their colonial profits on local education, or to over-educate a populace they hoped would attend mainly to growing the cocoa crop when it was not mining gold. "The process of educating the Protectorate as a whole is dependent on the financial resources of the Native Administrators and the supply of trained teachers," a 1938 report noted, expressing the belief that the colony should pay its own way. The report also showed a certain contentment with these limitations: "It is not to be expected that there will be any startling or sudden expansion in either direction [i.e., resources or teachers], nor is it considered desirable that there should be."[22] A few years later, in 1941, another report on the colonial school system noted the concern that "Native Administrators . . . [need to] have the right attitude towards the soil if their people are not to become alienated from farming through education."[23] The result: in large areas of the country, less than one-half of one percent of the population attended school.[24]

To Ghanaians, especially those educated enough to recognize the self-serving limits of imperial largesse, such caps on the development of the country were intolerable. After 1951, by expanding the educational system, Ghanaians attacked the structures of colonialism most tangible to them. It was, in Kojo Botsio's words, one of Nkrumah's "first targets: education of the masses. With that, he would be able to embark on his economic program."[25] Using American techniques of mass, progressive education, Nkrumah hoped to lead his country to socialism.

All this meant that when the *Ghanaian Times* denounced the Peace Corps, Kwame Nkrumah was horrified. Leaving an urgent message for the U.S. ambassador to call him, Nkrumah told the startled official who returned the call that he "deeply regretted" the editorial, that his cabinet was unaware the "press would launch such an attack," and that he wanted his feelings to be conveyed to Kennedy at the "soonest" opportunity. He would be happy to receive Shriver and judge the Peace Corps proposal on its own "merits."[26]

Once Sargent Shriver and his four aides arrived the next day, Nkrumah could hardly have given them a warmer reception. Although Nkrumah's lectures on Western imperialism made him seem ambivalent and even a little coy to his American visitors, his own staff recognized that Nkrumah was exceptionally enthusiastic.[27] The president called the Peace Corps a "bold, splendid idea," suggested that teachers would be most helpful, and after a friendly discussion, escorted Shriver to his car and insisted that the press take photos of them together.

Shriver subsequently met with the minister of education and the head of the influential Trade Union Congress, both of whom by then, according to the U.S. embassy, "strongly seconded [the] Nkrumah line." The minister of education in particular stressed Ghana's "desperate" need for secondary schoolteachers in math and science and requested 270 volunteers by the start of school in September, then five months away. The head of the Trade Union Congress assuaged any lingering doubts the delegation may have had, saying that the statements of "super-nationalistic radicals . . . should not be confused with responsible positions of their governments."[28]

While in Ghana, Shriver also met Prime Minister Julius Nyerere of Tanganyika, who was visiting Nkrumah and received Shriver cordially. Nkrumah's and Nyerere's simultaneous endorsement of the Peace Corps was "great," said a U.S. official in neighboring Nigeria, adding that if anything the "local editorial attacking PC [Peace Corps] just

before arrival added to [its] impact." Shriver's subsequent meeting with
the prime minister of Nigeria was "most satisfactory" as a result, the
diplomat concluded.[29]

From Africa, Sargent Shriver and his entourage went on to India,
which they considered "the hardest and most critical test of the trip"
because of its immense population and size, its importance as the first
British colony to achieve independence after World War II, and its role
as the world's largest democracy.[30] The Kennedy administration had
placed a high priority on cultivating cordial relations with India from
the start. John Kenneth Galbraith, the liberal economist, acted as ambassador. The historian Dennis Merrill notes that in cold war terms,
"Kennedy viewed a strong and rapidly developing India as a counter-
balance to the influence of the People's Republic of China."[31]

Yet Shriver and his aides received a comparatively tepid welcome in
New Delhi. Indians with whom Shriver and his aides met in New Delhi
gave them a mixed reception. Officials of the Punjab Ministry for
Community Development took the Americans on a tour of rural projects, and said they could use a couple dozen volunteers with expertise
in poultry production. One Indian acquaintance of Harris Wofford
expressed concern about America's imperial intent; a former companion of Gandhi hailed the Peace Corps as an expression of the independence leader's own philosophy of public service. Prime Minister
Nehru received Sargent Shriver wearily, appearing barely to listen to
Shriver's enthusiastic monologue. In the end Nehru responded that
India would accept a small number of volunteers, saying, "I am sure
young Americans would learn a great deal in this country and it could
be an important experience for them." But, he added prophetically, "I
hope you and they will not be too disappointed if the Punjab, when
they leave, is more or less the same as it was before they came."[32]

For a nation many times the size of any of the African countries,
without a specific, urgent need for volunteers such as Ghana had identified, the Peace Corps would inevitably be more a symbolic gesture
than a practical help. The expression of altruism in India probably did
more to strengthen American national identity than it did to promote
local development—and more to soften the frequently brittle relationship between the two nations than to soften the brittle class structure of
India itself. But symbols could be critical, and Kennedy manipulated
them masterfully. Skeptics would later dismiss this as nothing more

than the Kennedy "image," but in international relations image is one form of reality. Frank Ninkovich notes that in the twentieth century the "self-defeating capacity for [mass] destruction" led statesmen increasingly to recognize "world opinion" as often "the only possible solution to many of the world's problems."[33]

India's and Ghana's endorsements meant that the Peace Corps now had the blessing of the leading unaligned nations in Asia and sub-Saharan Africa. Ghana's endorsement was especially electrifying. Africans and Americans both were surprised that, as Kojo Botsio put it, "Nkrumah of all people would invite the Peace Corps."[34] K. B. Asante thought that for the newly independent Anglophone countries which "looked to Ghana," Nkrumah's imprimatur meant the Peace Corps was "a good thing."[35]

Nkrumah's approval also bolstered American public confidence in the inherent rightness of the Peace Corps and its use in the cold war. An article in the *St. Louis Post-Dispatch* commented smugly the next year, "The source of some of the requests is rather surprising . . . Ghana, whose President Kwame Nkrumah received the Lenin peace prize from the Soviet Union this spring, has requested 185 additional teachers to supplement 51 already sent there."[36] John Kennedy himself jotted in an early note to Secretary of State Dean Rusk, "Ghana has accepted 50 to 70 Peace Corps volunteers. Guinea is asking for 40 to 60 road builders and engineers from the Peace Corps. If we can successfully crack Ghana and Guinea, Mali may even turn to the West. If so, these would be the first communist-oriented countries to turn from Moscow to us."[37] Americans from the president on down assumed that the inspired thinking that produced the idea of teachers for Africa was their nation's own. Little did they realize that it was the point in the road where Ghana's and America's needs crossed.

When the first Peace Corps volunteers stepped off the Pan Am prop jet on August 30, 1961, wearing summer suits and light cotton dresses, the steamy, wood-smoke-tinged air of Accra signaled their arrival in a place far, far from home. The same minister of education who had sprung from his sickbed earlier in the year and who had met with Shriver only a few months later waited on the sizzling black tarmac with other dignitaries to greet them. Quietly forming themselves into a group, the volunteers sang as best they could the Ghanaian national anthem "Yen Ara Asaasa Ni" (This Is Our Homeland) in Twi, the local language they had studied. A gesture that appeared corny and inept to a later, more bruised generation of Americans struck Ghanaians as original and heartfelt—which is undoubtedly how it was meant at the time.[38] Radio Ghana taped the performance and aired it repeatedly. Years later a Ghanaian associate of the Peace Corps program called it "a singular gesture of friendship, goodwill and understanding which . . . more than any official statement could convey, signaled to Ghanaians and to the world the deep respect and concern that the very first group of volunteers had for the people of the first country it was to serve."[39]

The Peace Corps, like most development agencies, had few exact ways to measure its usefulness or to predict the long-range consequences of its intervention. In the field of education, particularly, to which roughly 50–80 percent of all volunteers in West Africa were assigned for more than three decades, it was difficult to determine how well students learned, how well teachers taught, how quickly a society advanced or fell back as a result of the quality of its mass education, and how education affected (if at all) the larger political culture upon which development was dependent. One volunteer ironically commented to another when being told in the early 1980s that the brutal dictator of Liberia on a visit to the United States had asked to see the Peace Corps volunteer who had taught him in grammar school: "Yes, maybe one of *your* students will grow up to disembowel a president and line up ministers on the beach to be shot."[40]

In Ghana, as in many other African countries, the Peace Corps knew that it was giving hundreds of thousands of students an education they would otherwise not get at all. The work seemed of value in itself. Not dramatic, and certainly not sufficient to produce development, but probably a necessary prerequisite. Even so, as Eric Sevareid commented about Peace Corps education programs as early as 1962, "the end results of such efforts lie far beyond the mistiest horizons."[41]

By American standards, and by the British standards that Ghana's Ministry of Education struggled to maintain, the majority of Peace Corps teachers were not qualified for the job. Most were neither education majors nor majors in the fields they were assigned to teach. But by the standards of Ghana's secondary schools, the volunteers were far better qualified than the local peer instructor alternative. The teachers were needed, and their willingness to try scaling the cultural barrier—to sing in Twi, as it were—was deeply appreciated. But perhaps the strongest proof of the value that members of the government placed on Peace Corps volunteers was the fact that Kwame Nkrumah never asked them to leave.

The government of Ghana had accepted word for word the Peace Corps contract presented by the American ambassador, with one amendment: "The Peace Corps program in Ghana may be terminated by either government ninety days after the date of written notification of such intent."[42] Nkrumah made it clear that the Peace Corps would not be tolerated if volunteers sought to have a political effect or tried to "propagandize or spy or . . . subvert the Ghanaian system."[43] The minister of Nigeria commented, when pressed by U.S. officials to commit to the program, that it was "naive to assume that for a government to invite the Peace Corps into its country was not a political act."[44] For Kwame Nkrumah, under whom 93 percent of the National Assembly voted for socialism and one-party rule in 1962, this "political act" contradicted his economic policy at the same time that it moved forward his educational policy. It contradicted as well the trend of his foreign policy, which became increasingly cool toward the United States.

Answerable only to himself once "insults" of the "Osagyefo" were outlawed in 1961, Nkrumah never had to resolve these contradictions to anyone's satisfaction but his own. The result was that he kept the Peace Corps, even praised it, while taking steps to minimize its potential to stir dissent. At first, Nkrumah welcomed the volunteers enthusiastically. He gave them a party on arrival at which, one volunteer later recalled, "he danced with us and taught us the 'high life,'" then a popular dance step. On the following New Year's Day, without mentioning the Peace Corps by name, the president broadcast to the nation his expectation that Ghanaians would embrace volunteers who had "left homes and friends to come work among us." Ghana, he noted, had "invited [them] here to assist us to develop our country . . . Those who have such a spirit deserve our co-operation and support in all they do for the good of the nation, and we should do nothing to discourage them."[45] At the end of the volunteers' first term, Nkrumah gave another party at his personal residence for those who had served in "Ghana I." U.S. embassy personnel noted that the usually anti-American Nkrumah seemed genuinely "impressed by the sincerity, dedication, and attractiveness of the PCVs."[46]

Sargent Shriver also received this impression, noting after his second trip to Ghana in 1962 that "the foreign minister, the minister of information, the minister of interior, and other cabinet members said of the Peace Corps: 'That's one thing your country is doing properly.'"[47] Nkrumah's satisfaction with the Peace Corps could also be seen through the press, controlled by the government. Yaw Agyeman-Badu has noted in his research comparing attitudes toward the United States in Ghana and Nigeria from 1960 to 1977 that Nkrumah's pan-African, socialist policies constantly "put him at variance" with American policies toward Africa. The only aspect of U.S. policy toward either Africa or third world development given even "neutral" press coverage in the Nkrumah years was the Peace Corps.[48]

Agyeman-Badu's assessment of the press coverage as generally "neutral," rather than actually "favorable" up until the president's overthrow in 1966, reflects Nkrumah's growing suspicion after 1962 that the Peace Corps was a front for the Central Intelligence Agency. "Nkrumah was made to believe," according to K. B. Asante, "that many of them were CIA agents. Therefore he became very cool." Rumors of a link between the CIA and Peace Corps persisted for decades in many countries, and could at times approach the absurd—as when soldiers in Zaire confiscated one volunteer's maps of Africa and then examined a tampon from another one's suitcase. ("They dropped it like a hot potato when they found out what it was for," a compatriot wryly noted.)[49] Such misgivings were natural considering the infamy of the agency's covert techniques. In the pursuit of victory in the cold war, the United States would stop at nothing to beat the Soviet Union, third world countries well understood. Even though the Ghanaian government never uncovered any evidence of CIA infiltration of the Peace Corps, and members of the regime later concluded that it had likely never occurred, in 1963 a suspicious Nkrumah took steps to counter the volunteers' influence.[50]

One step was to bar the Peace Corps from teaching English and history. Nkrumah pointedly did not extend the restriction to Canadian volunteers. According to George Ayi-Bonte, an associate director of the Ghana Peace Corps program for twenty years, some of the Americans had been using George Orwell's *Animal Farm* in their classes and members of the government got wind of it. Peace Corps country director George Carter never knew, however, what precisely made

Nkrumah believe that the volunteers had overstepped the bounds of math, science, and "neutral" English language instruction. Without warning, Carter found himself summoned to Flagstaff House (the Ghanaian presidential residence) one morning. Breaking diplomatic protocol, Nkrumah contacted Carter directly, rather than through the ambassador. Carter and the ambassador went to hear Nkrumah out.

According to Carter, an African American who had met Nkrumah socially several years before the Peace Corps started, "He was very pleasant, remembering vaguely our first meeting." Still, the president lectured Carter about his resolve not to allow young Americans to proselytize their way of life, warning that if they did so the Peace Corps would have to leave. Carter listened "attentively," as he later put it, agreed to Nkrumah's request that PCVs be taken out of English and history classes, and then tried to figure out how to stall for time "without being caught again."[51] Carter knew that it would not be easy to cancel classes mid-year, especially in such a universal, fundamental subject as language instruction.

So, publicly, the Peace Corps acquiesced to Nkrumah's directive in keeping with its own broader policy of going only where invited but also in recognition, as George Carter had told Shriver the year before, that "sensibilities are such that one significant mistake will mean the end of the Peace Corps in Ghana."[52] In practice, however, it took time to shift volunteers out of the assignments given them by the Ministry of Education.

At the level of Nkrumah and his cabinet members it was possible to set goals without giving careful thought to how they would be accomplished—like compulsory education within one year without additional teachers. According to Carter, however, the Principal Secretary of the Education Ministry, "who actually ran things," knew better and simply worked around the fact that "Nkrumah would have been upset" had he known all the details of the Peace Corps placements. Thus, while Nkrumah demanded "perfectly credentialed" Americans teaching only math and science, the Principal Secretary and the Peace Corps country director quietly continued a program of American noneducators, bachelors of arts generalists, teaching everything from geography, history, and English to physics, mathematics, and chemistry. "We worked well at it together," according to George Carter, and the teachers themselves proved a credit to both the ministry and the Peace Corps.

Volunteers were also gradually transferred to schools where they would not be asked to teach English or history. In the words of one such volunteer, the country director took great pains to avoid being "caught in the middle of this struggle between the president and his Ministry."[53]

In 1963 Nkrumah also took the second, more dramatic step of inviting young Russian "volunteers" to Ghana along with the Peace Corps and other Western volunteers from CUSO and VSO. It was "an obvious effort to neutralize the luster of Peace Corps teachers," wrote an American evaluator—one that Nkrumah viewed as a "brilliant ideological coup."[54]

The high morale of the U.S. volunteers led them to welcome the challenge, however. Indeed, the founding philosophy of the Peace Corps emphasized "promoting a better understanding of the American people," and what better way to show the differences between American youth and Soviet youth than by juxtaposing them? The volunteers' attempts to be friendly toward the Russian youth would also prove the intention of the United States to wage the cold war peacefully (even though it was already fighting in Vietnam). "The volunteers are delighted," an evaluator noted. "They consider this professional fraternization a major bonus of their assignment to Ghana." The Peace Corps teachers, who shared accommodations with volunteers from other countries, reported that the Russians returned their sociability.[55] One Soviet and one American volunteer even fell in love and married.

Still, the Peace Corps took the challenge seriously. The Soviet strategy, one report speculated, was "to win [a] position [of] strong influence in Ghana, using [the] country as a bridgehead for the rest of Africa."[56] Peace Corps staff thus kept a close watch on the Russian initiative, trying (unsuccessfully) to determine if the volunteers had really elected to come (probably they had), and attempting to assess their effectiveness compared with the American and other Western youth. The Russian volunteers struggled against the handicap of poor English, which was the national language of instruction in the former colony comprised, like India, of many different tribal and language groups. In the first contingent, 15 Russians came. The second contingent brought 98 Russian teachers, making it the largest contingent of volunteers after the Peace Corps, which had 108 volunteers in education.

In spite of the obvious attempt to attain numerical parity, however,

Russian volunteers were widely recognized to be less effective than the Western volunteers. They "were not such a success," then Foreign Minister Kojo Botsio later acknowledged. Their lack of English language skills held back the Russians, even though they were sometimes better trained in their specialties. One Peace Corps evaluator concluded with some satisfaction: "PCVs are better teachers, are better liked, have more Ghanaian friends, and have fitted more fully into the fabric of Ghanaian life." Still, he worried, it was "fair to assume that Russian training will improve and that in the future our superiority will not be so marked."[57] The future was not to come, however. After a military-police coup overthrew Nkrumah's regime while he was on a trip to Hanoi and China in February 1966, the Russian volunteers were quickly pulled out. The new government of Ghana asked the Peace Corps to send 50 more volunteers to take their places.[58]

The Ghanaian public overwhelmingly supported the coup. A 75 percent collapse in world prices for cocoa, Ghana's chief export, had led to economic stagnation, a scarcity of goods, and high inflation. Bribery and conspicuous consumption within the regime, along with inefficient state industries and spending on costly prestige projects (like expensive government conferences, large official buildings, and an underutilized superhighway), fueled the perception that Nkrumah's government would not deal fairly and prudently with the crisis. After a failed assassination attempt in 1962, Nkrumah had retreated from public contact and become more and more harsh toward opponents and rivals. When former independence leader Dr. Joseph Danquah died while in solitary confinement at Nsawam prison in February 1965, the popular base of Nkrumah's government withered away and surreptitious planning for a coup began. Ironically, among the placards which joyous groups of Ghanaian demonstrators later took to Flagstaff House after the overthrow were ones stating "No More Animal Farm." Perhaps Nkrumah had been right to worry about the possible ill-effects of English literature.[59]

From 1957 until 1966 Kwame Nkrumah grew increasingly hostile toward the country where he had lived in his youth. Yet he also retained for it a certain "tenderness," according to Kojo Botsio, who was with Nkrumah when he died in Romania in 1972. Nkrumah had seen both the kind and the cruel sides of the American character. The United States had given him an education and had given Ghana the Akosombo

Dam and the Peace Corps. The United States had rained abuse upon its own black citizens and death upon the Congo and Vietnam. Malcolm X, who arrived in Ghana to a hero's welcome in November 1964, in an interview with the *Evening News* of Accra, reminded Nkrumah that President Johnson "sends peace-corps teams to Africa but pays South African mercenaries to kill Congolese citizens fighting for the liberation of their country." Why did Kwame Nkrumah never expel the Peace Corps, which he thought might be CIA-infiltrated, as neighboring Guinea did when it was annoyed with U.S. policies? Perhaps because, as one of the volunteers suspended from teaching English said, "If it were really thought we were 'agents' of the C.I.A. type, I don't think we would be in Ghana at all."[60] But the most important reason was probably just that the Peace Corps was too helpful.

To the volunteers, however, many in tiny villages miles distant from Accra, the vividness of daily life dwarfed Nkrumah's political hostility. If they even felt the Osagyefo's coolness, it was quickly dispelled by the warmth of the people. One volunteer in neighboring Togo told his personal story many years later: "I was one of them [the chief said]; I should stay here with them. I only needed to have my body covered with charcoal, he told me, and I would be his true son. The hand lay on my shoulder like a blessing."[61]

A Peace Corps proverb in the sixties, often repeated by veterans, was that volunteers who went to Asia came back meditating, volunteers who went to Latin America came back as revolutionaries, and volunteers who went to Africa came back laughing.[62] Volunteers in Africa left "laughing" for various reasons, and one of them is the attitude expressed by the proverbs of the Africans themselves. As the scholar Kwame Gyekye has observed, the philosophy of the Akan (a collection of tribes encompassing the Ashanti, among others) has been handed down to each generation through proverbs that are both spoken and printed. The proverbs are guides to personal and collective behavior, reinforcing the values esteemed by the Akan. Chief among them is care of the family and the community. This value led many African villages to embrace young volunteers as one of their own, turning odd-looking "obroni" (whites) into members of the community addressed as "brother" and "sister."

These West African cultural traditions, combined with clearly structured assignments responding to obvious needs, led most volunteers there to complete their assignments with a sense of having served for a purpose, and happier for it. Between 1961 and 1990 the Peace Corps placed volunteers in more than one hundred nations—of which only fourteen countries had volunteers every single year for thirty years. Useful work combined with a receptive environment may help account for the remarkable fact that of these fourteen countries, scattered around the globe, six (43 percent) were on the fringe of West Africa.[63] Certainly, need alone cannot account for the continuous Peace Corps presence there, since disabling poverty could be found in all parts of Africa and the third world.

The cultural traditions of Ghana, in particular, made for a hospitable environment. "Within the framework of Akan social and humanistic ethics," according to Gyekye, "what is morally good is generally that which promotes social welfare, solidarity, and harmony in human relationships." This emphasis on collectivity and reciprocity, rather than individuality and autonomy, was expressed in proverbs such as "the left arm washes the right arm and the right arm washes the left arm," and "man is not a palm tree that he should be . . . self-sufficient."[64] For volunteers, this meant entering into a society that welcomed, accepted, and cared for them as members of a community quite unlike the industrialized societies from which they had come. One volunteer later summed up an experience common to many: "I was well looked after by concerned Ghanaian friends. One of the most remarkable and wonderful characteristics of the Ghanaian people is the way they look after their guests."[65]

The other aspect of Ghanaian communalism that enhanced the volunteer experience was the cultural openness to "help." Ironically, the volunteers themselves came from a cultural context where the need to be helped was frequently interpreted as a sign of weakness or insufficiency. Symbols like the frontiersman bespoke a cultural admiration for "going it alone," for helping others, perhaps, but not needing help oneself—for being, in the words of Ralph Waldo Emerson, "self-reliant." Fortunately for the Peace Corps, the cultural ethos in Ghana was nearly the opposite.

Akan philosophy, while recognizing that not everyone contributed equally to society, still asserted the necessity, dignity, and rights of each member. "The fingers of the hand are not equal in length," one proverb said, complemented by the related saying, "One finger cannot lift up a thing."[66] In Ghanaian society, gift giving and mutual aid were customary. And when a gift was given, it was considered rude to reciprocate too quickly, lest one appear to be trying to "pay off" the obligation of friendship. Thus aid that might have been resented in other cultures seemed natural to many African villagers who, having welcomed volunteers into their midst, accepted and appreciated the Americans' contributions to the life of the group.

Peace Corps volunteers as well as volunteers from other Western countries were struck by these qualities. One early British VSO volunteer in nearby Cameroon said, "I began to realize the value of human relationships, of mutual trust and faith, as I had never done before. So many of my relationships with other people had been on a basis of mutual irony and cynicism, that to find that this was not even understood, let alone common, was at first very jarring."[67] It was also inspiring. One Peace Corps evaluator reported in 1968 that volunteers came to appreciate more their own "American ability to organize," but also the "traits of generosity, geniality, and hospitality they had learned here."[68]

Volunteers raised on stories of hardy pioneers and frontier heroes also admired, as they frequently reported, the extraordinary work ethic of West Africans. Teachers noted that students worked in the fields before and after class. Community development workers were often amazed at the Herculean efforts of those students' parents to wrest sustenance from the sea or soil. Mike Tidwell, who advised the local chief on building his own fish pond, later said: "I knew that no man would ever command more respect from me than one who, to better feed his children, moves 4,000 cubic feet of dirt with a shovel."[69]

One result was a significantly lower early termination rate in Ghana than in many other countries. Worldwide, the rate of early termination for Peace Corps volunteers, including those who did not make it through training, averaged 30 percent by the mid-1990s, whereas in Ghana the rate hovered around 20 percent.[70] The reason for this, in addition to Ghanaian hospitality, was the placement itself, usually in teaching. According to Charles Peters, the happiest, least frustrated volunteers on average were teachers—"most were in Africa"—who had "structured jobs with a clear set of tasks to perform."[71] In Africa, work usually consisted of six periods of high school English, algebra, or chemistry—enough to satisfy the passion of almost any idealistic college graduate.

Reasonable living conditions also helped ease the path of the Peace Corps in Ghana. For most Americans, far away and with almost no history of trade or missionary work there, Africa was truly *terra incognita* in 1961. Tarzan movies, museum exhibits, and *National Geographic* photo displays of bare-breasted villagers were as close as most Americans had ever come to the mysterious "dark continent."[72] Volunteers and their terrified parents knew somewhat more, much in the form of medical horror stories told by trainers determined to lose as few young Americans as possible. In addition to prescriptions on how to minimize the risk of cholera, malaria, yellow fever, typhoid, rabies, dysentery, meningitis, and giardia, which one could catch in any third world country, Peace Corps staff warned volunteers going to Africa of the even stranger maladies and dangers to be found there: the guinea worm, which could grow up to a meter long in the body before emerging from a skin blister (through which it could then be extracted by wrapping the worm around a matchstick and carefully pulling on it for a month, wrapping a little more of its length each time); or "schisto" worms, which burrowed into the skin in five minutes but stayed thirty years, rapidly aging the unlucky host; or "oncho," also called river blindness, whereby one could lose one's sight forever by taking an ill-considered dip in a lake or river. Going to Africa in the early 1960s "took a bunch of guts," in the words of George Carter, whose number one concern was "that I come back with [the same] 52 kids."[73] And not all volunteers to Africa did return. The worst that usually happened was a case of malaria or severe dysentery. But over the years a number died in motorcycle or car crashes, and one twenty-five-year-old volunteer in Ethiopia even suffered the gruesome fate of being eaten by a crocodile.

Thus when daily conditions for teachers in Africa turned out to be relatively "civilized"—bungalows built for British teachers and other expatriates—volunteers gained confidence in their ability to endure the experience. "What they found when they got there was such a relief!" Carter recalled. Although some had to dig their own latrines, most volunteers were issued small gas-powered refrigerators, kerosene lamps, and rooms complete with screens against mosquitoes. Food was simple and strange, but plentiful and often wonderfully tasty—pineapples so sweet that they smelled like coconut, chicken stewed with red peppers and peanuts, plantains fried until the natural sugar in them crystallized, bland cassava pounded into gelatinous "fufu" and served with steaming palm fruit soup.

Not all African countries could provide such fare, of course. A later volunteer in Zaire, Tim Wilkinson, admired the Peace Corps volunteer who had come the year before him for her tough adaptability to local tastes. She liked the dog meat that he found greasy and smelly. "I guess I haven't been in Zaire long enough," he wrote home cheerfully. Wilkinson did eventually come to enjoy crunchy fried termites, though, especially since it was such perfect revenge on the populous pests that threatened to eat his house before he even got a chance to live in it.[74] For volunteers like Wilkinson, dreams of home revolved around food.

But even in Ghana not every volunteer developed an appreciation for local dishes like the cassava-based fufu. "If 'yer a hankerin' for a Ghanaian meal," Tom Livingston wrote back to the Washington staff eagerly awaiting news from an official "first" volunteer, "just chow down on an art-gum eraser soaked in tabasco sauce." The Peace Corps deleted this comment from Livingston's letter when they released it to the press, along with the volunteer's reference to his cook, whose name, unfortunately for the Peace Corps image, was Comfort.[75]

For many volunteers, the physical pleasures they experienced were sometimes tinged with guilt or at least uneasiness. Throughout the 1960s volunteers battled within themselves and with Washington over the expectation that being in the Peace Corps meant living in mud huts, being best friends with the natives, and generally changing the world single-handedly. Physical comfort did not fit the Peace Corps self-image, especially when Comfort was doing the work. Sargent Shriver made his first trip to inspect the volunteers' assignments in 1962, and he challenged the volunteers to reject the amenities offered by the Ghanaian community. One volunteer later recalled a very "tense" meeting that went late into the night.

Shriver charged that living in Western-style teachers' quarters provided by the government separated the volunteers from the community. The volunteers countered that not to do so would be "perplexing and insulting" to their fellow teachers, many of them Ghanaians. When Shriver demanded that they at least dispense with servants, the volunteers responded that the people they paid from their own meager wages saved them precious time to prepare for teaching. Shopping frequently required a walk of several miles to an outdoor market two or three times a week, and unprocessed foods were labor-intensive to prepare. (Fufu, for example, required hours of pounding with a shoulder-high pestle.) Getting rid of these helpers would also have meant firing individuals who depended on the income. Many had cooked and washed for previous teachers. The meeting did not result in any changes for Ghana I volunteers, but over the next several years Peace Corps administrators gradually fine-tuned policy by further reducing volunteer living stipends and taking away jeep privileges from the few volunteers who had them.[76]

Beyond the occasional defensiveness over "Sarge's" disappointment that they were not really roughing it, many volunteers were disturbed by the sense that the Peace Corps administration did not value teachers nearly as much as the heroes of community development. Both the American media and the Peace Corps newsletter, *The Volunteer*, tended to highlight those volunteers who either were in unusual or daring placements, or who—quite aside from their demanding jobs as teachers—had also managed to start so-called secondary projects such as libraries, craft cooperatives, adult literacy programs, or community gardens. From the attention these projects received, many volunteers drew the conclusion that the Peace Corps considered these projects not secondary but, rather, as the primary justification for placing young Americans in what otherwise seemed rather staid jobs. The volunteers felt that the newsletter "was implicitly criticizing them," George Carter wrote to Washington headquarters in 1962, "because they were not involved in a project which involved hacking one's way through the bush with a bolo knife."[77]

The volunteers' assessment was correct. In internal policy debates, Shriver and his staff tussled seriously over whether education "should" be a focus of the Peace Corps in Africa, especially since so many rural schoolchildren would never use the seemingly rarefied skills that schools taught and many, in fact, would never even pass their courses or graduate. In addition, instructors who taught English taught the language of colonialism, and in the French-speaking countries it was even the wrong colonial language. Peace Corps officials, appreciating only superficially that a common language (or access to an international language) was one vestige of colonialism that local peoples put to their own use, questioned how such activities could help with decolonization. But for Ghanaians the significance was clear: an official language to which no one tribe could lay claim was an important equalizer.

The Peace Corps stayed in education because African governments requested it and because Sargent Shriver himself strongly supported the Peace Corps role in education.[78] A former chairman of Chicago's Board of Education, Shriver had a natural compatibility with the emphasis of the Kennedy family and the Kennedy administration on achievement through education. Joseph and Rose Kennedy had sent their sons to the best schools money could buy and, having attained the presidency, John Kennedy built his Cabinet with professors from the Ivy League. In the United States as a whole, this was the post-Sputnik era of the "new math" and the "new physics," the era of the president's Commission on Physical Fitness and of growing federal aid to colleges, universities, and medical schools. Indeed, free compulsory education was the oldest of Yankee traditions.

None of this kept Peace Corps teachers from feeling like second-class citizens, however. They knew they were not in the glamour jobs. George Carter, who became the director for all of Africa, found in the often intense competition for volunteers among different divisions of the Peace Corps that his position "was a lot less dramatic" than that of the director for Latin America, who promised volunteers that they would revolutionize the continent. Carter described his task as "keeping the schools open."[79] Teaching, an inherently gradualist approach to social change, could never match in excitement the growing preference in the 1960s—both in America and in the third world—for immediate and dramatic transformations.

Some volunteers blamed themselves for their lack of heroic accomplishment. One evaluator noted in 1969 that the volunteers in that year "suffered from a major collective guilt complex." Volunteers made comments such as "I couldn't enjoy my teaching because I felt I should be digging latrines," or "I taught a lot of kids to read but I've left no bridges as monuments to my two years in Ghana," or "if I just teach, I feel like a crumb—Shriver wants me to build a mud hut in the backyard." The evaluator noted that if the volunteers had not been "so embittered over their inability or unwillingness to find satisfactory secondary jobs, these PCVs would have been a completely satisfied group."[80] Two years earlier a different evaluator made a similar observation, urging Washington to give more thought to representing in affirming ways the reality of West African teaching assignments. "The projects are immensely valuable to the countries and to the US but the combination of guilt and resentment over the nature of the 'outside' work of the PC and the living standards, etc., seems more disruptive than it has to be."[81]

Some evaluators did blame the volunteers, however. An evaluator in 1967 called that year's Ghana volunteers a "dull lot" who spent too much time teaching and not enough time dreaming up community development projects. If it were not for their own lack of spark, they would be naturally able to put into effect "that intangible which makes the Peace Corps special." That intangible, he added vaguely, was the "dream" that distinguished American volunteers from those sent by Canada, Britain, or other countries.[82] In other words, Peace Corps volunteers were right when they alleged that part of their guilt complex stemmed from staff who made them feel that "the guy who is sweating out the first good math syllabus twenty-four hours a day is a flop."[83]

Many volunteers, in return, "expressed cordial contempt" for the image of the "Super Volunteer" portrayed in Peace Corps publicity, contrasting it both with the solid job many of them felt they were doing and with the more realistic self-images of Canadian and British volunteers.[84] When the number of CUSO and VSO teachers rose to and exceeded the number of Peace Corps teachers in the mid- and late 1960s, American volunteers repeatedly brought to evaluators' attention that they were doing the same job as the others, as well as making the additional effort to learn local languages and meet villagers. "What's the main difference between CUSO, ex-patriots and PC?" a popular riddle made up by Ghana volunteers asked. "CUSO are teachers, ex-patriots are teachers and PCVs are teachers but are ashamed to admit it."[85]

Americans wrongly concluded, however, that other volunteers were under no pressure to be supermen and superwomen. Alec Dickson of VSO lectured British recruits that "they were to consider themselves on the job all the time, twenty-four hours a day, seven days a week for the whole year." When they had time off, he told them, "it was to be spent among the community with whom they worked—the Dayaks, the Kenyahs, the Nigerians, the Ghanaians." If they had holidays, they should organize "exciting expeditions . . . [and] take their pupils." The American Peace Corps, especially at the ideological core of the top leadership, was better known for its "gung-ho" attitude than the more circumspect British and Canadian organizations, but it certainly had no monopoly on this type of idealism.[86]

In all, most volunteers appeared to slough off what they saw as the irrelevant, "meretricious" Washington emphasis on nonteaching achievements. "Job-oriented and battle-hardened," the sturdiest volunteers adopted attitudes toward Washington ranging from "defensive to defiant to fairly riotously humorous," according to one staff member.[87] John Demos, a Ghana volunteer who went on to become a Yale history professor, wrote, "We held to a sharply restricted view of our role as Peace Corps teachers. Indeed, this soon became a source of pride, and around it there developed a remarkable kind of group loyalty. Probably we were sensitive to public criticism of the Peace Corps as opening the floodgates to youthful, naive idealism; in any case we struck the exact opposite pose. We were 'hard-headed.' . . . First and last, we aimed to succeed simply as teachers."[88]

One result was a program in which, by the end of the 1960s, 90 percent of volunteers reported that they were "moderately" or "very" satisfied with their Peace Corps experience.[89] Clearly structured jobs in response to a clear need, plus the support of the local culture, made the experience a good one in spite of occasional guilt about not doing enough, or loving enough, or sacrificing enough. One volunteer who taught high school English and ran an enormously popular Shakespeare festival in the nearby Nigerian bush said decades later: "My Peace Corps assignment was so perfect I hesitate to talk about it even now, fearing that someone will yet take it away." One woman wrote home from Ghana in 1962, "I'm more pleased with the world and humans and myself than previously."[90] From Africa, volunteers came back laughing.

In the decade and a half that followed the first Peace Corps forays into Ghana, the country (like much of the continent) struggled through repeated changes of government, from military to civilian and back. After the fall of Nkrumah, the Ghanaian military returned the country to civilian control within three years, but then took over again in 1972. Between 1966 and 1981, the nation endured six governments, all but one corrupt or incompetent. The exception was the

three-month rule of a group of young officers led by Flight Lieutenant
Jerry Rawlings in 1979. Rawlings took over briefly to oust and punish
the most corrupt of the military officials, who had bled the country to
pad their own foreign bank accounts. Rawlings then turned the government over to civilian control. The new president failed to arrest the
economy's downward spiral, though, and Rawlings staged another
coup at the end of 1981. The economy bottomed out in 1983, but
began growing at the rate of 5 percent a year in real terms after that. By
1988 the once-depleted government budget had a surplus and in the
1990s Ghana became an exporter of food to its neighbors.[91] During the
roughest years the Peace Corps struggled along with the nation, its
own programs responding to changes within the United States, to
changes in the whole Western debate over development, and to changes
within Ghana. One effect of all this was a continued commitment to
teaching, accompanied by a growing commitment to well-defined community and economic development.

For the Peace Corps, the 1970s began in 1969, when Richard Nixon
assumed the presidency. Joseph Blatchford, appointed by Nixon to run
the Peace Corps, increasingly deemphasized B.A. generalists (who
could most easily be placed into teaching) in favor of older, more
technically skilled volunteers. Part of the idea was to get away from the
"hippie" types Nixon was sure infested the Peace Corps by 1969, but
this trend also reflected a larger concern that the Peace Corps respond
more specifically to the third world's increasingly urgent needs in the
areas of health, food, sanitation, and business development.

From their vantage point Ghanaians encouraged the shift also. In
1970, when Nixon appointed a new National Advisory Council for the
Peace Corps, the council invited Ghana's deputy minister of education
to Washington. In the words of Minister Sebastian Opon, a graduate of
the University of Chicago, Ghana wanted a greater number of "ma-
ture" and "professional" volunteers. The Peace Corps had accomplished much in the field of education. Native teachers were more
numerous than before. And in the midst of a fifteen-year economic
nightmare that would culminate in 12 percent inflation a month and
shortages of many essential foods and supplies, the nation sought volunteers who could help its people with elemental survival.

Opon had seen the Peace Corps in action from the very beginning. A
former high school headmaster, he had hosted Sargent Shriver's second

visit to Ghana in 1962. After a long journey over a treacherous dirt road, Shriver arrived at the school in his usual and typically American fashion: enthusiastic, high speed, ready to pump hands, spread the word, and press onward. Sebastian Opon delayed him in typical African fashion. Hours of drumming, dancing, and singing followed, requiring Shriver and his entourage to stay the night. Shriver accepted the detour with zest, joining in the dancing, "with more enthusiasm than rhythm," a delighted African observed. To Opon, with the deeply religious outlook characteristic of Ghanaians, Shriver's Peace Corps "evolved a Christian solution to the problem of foreign aid by seeking to infuse into its practices broader and loftier ideals of morality."[92] At the same time, Opon could see room for improvement. Specifically, in 1969 he recommended in-country training of volunteers by Ghanaians as a step toward greater local participation in the program.

The Ghanaian government released four of its staff to work with the country director to coordinate training, tribal language instruction, and relations with local officials. One of these individuals, Samuel George Ayi-Bonte, worked as an associate director for the Peace Corps for the next two decades. Country director Eugene Martin also invited twenty-seven prominent Ghanaians to help start a national advisory board. By spring 1970, the new look of the Ghana Peace Corps included the first Ghanaian training program, held for two weeks at a teachers college in the small beach village of Winneba (site of an annual festival honoring the hunting of antelope), then moving to the University of Cape Coast, within sight of the old slave castle.

In addition to the mainstay of teaching, approximately 20 percent of volunteers took jobs with irrigation projects, game and wildlife agencies, credit cooperatives, small business bureaus, food research institutes, and forestry concerns. The Peace Corps had always placed some of its volunteers in economic development (one volunteer who began with the Geological Survey in 1963 became a paid staff member and was still working in Ghana in the 1990s), but eventually, as the program approached and passed its thirtieth anniversary, 50 percent of volunteers worked in health, the environment, or small business development.[93]

Still, as always, education volunteers constituted the largest category. Ghana knew what to do with them, and they knew what to do with themselves. By contrast, volunteers in areas like small enterprise development occasionally had to make up their own jobs, sometimes fashioning a silk purse out of a sow's ear and sometimes not. In the early 1990s, for example, the Ghana Credit Union Association requested and received a contingent of volunteers, several of whom were women. The female volunteers found themselves consigned to clerical positions, unable to utilize the business degrees or prior work experience they had brought to Ghana. Fearful of jeopardizing the more innovative jobs that male volunteers had landed, the women had to find ways of diplomatically extricating themselves from their sponsor.

One woman went on to establish a self-sustaining women's credit union and vocational training program. Together with Ghanaians, and with start-up donations from Women's World Banking and Peace Corps alumni associations in Oregon, North Carolina, and Minnesota, she obtained a building for a women's center in Cape Coast. The center included a restaurant, a store for selling products made by trainees, a meeting hall, and an office for the credit cooperative. Another volunteer developed her own placement with Aid to Artisans, Ghana, where she used her previous years of experience as an international buyer for a large (and unscrupulous) U.S. firm to teach local producers how to obtain a fair price from foreign companies. As one of these women commented, however, the challenge for small enterprise volunteers was that Ghanaians were not always sure in advance what the volunteers could do and what the value of their work would be.[94] The Peace Corps had to sell the program anew each time.

The demand for teachers, in contrast, continued. Ghanaian government policy refocused on the national importance of education in 1987 as part of Rawlings's official "Economic Recovery Program." Once more, there were not enough teachers to go around. The economic and political instability of the 1970s and early 1980s had sent thousands of teachers fleeing to Nigeria, Liberia, and Gambia in search of higher pay and better living conditions. Acute teacher shortages, especially in the rural areas, again plagued Ghana. "Any number that the U.S. government could send would be welcome," one Ghanaian stated in 1995.[95] The Rawlings regime additionally emphasized the importance of "equal opportunities for boys and girls," an area in which the Peace Corps, with its high number of women, could provide important role models.[96]

Canada and Britain also continued to send volunteers to Ghana, and their experiences in many ways paralleled those of the Americans. Indeed, what was perhaps most remarkable about the overlap among the Peace Corps, Voluntary Service Overseas, and Canadian University Service Overseas was how similar they were, quite unintentionally, in their placements, organizational cultures, and political outlook. At the same time, the programs had differences. Those differences place in perspective the sometimes hypercritical treatment of the Peace Corps by scholars who wish to demythologize Kennedy's Camelot or to show the essential flaws of all U.S. foreign policy during the Vietnam era. Comparing the Peace Corps with its Anglo counterparts alters the significance of some of these complaints.

The historian Gary May, for example, says that Peace Corps language instruction "was almost legendary for its poor quality" and that "Peace Corps incompetence and ignorance" in the field of volunteer health created a "nightmare."[97] In comparison with other programs, however, the Peace Corps not only gave volunteers extensive training on safety and hygiene (too much, some volunteers protested), but also innovated the practice of preventive gamma globulin shots (later adopted by the Canadians) and sent medical personnel to each country to attend to the volunteers. CUSO and VSO volunteers received relatively little of this kind of staff support, with the result that they suffered from a much higher incidence of potentially deadly hepatitis, dysentery, and malaria in the early 1960s than did Peace Corps volunteers. VSO volunteers thirty years later still complained about the lack of medical support compared with that given to American volunteers.[98]

The author Karen Schwarz, though not as critical as Gary May, leaves the impression that early volunteers could not "muster more than a few words" of a foreign language.[99] The inference to be drawn is that the Peace Corps was not as committed to its ideal of intercultural communication as it pretended. But notably (consistent with the organization's goal of getting volunteers to mingle with the population and erase the "Ugly American" stereotype), Peace Corps recruits received ten times the language training of Canadian and British volunteers. In the mid-1960s, CUSO gave its volunteers thirty hours of training in local languages compared with the three hundred hours volunteers received in the Peace Corps.[100]

By the mid-1990s, the ratio had changed little. Later CUSO brochures assured prospective volunteers that most of them would not have to learn a second language (though it would make their stay "more rewarding" if they tried). And in Ghana in the 1990s, where both Peace Corps and VSO still fielded volunteers, Americans received one hundred hours of language instruction to the British ten.[101] Although it is certainly true that many volunteers struggled deeply with language acquisition, the Peace Corps cannot be faulted for failing to make fluent speakers out of volunteers in eight weeks. Moritz Thomsen, a forty-eight-year-old farmer who served in Peru, ruefully remembered that although his training group practiced Spanish nearly around the clock, "We twisted and mauled that beautiful language into a million distorted shapes and watched our instructors, sensitive and dedicated people all, wither and age before our eyes." The most that any crash program could hope for was to give students a rudimentary vocabulary and grammar upon which to build. Attaining fluency took months of service in-country.[102]

In spite of the differences among their sponsoring organizations, most Western volunteers were initially thought of as "peace corps." Nkrumah's highly public acceptance of the Peace Corps, along with the broad, worldwide recognition of John Kennedy, immediately gave the American volunteers a place of prominence alongside their British and Canadian counterparts. Although the Americans were the most numerous at first, the numbers gradually evened up. Yet Ghanaian newspapers and even public officials indiscriminately called them all "Peace Corps volunteers," and occasionally even other expatriates used the term as a kind of shorthand. "This confusion is widespread," one Peace Corps evaluator reported, commenting:

> When I was talking with . . . [a] representative of the British Council . . . which oversees the British teachers of Voluntary Service Overseas, he remarked, "Our Peace Corps Volunteers teach. . . ." He smiled a bit sheepishly, and corrected himself, "I mean our V.S.O.'s. . . ."[103]

The fact that the volunteers frequently roomed together deepened the confusion. Throughout West Africa, teacher compounds housed Americans with Canadians, Britishers, Russians, and any other foreign or local instructors. This was also true in Asia. One volunteer teaching English in the jungle of Sarawak noted in a colorful article for *Cana-*

dian Geographical Journal in 1966, "There are four of us living in these two houses—three Peace Corps girls and myself."[104] Small wonder that local peoples had trouble telling one "peace corps" from another.

Still, naturally enough, many volunteers did not welcome being lumped together with the Americans. In Sierra Leone, some CUSO volunteers printed T-shirts using Creole dialect that announced, "Me notto Peace Corps." The Canadians cultivated a particularly strong sense of their distinctiveness from the Peace Corps which may have been useful in shoring their own national identity. The Peace Corps volunteers, they thought, presented a poor image—their tennis shoes were grubby, they wore their hair long. Peace Corps "gave away" its volunteers for free; CUSO required the host country to pay for volunteers' maintenance (which to them proved that the Canadians were wanted and valued). CUSO placements were carefully designed; Peace Corps workers were underemployed. CUSO was a neutral, nongovernmental organization; Peace Corps was "a political football."[105]

Such were the truths and partial truths that some Canadians held dear. In fact, at least some of the assumptions were false. In Ghana the Peace Corps volunteers were not free. Out of a sense of national pride, and the desire to better control the volunteers, Ghana in the 1960s paid the Americans' full monthly living allowance of $162 per volunteer. After Nkrumah, the extent of the Ghanaian contribution dropped steadily as the economy worsened—down to $10 out of a total monthly allowance of $156 in 1995—but Ghana nevertheless continued to pay something.

CUSO volunteers and staff probably took greatest pride in what they considered their independence from the sordid politics of the cold war. "CUSO is essentially free from any serious charge of being an arm of Canada's foreign policy," former volunteers stated in a 1968 book published at the height of American involvement in Vietnam.[106] "Our volunteers . . . go abroad not as Canadians, or as champions of our social and political way of life . . . but as individuals," their founder Francis Leddy claimed, arguing that the Peace Corps had an "overt political and national bias." Not surprisingly, he also noted that Peace Corps members sometimes "expressed resentment and irritation at what they considered the 'elevated' attitude of our volunteers."[107]

Still, in fundamental ways, the experience of American, Canadian, and British volunteers in Ghana paralleled one another remarkably, and they generally got what they came for: a chance to know the existentialist "Other" and to deny his or her essential differentness; a chance to express the individual initiative central to their own Anglo-derived cultures yet seemingly threatened by mass society; a chance to try on preindustrial life and the values of communalism often associated with it; and, last but not least, a chance for old-fashioned adventure and heroism.

As to what Ghana or Ghanaians got from the infusion of youthful labor, most volunteers and even their sponsors made few claims. In the words of one Canadian veteran, "Returning, there is only one clear, overwhelming thought: gnat against elephant. Your work has been that of a gnat, clean-faced and valiant, straining at the end of a tugrope against a dysenteric, powerful, embittered, starving, self-tortured, awakening, ancient, immensely humane, knowing and surprisingly unembittered elephant."[108]

Indeed, it would be hubris to think that any group of volunteers could change the life of a country. Volunteers generally developed a more realistic understanding of the limits of U.S. influence than most Americans ever could. The denizens of Washington could push a button and destroy the world. But creating successful new nations, or aiding old ones in the hope of remaking their destiny, required persistence, patience, and a willingness to tolerate frequent defeats and only occasional victories. Of course, as hard as they tried not to be, Peace Corps and other volunteers were also to one extent or another guilty of hubris. If they did not believe they could change the world, they would not have undertaken the effort and risk. Out of this optimism came some small but significant successes.

For their part, Ghanaians welcomed the assistance of VSO in 1958 and the Peace Corps and CUSO in 1961. They continued to welcome volunteers decades later. The contributions in education stood out especially to Africans. "The importance of the Peace Corps programme to Ghana cannot be over-emphasized," the national director of secondary education told volunteers in 1995, echoing the assessment of other officials.[109] Sheer numbers told part of the story: approximately 675,000 Ghanaians had American teachers between 1961 and 1991. Out of a population of 14 million, this equaled roughly 5 percent of all

Ghanaians. Indeed, in Ghana it was difficult to find a person who had achieved white-collar status who had not had a Peace Corps teacher at some point.

Peace Corps also helped introduce educational innovations, such as the "new math" and learning by reasoning rather than by rote. These innovations did not all spread, however. Lacking books that could serve as an aid to memory, Ghanaian students continued to rely on copying down and memorizing the facts necessary to pass state exams. Julius Amin, a former Peace Corps student in nearby Cameroon, later wrote: "Memorization provided the . . . [village] student with a feeling of being knowledgeable" in an environment that was otherwise unfamiliar and intimidating. Still, he noted in in-depth research on Cameroon, the volunteers designed both textbooks and curricula more attuned to the needs of the rural students than those of the British system they helped transform, and laid the foundation for a national testing center that replaced the London-based exam board in 1977. Throughout West Africa, volunteers also started libraries, equipped rudimentary science labs and technical workshops, built school latrines, initiated athletic programs, conducted science fairs, and organized academic clubs. Even though many Peace Corps teachers taught subjects for which they had not prepared in college, "they made a difficult job look easy," according to Julius Amin. "Whatever the weaknesses of the volunteers, it remains true that their services were essential."[110]

The Peace Corps never had the intense concentration in any field of community and business development that it had in secondary education, with the result that its cumulative impact was less discernible. Along with CUSO, it fielded a fair number of volunteers in forestry and fisheries (building village fish ponds and conducting zoological research on fishing in Lake Volta). VSO volunteers, generally older and more highly trained than Peace Corps volunteers by the 1990s (but still living on volunteer "pay," unlike the Canadians), assisted as well with the development of Ghana's own National Service Scheme, which beginning in 1973 required all secondary school graduates to give one year of service to the nation, and university graduates to give two. Other contributions included a Peace Corps volunteer's invention of a simple mechanism to make cement blocks. Developed at the Kumasi University of Science and Technology, the machine was eventually adopted all over Ghana. In the early 1990s, the forestry division of Peace Corps

Ghana planted 800,000 seedlings in one year and started a nursery program.

Perhaps the most compelling contribution of the Peace Corps, however, was indeed its simple existence. As one Cameroonian later expressed it, "These Americans had their weaknesses but just the fact that these Kennedy boys came to struggle with us, I think, is the most important thing."[111] Ghanaians often characterized the Peace Corps meaning to Ghana as one of morale. From the first singing of the national anthem in Twi to the volunteers in the 1990s who still reported to village chiefs before starting their assignments, the Peace Corps continuously impressed West Africans with its willingness to enter into the life of the villages "under all sort of conditions."[112]

To K. B. Asante and Kojo Botsio, the individual, intangible effect had enriched particular lives as well as the life of the nation. Ghana, in its totality, may not have become measurably different, but many Ghanaians had. "The individual's effort seeps into society," according to Asante. Asante himself served a stint as Ghana's education minister in the 1970s and was "so impressed" with the American Peace Corps volunteers—working in remote places "where Ghanaians wouldn't go"—who came to his office to ask for supplies for their schools.[113] To Kojo Botsio, who had weathered every political and economic crisis between 1951 and 1991 (from imprisonment by the British to a death sentence by a post-Nkrumah regime), the final judgment on the Peace Corps' thirty years in his country was simple: "We wanted to bring up the standard of education of the people and it contributed quite a lot . . . no doubt about it."[114]

Newspaper articles and editorials seconded Botsio's and Asante's assessment that the Peace Corps was "etched in the Ghanaian mind."[115] According to Agyeman-Badu, after Nkrumah's downfall "the attitude [of the press] toward the Peace Corps changed from indifference to favorable." In both Ghana and Nigeria between 1960 and 1977, the Peace Corps was the only part of overall U.S. policy toward the continent that Africans viewed favorably.[116]

In Ghana, the Peace Corps had not changed the world, but it had met its own stated goals: to serve the needs of another country, to promote local understanding of America, and to foster Americans' understanding of other people. Indeed, it had triumphed. The Peace Corps had proved that in order to achieve those goals, "all" you needed was love—*and* a good job, *and* a culturally receptive people, *and* a government whose own vision coincided in one or two critical ways with your own. These conditions would not be met everywhere. But when they were, they would do much to meet the larger aims of U.S. foreign policy toward the unaligned world. Peace Corps successes, even modest ones, would also help some Americans keep alive a belief in their nation's goals as the sixties rolled on.

7

Slippery
Slopes

———— ✸ ————

The Peace Corps is part of the establishment . . . The Peace Corps
doesn't have time for establishments . . .
Whether the Peace Corps is good or bad just depends
on how you look at things.

YOUNG & RUBICAM ADVERTISEMENT, 1968

On March 1, 1968, President Lyndon Baines Johnson wrote to a
troubled and nearly mutinous Congress, "If you would confirm your
faith in the American future—take a look at the Peace Corps." On the
last day of the same month he told his colleagues and a startled nation,
"I shall not seek, and I will not accept, the nomination of my party for
another term as your president."[1]

Johnson had lost faith in his own ability to unite the country, but he
remained convinced that the Peace Corps offered a small light in the
darkness. The commander-in-chief retreated ahead of his armies in
Vietnam, who would be led through five more years of stalemate by
Richard Nixon until the troops finally came home. He was right, however, that the Peace Corps would remain a part of America's future. It
would help many sustain a belief in the potency of American ideals. But
its power to generate popular consensus on the values of the nation
would never be the same. By 1968 citizens could no longer easily trust
the motives of their government. In Vietnam, the consequences were
horrendous. A pervasive sense of betrayal devastated troop morale,
leading to the assassination of officers in the field and to long-term
psychosis for many combat veterans.[2] Like these men, Peace Corps
volunteers had a relationship with their leaders that was founded upon
trust. When perceived government fidelity to national ideals floun-

dered, the Peace Corps did so along with it. Fewer women and men volunteered, and the beacon of the Peace Corps shone less brightly.

Of course, none of this was as Johnson intended. The thirty-sixth president had shown a strong attachment to the Peace Corps from its beginnings. As he was to do with civil rights, poverty, education, the environment, and so many other areas of reform that John Kennedy helped inspire, Lyndon Johnson set to work to fulfill as completely as possible the promise of the Peace Corps. He had already secured Peace Corps autonomy, lobbied the Senate for passage of the Peace Corps Act, hosted the International Conference on Middle-Level Manpower, and served as chair of the Peace Corps Advisory Board. But as vice president, there was little more for Johnson to do. The day before Lee Harvey Oswald shot John F. Kennedy in Dallas, Johnson composed a note to Sargent Shriver regarding upcoming appropriations hearings. "I certainly hope that it works out all right," he wrote tentatively. One week and what must have seemed a lifetime later, the president sent another kind of letter. "Good luck," he stated assertively, "and let me know if there is anything I can do."[3]

Lyndon Johnson's knowledge of poverty went deep, antedating his experience as a New Deal administrator during the Great Depression. Johnson's own family had been of middling though never very secure means. His father's farming failures, driving the family to the edge of bankruptcy, were not uncommon among Texas families in the 1920s. But it was the school year that Johnson spent teaching in the isolated, rural Mexican *barrio* of Cotulla, Texas, when he was twenty that taught him what poverty really looked like. His twelve- and thirteen-year-old students often came to school hungry. The local teachers were surprised that Johnson thought these brown-skinned children could learn anything. He asked his mother to ship him two hundred tubes of toothpaste, organized extracurricular activities, convinced other teachers to supervise games at recess, worked the students feverishly, and tutored the school janitor in English.[4]

Like American volunteers nearly forty years later, Johnson probably gained even more self-confidence and cross-cultural understanding than his students did. But they never forgot him, nor he they. As president, Johnson made frequent reference to his Cotulla experience as a touchstone for his reform policies. Like many returned PCVs, Johnson used the experience whenever he wanted to visualize the poor or to take a moral stand in relationship to them. Following Johnson's passionate address to Congress after the 1965 civil rights march on Selma, Alabama—when he asked for passage of the Voting Rights Act—someone asked him who had written the lines, "I do not want to be the president who built empires . . . I want to be the president who helped to end hatred among his fellow men and who prompted love among the people of all races and all religions." According to Harris Wofford, Johnson reached for a photograph of his students in Cotulla and answered, "They did."[5]

Johnson thought of Peace Corps veterans in terms that could easily have described himself in 1929. "It is fair to say that the lives of virtually all Volunteers have been changed by their service in the Corps," Johnson told Congress. "They have become aware—in a unique and profound way—of the bond of suffering and hope that unites men and women on every continent . . . No more valuable experience can be gained by any man."[6] Johnson's junior military aide who accompanied him on vice-presidential trips later claimed that Johnson believed that the Peace Corps was "one of the great things that this country ever did . . . to send its young people . . . to get to know people in developing countries and to make friends . . . The actual programs . . . were really secondary to this idea of personal involvement and contact with the people overseas."[7]

After the tragic death of John Kennedy, the Peace Corps had greater access to the White House than ever. The organization's two most visible leaders became two of Johnson's chief advisors. Peace Corps deputy director Bill Moyers was in Austin at the personal request of the president on the morning of November 22 to smooth over the rivalries of Texas politics, which he knew well. When the Secret Service called Moyers to report the shooting, Moyers flew to Dallas, where he slipped a note to an agent guarding Johnson's plane. "Mr. President," it read simply, "I'm here if you need me." Johnson asked the younger man to board Air Force One. Moyers remained in the president's inner circle until 1967. He did not, however, fail to return to the Peace Corps for want of trying. "Time and again I would petition him to let me go back to the Peace Corps," Moyers later said. The president, however, eventually told him flat out, "Don't ever mention that to me again."[8]

In the weeks following John Kennedy's assassination, Johnson took the tack with the Peace Corps that he took with all of the initiatives

Kennedy had hinted at or, in the case of the Peace Corps, actually
enacted: with the justification of continuing Kennedy's reforms,
Johnson greatly amplified them. To Shriver, the president wrote, "I
need you—and I need the services of the splendid group that was
knitted together under your leadership—even more than they were
needed by the man whom I have succeeded." Understanding that
Shriver had just buried his brother-in-law, Johnson added, "I hope and
pray that I can carry on the work which he began and with the help of
the people like you who meant so much to him."[9]

The next day the president sent a similar telegram to volunteers
worldwide, assuring them that they, too, had been special to their slain
hero. "Across the length of our nation people are asking 'What can I
do?'" Johnson told the volunteers. "You have already chosen to serve in
an enterprise which was as close as any I know to President Kennedy's
heart."[10] To members of Congress considering appropriations for the
Peace Corps, Johnson called it "a living memorial to the 35th President
of the United States."[11] Congress could not have turned him down,
even if it had been tempted.

Because he had not created the Peace Corps and because it functioned smoothly, Johnson never gave it the time he gave the War on
Poverty or had to give the war in Vietnam. It did not demand his
attention from either a domestic or geopolitical point of view. But the
president's support for it did not waver, and he sought in a few ways to
make it his own. Sargent Shriver and Bill Moyers sought the same
thing, undoubtedly to reinforce Johnson's commitment. Working from
within, Moyers periodically reminded the president of the need for
"physical . . . contact with that organization" and encouraged him to
meet volunteers. Shriver reassured the president of the Peace Corps'
compatibility with Johnson's own style. In the first months of 1964,
when the deliberately homespun president went around turning off
lights in the White House to demonstrate his frugal approach to public
funds, Shriver made a point of letting Johnson know that the Peace
Corps had come in under budget. The president reported to Congress
with pride in May 1964 that the Peace Corps had effected "an estimated savings of $8,964,000 to the American taxpayers and will return
that amount to the Treasury . . . in keeping with my repeated stress on
economy in government."[12]

But Johnson struck off on his own as well. Six months into office the president sent a memorandum to the heads of all agencies and departments within the Executive Branch, telling his appointees that he wanted them to make every effort to hire returned Peace Corps volunteers. The volunteers, he said, had "already fully demonstrated their dedication and intelligence in the service of their country." Like Kennedy, Johnson believed that the kinds of people who had gone into the Peace Corps and whose values had been shaped by it were precisely the people he needed in his administration. "For the Great Society requires first of all Great Citizens, and the Peace Corps is a world-wide training school for Great Citizens," the president said.[13]

Johnson gave federal agencies a little over three months to make some progress in hiring volunteers, and asked to be "personally informed" by the end of that time about how many Peace Corps veterans they had on staff. Peace Corps officials in turn wrote volunteers in the field to encourage them to think about government employment upon return. Within a year the civil service had hired nearly a fourth (22 percent) of the returned volunteers, many for AID, the State Department, the U.S. Information Service, the Peace Corps itself, and the newly created agencies of the War on Poverty, like the Job Corps.[14]

Johnson also encouraged expanding the Peace Corps mission, and specifically those aspects that would more fully integrate the Peace Corps into the life of the American nation. Johnson gave Sargent Shriver, whom he recruited at the start of 1964 to run the War on Poverty, the task of creating VISTA (Volunteers in Service to America) through the Economic Opportunity Act of 1964. VISTA volunteers exemplified Johnson's conviction that America needed to reform itself, too. Like young Lyndon in Cotulla, Texas, the generation of the 1960s would cross the tracks to develop compassion for those who lived on the wrong side. Although organizationally separate from Peace Corps, VISTA became known as the domestic Peace Corps and a number of volunteers returned home from overseas to give another year in the United States.[15]

The next year Johnson proposed that American schools be brought into the Peace Corps effort. In a 1965 speech at the Smithsonian, the president introduced the idea of a "School Partnership Program" in which American children would raise money for the bricks and mortar to build classrooms overseas, with poor villages providing their own land and labor. Hundreds of U.S. schools entered enthusiastically into the new Peace Corps initiative and sent an average of $1,000. Within two years, five hundred new schools had been built by adopted communities in Latin America, Africa, and Asia.

In February 1966 Johnson proposed yet another addition to the organization's mandate: an "Exchange Peace Corps." With this suggestion the president moved out ahead not only of Congress, but of the Peace Corps administration itself. "Our nation has no better ambassadors than the young volunteers," Johnson wrote Congress. "I propose that we welcome similar ambassadors to our shores." Demonstrating a remarkable willingness to bare America's soul (and dirty laundry) to the world, Johnson added, "We need their special skills and understanding, just as they need ours." Getting the Congress to accept this premise was not easy, though, as Peace Corps lobbyists on the Hill soon found out. "Congress didn't buy it," one official wrote Bill Moyers. Apparently, elected officials did not express enthusiasm for "welcoming foreign volunteers into our slums, mental hospitals and onto Indian reservations," he reported. "Visions of the Job Corps camps and Indian Reservations or Watts don't rest comfortably with most of them as it is."[16]

The Johnson administration eventually surmounted congressional reluctance, however. Through the State Department's Bureau of Educational and Cultural Affairs, "Volunteers to America" invited men and women from twelve foreign countries in 1967 to help the United States. The volunteers, thirty women and thirty-four men, arrived in July that year from nations as different from one another as Argentina and Ghana, Nepal and the Philippines, Iran and Israel. As in the Peace Corps, the majority of the volunteers taught school, while about one-third joined in projects of the War on Poverty. A few helped train Peace Corps recruits going to the countries from which they themselves had come. One of the volunteers, a sociologist who had done community development work in the slums of Manila, started a popular clean-up project in Harlem which he kicked off by parading down the block with a small group of dedicated residents clanging trash can lids. A Ghanaian volunteer applied in Temple City, California, the techniques used by Peace Corps volunteers in Accra and Kumasi. In addition to his regular teaching responsibilities, he devised new social studies curricula for the lower grades and at night started an adult education course on Africa.

Local residents learned how to make peanut soup and met their first African.[17]

Sixty-four "Volunteers to America," of course, sprinkled among 200 million citizens, had no chance of effecting deep change in the United States. Neither had 10,000 Peace Corps volunteers sprinkled among the 3.1 billion people inhabiting the globe in the early 1960s. But they had faith in the power of example, what Sargent Shriver called "a working model, a microcosm, a small society representing the kind of world we want our children to live in." This faith, as old as the Puritans' City on a Hill, would soon vie intensely, however, with the even older belief in the power of guns.[18]

In July 1965 Lyndon Baines Johnson gave the order for a massive troop mobilization for Vietnam. Two months earlier he had ordered the marines to the Dominican Republic. These events began a process that cut the Peace Corps in half in six years. But in the middle of the 1960s, specifically from 1964 to 1966, the organization enjoyed a heyday of size and prestige. Pushed by the president himself, the Peace Corps grew from 10,000 to over 15,000 volunteers. Johnson wrote to Vice President Hubert Humphrey, new chair of the advisory committee, that he wanted to see the Peace Corps increase to 20,000 volunteers so that "it continues to make history."[19]

Applications poured in. From 1964 to 1966, over 42,000 Americans applied each year (more than double the number who had submitted their forms in 1962). At first, the escalating war in Vietnam appeared not to contradict the idealism of the Peace Corps. Troops did not arrive in Vietnam in substantial numbers until after July 1965, and it took a year or more for the disillusioning effects to set in. By 1967 it became apparent that the war was deterring some Americans from volunteering for the Peace Corps, while encouraging others to join it for a draft deferment. But in the mid-1960s, these events had not yet happened. It still seemed possible to trust the liberal government that had passed the Civil Rights Acts of 1964 and 1965.

Indeed, the volunteer program remained a way for Americans to keep their ideals intact through a personal commitment abroad or through a friendly insurgency within the United States government itself. John Kenneth Galbraith, speaking to a Peace Corps staff meeting in 1965, revealed the attitude common among leading liberals. "If you design programs to promote social change in Latin America, word will drift back to Congress; some won't like what you do," the famous economist told the staff. But, he added, "the Peace Corps must be on the side of economic democracy . . . There is no alternative for the Peace Corps to political sophistication."[20]

For Galbraith and his listeners, sophistication meant living with a set of contradictions finessed through political manipulation. Promoting "revolution" in Latin America contradicted the war in Vietnam; promoting domestic upheaval in the United States contradicted the goal of holding onto the mandate that American voters had given the Democratic Party. The Peace Corps and Shriver's Office of Economic Opportunity were both characterized by their attempt in the middle 1960s to bring dissent into the heart of the government, while husbanding the resources of government to effect social change. Hugh Heclo notes that this was a "central paradox" of the decade, with ill portent for the future: challenging the legitimacy of government while expecting it to do more than ever. It was a little like combining nitrogen and glycerin. But who said that holding the globe in your hands would be easy?[21]

The president had his own contradictions to finesse as well, and the Peace Corps allowed him to fend off complaints about his military policy by pointing to international aid and cooperation. In November 1965, when protesters at the University of Michigan and at Berkeley mounted demonstrations against Vietnam, the Peace Corps represented the president's views to student radicals. At Berkeley, "our recruiting team was confronted on arrival with an organized effort urging students not to join the Peace Corps as a protest to our Viet Nam war effort," Shriver told Johnson. "Face-to-face, Peace Corps Representatives debated in front of large student crowds. And we won. They finally abandoned the field to us and we succeeded in signing up more students than ever before."[22]

But while Shriver decried "irresponsible campus agitators" to Lyndon Johnson, his lieutenants nonetheless actively wooed these same individuals, hoping to turn them from one version of political activism to another. Warren Wiggins went to Berkeley at the start of the Free Speech Movement to meet with members of the Students for a Democratic Society (SDS). In a speech soon thereafter, Wiggins revealed his ambivalence about radicals. "If you become an advocate of change outside the respectable limits you enter dangerous territory," Wiggins warned. "You may discover why we burned witches in Salem." At the same time, he added, "we need more people willing to commit those sins."[23] Wiggins and most other Peace Corps officials thought that "angry young men" could bring a bright spark to the task of reform. Had these administrators been twenty years younger, they would likely have been on the other side of the campus debate. They wanted to utilize radicals who defended in a more volatile way the ideal that they all shared of a moral foreign policy.

Harris Wofford and Frank Mankiewicz reportedly offered a job in 1965 to the SDS leader Tom Hayden to foment social change in Peru (perhaps because it was farther away). In sync with student leaders, they also increased the intensity of their rhetoric. In 1964 Mankiewicz wrote a widely circulated discussion paper calling the Peace Corps a "revolutionary force" and asserting that its volunteers did much the same kind of organizing as the Student Non-Violent Coordinating Committee (SNCC) in Mississippi. The Peace Corps was an "international sit-in," Mankiewicz said. Wofford called the Peace Corps a "University in Dispersion"—a phrase of particular appeal to those who had begun attacking colleges for their hierarchical structures.[24]

Robert Satin, a Peace Corps public relations officer, told the Associated Press in 1965 that campus protesters were considered "high risk, high gain" recruits. "They'll either blow the place up or they'll get something done." In comments that would alarm Shriver, Satin asserted that the Peace Corps wanted to recruit "the people who can get thousands of demonstrators to turn out, because they have the kind of organizational skills that can make democracy work in underdeveloped nations." Worried that newspapers might interpret Satin's comments to mean that the Peace Corps provided a haven for opponents of the draft, Shriver issued a denial which he sent to the president. "I plan to continue this policy of immediately and forcefully clarifying our position whenever it is misstated," the director told Johnson, laying the blame for any confusion at the feet of the press.[25]

The Peace Corps could credibly claim to the president that it could handle campus radicals because the organization had an edge over dissidents whose views had yet to gain wide currency. The national press still gave much more serious coverage to Johnson than to those who criticized his war. The media also continued to give much positive attention to the Peace Corps. Even though the "numbers game" continued to produce placement disasters abroad, these failures were not as widely known as Peace Corps successes. For example, in 1966 the Peace Corps sent 700 volunteers to tiny Micronesia (population 90,000), creating a foreigner-to-native ratio of 1 to 130. Many of the volunteers spent more time bumping into one another than doing anything useful. Disillusionment followed. In India, where Johnson had called in 1966 for a U.S. aid effort that would be "small neither in its magnitude or concept," the Peace Corps responded to the president by expanding from 700 to 1,700 volunteers. Confusion reigned. Yet at the same time the Peace Corps continued to receive positive reports from many of its other projects abroad, and Shriver assiduously fed them to the president and to the press.[26]

In India, a year before the ill-fated expansion in 1966, the national Planning Commission gave the Peace Corps high marks for its teaching and community development programs and for the "fresh spirit" and "idealism" of its volunteers. One nurse helped set up the first open heart surgery unit, the Indian report noted. Another volunteer organized an emergency effort and saved a village from a flood. Other volunteers started a business in agricultural implements, introduced the use of plastic water pipes for irrigation, and built generators that turned cow dung into gas. The commission gave particularly high marks to the Peace Corps' work in poultry production, an important contribution in a nation with food shortages and where the dominant religion prohibited the killing of animals. Peace Corps volunteers coined the phrase "vegetarian eggs" to help poultry producers explain that an unfertilized hen's egg could not be considered to have life.[27]

Other nations also praised the Peace Corps in the mid-1960s. A study of Colombians found that 94 percent of villagers interviewed believed that the Peace Corps had made a visible, worthwhile contribution. The minister of development of Botswana wrote a U.S. senator that he could not "help wishing that there were a few more people who could recognize the impact which fifty-two young men and women are capable of making in a country such as mine." In Nigeria, when Malcolm X made speeches denouncing the Peace Corps, the local paper rebutted his charges of neo-imperialism and asserted that Nigeria had "benefited immensely" from the Peace Corps, whose volunteers represented 25 percent of all teachers in the newly independent nation.[28]

State and national leaders in Brazil credited Peace Corps organizers for multiplying the number of 4-H clubs from 207 to 538 in three years, and increasing government respect for "the ability of the rural people."[29]

In 1965 such reports could still shame self-identified radicals like Paul Cowan who realized that the easy comforts afforded to them by life in the United States meant that they were not quite living "the committed life that Camus had described." When an antiwar, antiracism song called "Eve of Destruction" made the radio hit list, a Peace Corps publicist noted with satisfaction that another band had come out with a song called "Dawn of Correction" which listed the Peace Corps as one of the many signs of hope in the world.[30]

In the mid-1960s, therefore, the Peace Corps entered an especially tricky phase of existence, placing itself in between protesters whom it hoped to win over and a government whose foreign policy it could not always endorse. Initially, this won the Peace Corps much admiration. The leftist commentator Andrew Kopkind wrote in 1966 that "the very idea of different agencies of the same government consciously exploring opposite approaches in foreign affairs at the same time is worth the whole Peace Corps business." In Britain Alec Dickson noted with approval the recruitment policy of VISTA, though he could as easily have been speaking of the Peace Corps. "Such audacious, collision-bound roles are the more piquant in that the volunteers are, for the duration of their service, Federal employees," Dickson stated. "One cannot help but admire the government attitude that authorises, even condones, the challenging of officialdom."[31]

With the creation of the Office of Economic Opportunity (OEO), Sargent Shriver and his aides widened dramatically the scope of this challenge. Lyndon Johnson had launched the War on Poverty with his first State of the Union address barely a month after the shooting in Dallas. Books like John Galbraith's *The Affluent Society* (1958) and Michael Harrington's *The Other America* (1962) had made increasingly visible the problem of poverty in the United States. The Kennedy administration had undertaken studies of the issue, and the president himself had expressed compassion for the plight of the unfortunate. "Imagine," he said, "just imagine kids who never drink milk." Johnson, with his extraordinary legislative skills, decided he could do something about it. One-fifth of all Americans lived "on the outskirts of hope," Johnson told the nation, in "inherited, gateless poverty." On February 1, 1964, he named Sargent Shriver to head the ambitious effort.[32]

The appointment of Shriver was logical: the Peace Corps had earned renown for its battle against world poverty. Shriver continued as director of the Peace Corps, and brought with him much of what he had learned there. Like the Peace Corps, the OEO would emphasize bigness, speed, and grass-roots social change. Like the Peace Corps, it would especially aim to channel the energies of young people in programs like VISTA, the Job Corps, and Head Start. Like the Peace Corps, it would mix widely supported education programs (which continued for decades after the Johnson administration) with highly controversial programs in community development (which did not).

The most controversial of all the OEO initiatives by far was the Community Action Program (CAP). Community Action was set up to provide funds on a large scale to governments and private organizations across the country to develop projects that would organize people to eliminate poverty. Shriver and the first staff of CAP required those who wished to apply for the funds to demonstrate that in designing and running their programs they had the "maximum feasible participation" of the poor. The programs themselves could vary widely, depending on the "felt needs" of the communities themselves.

CAP jargon echoed that of the Peace Corps, leading to a still unresolved historical dispute about who first employed the phrase that Senator Daniel Patrick Moynihan later ridiculed as "maximum feasible misunderstanding." Frank Mankiewicz sat in on Sargent Shriver's early planning meetings for the War on Poverty, and he remembered the phrase as coming out of discussions of the experience of the Peace Corps in Latin America. Harris Wofford gave credit for the concept to Richard Boone, who insisted that "the poor themselves must be involved in the planning, so that programs were not imposed on them by existing organizations, city hall, or the federal government." Boone had been earlier recruited into the Kennedy administration by David Hackett, a friend and confidant of Robert Kennedy since boarding school. Together Boone and Hackett developed the outlines of what would become CAP when they worked on the president's Committee on Juvenile Delinquency and Youth Crime. From 1961 to 1963, chaired by Robert Kennedy, the president's committee funded pilot projects in poor neighborhoods across America to test the concept of community development. When Johnson instigated the War on Poverty, Robert Kennedy asked Boone to represent the Justice Department on the planning committee. Boone harped on the idea of involving the poor until other committee members finally took note.[33]

Richard Boone, like Frank Mankiewicz, brought an awareness of domestic injustice to the task. Two concerns animated his insistence on "maximum feasible participation of the residents." First, he shared in the antiprofessional bias increasingly typical of the sixties. But more specifically, he had been influenced by an anthropologist on the Navajo Reservation who had impressed him with the folly of outsiders trying to decide how to remake Indian communities. "Don't plan *for,* plan *with,*" Bob Russell told Boone. Second, in hailing from the state of Kentucky, Boone understood how federal largesse to the South usually got funneled through all-powerful petty officials who doled out patronage according to race, kinship, and class rather than according to need. Daniel Patrick Moynihan, charged by Shriver to organize the jobs component of the War on Poverty, remembered this aspect of Boone's plan best: that maximum feasible participation would "ensure that persons excluded from the political process in the South and elsewhere would nonetheless participate in the *benefits,*" unlike what had often happened during the New Deal, when blacks received little of the emergency aid directed southward.[34]

Shriver thus encountered two powerful influences when crafting the Community Action Program. He drew upon what he had been hearing from Frank Mankiewicz for the preceding three years: that community development had greater potential to challenge entrenched inequalities than any other activity of the Peace Corps. Shriver also drew upon a set of working plans that administrators under Robert Kennedy had begun developing months before. Neither the Peace Corps nor the younger Kennedy's assistants had arrived at any sure-fire ways to mobilize the poor, or channel that mobilization in the best possible ways, or eliminate poverty. But like many in the 1960s they reasoned that experts did not have all the answers, and that the poor were likely to know more about poverty than the rich.

Community Action drew fire immediately. When OEO staff returned proposals submitted by the city governments of Cleveland, Philadelphia, New York, Los Angeles, and San Francisco because they did not document participation by the poor, elected officials were incredulous. Worse yet, when organizers of the community action agencies that did obtain funding began criticizing city mayors for being deaf to social problems, politicians struck back hard. In Syracuse, CAP funded Saul Alinsky to train community organizers to form tenants' unions and mount voter registration drives. The angry Republican mayor, aware of a gathering threat to unseat him in the next election, warned, "I'm not going to take this lying down."[35] In other cities Democrats similarly found that CAP gave publicity and powers of patronage to activists who could then run against them, claiming even greater dedication to the liberal cause. The funding for such insurgency could not last. Frank Mankiewicz later observed, "You can't ask congressmen for long to appropriate money to set up alternate power systems in their own district."[36]

Officials were especially not amused by what one observer called the rapid "progression from a politically neutral concern with organizing the slums to a fully engaged animus for the city 'Establishment.'"[37] CAP bore responsibility as one contributor to political polarization in the 1960s, but there were many groups on both the left and the right that hastened this process. Some of it went back to Saul Alinsky himself, who had done much to popularize the conflict approach to organizing that originated in the 1930s with the Congress of Industrial Organizations (CIO). According to Neil Betten and Michael Austin, "Alinsky's tactics permitted no 'middle ground;' the opposition was clearly the enemy" and should be attacked personally.[38]

Alinsky's in-your-face tactics, however, had counterparts elsewhere in American society: from segregationists who personalized their opposition to civil rights to the point of murdering black leaders, to "doves" who held Johnson responsible for a Vietnam policy developed under four presidents ("Hey, hey, LBJ, how many kids did you kill today?"). For people as different from one another as George Wallace, Spiro Agnew, Eldridge Cleaver, Stokely Carmichael, Jerry Rubin, and the Weathermen, conflict increasingly became the tool of choice. The pendulum swung from "love is the answer" to "hate is the answer." Martin Buber's repudiation of the "I-Thou" dichotomy was effectively repudiated. Peacemakers and coalition builders like Martin Luther King, Jr. (who rejected demonizing the opponent) and Malcolm X (who learned to) were rare, and both King and Malcolm X were killed.

CAP, however, was the only *government*-sponsored program that actually sought to inspire broad-scale activism—aside from the tamer and much farther away Peace Corps. The annual meeting of the U.S. Conference of Mayors in St. Louis in June 1965 barely stopped short of denouncing CAP for its promotion of "class struggle"—practically an accusation of treason in cold war America. Allen Matusow later wrote that remarkably, no one outside the agency "divined that one consequence of community action might be to ignite, at the local level, political and social conflict." Lyndon Johnson, according to Matusow, realized too late "that loyalists of Robert Kennedy had planted a time bomb in *his* antipoverty program."[39]

Frank Mankiewicz later asserted that Shriver was fully aware, however, of the social-change emphasis of CAP. Shriver was entirely loyal to Lyndon Johnson (at the cost of some tension within the Kennedy family), and he viewed CAP's work as the logical extension of what the Peace Corps was doing abroad. When an official from New Mexico berated Shriver because an ex-PCV working for CAP was leading protests at city hall, Shriver told Mankiewicz: "That's the best evidence I have that both of the agencies I'm running are successful. A guy who agitated for the poor in Peru for two years took that training and used it, and is now working for OEO to get the poor to demand that they be allowed to participate in city council meetings."[40]

Moynihan disputes the idea that Shriver himself sought to create a "radical" program that would undermine the nation's political consensus and weaken the Democratic Party. The subordinates who organized the Community Action Program gave it "a structure that neither those who drafted it, those who sponsored it, nor those who enacted it ever in any way intended."[41]

But Shriver was not simply the innocent victim of idealists whose goals he did not understand. Shriver, a typical New Frontiersman, supported activism. Supremely conscious of building consensus through public relations and lobbying, he nevertheless eschewed the bureaucratic ethos of backing only "safe" programs. Since 1961 the job descriptions of individuals like Larry Radley and David Crozier had included grass-roots organizing to stir local participation in both economic development and self-government. *Juntas* formed the basis of community development abroad: poor people organized into groups to create new institutions and demand, implicitly, a more just social order.

The Peace Corps of Latin America simply came home. Although he said "the word 'revolution' made him uneasy," no less an establishment figure than John Kenneth Galbraith told the Peace Corps in 1965 that its job was to facilitate precisely that.[42]

According to Richard Boone, Shriver's primary worry about CAP, from the start, was that it was too hard to implement, not that it was too radical. Community Action relied upon the cooperation of disparate agencies and individuals in each American town. It sought to bring together the schools, the police, local governments, nonprofit organizations, businessmen, and residents to develop strategies for eliminating poverty. Boone remembered Shriver saying, in the negative, "I've been through that with the Chicago school system . . . You'll spend all your time coordinating." Shriver also had to concern himself with selling Community Action to the U.S. Congress, not easily impressed with vague reform measures designed to share power. The OEO director vastly preferred projects like Job Corps, Foster Grandparents, Head Start, and Upward Bound, which yielded the type of compelling human interest stories that had made the Peace Corps famous. Nonetheless, Shriver listened to the aides who urged him to attempt more experimental programs. CAP "wasn't what you would call a safe program," Boone recalled, "but we had many, many safe programs that never helped poor people . . . that didn't reach down to people." It was the argument that had launched the Peace Corps—and distinguished it from AID.[43]

Shriver, Boone, Mankiewicz, Wofford, and even bureaucrats like Wiggins and professional politicians like Robert Kennedy epitomized a kind of zeal abroad in the land that inspired immense dedication in many Americans and zealotry in others. "The problems are too large and too important to be left to normal political methods," Shriver wrote in *The Point of the Lance*. "The point of the lance is lean, hard, focused," Shriver wrote, using imagery that Ernest Hemingway or T. E. Lawrence might have picked to describe a manly hero. "It reaches its target."[44] Under Sargent Shriver, philanthropic service would be anything but "ladies' work." But a Don Quixote jousting his way through sub-Saharan Africa or the trackless Amazon was one thing. Set upon city hall he was quite another.

Harris Wofford summed up the critical difference between the Peace Corps and the Office of Economic Opportunity. The War on Poverty, he noted in his memoirs, "took place close to home."[45] The Peace Corps always knew that it could get kicked out of a country if it made itself too unpopular. Whatever volunteers and staff may have thought privately about Kwame Nkrumah or Anastasio Somoza Debayle or the Shah of Iran—and regardless of how many citizen's groups they organized—Peace Corps representatives exercised great caution when it came to local politics. CAP organizers, in contrast, worked in their own nation. They were bolder, and mayors could not simply wave charges of foreign imperialism over the heads of Shriver's emissaries when they wanted and make them disappear. The word "revolution" did not receive as happy a reception when applied to the United States.

In addition, although both the Peace Corps and the OEO suffered from too-rapid expansion and consequently thin planning, the OEO's promises to conquer poverty were less tentative and its inability to do so was more easily observed. Sargent Shriver had much company in the mid-1960s, of course, when expectations of political reform and economic growth crested throughout the world. At the outset President Johnson declared that the War on Poverty "had to be big and bold and hit the nation with real impact."[46] Indeed, this was Johnson's approach to nearly everything. Shriver was ideal for the job. No one knew better how to set a fast pace. But nowhere in its literature did the OEO widely advertise before-and-after pictures of the War on Poverty like the ones that posters had portrayed of the unchanging Andean village before and after the Peace Corps. Neither agency—and no agency among the United Nations—had arrived at a miracle cure for poverty, foreign or domestic. But from a political point of view, it was not permissible to tell voters in the United States that poverty could not be eliminated anytime soon, when presidential elections arrived like clockwork.

Johnson's most grandiose goals for the OEO were not to be fulfilled, and anyone who bothered to open the newspaper knew it. The president first refused to raise taxes to support the War on Poverty (rejecting even a 5-cent tax on cigarettes), and then turned his back on CAP when the mayors began to complain. The expensive war in Vietnam brought a halt to attempts to expand the employment programs of the OEO, which would have done much to further alleviate poverty. Congress reduced funding for Community Action in 1966 and 1967. Although VISTA, Head Start, and Job Corps provided substantial services and were widely admired, CAP struggled awkwardly in full view of the public, the victim of turf wars and racial politics at the local level. The Peace Corps could fail, and for the most part only the volunteers knew it. In addition, they usually blamed themselves. When the OEO failed, the public blamed Sargent Shriver.[47]

At the same time, the Great Society accomplished a great deal. According to the U.S. Census, the percentage of persons of all races living below the poverty level in the United States declined from 22 percent to 12 percent between 1959 and 1969, and among blacks the numbers declined from 55 percent to 32 percent. Some of this decline must be attributed to the temporary expansion of the economy during the Vietnam War and to rural migration to booming cities, but the reduced figures nevertheless held through the 1990s, in part because of the solid gains made by senior citizens. Great Society programs like Medicare and the new minimum payment requirements of the Social Security Act reshaped millions of lives. Yet to those for whom the glass was still half empty rather than half full, the sense of relative deprivation remained. Poverty existed, and its skewed racial distribution became ever more visible once the elderly largely exited the ranks of the very poor.[48]

Activists claiming to represent the impoverished made perhaps the most painful accusations. "That was always the hellish problem we had in this business," according to William Kelly, director of Job Corps. "We'd find our friends picketing the front of the building."[49] Shriver in particular bore the brunt of the accusations. Three days before Christmas in 1967 a busload of the "vocal poor and their representatives" stood outside the home of Eunice and Sargent Shriver caroling them and their children:

> O come all ye poor folk,
> Soulful and together
> Come ye, O come ye to Shriver's house.
> Come and behold him, politicians' puppet.
> O come and let us move him,
> O come and sock it to him,
> And send him on his way to L.B.J.[50]

The antibureaucratic tendency of the Peace Corps expressed itself in a mostly good-humored irreverence, encouraged by the informality of the director. In the War on Poverty, irreverence turned to disrespect.

Organizers did not undergo group training together in the way that Peace Corps volunteers did, and so never developed a sense of loyalty to the larger organization, its mission, or its director. The antibureaucratic impulse remained, expressed in maximum feasible participation of the poor and the delegation of planning to local Community Action agencies. These agencies encouraged loyalty to the issues as they defined them and to their constituency. Shriver, far away in Washington and striving to defend the OEO from critics on the right and the left, became (in sixties parlance) "The Man," or the establishment.

The consequences of OEO's disasters did not directly touch the Peace Corps. Sargent Shriver remained personally popular within the agency, which he left in early 1966 when President Johnson realized that the embattled War on Poverty needed its director's undivided attention. To take Shriver's place Johnson appointed Jack Hood Vaughn, a former Peace Corps staff member whom he had earlier made assistant secretary of state for inter-American affairs. Vaughn was not an obvious choice from the perspective of other Peace Corps staff. Rather quiet and even shy, Vaughn seemed Shriver's opposite. But the choice fit with Johnson's growing insistence on loyalty from subordinates. During the Dominican crisis, Vaughn among others came under attack for Johnson's policies, but he stalwartly defended his president. Within the Peace Corps he became known as a disciplinarian, angering volunteers by lecturing them against sloppy dress and instituting an absolute ban against beards, especially in Latin America. At the same time, many would later admire Vaughn for fighting some of the hardest battles for the agency, keeping it going during the rough years, insisting that it develop better jobs for volunteers, and communicating—quietly, individually—a deep belief in universal solidarity and the possibility of love for one's fellow humans.[51]

With enormous goodwill toward its founder, Vaughn's Peace Corps wrote Shriver a letter of recommendation upon his retirement. The letter attested that Shriver had satisfactorily completed a training course in "How to Persuade United States Congressmen to Vote for an Underdeveloped Program" and had "challenged great numbers of people to leave their campuses and jobs to go abroad to perform strange tasks for no pay." Playfully, the letter concluded that as "an agent of change, Mr. Shriver . . . reduced the maximum penalty for the crime of bureaucracy from life imprisonment to five years, and otherwise subverted public order and complacency." It was a high compliment, undoubtedly taken as such, even though such subversion at home had exacted much from Shriver and the Kennedy family.[52] Vaughn took over from Shriver optimistically, pledging to expand the Peace Corps while diminishing the number of phony jobs.

But what OEO embarrassments and Shriver's retirement could not accomplish, the Vietnam War did. The War on Poverty and the Peace Corps, like most reforms of the 1960s, would surely have looked much different in the end had "Lyndon Johnson's War" gone differently. In 1966 the Peace Corps had 15,556 volunteers. In 1972, a year before Richard Nixon withdrew from Vietnam in a putative "peace with honor," the Corps had declined by 56 percent to 6,894 persons in the field. In dollars adjusted for inflation, Congress had cut its budget 33 percent. Daniel Patrick Moynihan, questioned by the Nixon administration about how it could create a stronger spirit of service among young people, replied that he doubted "any action by the government could persuade any students to serve their country as long as the war lasts."[53]

Early on, Peace Corps officials were convinced that they could contain the damage. When the marines invaded the Dominican Republic, Frank Mankiewicz persisted with the agency because he believed that most people in the Peace Corps dissented from the president's policy as he did and because, as he later put it, "I thought I could do something in that particular case—Latin America." Political sophistication meant cooperating with the president even when you did not fully agree with him, so that you could get your way on larger matters (like community development) at which he would not look too closely. Still, the Dominican invasion opened a Pandora's box of doubts. The U.S. army, supposedly a neutral force present simply to evacuate Americans and protect their property, in reality gave aid to the military government against the forces of the exiled president, Juan Bosch. "It suddenly occurred to me that maybe they weren't telling the truth in Vietnam either," Mankiewicz said.[54]

Volunteers who doubted the wisdom of the invasion persisted as well. Kirby Jones, a twenty-three-year-old volunteer who held a flashlight for surgeons during the fighting in Santo Domingo, reenlisted in the Corps and then joined the staff because he "felt very proud to be part of a U.S. organization that was totally accepted in a situation where there was such anti-American feeling, and I felt this is what the Peace Corps really means. It really gets to the people." Jones's statement showed his belief that, at base, anti-Americanism was misguided. In 1965 he was one of sixteen volunteers who signed up to serve again in the Dominican Republic, proud representatives of a "better" America. Two years later, though, Jones would help organize a Peace Corps protest of Johnson's policies in Vietnam.[55]

Around the globe, program officers and field representatives worked to keep criticism of Washington within limits acceptable to both the president and the Congress. "It is irrelevant whether I or anyone else in the agency agrees or disagrees with you about the U.S. position in the Dominican Republic—or Viet Nam," the head of the India program, quoting Warren Wiggins, told his area's volunteers. Volunteers could have their opinions, as long as they did not try to organize support for those opinions overseas. "Exporting political opinions of any sort is imperialism," Wiggins asserted, using a term guaranteed to instill self-doubt in any volunteer. "It involves a colonialist mentality which is inept, out of date and offensive to people who can think." It was another version of sophistication bordering on sophistry: only a volunteer with a colonialist mentality would think of imposing his views about Vietnam on local peoples. What the U.S. government might impose on Vietnam was another matter.[56]

But the Peace Corps was too important a symbol to be let alone. Volunteers and staff who believed their work stood for what America *should be* felt increasingly compelled to announce which side they were on. Liberal politicians who had long admired the Peace Corps felt similarly compelled. In 1967 the antiwar activist Allard Lowenstein approached Kirby Jones, then Peace Corps desk officer for Ecuador, to help organize a letter-writing campaign against the war. Lowenstein and Jones drafted what they hoped was a reasonable letter, but one that stated openly their conviction that the war in Vietnam was "causing an erosion of trust in our Government . . . among those Americans who, like us, want to believe in the high purpose and constructive world role of the United States." Jones then contacted former volunteers around the country, 800 of whom signed the letter to Johnson which was sent on March 6, 1967.[57]

Jack Vaughn told Jones, "You've got to stop," but declined to stop him. A few months later the director took more decisive action when

92 out of 317 volunteers on active duty in Chile signed another petition expressing their opposition to the war. Peace Corps administrators
in the country told the volunteers that they could not sign a petition
that identified them as Corps members because it violated their obligation to remain politically neutral. The United States ambassador to
Chile, Ralph Dungan, told the volunteers to resign if they could not
abide by this requirement. The volunteers chose not to release the
petition, but PCV Bruce Murray, a music instructor, wrote to Jack
Vaughn, the *New York Times,* and the Chilean newspaper *El Sur* to
protest the Peace Corps gag rule.

Sounding like a training officer, Murray argued that "part of the job
of a Peace Corps volunteer is to give an opportunity to citizens of a
foreign country to know an American citizen in all the varied aspects of
his personality including his thoughts on important issues." The Chilean volunteers had been taught from the beginning to explain America
to their hosts and to be an example of the United States' willingness to
acknowledge bravely how it wanted to do better on race, poverty, and
social injustice worldwide. With this mandate, some volunteers found it
nearly impossible to keep their mouths closed. In the middle of the
semester at the Chilean university where Bruce Murray worked, Peace
Corps representatives told him to pack his bags. His contract was over.
Murray claimed he had been an apolitical fellow until he was told by the
Peace Corps what he could not say, but Vaughn asserted that Murray
was acting as a "full-time propagandist."[58]

Abridgments of First Amendment rights had plagued U.S. domestic
politics since the Berkeley Free Speech Movement of 1964, when campus administrators banned certain groups from setting up tables to
distribute civil rights literature. In the pre–Civil War period, the gag
rule in Congress had similarly radicalized the debate over slavery, leading moderates like John Quincy Adams to take up a political issue they
had previously shied away from. When the Peace Corps—which had
always emphasized that its volunteers were free men and women, free
to express their own views—tried to control volunteer speech, the
organization slid into the credibility gap.

Jack Vaughn tried to reverse the damage done to the agency's reputation, and a month later the Peace Corps announced that volunteers
would not be prohibited from submitting petitions or letters to their
own nation's newspapers, but simply from publishing their views in the

host country. Still, as Karen Schwarz notes, the Peace Corps was perceived differently afterward. In 1966 a Harris poll had found that only 3 percent of college seniors believed that the Peace Corps limited volunteers' freedom of speech, but in 1969 at least 70 percent thought so.[59]

Meanwhile, the vise closed on Bruce Murray. The Peace Corps informed Murray's draft board that they were terminating him and the draft board called Murray's mother while he was still in Chile to inform her that her son had been reclassified 1-A (available for immediate service). Murray sought the help of the American Civil Liberties Union, and two years later a judge in the United States district court in Rhode Island ruled on Christmas eve 1969 that both the Peace Corps and the local draft board had violated Murray's rights to due process.[60] The Peace Corps, caught between President Johnson's insistence on loyalty and its own unwillingness to be a tool of the cold war, edged closer to the controversial administration. Jack Vaughn showed Lyndon Johnson he knew how to play hardball.

Applications for the Peace Corps began declining the year that Bruce Murray was terminated. In 1967, the number fell by 7,000; in 1968, the figure fell another 5,000. When Richard Nixon came into office in 1969 applications dropped another 6,000; and in 1970, the Corps received 5,000 fewer yet. That year, only 19,022 individuals applied to join the Peace Corps, well below half the number who had applied in 1966. Simultaneously, the ratio of male to female volunteers crept increasingly out of balance. By 1970 males were 70 percent of all volunteers, up significantly from the average of 55 percent in 1965. The percentage of male volunteers remained high throughout the draft.[61]

The Peace Corps sought to shelter its volunteers from military service to the extent possible. "I spend most of my time writing letters to draft boards," Jack Vaughn candidly briefed the president's Cabinet in late 1968, arguing that Peace Corps service ought to entitle volunteers to a deferment until they completed their assignment. Sponsors, Vaughn pointed out, frequently became irate when their volunteers were yanked away to be sent to Vietnam. It was not fair to the host, volunteer, or the Peace Corps, all of whom had invested significant time in preparing for the placement. Vaughn did not mention, although all the Cabinet members knew, that a two-year deferment could easily place the returned volunteer beyond the magic age of twenty-six, after which he was no longer draftable. Physicians, draftable even after age twenty-six, were the only exception, and (until the conservative American Medical Association opposed it) the Peace Corps was able to win a draft exemption for its doctors.[62]

Vaughn never got an automatic deferment for volunteers in general, however, nor did Joseph Blatchford, Richard Nixon's appointee. But both Peace Corps directors during the draft devoted countless hours to negotiating with local draft boards, the national Selective Service, and the House Armed Services Committee on behalf of volunteers. When the Nixon administration began tightening up even further on Peace Corps deferments, Blatchford struck back, saying that Peace Corps deferments should be eliminated only if the student deferment (a sacred cow to the middle class) was eliminated as well. Some volunteers did get drafted out of their Peace Corps assignments anyway, and shipped to Vietnam. They fought; some died. But the majority of volunteers found, as one engineer who joined to avoid the war later said, "The word was that if a guy joined the Peace Corps, most draft boards would just forget about him."[63]

General Lewis Hershey, head of the Selective Service, leniently interpreted Peace Corps service as important to the national interest. Local draft boards had the discretion either to honor this interpretation, and defer an individual's military service until completion of his Peace Corps assignment, or to draft him if they deemed it imperative. Many let volunteers slip through, but some did not. Tom McGinley, a volunteer in Micronesia, found his draft board extremely resistant. "I'm from a small town in Texas," he later recounted, "and my board's feeling was, 'None of this Peace Corps shit. You go fight like a man.'"[64] In the first year of the Nixon administration, 150 out of 7,800 male volunteers were drafted out of their assignments. Probably more would have been had it not been for the 1969 precedent of the Bruce Murray case, of which Blatchford reminded General Alexander Haig and Henry Kissinger when they asked him how the Peace Corps could "eliminate" the problem of obstreperous volunteers.[65]

Volunteers who came to the Peace Corps to avoid the draft were often not the best. The draft pushed Paul Cowan into the Peace Corps, who felt adrift and afterward wrote a scathing denunciation of the program. A British volunteer recalled a song that happily underemployed Peace Corps draft resisters in Guatemala used to sing, which they had set to the tune of "If I Were a Rich Man," from the popular musical *Fiddler on the Roof*. "If I joined the Peace Corps, I'd just idle, idle, idle, idle, idle, diddle-dee," the Americans taught the amused Englishman. "And have my Indian coop in Tecpan, Growing marijuana in the spring." The refrain ended, "Please don't send me off to Vietnam; Let me be a Peace Corps man!" Another volunteer who went to Thailand summed up his level of enthusiasm for the assignment by saying he hadn't specified a preference as to placement, since he "figured one foreign country would be as foreign as another." That he had fooled even the Peace Corps deepened the volunteer's alienation. Abroad, such volunteers tarnished the image of the agency and sometimes embarrassed those who had joined for better reasons.[66]

Not all male volunteers from 1965 to 1973 entered the Peace Corps to avoid the draft, of course, and of those who did, not all were poor volunteers. Some joined the Peace Corps because it seemed a more noble way to avoid the draft than others, and because they felt that their service had purpose. "I like to think I would have gone into the Peace Corps even if there hadn't been a Vietnam War," one volunteer later recalled. Another volunteer had an attack of conscience during training in Maine and dropped out to enlist in the marines. "It was more wrong for me to avoid the draft and let someone else go fight in my place than it was for me to go," Bill Broyles recounted. Yet another volunteer in the Marshall Islands also left to enlist, having decided it was unfair to allow other men to die while he enjoyed a South Sea "paradise."[67]

Still other men, unable to believe there was any honor in killing Vietnamese, even to save misspent American lives, genuinely looked upon their Peace Corps years as a form of compensation to their country—and worked even harder to make their assignments meaningful. George McDaniel, who served in both Togo and Vietnam (where he took shrapnel in the face), later said he felt the Peace Corps had been more effective at its job than the army. "The Peace Corps," he observed, "trained us to learn about people, to try to think as they do in order to understand problems and solve them." The army distanced its soldiers from the "gooks." In the end, after all the bloody sacrifice, the Vietnamese won.[68]

Not all volunteers opposed the war, as correspondence in both the

Johnson and the Nixon archives attests. One angry returned volunteer
wrote Johnson that the antiwar organizing of some Peace Corps
officials ought to be investigated. Another volunteer in Kenya wrote
Nixon that he was a proud member of the "silent majority" who found
it humiliating that local peoples would place him, in their minds, alongside the less responsible young men then joining the Peace Corps
simply to avoid military service.[69] These volunteers reflected the diversity of opinion within mainstream America, of which the Peace Corps
was a part. Their letters were also the sort most often forwarded to the
president himself.

Still, on average, people who considered being in the Peace Corps
were more likely than other college students to oppose the war. An
opinion poll conducted by Louis Harris in 1969 found that college
seniors with the highest level of political activism were also the ones
most likely to sign up for volunteering abroad. Harris reported that 35
percent of students overall in the West, Midwest, and East said they had
participated in antiwar demonstrations, but of those people who said
they were considering the Peace Corps, 48 percent had acted on their
opposition to the war. College seniors still rated the Peace Corps as
"the program doing the most to help the reputation of the U.S. in the
world today," and many who detested the war viewed the Peace Corps
as perhaps the only way to be a decent American in a world context.[70]

While Lyndon Johnson pondered his decision not to run for reelec-
tion, Americans undertook the slow evolution that by 1971 would lead
65 percent of the population polled to define the war as "morally
wrong." In early 1968, it was only a minority who would yet go so far
as to equate the United States with what was then still considered the
epitome of evil, Nazi Germany. But one Peace Corps officer, the education specialist Robert Greenway, acknowledged to the deputy director
that many people like himself had begun to "feel a sickness in their
hearts" when they heard the accusations of more radical campus organizers who said that the Peace Corps was mere window dressing on U.S.
foreign policy. As one Harvard student put it, Greenway reported,
"Yes, in the year 2000 some will ask, 'did you join?' But many will ask
also, as they ask now in Germany 30 years later, 'Why didn't you
leave?'"[71]

The Peace Corps wrestled openly with the paradox of U.S. policies.
In 1968 Young & Rubicam came to the service of the organization

again with a series of dramatic advertisements that squarely confronted viewers, imploring them to continue to believe that, at least through the Peace Corps, Americans could hold their government to its stated ideals. "The Peace Corps is bad; The Peace Corps is good," one ad expressed the dichotomy, urging readers not to dismiss the agency as hypocritical even though there was a war on. "Make your own peace," another ad challenged youth who "would rather do something . . . Instead of nothing." Another ad showed a young white woman holding an infant Nigerian in a maternal embrace, and ran alongside it her statement, which ended: "I never seriously thought I would change the world. Does anyone believe it any more? Then I came back. And I'm a teacher. And I've been seeing this guy, Ronnie. He's a teacher. We teach at P.S. 201. It's in Harlem."

But even honest advertisements could not paper over the damage. To some young people, the immorality of U.S. policy in Southeast Asia hopelessly tainted even a "good" program like the Peace Corps. Johnson bequeathed to Nixon an organization that was, indeed, sick at heart over the war, and over a number of other things as well. Joseph Blatchford attributed much of the decline in applications to the Peace Corps to the proliferation of competing opportunities for activism and service, but he nonetheless attached central importance to domestic conflicts and the Vietnam War.

The assassinations of Martin Luther King, Jr., and Robert F. Kennedy in 1968 did much to shatter the hope that people of good will could work through the problems of the nation. Race riots and the separatist ideology of Black Power further degraded the ability of many Americans to believe in the possibility of racial harmony or the idea that the moral goodness of one person could make a difference. The Peace Corps and its counterparts abroad, founded on the notion that love and universal human rights were the rocks on which a new world order could be based, had the ground under them rudely shaken by the Vietnam War and all the other disintegrating factors of the times. "Forced to lay money on two horses," a Canadian volunteer wrote in 1968, "—a CUSO motivated by rational and idealistic norms of human behaviour or a United States Air Force obviously motivated by aggressive patterns of behaviour reaching back into the Stone Age—a man would have to be an idiot to select the CUSO horse."[72] Violence seemed to be winning.

The Vietnam War also provoked a crisis of confidence in the meaning of foreign aid that lasted far longer than the fighting in Southeast Asia. When Lyndon Johnson said that all he wanted to do was to help the people of South Vietnam, he gave help a bad name. In 1965, speaking at Johns Hopkins University, the president described the carrot he was offering the Vietnamese people, including the development of the "vast Mekong River . . . on a scale to dwarf even our own T.V.A." Although the president himself was likely not cynical in his offer, it nonetheless prompted much cynicism when he ordered the defoliation of the shores along Vietnam's waterways in following years.[73]

Lyndon Johnson's extravagant rhetoric about the downtrodden, in his own country and abroad, increasingly did not ring true for many who heard it, leading some to reject the language of paternal love upon which he relied. "These Greek people love you," Johnson told a balking Harry Truman when he tried to convince the eighty-year-old former president to attend a state funeral in the nation that had prompted the Truman Doctrine. "There's a few crackpots, but they love you . . . And I want to show them we love them," Johnson said, creating a lavish description of international affection that hardly fit the father of the cold war. It was vintage Johnson: emotional, sentimental, and filled with the imagery of help given and filial love returned.[74]

But "aid" to Vietnam did not produce a happier Vietnam. Nor did aid to Latin America in the 1960s, which though it had been promised help with peaceful revolution underwent a series of coups that turned many countries into dictatorships. Electrical devices shipped by the U.S. aid program to promote communications were reputedly used to administer electrical shocks to the genitalia of dissidents. The U.S. military "School of the Americas" in Panama, set up to train Latin American officers in counterinsurgency techniques, became more popularly known as "Escuela de Golpes" (School of Coups). The Alliance for Progress fell apart under Johnson. The Latin America to which Larry Radley had been posted, in which the Democratic left seemed to be in the ascendancy, was gone. Gone also was the optimism that Kennedy had generated for the so-called Development Decade of the 1960s. Instead, it seemed that the regions which the United States had done the most to "help" had suffered the most egregious damage.

Similarly, at home, the more that Johnson had done to eliminate the wrongs of racism—in the civil rights acts of 1964, 1965, and 1968—

the more that some African Americans, especially in the Black Power movement, gave him and the entire country the message that there was nothing he or any white person could ever do to "make things right." The ethos of Black Power, unlike the ethos of the strongly religious early civil rights movement, did not embrace the concept of personal redemption for whites. In 1966 the Student Non-Violent Coordinating Committee expelled all of its white members on the premise that the financial support of any such person was an extension of "the tentacles of the white power complex that controls this country."[75] So much for the power of the one righteous person.

Americans were not the only ones who doubted the efficacy of their attempts to "do better." Other predominantly white nations also sometimes found their overseas aid efforts spurned or defined as neo-imperialism. Sekou Touré informed de Gaulle that he had no desire to be part of the French Community. Demonstrators in Trinidad spat on the car of the Canadian governor-general. Other African, Latin American, and Asian nations sharply and frequently criticized their former masters. For volunteers in many countries, the result was a growing fear that their own efforts were part of the corrupting effect of the West. The Peace Corps had always preached that volunteers should not consider themselves better than natives, but now volunteers began to doubt they were as good. Some critics of Western influence argued that no matter what volunteers did, their presence robbed local people of initiative, or introduced inappropriate technologies, or served as a cover for white imperialism.

A study of Peace Corps volunteers in Ethiopia in 1968 found that volunteers had been socialized so strictly on the dangers of "arrogant imperialism" that they had been "left with fundamental and perhaps irrevocable doubts about the legitimacy of their roles as helpers." Canadians experienced a similar problem. According to Ian Smillie, a CUSO volunteer to Sierra Leone, orientations "were so intense that many candidates would 'deselect' themselves before departure" in the face of guest lecturers who strongly criticized "neo-colonialism, neo-imperialism, 'do-gooderism' and aid in general." A 1969 training for East Africa featured Black Power activists who, according to Smillie, "spread doubt and guilt among the middle-class Canadians as though they were sprinkling herbicide on a weed bed." Parallel orientations occurred in the United States. One San Diego session featured speakers who told volunteers that regardless of their best efforts, they would always be tools of U.S. imperialism.[76]

In extreme form, as two researchers noted in 1968, this worldview was "based on a fantasy of omnipotence that suggests the 'helped' are incapable of resisting the unwanted effects of the helper." In actuality, volunteers were far more likely to encounter villagers who flatly rejected concepts they found alien than villagers who slavishly implemented every suggestion. Critiques of this sort also did not squarely face the fact that volunteers had been requested. Presumably not all third world leaders were dupes, and based their requests on reasonable calculations of national interest.[77]

But careful, dispassionate analysis was not a hallmark of the late 1960s or early 1970s. The moral outrages of the period and the images that went along with them overwhelmed such thinking. Photojournalism flourished and brought forward pictures that traumatized the American psyche: a naked nine-year-old girl on fire in Vietnam, Coretta Scott King in a black veil, the funeral train of Robert Kennedy, American athletes with their fists raised in a Black Power salute at the 1968 Olympics, a kneeling Viet Cong prisoner shot in the head on a Saigon street, a woman with her arms outstretched in shock over a dead body on the ground at Kent State University. Such images made many impressionable and morally acute young people feel that far from being heroic, if anything their nation was demonic.

As a result, a number of potential volunteers accepted the idea that they and their nation were deeply culpable for all the power inequities of the world. Glyn Roberts, a British author, did much to popularize this view among volunteers throughout the West with his 1968 book *Volunteers and Neo-Colonialisms* and a later pamphlet for Paris UNESCO, *Questioning Development*. CUSO held a forum on the writings of Roberts, and many Peace Corps volunteers read them as well. Typical of his generation, Roberts was sensitive to the ways in which personal behaviors made political statements. "I am convinced that the majority of Europeans become *markedly more authoritarian* during a stay in an underdeveloped country," Roberts wrote, basing his observations on interactions with volunteers from a broad cross-section of countries. "Even the average volunteer nowadays seems to have a cook/housekeeper," he noted.

Roberts also rejected capitalist modes of development, praising

China, Cuba, North Vietnam, and Tanzania, instead. Every volunteer, he argued, was in some small way an extension "at the individual level" of the capitalist power of the oppressive North. "Visit one of the 15,000 prostitutes in Addis Ababa, use a rickshaw in Calcutta, climb Kilimanjaro with hired porters, and you exercise your economic superiority without promoting the more equal distribution of power." American and other Western volunteers, without a doubt, had done all of these things at one time or another. Everyone slipped in some way.[78]

Roberts's preference for socialism over capitalism reflected yet another trend pushing many young Americans to the left, both in the Peace Corps and at home. Following the passage of laws that outlawed public segregation and voting fraud in the United States, the civil rights movement had turned its attention to economic inequality. Martin Luther King, Jr., had pointedly called this effort a "Poor Peoples' Campaign" rather than a black peoples' campaign, and he was shot while in Tennessee supporting a sanitation workers' strike. African-American groups with separatist policies, like SNCC, the Black Muslims, and the US organization in California, went further and equated poverty with racism. Poverty, however, was more intractable than racism. It was older, and had its own history. When poverty refused to yield, many activists concluded that racism was at bottom and their anger with "the system" grew. Still others concluded that the fundamental problem lay with capitalism.

Members of the Peace Corps had greater personal experience with intractable poverty than most Americans. Every individual who entered the Peace Corps came out knowing that there were few immediate solutions to misery in the world. Because of their contact with foreigners, volunteers also had more knowledge than most Americans of alternative explanations for this situation. By the late 1960s, capitalist modes of development had come under wide criticism in the third world. In Africa and Asia, the newly independent countries almost all went through a socialist phase. In Latin America, dependency theory crowded out liberal economics by the end of the decade. Well-known theorists like Raul Prebisch of Argentina and Celso Furtado of Brazil, along with northerners like André Gunder Frank, argued convincingly that the underdeveloped world was impoverished not because it had failed to enter the modern world of capitalist development, but because of the specific role it played as the provider of raw materials. According to dependency theorists, those "satellite" regions of the world's economic periphery that suffered the most greatly were "the ones which had the closest ties to the [world] metropolis in the past."[79] Many Latin American intellectuals arrived at the conclusion that their nations were the proletarians of world capitalism—and they had nothing to lose but their chains.

The prescription of the *dependistas* was therefore greater separation from capitalist economies rather than greater integration. Here, again, the touch of Americans (even Peace Corps volunteers) came to be seen as potentially corrupting. Volunteers at the start of the decade had been much hailed for their simple willingness to reach out to poor people of all races, and not make themselves out to be "too good" to socialize with local peoples. Ten years later, it seemed that they might be "too bad." Not, of course, as individuals—but in a Marxist worldview individual volition counted for little. The relations of production determined who was rich and who was poor, and volunteers who dug wells or taught English were, at best, naifs on a fool's errand. At worst, they perpetuated inequalities of power by encouraging false hope and luring third world countries closer to the existing capitalist system.

Volunteers split over how to view these critiques. Many ignored them, and in the initial days of Nkrumah in Ghana, volunteers probably without exception believed that their system had socialism beat, hands down. But as the sixties wore on, a number of volunteers moved from simply tolerating socialists to openly sympathizing with their goals and even their methods. The Committee of Returned Volunteers, formed in 1966 as the first alumni association of volunteers, entertained radical solutions in the belief that they owed it to the peoples whom they had served to get to the bottom of the underdevelopment mystery. Following a trip to Cuba in 1969, a group of thirty-nine ex-PCVs endorsed "revolution which carries out an equitable redistribution of economic and political power."[80] Although their posture was more radical than that of the vast majority of volunteers, the Committee of Returned Volunteers had simply taken the logic of the Peace Corps one more step: the short distance between disdain for exploitative upper-class elites of the third world and a disdain for exploitative upper-class Americans.

Canadian volunteers became even more radicalized. The Latin American field staff of CUSO took to calling itself a "collective," resisting direction from the head office in Ottawa which members identified with the capitalist status quo. According to Ian Smillie, returned volunteers who had seen conditions in the third world first-hand found CUSO's apolitical character maddening, and did their best to awaken the organization. "Many wanted to slap the rose-coloured glasses off the technocratic face of development and say loudly what they had seen: that the gaps, rather than narrowing, were widening to reveal a terrible chasm of poverty and despair that demanded urgent attention." David Beer, one of the two teenagers whom Guy Arnold had taken to British Guiana in 1960, argued in 1969 that anything less was "naive wishy-washy liberalism."[81]

Not everyone responded this way. The sixties and early seventies were characterized by a storm of divergent opinions on profound issues. Many North American volunteers balanced radical critiques against what they also knew of the third world from first-hand experience: that local peoples bore some responsibility for their situation and that an individual could, sometimes, make an important difference. A Peace Corps volunteer architect in Tunisia noted with frustration in his journal that it always seemed to be the foreign technicians who actually got "the lead on the paper." Local people, with a looser work ethic than the North American one, "can't or won't bother." A Canadian volunteer engaging in a debate of Glyn Roberts's work countered the negative view of volunteers put forward by the "realist" contingent of CUSO radicals. "I believe that the spirit of working-while-doing-without is central to voluntarism," Peggy Buckley wrote, claiming that volunteers set a standard for new types of behavior. Rich countries and their citizens needed to learn how to make some sacrifices.[82]

The clouds of dissension that had gathered over the Peace Corps by the end of Lyndon Johnson's presidency broke with fury during the first half of Richard Nixon's only full term in office. The Republican president swept into power over the imploded remains of a Democratic Party that had seen its most popular candidate assassinated (Robert Kennedy) and its eventual nominee (Vice President Hubert Humphrey) saddled with the burden of Lyndon Johnson's war guilt. Nixon's victory was made surer by his appeal to "law and order." Radicals given safe harbor by the Democrats, Nixon claimed, threatened U.S. stability.

But radicals, and even the relatively mild-mannered Peace Corps, had simply given voice to the real cause of this instability. Faced with the shocking facts of the U.S. war in Vietnam, a growing number of Americans could not see in reports on the conflict the face of a nation they recognized as their own. The early Peace Corps confirmed American identity. The Vietnam War undermined this identity and the stability it had long conferred. Over the normally optimistic American people—unable to believe in their country's mission, unable to trust their government to carry it out—self-doubt cast a pall. The nation longed to be restored to itself. Nixon promised he could do that. What he did not say was that one casualty might be the Peace Corps.

8

Under
Attack

We went abroad to help Asians, Africans, and Latin Americans
develop their resources and become free people. Once abroad,
we discovered that we were part of the U.S. worldwide pacification
program. We found that U.S. projects in these countries are designed
to achieve political control and economic exploitation: to build an
Empire for the U.S. As volunteers we were part of that strategy;
we were the Marines in velvet gloves.

COMMITTEE OF RETURNED VOLUNTEERS, MAY 1970

Bust the Peace Corps.

H. R. HALDEMAN, MAY 1970

Hardly sympathetic to John Kennedy's creation, Richard Nixon was
willing to tolerate the Peace Corps only as long as it behaved. Hardly
sympathetic to the incoming Republican and in direct opposition to the
Vietnam War, members of the mostly Democratic Peace Corps staff
braced themselves for the worst. When the newly appointed Joseph
Blatchford arrived at his offices in 1969 he looked vainly for the portrait
of the current president that traditionally graces the foyer of every
federal building. All he could find was an old picture of Kennedy. A
staff person dug Nixon's framed portrait out of the trash.

Richard Nixon was in many ways a very practical man. He did not
evince ideological fervor for or against the Peace Corps. Rather he
believed that, like all parts of U.S. foreign policy, it should serve specific
ends. Too much fervor had led to unrestricted interventionism culminating in Vietnam. Like Henry Kissinger, his chief foreign policy advisor, Nixon believed realpolitik was a surer guide to the nation's interests
than a policy of promulgating its domestic ideals in the world arena.

All You Need Is Love

His was a policy of increased international restraint. Had Nixon reserved that policy for foreign nations alone, and not used the most cynical devices of realpolitik on his domestic opponents (as the Watergate scandal revealed), the president would have finished two terms in office. His contributions to foreign policy would have been more secure. But Nixon's actions compounded the doubts raised under Johnson, leading even more Americans to question whether the nation's ideals had any substance left at all.

Initially, the Nixon administration appeared accepting of the Peace Corps. It placed a high priority on finding a qualified person for the job of director. In Joseph Blatchford, Nixon's staff found not only a competent director but someone who, unlike almost anyone else in the conservative administration, actually looked like a sixties kind of guy. An exhibition tennis player and jazz musician, Joseph Blatchford had dark curly hair and fashionably long sideburns. He rode a black motorcycle to work, which he pulled into the Peace Corps lobby. At age thirty-four, he was a decade younger than either Sargent Shriver or Jack Vaughn had been at the time of appointment. Blatchford also had had more pertinent job experience. Ten years earlier, while in law school at Berkeley, Blatchford had organized Acción, a community development organization utilizing U.S. volunteers in Latin America. Blatchford had not campaigned for Nixon (unlike some applicants for the job), and in fact was in São Paulo, Brazil, when he got a call from the White House asking him to come for an interview.

"The Director of the Peace Corps must be a strong individual—one who can and will assert himself in the face of what will often appear to be overwhelming odds," the Nixon aide Alexander Butterfield wrote to the subordinate who was coordinating the search. "Thus, if you can come up with some proof as to his strength of character and his general 'toughness,' we may have a winner." Butterfield's assessment was prophetic, and the choice of Blatchford a lucky one for the Peace Corps. The organization was assaulted immediately: first by its volunteers, and then by the president.[1]

"We have come to the unavoidable conclusion that the Peace Corps should be abolished," the Committee of Returned Volunteers (CRV) announced in September 1969. The United States perpetuated underdevelopment, the committee asserted, and the Peace Corps itself was nothing more than a "graduate school for imperialism." According to

the committee, it was the responsibility of current volunteers "to subvert the Peace Corps and all other institutions of US imperialism."[2]
When it began in 1966, CRV had declined to make statements about
Vietnam and instead set up a study group on the subject. The group
numbered only 75 out of a population of approximately 33,000 returned volunteers. But in August 1967 the committee published its
Vietnam study group's findings in the leftist journal *Ramparts* and
obtained endorsements from 659 other former volunteers.[3]

"For those of us who worked to build a school or a dispensary, for
those of us who saw dysentery decrease because we helped the people
dig a well, for those of us who helped a village realize its ambition to
have a bridge to get its goods to market, for those of us who helped a
child discover the meaning of electricity, each bomb in Vietnam that
destroys a school, a well, a bridge or a child destroys the very kinds of
things which we considered most important in our service as volunteers," the committee stated, relying on a simple logic of bridge for
bridge, child for child. By 1969, however, when President Nixon began
a secret bombing campaign in Cambodia, the CRV had gone from
conceiving of the war as a tragic mistake by a liberal administration
otherwise committed to human rights to seeing the war as part of a
deliberate strategy of U.S. hegemony.[4]

Other volunteers also recommended phasing out the Peace Corps,
though for different reasons. In September 1970, twenty-nine volunteers in Malaysia wrote Richard Nixon that the Peace Corps ought to
be replaced with an occupational exchange program. "We feel our
presence often inhibits Malaysians' awareness of their problems and
priorities in their nation's development and the ability to formulate
Malaysian solutions to Malaysian problems," the volunteers told the
president, expressing a frustration common to development workers.
"It is a patronizing role for us to assume, however well meaning." The
Malaysian volunteers had encountered an endemic dilemma. Helping
people help themselves could be subtly contradictory—and in some
cases gave them no motivation to solve their own problems. Confronted with stubborn poverty, corruption, and resistance to change,
many volunteers now rejected the optimistic assumptions with which
Shriver had begun. "The world has changed since the Peace Corps was
first established," the Malaysian volunteers warned the new president.[5]

Even the Washington headquarters of the Peace Corps appeared

ambivalent about the future. Coming to work each day, Joseph Blatchford was struck by the strong feelings of staff members who had seen
both Kennedys killed and who now saw themselves in the clutches of
Richard Nixon. They preferred to dissolve the Peace Corps rather than
have it wither slowly under the Republican president. "This belongs to
us," Blatchford later paraphrased staff sentiment. "This is our emotional framework. This is our life. Nixon is not going to be the head of
the Peace Corps. Let's close it. Let's stop. Let's bury it. Let's end it. Do
not let him touch it. Get his hands off it."[6]

Joseph Blatchford, however, was by no means ready to close down
the Peace Corps. His own first volunteers with Acción had gone to
Venezuela just a few months before the Peace Corps started in Ghana.
Since then Blatchford had had numerous occasions to talk with Peace
Corps volunteers in Latin America, many of whom he thought were
seriously underutilized. Having fielded over a thousand volunteers himself in the preceding nine years, Blatchford was deeply committed to
the concept and looked forward to making it work better. He thought
he had the president behind him, and for a short while he did.

Blatchford had to undertake several tasks at once. If the organization
were to continue beyond the sixties, it would need to give Republicans
a greater stake in its survival. It had to find, in the words of one White
House aide, some "good staunch Republicans" to serve as country
directors and staff officers when positions became available. It also
needed, as Blatchford was later to direct his staff, to devise a program
"which bears the stamp of this President." If the Peace Corps failed in
these tasks, it would fail an elementary test of the American political
system as it had evolved since the nineteenth century. Republicans had
to be allowed the spoils of the election—and the Peace Corps, like it or
not, was one of them. Shriver and Vaughn, after all, had filled the Corps
with Democrats. Still, Blatchford showed a restraint that earned him a
few points with older Peace Corps staff by agreeing to take on only
those Republicans with demonstrable qualifications for the job. Blatchford enforced the five-year rule to a greater extent than Vaughn, but
when key staff resigned or had their terms expire he also promoted
from within.[7]

Blatchford's other major challenge was to meet what he delicately
called the "problem of political involvement." From the outset Blatchford had to respond constantly to detractors of the Peace Corps in the

White House who watched it hawkishly. Barely a month in office, Blatchford was called on the carpet by presidential aide John Ehrlichman to explain what the Peace Corps was up to in Micronesia, where volunteers for the previous year had been complaining of the islands' poor treatment as a trust territory of the United States. Hope and Todd Jenkins, volunteers on the island of Kili, had even written a letter (leaked to the *Washington Post*) to the United Nations Trusteeship Council. Blatchford denied, however, that there was a significant problem of volunteer interference or that Micronesian concerns about their twenty-year banishment from the mother island of Bikini (devastated by the testing of U.S. nuclear bombs) were due to Peace Corps influence. Blatchford argued that to look at volunteers as outside agitators suggested "a dependency by the Micronesian leaders which does not in fact exist . . . They know exactly what they are doing."[8]

At the same time Blatchford recognized that he had to curtail protesters of U.S. policy to the extent he could if the Nixon administration was going to let the program live. Vaughn had had to do the same. Vice President Spiro Agnew, appointed chairman of the Peace Corps Advisory Board according to precedent, presented an important obstacle. Agnew brashly characterized student protesters as an "effete corps of impudent snobs," and freely admitted that his statements might "polarize the American people." His image hardly set well with the Peace Corps. When Agnew heard of Peace Corps protests against the war he told Blatchford simply, "Fire them all." The vice president's continuing presence on the board could only fuel unrest. Blatchford considered whom the president might consider an appropriate alternative, without giving offense to Agnew. When Captain Neil Armstrong took the first steps on the moon in July 1969, Blatchford had his man. Eisenhower had *said* they ought to send volunteers there. Agnew cared little about being relieved of the Peace Corps, and Nixon relished Blatchford's political finesse.[9]

Blatchford strove to bring Nixon together with the maverick agency in ways that would offend neither. One activity in September 1969 was a touch football game to which the Peace Corps challenged the White House staff. (Nixon was known to be a keen football fan.) That same month Blatchford and Nixon together planned a prayer breakfast for Peace Corps country directors and host ambassadors. Prayer breakfasts were not typical of the devoutly secular Corps, but agency staff followed Blatchford's lead. Harder to sell would have been Nixon's initial suggestion that the event feature music by the Army Band and Chorus, one of the president's favorites. "How do I tell him it would not be good to have the Army Band and Chorus and the Peace Corps during the Vietnam War?" Blatchford thought to himself. "How about the Howard University band?" the director suggested, cleverly substituting a safe choice designed to make the president look good on race relations.[10]

The September breakfast was a great success if one ignored the protesters from the Committee of Returned Volunteers across the street in Lafayette Park. As guests and reporters left the White House, CRV did a spot of guerrilla theater equating Peace Corps nutrition programs with Coca-Cola and its education programs with *Time* magazine. "Gosh, golly, gee whiz, wow," the chorus chanted in the background, mocking Peace Corps naiveté.[11] When two hundred volunteers from around the world joined in the Vietnam Moratorium on November 15, 1969, the administration's brief honeymoon with the Peace Corps ended. Although the moratorium was a peaceful affair that attracted sober, middle-class citizens across the country and involved a number of churches, the administration saw participation in it as evidence of radicalism. Small Peace Corps contingents in Asia and Africa filed respectful antiwar petitions with their ambassadors, to the shock of the White House. It mattered little that fewer than 2 percent of the 12,000 volunteers overseas participated.

Blatchford tried to turn the Peace Corps in midstream in directions he saw as compatible with the administration, but he was not quite in time. Some of these "New Directions," as Blatchford called them, were designed specifically to decrease the number of disenchanted youth in the Peace Corps. Others were to correct problems with the Peace Corps of which Blatchford had been aware for several years. Indeed, Jack Vaughn had first pointed them out. Vaughn, for example, had done much to cut back on urban community development in Latin America, which had a high rate of attrition. "As in the United States, we don't know how to do urban community development," Vaughn told Johnson in 1968 in a clear reference to both the OEO and the Peace Corps. "We haven't found a handle . . . But we keep experimenting."[12]

With regard to dissidents then in the Peace Corps, Blatchford told

Henry Kissinger that "in the final analysis," since the courts had elected to stand behind the free speech and due process rights of volunteers, there was not much a Republican Peace Corps could do other than to recruit different kinds of people in the future. From the start, Blatchford adopted a policy of recruiting a "broader range" of skilled Americans with an "emphasis on maturity." These people, Blatchford assured the administration, would "emphasize technical assistance more than simply good will." (In other words, the emphasis would be on apolitical aid, as opposed to political solidarity of a sort that might lend itself to criticism of the United States.) The agency also stopped sending each volunteer abroad with a locker full of books. Although Blatchford did this to diminish paternalism in the agency, it reduced the socialization component of the Peace Corps as well. Volunteers no longer had liberal tracts to meditate on in the bush, unless they obtained them themselves.[13]

Blatchford brought an older group to the Peace Corps. For the first time, the Peace Corps specifically recruited families with children, focusing on individuals with specific technical skills and experience. Critics of Blatchford interpreted these moves as designed to get rid of recently graduated B.A. generalists who were considered troublemakers. "He and the Nixon Administration are bent on turning their backs on the young people who have hitherto been responsible for the Peace Corps's unique contribution," the returned volunteer Robert Jachnig wrote the *New Republic* in 1969. Opponents correctly perceived that Blatchford sought to lower the number of potentially leftist volunteers; but they wrongly assumed that his policies were designed primarily for that purpose. That was mostly (in Republican terms) a lucky side effect.

Like many people working in development in the 1960s, Blatchford had been quick to perceive the growing disillusionment in third world countries by the end of the decade. Love was not enough. Idealism was not enough. The gap between rich and poor had not narrowed. A number of host governments, especially in Africa, told Blatchford explicitly on his first goodwill tour in May 1969 that while they liked the Peace Corps, they needed more skilled people in more focused assignments. Blatchford did not assume that people over thirty could not be trusted, and he disagreed that ideals burned only in the hearts of college students. "It was elitism at its worst," Blatchford later said of the emphasis on nontechnical college graduates. The approach hid the assumption, he felt, that "if you went to trade school you knew nothing about the world; you couldn't learn a language."[14]

Blatchford's emphasis on the job to be done, rather than on the spirit that young people might take with them, registered some notable successes. In the Philippines, for example, the Peace Corps switched its emphasis from education to agriculture at the urging of the Philippine government, which was poised to reap the benefits of advances in rice production that had come out of experiments over the preceding decade. Blatchford's New Directions brought technicians with rare skills to the Philippine program, along with a batch of recent college graduates trained as extension agents in rural credit, sanitation, nutrition, and basic agriculture. Older volunteers, some with thirty years of experience as farmers and livestock producers themselves, brought their families and contributed enormously to program maturity.[15]

At the same time, the organization found that technical skills were not a panacea for all that troubled the development process. The Peace Corps was never perfectly organized, and neither were its hosts. PCV Arthur Wild, one member of a group of credentialed architects posted to Tunisia under Blatchford, vainly pursued the hope that every hour of his valuable time could be well spent. The "prison" term of two years of poor food and unsanitary conditions would be worthwhile if he could really be "useful in the society." Upon arrival, he waited eagerly to be placed. But the Tunisian government did not need as many architects as it had requested. He finally found a placement with a private firm, but soon discovered that the architecture he knew how to do and the architecture his supervisor wanted did not coincide. "All he wants is the cheapest most unimaginative thing he can find," Wild moaned to his journal. Design seemed to be stuck in the 1940s, and local architects appeared to have no consciousness about environment or pollution. He concluded that the "cultural base of architecture is impossible to transfer." Wild completed his simple drafting assignments patiently, but without enthusiasm. When his Peace Corps supervisor told him in disgust a year later, "Anybody could be doing this," Wild asked in his diary, "What should I be doing? Quitting?"[16]

Arthur Wild, like most volunteers, lost weight during his two-year tour in Tunisia, dropping from a bantam 137 pounds down to a scrawny 124. His frustrations also became lighter, though, largely because he embraced the Shriver-like notion of a Peace Corps "spirit." It turned out that his Tunisian supervisor, a "big, husky Turk full of hair which sticks out all over his shirt," was the grandson of a Barbary pirate, and an amateur philosopher. "Little by little, some each day, ideas come," Raouf Erraïs told Arthur. Be patient. "From the discussion comes the light," he reminded the young American. "It's not so important that we put up some buildings. It is important that we get to know each other and that you get to know Tunisia." Near the end of Arthur Wild's placement, Raouf took him to talk to young Tunisians at an architecture school. "Okay," Arthur Wild began his lecture in 1973, "even though my architecture can't be your architecture, at least we can pay attention to orientation and climate."[17] The highly skilled Wild won a small victory for himself by focusing on simple principles. Diana Louise Stahl, the "unskilled" B.A. generalist in the Philippines who developed rabbit farms for lepers and others in the same year, showed what could still be done by creative individuals. Blatchford's Peace Corps found room for them both.

Still, in the words of Philippine country director David Searles, "New Directions unquestionably tipped the balance in favor of jobs" over spirit. In the long run this may have helped ensure the continuing relevance of the Peace Corps as succeeding generations of volunteers questioned the validity of the universalist assumptions so prized during the Shriver era. In the 1980s and 1990s, "multiculturalism" contributed to a critique of ethnocentric do-gooders who wanted to change the world until it mirrored themselves. Few volunteers or staff were ever as ethnocentric as this stereotype implied. Indeed, the Peace Corps had done more than any other government institution to recognize the value of every language, the dignity of every people, and the limits of Western understanding. But New Directions even more explicitly rejected any assumption that the Peace Corps had a monopoly on development ideas or that its volunteers had some indefinable pioneer essence which set them apart from other, more plodding nationalities. Blatchford and his staff took pains to welcome average Americans, not just Paul Bunyans.

In line with this more unassuming approach, Blatchford increased the range of opportunities for local people to give feedback to the Peace Corps. In 1970 he set a goal of paid country staffs "composed of fifty percent of local citizens." In countries like Ghana the Peace Corps also formed unpaid advisory councils with the idea of conducting "foreign affairs in a greater spirit of partnership." With Nixon's support, Blatchford took yet another step to internationalize the Peace Corps idea, consistent with earlier efforts under Shriver. One of Blatchford's proudest moments in the Peace Corps came when he turned over to the UN a check for the first installment on $200,000 to help start United Nations Volunteers.

All of these actions, Blatchford felt, had the additional benefit of making the Peace Corps more consistent with the Nixon Doctrine. The United States would continue to support its friends, Nixon stated on the island of Guam in 1969, but "cannot—and will not—conceive all the plans, design all the programs, execute all the decisions and undertake all the defense of the free nations of the world." In the president's scheme that meant giving support to authoritarian regimes like Iran and South Africa which could keep the peace in their regions. In the Peace Corps that meant giving more authority to local peoples.[18]

Blatchford disagreed philosophically with what he saw as the early Peace Corps's paternalism, expressed not only toward its hosts but even toward its own volunteers. The Corps had been established when the policy of *in loco parentis* was still unquestioned on college campuses. Universities at the start of the 1960s, acting as surrogate parents, supervised student dating, dress, and living arrangements. Similarly, Shriver's and Vaughn's Peace Corps treated its "boys and girls" (a phrase Blatchford despised) as wards, doling out separate allowances for living expenses, clothing, vacation travel, and household supplies. The Peace Corps even handled volunteers' luggage, not quite trusting "Kennedy's kids" to ship it to the right spot on their own. By the late 1960s these policies seemed out of date for college graduates and insulting to the older candidates whom Blatchford hoped to attract. "The volunteer is a responsible individual, well able to manage his own financial and logistic affairs," Blatchford told his staff.[19]

Blatchford also eliminated psychological evaluation during training—again with the idea that recruits were responsible adults capable of knowing their own minds. One result of this change was to increase the Peace Corps retention rate, enabling Blatchford to reverse temporarily the downward slide in numbers. Volunteers did not have to be members of an elite group resistant to psychological "torture." Normal Americans need apply. More volunteers also stayed in the field once there. The Peace Corps, one official under Blatchford later asserted, ceased blaming volunteers for failing to live up to unrealistic expectations and instead focused more of its energy on giving them good jobs and involving volunteers in larger program decisions they were capable of making. The organization stopped insisting that every volunteer be extraordinary.[20]

Blatchford's statements on paternalism and elitism undoubtedly seemed opportunistic to those Peace Corps veterans who would never trust a Richard Nixon appointee, even when he was an ally. "Under attack in Congress for being too sympathetic to campus hotheads, under attack on the campus for being a tool of the system," one CBS reporter noted in 1970, "Blatchford, meanwhile, quietly tries to tell both sides there is something in what the other believes." In fact, there is little reason to assume that Blatchford was not entirely sincere. A liberal Republican and an internationalist of the Rockefeller-wing persuasion, Blatchford was part of what was becoming a bipartisan consensus on many of the issues of the 1960s: that the war was going nowhere, that universities should treat students like grown-ups, that men who could be drafted should have the right to vote, that segregation violated American values, and that foreign aid should be less interventionist and rely more on local people. The jazz-musician-turned-government-bureaucrat even quoted Camus to Nixon at Christmas: "In the midst of winter I found that there was in me an invincible summer."[21] Blatchford actually deserved credit for revising obsolete procedures and insisting that the organization strive to fulfill its potential to help struggling nations.

Blatchford's New Directions did not satisfy Richard Nixon, however. Within the space of a year, and without telling his appointee, the president decided to eliminate the Peace Corps. At first Nixon contented himself with cutting back the Washington staff. Through Henry Kissinger the president conveyed a formal request in July 1969 that the administrative staff be reduced by one-third. Blatchford agreed with Nixon that there was waste in the Peace Corps budget, and had already set such a goal. A few months later, the president met with Blatchford personally and, according to minutes of the meeting, told him "to keep on cutting, to get more young men like Mr. Blatchford, and to 'get rid of the other sort.'"[22]

In the winter of 1970 Nixon decided that this was not enough. "You are . . . to go to work quietly to begin an effort to phase out the Peace Corps and Vista," the White House aide Lamar Alexander wrote Bryce Harlow, assistant to the president for congressional affairs, on March 26, 1970. "The best place to begin this effort, says the president, is to get an appropriations cut," Alexander reported.[23]

The secret directive came straight from the president, who had polled his closest aides and supporters in Congress on how to get away with it. "I would not counsel such drastic action," the speechwriter Pat Buchanan wrote Nixon a month earlier. "It would put us crosswise with a number of our friends who have swallowed the propaganda that this is the greatest thing since sliced bread," he said, adding "the Kennedyites would create a real storm." Senator Bob Dole, Buchanan reported, suggested a more indirect approach. Expose some "Peace Corps blunders," Dole had advised, and then turn "them over to our Republicans on the Hill to investigate." If the administration "leaked the blunders again and again," Buchanan pointed out, it might "create a climate of opinion that would receive the executive a little better." Still, the conservative speechwriter himself thought the president would get more political mileage, and risk less exposure, if he went after "the more offensive OEO operations" instead. Two weeks later Buchanan sent Nixon another memo detailing the antiwar activities of volunteers.[24]

A *Wall Street Journal* article on the Committee of Returned Volunteers that same month further alienated Nixon from the Peace Corps. A presidential aide, John Brown, told Ehrlichman and Kissinger that Nixon felt that disillusioned volunteers' rejection of "JFK idealism" as a form of imperialism was a "powerful problem" for the Corps. Like other assistants in subsequent memos, Brown relayed that the president wanted the agency phased out—"quietly."[25]

A dramatic protest that spring by the Committee of Returned Volunteers undoubtedly stiffened the president's resolve. In early May, Nixon announced that he had taken the war into Cambodia. Protesters turned out in record numbers, and National Guardsmen killed four student demonstrators at Kent State in Ohio and two at Jackson State in Mississippi. Four days later, CRV members distributed leaflets asking Blatchford's staff to go on strike in protest. When it became clear that they would not, CRV decided to occupy the Peace Corps headquarters. The morning of May 8, 1970, a small group of twelve CRV members burst into the fourth floor offices of the Southeast Asia division of the agency, escorted compliant staff members out, sealed off the wing, and hung a fifteen-foot Viet Cong flag out the window. Indignant staff members on the floor below hung out an American flag, while others on the floor above pulled in the Viet Cong flag through their own window with a nail-studded board. The fourth floor unfurled yet another Viet Cong banner. On the sidewalk below, a team of protesters started a picket line within sight of the White House. Using walkie-talkies, they communicated in Turkish with their comrades above.[26]

For the next thirty-six hours Blatchford staved off demands from the White House that he "bust the Peace Corps—get it rough." Blatchford later recalled that presidential aide Bob Haldeman and John Ehrlichman summoned him to the White House "three times, four times a day" to lobby him to eject the protesters forcibly. Blatchford kept telling them that he had one plan, then another, then another—anything to avoid an open and possibly bloody confrontation. Recalling the 1968 Democratic Convention in Chicago, infamous for its violence, Blatchford believed that such a confrontation would spell disaster for the Peace Corps on both the political right and the left. His common sense paid off. After a day and a half, the demonstrators quietly slipped out.

John Ehrlichman called shortly thereafter to give Blatchford a direct order to throw out the protesters. "They left," Blatchford informed him. "Why did they leave?" the startled aide asked. Blatchford replied, "John, I don't know. They didn't call and tell me good-bye."[27]

Although Ehrlichman complimented Blatchford on his cool approach, it may have been that the White House would have been equally pleased to see the Peace Corps shoot itself in the foot. Getting the public to equate his opponents with extremism was a typical Nixon ploy, dating back to his campaigns for public office during the McCarthy era. In minutes of conversations with the president soon after the aborted occupation of the Peace Corps, Haldeman recorded that Republicans must "polarize the electorate" if they were to win future elections. Sensing the distressed temper of the American public and correctly perceiving that there were now "more votes on the Conservative side," Nixon told his chief of staff that Republicans needed to force their opponents to the left and "put the opponent on the side of being for the protester, and our guy against them, don't let up on this."[28]

Nixon meanwhile constructed a careful timetable for dismantling the Peace Corps. In July 1970, the president instructed Bob Haldeman to keep Bryce Harlow on the task and get the Peace Corps and VISTA "chopped per the president's instructions." He also asked Haldeman to make other key staff understand "that this has to be done and has to be done now . . . We can't do it just before the '72 elections and we have to do it after November 1970," when congressional elections would be held. Haldeman instructed subordinates to cut the agencies by one-third to start. It would have to be done at a strategic moment, when voters could not hold the administration responsible.[29] In his diary Haldeman noted that the president wanted to cut the organizations' budgets "down far enough to decimate them."[30]

The president's henchmen kept to schedule. Two months after the November 1970 elections, in January 1971, Joseph Blatchford received the proposed federal budget for the coming fiscal year. To his surprise, the executive Office of Management and Budget (OMB) had cut the number of volunteers from 9,000 to 5,800 and reduced the agency budget from $90 million to $60 million. Blatchford was especially taken aback because only two weeks earlier the president had given a speech to students at the University of Nebraska in which he had urged them to commit to the idea of personal service. Nixon used the occasion to propose a merger of Peace Corps, VISTA, Foster Grandparents, and all other volunteer programs into one agency. The administration had already reorganized several agencies under the Executive Branch, and the president claimed that this move would more efficiently enlist "the dedication and idealism of those young Americans who want to serve their fellow man." This speech constituted another surprise for Joseph Blatchford, who had earlier made known his opposition to combining Peace Corps with the other volunteer agencies.[31]

Blatchford dashed off two memos on the same day to John Ehrlichman, who assisted the president on domestic affairs. "This must be a bold, affirmative new program," Blatchford wrote, indicating an eagerness to get in line behind the president now that Nixon had announced his intent formally. The director warned, however, that some cynics were poised to condemn the merger "as a disguised burial for existing programs." The report from the Office of Management and Budget would confirm "this negative diagnosis," Blatchford told Ehrlichman, who of course was aware of the presidential directives that the agency director had never seen. Perhaps with his own suspicions—not about Nixon but about the OMB—Blatchford added, "It will be quite evident to most Congressmen and to the public that the president's expansion of service opportunities has begun with a 30 percent cut over last year's request for the largest of the merged agencies." The director pleaded with Ehrlichman for the preservation of the Peace Corps at its current budget level, as well as decisive action by the president to get the new agency rolling.[32]

Congressmen certainly did perceive the president's deeper intent, and at least one of them was quite happy. "If I had to meet my Maker in three minutes and the last decision the Good Lord would let me make . . . it would be to abolish the Peace Corps," the conservative Democrat Otto Passman said during budget hearings the year before. The Louisiana congressman had opposed the agency since 1961. Unable to foil the original Peace Corps Act, Passman kept what pressure he could on the agency as chair of the House Subcommittee on Appropriations. When Jack Vaughn was Peace Corps director, Passman condemned Vaughn during public hearings for not pulling out antiwar volunteers "by the nape of the neck" as he would have done. "I was shocked to hear them expressing themselves vocally in opposition to our Vietnam policy," Passman said. "I would not do that any more than I would shoot my brains out."[33]

The year 1971 presented one trial after another for the Peace Corps. Opposition to the president's plans gathered force quickly. Eighty-seven organizations objected to the merger, including every group of volunteers and former volunteers from the Peace Corps and VISTA. At congressional hearings they testified extensively that the plan would destroy the distinctive identities of both organizations. Blatchford enthusiastically endorsed the new agency, called ACTION, unwilling perhaps to question too strongly any plan of the president, whom he thought supported the Peace Corps. Blatchford also believed that combining the Peace Corps with domestic programs might shield it from critics of foreign aid and add VISTA supporters to its constituency. The Peace Corps was isolated and vulnerable, Blatchford rationalized, and "would survive better under ACTION." Congress stalled, though, and did not pass legislation confirming Nixon's executive decision until July 1973—six months after Blatchford had resigned, having headed the unauthorized agency for more than a year.[34]

Congress also delayed passing a Peace Corps appropriation until halfway into the 1972 fiscal year. Otto Passman, charged with meeting the president's defense requests, told Henry Kissinger to "shut up the Peace Corps guys" who kept lobbying for a better budget. Once again Blatchford had to fight to keep the agency from going under.[35]

In February 1972, the House-Senate Conference Committee announced a compromise appropriation for the Peace Corps of $72 million dollars. Because the agency had already recruited and fielded volunteers on the basis of a $90 million budget, this meant it had to make severe cuts immediately. Blatchford first reduced salaries and nonpersonnel expenses, but ultimately found he had to delete another $5 million from the budget by June. Tired of the constant erosion of the Peace Corps' position, he went to the Congress and to the press and played his own kind of hardball. Blatchford announced that 2,313 Peace Corps volunteers, stationed in thirty-three countries, were being recalled. He did not have to spell out that their removal would be an international embarrassment of enormous proportions. Blatchford cleared the diplomatic cables with the State Department and arranged to send them at one minute past midnight on March 7. Volunteers were ordered to return home by April first.

"This country probably needs the Peace Corps as much, or more, than those countries in which corpsman are in action," the *Boston Globe* editorialized. "The United States needs to believe that it is not the murderous ogre depicted by its enemies. There is another side to the story, and the Peace Corps is one of the best ways of telling it, at home and overseas." Fittingly, the *Globe* commented, the administration planned to bring volunteers home on April Fools' Day. Otto Passman, unwilling to be made to look bad as chair of the appropriations committee, came through on the day the cables were to be sent with an offer to find extra funds. He called Blatchford and told him to take the heat off, but also warned the director, in effect, "You don't have as many friends in the White House as you think." Richard Nixon, unwilling perhaps to look worse than Otto Passman, came up with an identical offer out of his own budget three days later, canceling out Passman's.[36]

Blatchford never suspected that his problems originated in the Oval Office. He remained convinced that the president was a friend to him as well as the Peace Corps. Nixon played a role for the Peace Corps director as he did for nearly everyone. His aide William Safire said that the president could "don a personality by opening a door." His biographer Stephen Ambrose notes that it was "a mark of how many different Nixon personas there were that when the transcripts of the Nixon-Haldeman-Ehrlichman-Mitchell conversations were made public, many men who had had intimate contact with Nixon over long periods of time . . . were shocked. *They* had never heard Nixon talk like that."[37] Joseph Blatchford was among them.

Three months after the Peace Corps budget crisis, on June 17, 1972, police at the Watergate office building arrested five men equipped with cameras and electronic listening devices. For the next two years, Richard Nixon waged a losing battle against charges of corruption that led to the resignation of Vice President Agnew, the indictment and conviction of Bob Haldeman and John Ehrlichman, and finally to the resignation of the president himself. Richard Nixon's political career, including his back-door campaign against the Peace Corps, was over.

Like Lyndon Johnson, Nixon believed that young Americans ought to get out and know the peoples of the third world, many of whom, though desperately poor, "had a dignity and grace which was very moving."[38] But while raised as a Quaker and capable of rhetoric about spiritual values, Nixon never managed to make it sound authentic. The thirty-seventh president oozed realpolitik. Together with Henry Kissinger, Nixon pragmatically sought in the 1969 doctrine that bore his name to rein in American commitments abroad. Foreign interventionism on too broad a scale threatened the nation's power. The Vietnam War was a classic example, and Nixon tried unsuccessfully to diminish U.S. involvement in it by substituting South Vietnamese soldiers for American ones. Through détente with China and Russia, the president also labored to create a more stable world system that would not call as frequently on the resources of the United States to enforce peace. Even so, the expenses of war had already drained the U.S. economy, and Nixon abandoned the gold standard in 1971. The unparalleled economic strength and global approbation that had pushed Americans outward in 1961 were gone. Economic strain and worldwide disapproval now pulled them back. Idealism and interventionism cooled together.

Richard Nixon likely saw little place in his plans for a warm and fuzzy Peace Corps spreading goodwill throughout the world. If it could not fulfill a specific foreign policy function that gained the United States an advantage in the world, it should be "chopped." It was the president's way, because of his own lack of moral character, to do so conspiratorially. Stephen Ambrose notes that Nixon explicitly rejected virtue as a quality of great leadership. He rejected it for himself, and he could not respect it in others. It is hardly surprising that the president failed to appreciate the significance of a program whose meaning, at heart, was the inculcation of civic virtue.[39]

The cynicism wrought by the Watergate scandal, by Gerald Ford's pardon of Nixon, and by all the fruitless sacrifice of the Vietnam War seeped deeply into American life in the 1970s. The harm was done. Together with a new cautiousness about foreign adventures, this cynicism meant that the number of volunteers in the Peace Corps drifted incrementally downward through the 1970s and 1980s, hitting an all-time low of 5,219 in 1987. And yet Americans of both political parties continued to volunteer, convinced, as Lyndon Johnson had said at the end of his own career, that to do so expressed "faith in the American future." To most Peace Corps veterans, especially those who had come through the trials of the 1960s and early 1970s, it also confirmed their faith in at least one aspect of America's immediate past.

9
The Peace Corps Dilemma

———— ✻ ————

To many people, volunteer service is a suspiciously romantic,
unrealistic notion. But is it unrealistic . . . to recognize that the war
of development is a peoples' war, and that it has to be fought by the
people at the level of the people? And that the army that will win
such a war cannot be composed of officers only?

MICHAEL VON SCHENCK,
INTERNATIONAL SECRETARIAT FOR VOLUNTEER SERVICE,
GENEVA, 1969

The Peace Corps did not suffer confusion and disillusionment alone. It
remained part of a larger global movement of volunteers. Many of the
choices it faced after the sixties were shared by others, even though
perhaps only in the United States did these choices touch so painfully
on questions of national identity. Between the 1970s and the 1990s, all
volunteer service agencies came to a critical turn in the path that they
had followed together. The directions they went divided volunteer
groups into two camps with basic differences about the meaning of
development and the role of the West in promoting it.

In its own way, every volunteer group had to answer several fundamental questions, and place its emphasis on one or the other side of
certain dichotomies. Did it exist mainly to enable one nation to live out
its own values or to provoke other nations to change theirs? Was it a
school for citizens or a temporary agency for technical experts? Was it a
witness to the efforts of developing nations or a catalyst for their
transformation? Was it a means of demonstrating human solidarity with
the trials of others, or a means of implementing solutions? Were volunteers idealists or realists? Were they offering love or knowledge?

The volunteer was the pivot on which these questions turned. The Canadian, Dutch, and German organizations eventually stopped using what they had called "volunteers." The word implied human solidarity for its own sake, and they had come to the conclusion that this was not only *not* sufficient to produce development, but that it dishonestly substituted sentiment for solutions. The Americans, British, French, Japanese, and Australians maintained their commitment to the volunteer idea. For their own reasons, they were not willing to part with the idea of altruism as having a function in its own right. The histories of the American and British programs on the one hand, and the Canadian and Dutch on the other, demonstrate most clearly the alternative ways that social activism survived the 1960s—and the absence of easy answers to the question of how to "save" all those whom the Beatles and other sixties troubadors had said could be saved by "Love."

As a vehicle for American ideals, the Peace Corps traveled a particularly bumpy road. Now mistrustful of their own earlier altruism and of the global interventionism with which it had been intertwined, U.S. citizens looked hard at the Peace Corps if they took an interest in it at all. The organization struggled to prove that it was not merely high-minded, even though that may have been its best reason for being. And yet the Peace Corps ultimately refused to reject as "totally ludicrous," in the words of one returned volunteer, "the notion that any kind of social change can occur through the efforts of naive, well-intentioned American college kids."[1]

The number of Peace Corps volunteers hovered between 5,000 and 6,000 per year from the 1970s through the 1990s, reflecting the ambivalence of Americans about their world role. But even with its smaller numbers it continued to be the largest of the volunteer sending organizations. By the early 1990s, for example, VSO had 20,000 returned volunteers, the German DED had 10,000, and the Australian program had 2,200—compared with more than 140,000 returned Americans. The age of volunteers went up gradually, and the ratio of men to women achieved rough parity again after 1973. The Peace Corps continued to work on improving the quality of its recruits and the specificity of their assignments.

The organization became a fixture in Washington, attracting neither much good nor much bad attention in the 1970s as it suffered through six directors in nine years. Each director had to respond as much to the shifting fortunes of political patronage as to the constantly evolving development debate that took place in forums like the United Nations and the World Bank. When Jimmy Carter came into office in 1976, many Peace Corps supporters saw the election of a Democrat as an opportunity to recapture the organization's heyday. Carter sent shock waves through Washington by appointing the former radical activist Sam Brown to head ACTION. Brown had first made a national name for himself during the Vietnam moratoriums, and then eased into electoral politics as treasurer of Colorado. His appointment appeared a direct repudiation of the Nixon-Ford years.

But Brown had much less interest in the Peace Corps than in the domestic volunteer programs. He made no effort to restore the Peace Corps's autonomy (which would have diminished the size of his own agency), instead arguing that it was time to work "within the system." He waited five months to appoint a director for the Peace Corps (the first woman and first minority), and then ignored her counsel. Brown brought a leftist critique of the Peace Corps. He vowed to rid the agency of its cultural imperialism. An editor of the *Washington Monthly,* a magazine run by the former Peace Corps evaluator Charles Peters, observed that the liberal Peace Corps was an easy target: "the proudest creation of the generation people like Brown were dedicated to unseating from power and influence."[2]

Specifically, Brown insisted that all English-language programs be replaced with ones focusing on "Basic Human Needs" as defined by new World Bank policies that also influenced other volunteer agencies. The Peace Corps director he appointed, Carolyn Payton, agreed with him that development should start at the grass roots, be sustainable, and attack fundamental problems such as overpopulation, unsafe water, inadequate crops, and disease. The Peace Corps had always had these goals. But as a former country director who knew far more than Brown about the third world, Payton could not accept that teaching had no place in the Peace Corps. To Brown it was "non-negotiable," however, even though many countries, especially African ones, continued to press the Peace Corps for teachers. Country directors were reduced to bargaining. "I used to tell the government ministers, 'If you let me bring in five skill-trained volunteers, I'll get you ten more English teachers,'" the director for Kenya and Swaziland later recalled.[3]

Sam Brown subsequently announced that the Peace Corps would only work in the poorest of the poor countries, based on GNP. The policy ignored the distribution of wealth in these developing countries, all of which had severe regional poverty. Then Brown went even further and announced that the Corps would pull out, rather than phase out, of countries that did not meet *its* criteria for aid. (Under Shriver, Vaughn, and Blatchford, any country could receive volunteers.) The Peace Corps sent cables to directors in countries like Brazil, Côte d'Ivoire, and Malaysia telling them to close down. After only a year on the job, Carolyn Payton resigned in protest over Brown's unilateral moves. "Whether or not we could find satisfactory jobs for volunteers was a better criterion than how much money a country has . . . It's offensive to me to tell a host country what their needs are," she commented later.[4]

Sam Brown's ideological rigidity aside, at base of the Peace Corps dilemma was a continuing tension over the primary purpose of the program. In the pragmatic seventies, Peace Corps staff worried whether the organization should be expected to demonstrate a measurable impact on, say, the calorie-intake or pure-water quotient of a population, or if it should simply be expected to offer a good day's work in the service of another nation that had asked for help from America. Some staff recognized that, considering the extreme difficulty under which many volunteers labored (such as when villagers resisted planting trees to prevent deforestation because "Allah plants the trees"), it was not always reasonable to exact specific measures.[5]

Loret Miller Ruppe, a moderate Republican and friend of George Bush, pulled the Peace Corps out of its doldrums in the 1980s. Director for eight years, she served longer than any other head of the Peace Corps. Like Shriver, Ruppe made her political mark first as an astute party campaigner, and she brought these finely honed skills at a time when the Peace Corps badly needed them. Her Republican credentials were impeccable. Ruppe resold the Peace Corps to Congress, managing to overturn cuts requested by President Ronald Reagan's slash-and-burn budget director, David Stockman. Like Joseph Blatchford, Ruppe played heavily to her conservative constituency, telling the president's Bi-Partisan Commission on Central America that far from being sixties-type hippies, the volunteers of the eighties were "older and better-trained, with a higher percentage highly skilled." At the same time, borrowing from Shriver, she emphasized that volunteers showed the world a moral America. "They show something better than 'Dallas,' 'Miami Vice,' and 'Dynasty.'"[6]

Ruppe told Congress and the press that America should commit to fielding 10,000 volunteers overseas, and used her charisma and persona of maternal decency to shame anyone who dared dismiss America's volunteer tradition. When the White House liaison to the Peace Corps boasted at their first meeting that he had recommended abolishing the agency, she shook his hand politely and said, "I guess I'll have to request another liaison." Heiress to the Miller brewing fortune, Ruppe was deeply influenced by her mother, who had been a socialist and peace activist before dying young. "Loret was the most rational, most middle-of-the-road director since Shriver," said one country director who served during both the Carter and the Reagan administrations. "She cared about the Peace Corps first and that was her only agenda."[7]

Ruppe nonetheless recognized that she had to please her president. Under her directorship, the Peace Corps started a new division called Small Enterprise Development, sent high numbers of volunteers to Grenada and Central America, raised funds from U.S. corporations for Peace Corps projects, and once again lectured recruits on the evils of communism. The results were mixed. Ruppe was accused by some of prostituting the Peace Corps for conservative Republicans, and so many volunteers roared with laughter at the clichés in a new anticommunist training film that it had to be shelved.[8]

But Ruppe's moves also responded to the gradual rehabilitation of capitalism in the eyes of most liberals in the 1980s, as the economic weaknesses of state-run enterprises became apparent throughout the world. The international debt crisis further confirmed a trend that led many development agencies to place new emphasis on the creation of micro-businesses among the poor in the third world rather than on massive projects that ran up more private or government debt. Peace Corps volunteers, many with bachelor degrees in business (the most popular undergraduate major in the 1980s), consulted with artisans and other fledgling entrepreneurs on marketing, accounting, and production. Ruppe also developed a strong alliance with returned volunteers. "We are all in this together," she told veterans at the twenty-fifth

anniversary celebration in 1986. "You returned Peace Corps volunteers
. . . trod the path of peace once in a distant land. Now I must ask you
to tread it again."[9]

Ruppe reached out as well to the diplomatic community in an effort
to demonstrate to the president that the Peace Corps served U.S.
foreign policy goals. In a special report prepared by Ruppe and sent by
Secretary of State George Schultz, the Peace Corps reported that ambassadors from twenty developing nations agreed that the Peace Corps
presence was invaluable. The Peace Corps provided useful, appropriate
assistance and served as a bridge to nations to which the United States
could otherwise give little attention because of higher priorities elsewhere.

"In my judgment there is no U.S. overseas program that yields as
much return for the taxpayers' dollar as the Peace Corps," the ambassador from Kenya commented. "There is hardly a Tunisian in the twenty
to forty age bracket who has not had some contact with a PCV, and the
cumulative impact has been overwhelmingly positive," the ambassador
there reported. "The Peace Corps plays a central role in the U.S. effort
to bridge the chasm between what we can offer Mauritania and what
Mauritania can absorb," noted another ambassador, emphasizing that
weak national institutions meant that development support was best
transmitted "person-to-person." The ambassador to Paraguay commented that "the payoff in goodwill is extraordinarily high." Volunteers, he added, made their strongest contribution to U.S. foreign
policy by earning the respect not only of government officials but of
opposition groups and people at the grass-roots.[10]

The Reagan administration nevertheless gave only lukewarm support
to Ruppe's endeavors, and she went out on a limb more than once to
overturn its policies. In 1981 long-standing legislative efforts to separate Peace Corps from ACTION came to fruition. The collaboration
had never been smooth: ACTION directors had squelched even the
Peace Corps name, leading Sargent Shriver to comment that the "Peace
Corps isn't even listed in the telephone book anymore."[11] The White
House decided to oppose the bill. Ruppe lobbied hard for the legislation, efforts that led the arch-conservative Heritage Foundation to
criticize her as having done little to implement "the Reagan agenda."[12]
Ruppe laid her political reputation on the line partly because the president had appointed a former army intelligence officer, Thomas Pauken,

as head of ACTION—a direct violation of the traditional Peace Corps prohibitions on any connection to intelligence gathering. Congress supported Ruppe, and ten years after one Republican led the Peace Corps into ACTION, another Republican led it out. On February 22, 1982, the Peace Corps was reestablished as a separate agency under the Department of State.

The Peace Corps stepped back into genuine if fleeting prominence in the late 1980s when the cold war came to an end. Once again, it assumed its role as first-point-of-contact between "decolonizing" nations and the West. President George Bush asked Peace Corps volunteers holding the flags of more than sixty nations to march in his inaugural parade, and proudly announced during a July 1989 trip to Budapest that Peace Corps volunteers would leave soon for Hungary, the first Eastern European country to request them. Poland also requested volunteers. By the early 1990s it had the largest Peace Corps program in the world.

Volunteers in the three Eastern European countries rimming the West (Poland, Hungary, and Czechoslovakia) concentrated most heavily on English-language instruction, reflecting the heavy demand for this assistance from nations eager to reenter the Western orbit of commerce and ideas. A smaller number came as business advisors. In Romania, volunteers were assigned to orphanages that had moved the world to outrage after the fall of Nicolai Ceauşescu, and in Bulgaria volunteers concentrated in business and agricultural extension.[13] President Bush gave the volunteers a send-off in the White House Rose Garden, last used for that purpose by John F. Kennedy.

In 1992 volunteers went to the Ukraine and, in a supreme irony, one hundred business volunteers departed for Russia. American bankers, store owners, and salesmen, along with teachers of English, spread out across the steppes. Ron Seibel, a former marine turned businessman, started a class using Dale Carnegie techniques to show Kazaks how to turn "*nyet* profit into net profit." Joyce Elferdink, a banker, encountered resistance when she criticized the banking system that offered loans at 200 percent interest over a three-month term, but found an opening when she offered to help compile databases on local businesses. English teachers discovered, as always, that to their students they were "America in the flesh." In the former Soviet Union, where the United States had long been an object of deep fear, putting these fears to rest was particularly poignant for volunteers.[14] By 1993 a tiny contingent of teachers had left for China. The cold war was over—and the Peace Corps had survived with the concept of volunteering more or less intact.

Britain's VSO, refusing to be "hijacked" (as one veteran staffer put it) by development fads that valued technical experts over volunteers, also held tightly to the concept of volunteering that it had begun with in 1958. A private organization that received 75 percent of its funds from the British Overseas Development Agency, VSO's conservative internal structure helped it to retain this vision. Prince Philip acted continuously as patron of VSO from 1961 onward. By 1997 the organization had had only six directors in almost forty years, all of whom strongly supported volunteering as a British cultural value. When returned volunteers in the seventies formed their own organization, Returned Volunteer Action, VSO marginalized the input of radicals who considered the organization "unbearably stuffy." It also continued sending English-language teachers abroad when requested, like the Peace Corps but unlike any of the other British Commonwealth volunteer programs.[15]

The British commitment to volunteering, as a good in its own right, stemmed from the nation's deepest traditions. Inventors of the Boy Scouts and Outward Bound, the British had long grappled with the imperative of shaping useful citizens. From the outset, VSO comfortably acknowledged that volunteers got as much as they gave. But the organizations' leaders also stoutly maintained that volunteers offered qualities simply not found in professional development workers. Volunteers exuded a faith and optimism not as readily evident in experts—provided by many other agencies anyway—and were more willing to participate in the life of the entire community. Dick Bird, a VSO staff member in the 1990s, commented that with volunteers "you get someone who is there because they want to be there . . . Conditions in the third world need putting up with." One VSO volunteer, expecting her successor, made a similar point when she wrote to London: "Please send someone with a sense of humour, someone who won't mind having a go at anything from hair-cutting and burying pigs which are bad to helping in the dispensary—in fact almost anything."[16]

Notably, the British were not the only Europeans who believed that volunteers provided an especially useful work force. The French Ministry of Cooperation strongly endorsed the work of volunteers, who one spokesman noted were willing to do the hardest work and came with fewer personal restrictions than professional staff. Volunteers also brought back to France an "international conscience" that the nation valued.[17]

In the 1970s the British Ministry of Overseas Development under the leadership of Judith Hart pushed VSO to examine more closely the development strategies then being touted by the World Bank. Like other volunteer agencies in that decade, including the Peace Corps under Blatchford, VSO came to emphasize "qualified, experienced individuals, able to provide the specific skills needed by communities in the developing world." The age of volunteers went up correspondingly, and by the 1990s VSO had earned a reputation for people who were somewhat older and more job-ready than their American counterparts.[18]

Yet VSO never dropped the notion of volunteering for its own sake. "We remained like the British are, restrained and conservative," Dick Bird noted. Alec Dickson himself sounded a prophetic note in 1970 in a speech at Yorkshire that Joseph Blatchford kept on file. "Pulses may beat faster when Saul Alinsky exhorts us 'to rub raw the sores of discontent.' But not all may be able, or want, to sustain these abrasive roles indefinitely." Volunteer organizations, Dickson cautioned, would do well not to polarize "caring" and "confrontation."[19]

And so VSO refused to be drawn into the unruly debates that transformed other programs, and even looked askance at the turmoil which threatened the Peace Corps. "The present travail of American society," the VSO historian Michael Adams wrote at the end of the sixties, "where the most advanced, the richest, the most highly developed social organism the world has yet seen finds itself threatened with disruption from within, is surely a lesson which none of us can disregard." Liberal idealism remained at the core of VSO's philosophy through the 1990s and echoed in the gentle phrasing of its advertising, which used words like "disadvantage" rather than "oppression," and "friendship" rather than "social change."[20]

In Canada and Holland, however, volunteer programs followed a political trajectory that shot them to the left of where they had started. Each took a far less benign view of its nation's place in the global economic system than did the British or Americans. Because of

CUSO's decentralized structure, returned volunteers and domestic activists had a larger say in it than in any other comparable organization.
CUSO received up to 90 percent of its funding from the Canadian
government, but maintained its status as a private, nonprofit organization. Thus CUSO could always claim that it had no connection to
Canadian foreign policy. Nearly every supporter of CUSO believed that
this gave CUSO, as one of its first directors said, "definite advantages"
over the Peace Corps. Paul Martin, the head of the International Development Agency, concurred: "It is from its voluntary and non-govern-
mental character that CUSO gets its spirit and its impetus, and we must
do everything to make sure that this spirit and this impetus remain
undiminished."[21]

As the 1960s turned into the 1970s, CUSO underwent a series of
ideological transformations unrestrained by the Canadian electorate.
The Peace Corps had to conform to each incoming presidential administration, no matter how conservative or liberal. CUSO, however, could
maintain a separate vision. Returned volunteers whose anger at poverty
had been sharpened by leftist critiques and time abroad increasingly
influenced this vision. Murray Thomson, CUSO director from 1973 to
1976, encouraged a growing commitment to participatory democracy
in the organization through which this anger could be aired and placed
in practice. "Development is our business and development is disturbance; disturbance to ourselves and our organization," Murray wrote
shortly before taking office. "It means trying to define, isolate and
attack obstacles, barriers, roadblocks to real development: trade barriers, arms races, greedy multinational corporations, elites (including
ourselves) which are screwing up the process."[22]

One result, according to Ian Smillie, was that CUSO's annual general meetings "were no longer intimate gatherings of the founding
fathers, but large, brawling assemblies of returned volunteers, often
radicalized by their overseas experience and the apathy they found on
their return to Canada." At the same time, Murray Thomson continued
a trend started in the late sixties of greater emphasis on professional
skills, similar to that of Joseph Blatchford. The early CUSO motto "To
Serve and Learn" gave way to "Development Is Our Business." The
term "volunteer" fell slowly into disfavor, supplanted by the French
word "cooperant." Young people serving as teachers and nurses (typical

colonial missionary roles) came to understand that newer CUSO staff viewed them as the problem, rather than as part of the solution. Regional staff and a handful of guilt-stricken cooperants voted in the early seventies to close large programs in Malawi and Zambia. In 1980, in a gesture symbolic of its rejection of youthful "do-gooderism," CUSO formally adopted its acronym as its name—no longer Canadian University Service Overseas.[23]

Not everyone took these changes with equanimity. Factionalism tore into CUSO in the 1970s. The national debate over Quebec's autonomy had its parallel in the volunteer organization, culminating in a headquarters cut in half by a bank of filing cabinets running like a Berlin Wall between the English and French sectors. The two formally split in 1980, after many years of the French division calling the Anglo one racist and paternalistic. Meanwhile, CUSO itself frequently aimed the same accusations of paternalism at its own superiors in the government, including CUSO's founder Lewis Perinbam, then a vice president of the Canadian International Development Agency. Like Sargent Shriver in OEO, Perinbam found himself derided by the very people he had helped organize.[24]

Other Canadians sometimes expressed chagrin at the antivolunteer attitude growing in CUSO as staff sought to wring greater technical accomplishments from the development process. Instead of recruiting volunteers, CUSO began advertising specific jobs to be filled. In the early 1990s the average age of cooperants rose to thirty-eight, compared with twenty-nine in the United States and thirty-three in Britain. "CUSO is always eager to provide evidence that the average age of its cooperant population is rising. What was wrong with being young?" one Nigerian volunteer asked in 1984. "What was wrong with being 'a keen idealist filled with romantic notions of saving the world?'"[25]

What was wrong was liberalism itself. CUSO rejected the liberal economic view of development that had inspired the founders of all the Western volunteer programs. The only honest way to promote development, they thought, was to commit to overturning that system, both in Canada and in the third world. In 1975, for example, the CUSO Board of Directors voted financial support for the reconstruction of North and South Vietnam and to expose the profits made from the war by Canadian companies. Hugh Heclo notes that movements of the sixties in the United States "rejected not conservatives but the liberal consensus and its institutional structures." This attack was carried on throughout the West.[26]

In Holland, individuals at the top of the political hierarchy began the assault. The elections of 1972 brought the Socialist Party to power in Holland for the first time since World War II. Jan Pronk, a leftist social democrat, became minister for development cooperation. According to Will Erath, director of the Dutch volunteer program SNV from 1968 to 1975, Pronk drew inspiration from types as diametrically opposed as Mao Zedong and Robert McNamara (then head of the World Bank and architect of the emphasis on the "poorest of the poor"). Pronk helped develop and pass the government target of 1.5 percent of net national income for development aid, which was still in effect in the 1990s. Pronk also brought former volunteers onto the board of SNV in the name of democratization and helped broaden the types of volunteers recruited.[27]

Prior to Jan Pronk's intervention, SNV was allowed by the Dutch government to recruit only noncollege graduates to fill what the Puerto Rico conference of 1962 had dubbed "middle manpower" needs. Until the early 1970s, the relatively apolitical character of this group of lower-middle-class young people protected SNV "from getting at loggerheads with the Netherlands government," Will Erath later noted. Neither the government nor the receiving countries wanted university "radicals from Northern Europe." But Pronk, believing that one needed allies among the young whose social conscience had been stirred to action, hoped to involve precisely these types of individuals. Pronk acknowledged that, in effect, volunteer agencies asserted for themselves the "right to intervene if, in our view, the distribution of income, wealth and power within a developing country is too unequal." This intervention in others' countries could be justified only if volunteers were also willing to change "those structures within the rich countries which at present form the main bottleneck to the development of the third world."[28] Of course, the minister's emphasis on economic redistribution fit his political party's plans for Dutch society as a whole.

Pronk also supported the move within SNV to professionalize the staff so that they could better attack sophisticated problems. Over the decade of the seventies SNV gradually raised salaries until they could support a development worker plus his or her family in relative comfort, lengthened the terms of service, and required specific expertise for jobs abroad which often lasted as long as six years. Like CUSO, SNV formally dropped the term "volunteer" in 1985.[29]

This transformation came at what seemed a high price to some. Both Will Erath and Bert Barten, president of SNV from 1980 to 1989, later rued the radicalization over which they had helped preside. (Barten was a former garage mechanic and volunteer who took over as president of the board in 1980 from Prince Claus in one of the many attempts to break down the authoritarian tendencies of Dutch life—SNV's own version of maximum feasible participation.) Erath and Barten especially worried about using development workers to promote social change and unrest abroad. "It's putting too much responsibility on weak shoulders," Erath later asserted. Barten worried that "sending people with more and more education in higher and higher positions" inadvertently re-created colonial roles in which foreigners told host nationals how to run their countries. "You cannot develop other countries," Barten concluded; you could at best show solidarity with them.[30]

The SNV veterans who prevailed, however, believed that human service simply was not enough. By the 1980s many third world countries had sufficient numbers of middle-level workers, but often too few jobs for them. These nations did not need similarly skilled Westerners practicing "solidarity" with them. Living at the level of local people might give volunteers the satisfaction of an "idealistic ideal of solidarity," but it wasted time and talents that could be more strategically deployed. Ton Nijzink, the staff historian of SNV, noted that the organization was especially eager to disassociate itself from the image of immature, "frivolous" volunteers—like those of the Peace Corps. And so SNV sought to forge a harder wedge of activist professionals to cleave class structures at home and abroad.[31] As they veered to the left, both the Canadian and Dutch organizations implicitly rejected emotional idealism in favor of a sharply cognitive outlook that accepted realpolitik as the best description for how the world worked.

In spite of their split over the use of volunteers, the Peace Corps, VSO, CUSO, SNV, and other groups like them remained united in the 1990s by one overarching value—and lesson—which all had drawn from the sixties, even though they applied it in different ways. All persisted in the commitment to fostering participatory democracy, including the maximum feasible participation of poor people in their own development. "The emphasis is always on human development, self-improvement, local answers to local problems, and the substantive involvement of beneficiaries in the process of their own development," the U.S. ambassador to Paraguay wrote, using terms that any volunteer agency would have wanted applied to itself. The "Peace Corps is helpful in that volunteers are constantly setting examples and showing the way for democratic decision-making and joint problem-solving at the grass-roots level," he added.[32] Although it arose from sixties antiauthoritarianism, participatory democracy gradually became grounded in the notion of "sustainable development."

Concern for sustainable development deeply shaped the ideology of foreign aid in the 1990s from the World Bank and United Nations on down. Poor countries took up the banner, too. The president of Bolivia, who won wide admiration for his effective restructuring of government expenditures, created a system that sent 20 percent of revenues back to the municipalities to run their own services and for the first time gave an annual income to people over age sixty-five. The president placed the responsibility for health, roads, education, irrigation, and the stimulation of micro businesses at the local level, where the people could identify and meet their own needs. "Our whole administration is based on the principle that the people know best how to use the money, especially for the poor," Gonzalo Sanchez de Lozada told an American newspaper in 1997. Bolivia had not solved the problems of poverty, but its most promising methods were those that Peace Corps community organizers had struggled to introduce three decades earlier.[33]

By their very nature, volunteer-sending organizations had pioneered in sustainable development. They had never brought the funds, machinery, and advanced technology that developing countries found so hard to replace whenever rich country largesse dried up. "For forty-five years the major agencies have been doing the wrong thing," Peace Corps acting director Jack Hogan commented in the early 1990s. The largest foreign-aid institutions had barely begun to face the challenge, "How do you get people to accept some of the responsibilities for themselves?" Organizations like SNV phrased these ideas in sharper political tones ("the poor and the oppressed . . . target group must gain control of its own development"), but the message was essentially the same: power to the people.[34]

Oddly, though, after the Vietnam War the U.S. Peace Corps never fully recovered its sangfroid about volunteerism, especially when compared with the British or even the French agencies. The Peace Corps could still be successfully promoted by a director like Loret Ruppe as being as American as apple pie, but in the decades when animosity toward "big government" bloomed, it was perceptibly harder to square "volunteering" with federal expenditure.

In Britain, the government had cooperated with missionaries since the late 1600s when it sent them to convert renegade Protestant colonists in North America. Volunteering was embedded in Anglo-Saxon tradition. In addition, "doing the right thing" by the former colonies was part of the newer Commonwealth ideology and there existed a genuine sense of relatedness to poor countries that still claimed the same queen. For the French, who had no deep tradition of voluntarism or private philanthropy but who nonetheless retained a commitment to sending young people overseas through the 1990s, volunteering reflected the lessons of two world wars and modern colonial wars. Like the Germans, with whom they participated in many intra-European work camps, the French saw little alternative to human solidarity as a deterrent to destructive nationalisms.

For 60 percent of participants in Volontaires du Progrès (nearly all of the male volunteers), volunteering abroad also took the place of the national ten-month military requirement.[35] The French tradition of compulsory military service, dating back to Napoleon's citizen armies, had the effect of reinforcing programs like Volontaires du Progrès by linking them to the sacrosanct obligations of citizenship within the French Republic. Ironically, because of the French class system, only graduates of a handful of elite universities could obtain these coveted positions for substitute service. This made for a startling contrast with the Peace Corps, long associated with the rejection of privilege rather than the expression of it. But even so, the French appeared more confident in the rightness of volunteering as a good in itself than the many Americans who wondered into the 1990s if the Peace Corps did enough for development. Grasping for justifications of Peace Corps expenditures that could prove the agency's certifiable effectiveness as a development tool—and thus the *effect* of their altruism—many Americans overlooked the most important proposition of all. Perhaps training its own citizens as better servants of humanity was itself reason enough to send Americans abroad.

"We are in the least liked, least supported, least respected account in the . . . budget of the United States: Foreign Assistance—and Peace Corps is listed in that account under the grandiose title: Miscellaneous One," Ruppe observed in 1986.[36] But she showed that Congress and the American public could still be persuaded to support the Peace Corps, or at least could not quite bear to part with it. Like the idea of moral purpose in American foreign policy, it attracted admirers at the same time that it provoked their skepticism. Democratic ideals remained at the core of American identity. When these ideals weakened, identity and stability did so too. But many individuals also sensed that the exercise of these ideals, especially abroad, was connected in some way to the exercise of power. Unsure of what the connection meant, Americans did not know whether to celebrate or to forget John Kennedy's Peace Corps.

10

Balancing
Ideals and
Self-Interest

————— ❀ —————

The ancient phrases—"opportunity," "justice," "equality"—
seemed not ritualistic invocations, stock phrases from old
Independence Day orations, but guides to action.

RICHARD GOODWIN, *REMEMBERING AMERICA*

The Peace Corps was the first mass movement of young Americans in the 1960s. Although sponsored by their government, young people pressed John Kennedy for a Peace Corps and then volunteered for it. They made front-page news of what the *New York Times* later editorialized as the primary product of the sixties: a "morality-based politics that emphasized the individual's responsibility to speak out against injustice and corruption."[1]

How did that decade steal upon the world? The story of the Peace Corps reveals powerfully that the "sixties" was an event throughout the West triggered by global trends following World War II. One trend was the explicit arrival of mass society and, more specifically, the means of mass production and mass destruction. The gross national product of the United States quadrupled between 1940 and 1955. For the first time in human history, a majority of people in one of the largest countries on earth could have all of their needs and most of their desires met on demand. They paid for it with the knowledge that technology could obliterate them without notice.

The rebellion against mass society was deepest in America, but the rebellion had adherents throughout the West. In England, Alec and Mora Dickson worried over "the Welfare State that is Britain today." George Orwell wrote *1984,* inventing the term Big Brother. In France, Albert Camus pleaded poetically for the individual to take a stand against modern injustice, regardless of the outcome, regardless of impotence. In Italy, the novelist Alberto Moravia wrote the cautionary tale "The Conformist." In Germany, a nation nursed the deep wounds it had inflicted on itself and the world through its own form of mass regimentation. Out of this international consciousness came both the student movement against university authorities and the volunteer movement to experience the remaining preindustrial world *as* individuals.

The events and movements of the sixties also derived from the revolution in relations between whites and people of color between 1945 and 1959. The discovery of the Holocaust by the general public in 1945, the start of the cold war in 1947, and the decolonization of Asia and Africa between 1947 and 1960 combined to rend completely the tattered legitimacy of racism. In Australia this led to the reversal of the White Australia policy. For Britain this led to the expulsion of South Africa from the Commonwealth. In the United States this led to the implementation, at last, of constitutional amendments nearly one hundred years old. In all three countries there formed movements of young volunteers eager to become the nonracist women and men of the next generation. When these volunteers encountered resistance to their ideals, they sometimes sought more radical changes. They had learned from their parents and teachers, the World War II generation, that there should be no compromise with evil. The world entered the sixties.

Liberals made the initial critiques, whether they were writers like Paul Goodman, preachers like Martin Luther King, Jr., or politicians like John Kennedy. They believed in perfectibility, both moral and economic.[2] They demanded that America live up to its potential. But accomplishment could never equal potential. The demands grew and eventually spun far ahead of any administration's or movement's ability to deliver. To some extent, the leadership itself was to blame. Kennedy had the ability, reinforced by the sacrifice of his own life, to shame people for their selfishness. Johnson had the opposite effect: the more he gave, the more people wanted. Both men raised the ante, though, claiming in effect that America could be all things to all people. Like Sargent Shriver in the OEO, leading liberals did not insist *enough* that deep social change is usually gradual. But the compression of time brought about by rapid scientific advances and by catastrophic war in the twentieth century fooled nearly everyone. Kwame Nkrumah ordered a national school system in less than a year. Science demonstrated that anything could be perfected, and the cold war showed that it had to be. What else can account for John Kennedy's dubbing the sixties the Development Decade, as if hundreds of years of economic reality could be altered in ten?

Liberalism reaped the consequences of hubris when its extraordinary goals could not be met. Young people—who attributed failure to hypocrisy—heaped scorn upon their elders, and many turned to the left. Conservatives—who attributed failure to treason—won out in both the Democratic and the Republican parties. The middle of the road, once so wide, shrank. A smaller group of Peace Corps volunteers walked down it. Their experiences abroad schooled them to accept modest accomplishments, knowing they might never see the highest objectives to which they dedicated themselves. Collectively, they represented a little-seen seasoned liberalism. They shared this quality with volunteers from other liberal democratic nations.

When the sixties began, the preeminence of the United States was hardly questioned within the West and within the country. It seemed right for the nation to undertake the monumental tasks of world security and even world economic reform. Political and economic isolationism had been roundly discredited by World War II. Truman, Eisenhower, Kennedy, and Johnson all accepted the role of global banker and policeman, a role that represented an enormous expansion of U.S. power and responsibilities.

The country had gone through other cataclysmic periods of expansion. The Revolution doubled the nation's territory. The Civil War added no territory, but expanded the role of the federal government and confirmed its power over the states. World War I prompted the nation's first exercise of power in Europe, and World War II saw crushing displays of that power in both Germany and Japan. After 1945 the United States used its dollars backed by gold to reconstruct those nations, fight two wars in Asia, and build worldwide military alliances that ultimately squeezed dry its new enemy, the Soviet Union.

Alongside these periods in which the American government expanded its power, one can trace roughly corresponding peaks of social reform rhetoric and action. The Revolution gave rise to the Bill of Rights, the Civil War to the Emancipation Proclamation, World War I to the Fourteen Points, World War II to the Atlantic Charter, and the cold war to the Peace Corps and the sixties.

Founded explicitly on Enlightenment liberalism in 1776, the United

States has always had a relatively narrow ideological spectrum. Its government and people must rely heavily on one intellectual framework to explain the world and the United States' relationship to it. Liberalism, however, offers only weak justifications for the concentrated use of power, since historically it evolved from resistance to state monopoly of economic and political authority. Such justifications are in demand, however, when a great deal of blood and treasure must be sacrificed, and when the exercise of power may appear to tread on a cardinal rule of the nation's founding philosophy: the right of all peoples to self-government. In times like these, Americans appear to take solace in yet another Enlightenment doctrine, the belief in the innate goodness of humans. Translated into American English, this has meant the innate goodness of Americans and the innate goodness of their power. Thus when U.S. power has undergone periods of expansion, it has often been supported by an upswing in ambitious social reform. Americans have few other ways to justify power that are consistent with their comparatively homogeneous political culture, and they usually have not quite had the stomach to grab power openly for its own sake.

Idealism is a by-product of expansionist policies in a classically liberal nation. It is a sword that can cut both ways. When republican rhetoric simply palliates the American conscience by cloaking ambition, it subverts American ideals. But the "idealism" that accompanies an expansion of power is also sometimes grounded in a genuine attempt to use that power beneficently. In the Civil War Abraham Lincoln belatedly drew upon the ideals of abolition to explain the reasons for federal repression of states' rights—but draw upon them he did, with favorable consequences for humanity. In the 1960s, when John F. Kennedy pledged that the United States would "pay any price, bear any burden, meet any hardship, support any friend, oppose any foe to assure the survival and the success of liberty," the nation's people responded with the idealism to which their history had accustomed them. When the failed war in Vietnam made many of these same people suspect that the United States had intervened unjustly in another nation's civil conflict, the ability to sustain faith in America's good intentions all but collapsed.

The Vietnam War ended the blithe expansion of American overseas commitments. An internationally embarrassed United States withdrew in virtual defeat. Nixon curtailed U.S. responsibilities as world policeman, and subsequent presidents adjusted their ambitions to the constraints of the "Vietnam syndrome." The Peace Corps itself entered a decline that bottomed out in 1987. Suspicious of power, many Americans seemed suspicious of idealism as well. Either it was entirely false, or it had gotten the United States into the mess to begin with.

This post-Vietnam suspicion has found expression again and again. Numerous scholars have labored to show that U.S. presidents in the twentieth century have freely trampled on the self-determination of peoples who did not conduct their social reforms according to U.S. standards and whose skin color confirmed that their cultures were "backward or malleable."[3] One alternative frequently proposed is that the United States forgo its moralistic policies—based on delusions of grandeur and lack of respect for others—and substitute for them a careful, pragmatic, realpolitik. George Kennan argued even before the liberal consensus weakened that a "legalistic-moralistic" framework of international relations had led the nation into implacable conflicts with other nations from which it then demanded unconditional surrender. Ironically, a moralistic foreign policy, Kennan commented, "makes violence more enduring, more terrible, and more destructive to political stability than did the older motives of national interest. A war fought in the name of high moral principle finds no early end short of some form of total domination."[4] Vietnam tragically proved the point.

Richard Nixon would have concurred. The Republican president did his best to shape a foreign policy based on the reality of spheres of influence, manipulating them to the advantage of the United States to the extent possible. In the years since, Americans have alternated between admiration for Nixon's achievement and a stunned shock over the extent of his political corruption. Well into the 1990s new revelations of Nixon's cynicism made their way into newspaper headlines—from his orders to burglarize opponents' offices to his plans to bribe black politicians to run for office to split the Democratic vote. Reinhold Niebuhr had counseled Americans at the start of the heroic age that they would need "the wisdom of the serpent and the harmlessness of the dove . . . armed with the wisdom of the children of darkness, but . . . free from their malice."[5] Nixon showed both what could be accomplished with realpolitik and how degraded America could be by someone lacking the nation's finest ideals.

One result of the trauma wrought by Nixon was a deepened ambivalence over idealism and self-interest in foreign policy. Charles Krauthammer in *Time* magazine in 1993 bemoaned the type of post–cold war liberalism in which "self-interest is a tainted, corrupting motive for intervention" that is seen as "disqualifying" any assertion of American influence for the nation's own benefit. President George Bush split the difference in the Persian Gulf War by characterizing it as a war between good and evil fought in the world's largest oil field. But along with the distrust of self-interest came a distrust of altruism.[6]

The Peace Corps gave meaning to the goal of virtue in the American polis, imperfectly expressed in policy. Certainly Americans were not nearly as virtuous as they believed. In 1995 the United States spent only 0.1 percent of its gross national product on foreign assistance, the least of any developed nation in the world. Citizens guessed that the federal government devoted 15 percent of its budget to development, when in fact foreign aid accounted for one-half of one percent.[7] "Altruism" could also be a subtle form of social control. Give juvenile delinquents something to believe in and they won't make trouble for the country. Convince third world countries of American idealism and they will side with us in the cold war.

And yet the Peace Corps strove for something more as well. It allowed Americans to practice the principle of universal respect and trained citizens to give something to their own nation by serving the world. It was not part of a development ideology that extended, in one critic's words, "the long-established American views on race." Sargent Shriver and his colleagues in fact did all they could to overturn these views. The Peace Corps also learned early what too many American leaders failed to understand: that change and development were not "relatively easy."[8] Volunteers lived daily with the recognition that progress is grudging and that their own presence sprang from a mixture of altruism and self-interest. Self-interest, on the one hand, tempered a tendency to self-righteousness. They got at least as much as they gave. Altruism, on the other hand, tempered selfishness. Power *could* beget kindness (if one tried very hard), and not just complacency.

And so even after Vietnam and the cold war, the Peace Corps contained a spark that made it possible for cynics on the right and left, and chastened liberals in between, to believe that constructive ideals might play a part in at least one aspect of their nation's foreign policy. It was something most Americans wanted to believe of their nation. "No one could view this program without feeling a great sense of pride in his fellow American," one man wrote Shriver early on. "The Peace Corps is our dream of ourselves," *Look* magazine editorialized next to four portraits of volunteers it commissioned Norman Rockwell to paint in 1966. The Peace Corps is a "way of being in the world . . . that may yet save this fragmented and dispirited age," Bill Moyers told returned volunteers at the twenty-fifth anniversary celebration in 1986.[9]

In the mid-1990s, the number of volunteers slowly began increasing again, averaging 6,800 a year. Of the more than 145,000 returned Americans, 94 percent surveyed said they would make the same decision to join again and 93 percent said they would recommend the Peace Corps to a friend. Eighteen percent had married another member of the Peace Corps. Returned volunteers joined the ranks of elder statesmen to become senators and congressmen, heads of corporations, and organizers of nonprofit institutions. The largest number, more than one-fourth, became teachers of the nation's children. The second largest number went into business. Ten percent of the participants in each new class of foreign service officers were returned volunteers, and former volunteers made up 40 percent of AID staff. Over a dozen U.S. ambassadors were former volunteers.[10] Their understanding of third world issues, from poverty to environmental degradation, was based on an inherently deeper and more personal experience than that of their colleagues. Returned volunteers also brought home an appreciation of America's better qualities, tempered by respect for other nations. Joe Serna, a Mexican-American farmworker's son who was twice elected mayor of Sacramento in the 1990s, credited the Peace Corps for leading him into politics. "In Guatemala, I learned to appreciate all over again the value of democratic participation," Serna commented. "I saw people who walked for a day across the mountains just for the right to vote."[11]

The Peace Corps' primary contribution to nation building, therefore, was to the United States itself, by confirming its values and sense of mission as the world's first democratic country. "If she abandons her ideals she no longer exists," Pierre Ceresole said of his own nation.[12] Although this was hyperbole, there is truth to the notion that a state's cohesion depends on the clarity of its national identity. Tradition stabilizes. This is particularly true of a country as vast and heterogeneous as the United States.

Notably, other peoples have also at times depended on the good intentions of the United States in a chaotic, threatening world. What may be most remarkable about the American tradition when viewed in comparative terms is its unusual capacity to produce international heroes who the world community believes care about them. In the twentieth century, one need only mention Woodrow Wilson, Franklin D. Roosevelt, and John Kennedy to realize they have no equivalents. Willy Brandt, mayor of West Berlin when it was walled in, later wrote that he, himself, "felt emboldened to explore 'new frontiers'" by Kennedy, and that the most important quality which Kennedy communicated internationally was compassion. "The public sensed this quality in John F. Kennedy (and later in his brother Robert)," Brandt noted, "and it redounded to them in death like a mighty wave."[13]

While scholars may long debate to what extent Wilson, Roosevelt, and Kennedy truly cared about or did anything exceptional for the world community, what is undeniable is that the Fourteen Points and the Four Freedoms and the New Frontier were seen as having meanings that extended well beyond the borders of the United States. Provincialism keeps Americans from recognizing this at times—as well as the fear that the United States might have foisted an unwelcome influence upon the world. It is true that the United States avidly sought to expand its power after World War II with sometimes horrific consequences, but it is equally true that much of the world avidly pressed for U.S. assistance with sometimes beneficial consequences. Americans have had an ability to convey, convincingly, a sense of "promise" to the world. The Peace Corps in the 1960s was John Kennedy's chief instrument for doing so. It helped to unify the United States and, along with its counterparts in other countries, helped to strengthen in a small way the bonds of solidarity that, in Camus's words, may ultimately be humanity's only way to "negate frontiers and the crudest implications of history."[14]

In a new century the United States has new choices. The history of the Peace Corps demonstrates that power disparities do not inevitably produce oppressive outcomes, even though realpolitik wisely cautions that they usually do. Fear and greed have always been powerful motivators of human behavior. The values of self-determination and fair play are continuously compromised in a complex, competitive, and dangerous world. Sometimes they are compromised by plain arrogance.

But the story of the Peace Corps counsels us to be wary of theories that tend to simplify international relations either as a stacked contest for power in which the downtrodden never win, or as a contest for control between competing superpowers whose reality determines everyone else's. It also shows the limits of defining all foreign policy from 1947 to 1989 in cold war terms. The Peace Corps was a tool of this conflict, but we perpetuate a false dichotomy if we assume that this cancels out the organization's role as a purveyor of the ideas of freedom and equality. Like most human events—even including love, which is never purely selfless—it reflected a compound of motivations. The Peace Corps consciously sought to build upon the best traditions of the United States, including the belief in the right of all peoples to self-determination. Such was the spirit of the sixties. This spirit contrasted sharply with much foreign policy whose impact was far greater, but it was nonetheless real.

The Peace Corps demonstrates that constructive relations between nations of unequal strength and resources are possible, even during times of great international tension. It indicates that foreign aid can be moderately helpful, though it is never determinative of development. It exemplifies a form of humanitarian support that, unlike interventions in civil wars, entails no risk to U.S. soldiers. Its history reveals that some local elites are better at serving their peoples, and some U.S. presidents have been better than others at serving both their country and the world. Volunteers have shown that it is feasible for citizens to carry out the nation's ideals.

Volunteers have also found that the effort to achieve humane international relations is fraught with complications. But it is an effort worth taking up, with modest expectations and with the knowledge that it serves what might turn out to be the most important goal of all: human solidarity. This means accepting as valid the imperatives of national security and national economic interests—recognizing that while they sometimes contradict, they do not obviate the equal imperative of caring for the beliefs that define the nation to itself.

Appendix

Peace Corps Data

Volunteer Information

- Volunteers must be U.S. citizens, at least 18 years of age, and in good health.
- Volunteers serve 27 months: 3 in training, 24 on a tour of duty.
- Most positions require either a B.A., B.S., or comparable on-the-job experience.
- Average compensation of volunteers depends on country and locale (urban or rural) and is set at subsistence level. In addition, volunteers receive $200 per month (up to a total of $5,400, subject to federal tax) posted to a U.S. bank for use upon return home as a readjustment allowance.
- Vacation time: 48 days over two years.
- Volunteers may request a geographical region but are not guaranteed any country or continent, since placements depend upon country requests and volunteer qualifications.
- Average application period: 9 to 12 months.

Directors

1961–1966	R. Sargent Shriver, Jr.	1977–1978	Carolyn Payton
1966–1969	Jack H. Vaughn	1979–1981	Richard Celeste
1969–1971	Joseph H. Blatchford	1981–1989	Loret Miller Ruppe
1971–1972	Kevin O'Donnell	1989–1991	Paul D. Coverdale
1972–1973	Donald K. Hess	1991–1992	Elaine L. Chao
1973–1974	Nicholas W. Craw	1993–1995	Carol Bellamy
1975–1977	John R. Dellenback	1995–	Mark D. Gearan

Appropriations, Volunteers and Trainees, and Applications

Year	Appropriations (in thousands of dollars)	Volunteers and trainees (in the field, at end of FY)	Applications[a]
1961–1962	$30,000	2,940	32,692
1963	$59,000	6,646	33,762
1964	$95,964	10,078	45,653
1965	$104,100	13,248	42,125
1966	$114,000	15,556	42,246
1967	$110,000	14,968	35,229
1968	$107,500	13,823	30,450
1969	$102,000	12,131	24,220
1970	$98,450	9,513	19,022
1971	$90,000	7,066	26,483
1972	$72,500	6,894	23,849
1973	$81,000	7,341	33,637
1974	$77,000	8,044	30,158
1975	$77,687	7,015	28,761
1976	$81,266	5,958	20,641
1977	$80,000	5,752	13,908
1978	$86,234	7,072	13,661
1979	$99,179	6,328	18,159
1980	$99,924	5,994	16,195
1981	$105,531	5,445	15,527
1982	$105,000	5,380	14,577
1983	$109,000	5,483	16,835
1984	$117,000	5,699	13,917
1985	$128,600	6,264	13,975
1986	$124,410	5,913	12,200
1987	$137,960	5,219	10,300
1988	$146,200	5,812	12,700
1989	$153,500	6,248	13,800
1990	$165,649	5,583	12,677
1991	$186,000	5,866	13,272
1992	$197,044	5,831	17,749
1993	$218,146	6,467	13,787
1994	$219,745	6,745	10,107
1995	$219,745	7,218	10,498
1996	$205,000	6,910	9,187

Sources: All statistics are based on the fiscal year. Volunteer information from Peace Corps, Office of Planning, Policy, and Analysis. Budget figures from Congressional Budget Presentation, FY97.

a. Applications reflect the total received during each fiscal year for the number of new positions open during that period or, roughly half the number of two-year volunteers in the field.

Volunteers and Trainees, 1961–1996 (1997 regional classifications)

Year	Africa	Asia-Pacific	Inter-America	Europe/ Central Asia/ Mediterranean	Total
1961–1969	15,099	15,572	19,186	4,357	54,214
1970–1979	13,861	11,353	12,000	2,595	39,809
1980–1989	12,893	6,292	8,851	1,651	29,687
1990–1996	9,122	3,444	6,961	4,418	23,945
Totals	50,975	36,661	46,998	13,021	147,655
(percentages)	(34%)	(25%)	(32%)	(9%)	(100%)

Source: Peace Corps, Office of Planning, Policy, and Analysis.

Countries Where Volunteers Have Served since 1961, by Region

Africa	Asia-Pacific	Inter-America	Europe/ Central Asia/ Mediterranean
Benin	Afghanistan	Anguilla	Albania
Botswana	China	Antigua and Barbuda	Armenia
Burkina Faso	Cook Islands	Argentina	Bahrain
Burundi	Fiji	Barbados	Bulgaria
Cameroon	India	Belize	Cyprus
Cape Verde	Indonesia	Bolivia	Czech Republic
Central African Republic	Kiribati	Brazil	Estonia
Chad	Malaysia	Chile	Hungary
Comoros	Marshall Islands	Colombia	Iran
Congo	Micronesia (FSM)	Costa Rica	Jordan
Côte d'Ivoire	Mongolia	Dominica	Kazakstan
Equatorial Guinea	Nepal	Dominican Republic	Kyrgystan
Eritrea	Niue	Ecuador	Latvia
Ethiopia	Pakistan	El Salvador	Libya
Gabon	Palau, Republic of	Grenada and Cariaccou	Lithuania
Gambia, The	Papua New Guinea	Guatemala	Macedonia[a]
Ghana	Philippines	Guyana	Malta
Guinea	Solomon Islands	Haiti	Moldova
Guinea-Bissau	South Korea	Honduras	Morocco
Kenya	Sri Lanka	Jamaica	Oman
Lesotho	Thailand	Montserrat	Poland
Liberia	Tonga	Nicaragua	Romania

Countries Where Volunteers Have Served since 1961 (continued)

Africa	Asia-Pacific	Inter-America	Europe/ Central Asia/ Mediterranean
Madagascar	Tuvalu	Panama	Russia
Malawi	Vanuatu	Paraguay	Slovak Republic
Mali	Western Samoa	Peru	Tunisia
Mauritania		St. Kitts-Nevis	Turkey
Mauritius		St. Lucia	Turkmenistan
Namibia		St. Vincent-Grenadines	Ukraine
Niger		Suriname	Uzbekistan
Nigeria		Turks-Caicos	Yemen
Rwanda		Uruguay	
São Tome and Principe		Venezuela	
Senegal			
Seychelles			
Sierra Leone			
Somalia			
South Africa			
Sudan			
Swaziland			
Tanzania			
Togo			
Uganda			
Zaire			
Zambia			
Zimbabwe			

Total Countries: 132

Source: Peace Corps, Office of Planning, Policy, and Analysis.
a. Former Yugoslav Republic of Macedonia.

Notes

—— ❊ ——

Abbreviations

AID Agency for International Development
CNA Canadian National Archives, Ottawa
JFKL John F. Kennedy Library, Boston
LBJL Lyndon Baines Johnson Library, Austin
LRP Lawrence Radley Papers (private collection), La Jolla
NAG National Archives of Ghana, Accra
NMNH National Museum of Natural History, Smithsonian Institution, Washington, D.C.
NP Nixon Project, National Archives, College Park, Maryland
PCL Peace Corps Library, Washington, D.C.
PRO Public Records Office, London
SP Ian Smillie Papers (private collection), Ottawa
USNA United States National Archives and Records Administration

Prologue

1. George Washington in Felix Gilbert, *To The Farewell Address: Ideas of Early American Foreign Policy* (Princeton, 1961), 145–146.
2. Winston Churchill in Geir Lundestad, "Moralism, Presentism, Exceptionalism, Provincialism, and Other Extravagances in American Writings on the Early Cold War Years," *Diplomatic History*, 13 (Fall 1989), 540.
3. "Joseph Campbell and the Power of Myth," with Bill Moyers, no. 1 of 6, "The Hero's Adventure," Public Broadcasting System.
4. Alexis de Tocqueville, *Democracy in America* (New York, 1947), 334.
5. Bradford Perkins, *The Cambridge History of American Foreign Relations: The Creation of a Republican Empire*, vol. 1 (Cambridge, 1993), 16.
6. Michael Hunt, *Ideology and U.S. Foreign Policy* (New Haven, 1987), 190.
7. Richard N. Goodwin, *Remembering America: A Voice from the Sixties* (New York, 1988), 9.
8. Perkins, *American Foreign Relations*, 15.
9. William O'Neill, *Coming Apart: An Informal History of America in the 1960s* (New York, 1971), 427.

10. See, for example, Paul Cowan, *The Making of an Un-American: A Dialogue with Experience* (New York, 1969); David Hapgood and Meridan Bennett, *Agents of Change: A Close look at the Peace Corps* (Boston, 1968); Kevin Lowther and C. Payne Lucas, *Keeping Kennedy's Promise: The Peace Corps, Unmet Hope of the New Frontier* (Boulder, 1978); and Gary May, "Passing the Torch and Lighting Fires: The Peace Corps," in *Kennedy's Quest for Victory*, ed. Thomas G. Paterson (New York, 1989), 284–316. Ellis Briggs in Gerard T. Rice, *The Bold Experiment: JFK's Peace Corps*, Gerard T. Rice (Notre Dame, 1985), 61.

11. For a critical analysis of Kennedy's foreign policy, see Thomas Paterson's introduction to *Kennedy's Quest for Victory*, 3–23.

1. Love and Youth in a Brave New World

1. David Pollack, "John Kennedy in Ann Arbor," *Ann Arbor Magazine*, September/October 1985, 13.

2. Quoted in Coates Redmon, *Come as You Are: The Peace Corps Story* (San Diego, 1986), 4.

3. Quoted in Karen Schwarz, *What You Can Do for Your Country: An Oral History of the Peace Corps* (New York, 1991), 27.

4. Richard D. Mahoney, *JFK: Ordeal in Africa* (New York, 1983), 30.

5. Norman Mailer, "Superman Comes to the Supermart," *Esquire*, November 1960, 122.

6. Ibid., 122–123.

7. Quoted in Rice, *Bold Experiment*, 21.

8. Ian Smillie, *The Land of Lost Content: A History of CUSO* (Toronto, 1985), 13.

9. Akira Iriye, "Culture," *Journal of American History*, 77 (June 1990), 100.

10. William James, "The Moral Equivalent of War," in *The Peace Corps*, ed. Pauline Madow (New York, 1964), 28.

11. Neil Sheehan, *A Bright Shining Lie: John Paul Vann and America in Vietnam* (New York, 1988), 147.

12. Charles C. Moskos and John Whiteclay Chambers II, *The New Conscientious Objection: From Sacred to Secular Resistance* (New York, 1993), 12–13, 75.

13. Daniel Anet, *Pierre Ceresole: Passionate Peacemaker* (Delhi, 1974), 56, 67.

14. Jürgen Kuhlmann and Ekkehard Lippert, "The Federal Republic of Germany: Conscientious Objection as Social Welfare," in Moskos and Chambers, *Conscientious Objection*, 98.

15. Michel Martin, "France: A Statute but No Objectors," 84, and Anton Bebler, "Socialist Countries of Eastern Europe: The Old Orders Crumble," 167–168, in Moskos and Chambers, *Conscientious Objection*.

16. William Lederer, *A Nation of Sheep* (New York, 1961), 11.

17. Richard Hofstadter, *The Paranoid Style in American Politics, and Other Essays* (Chicago, 1964), chap. 2.

18. Louis Hartz, *The Liberal Tradition in America* (New York, 1955), 59.

19. Frederick Jackson Turner, in *The Frontier Thesis: Valid Interpretation of American History?* ed. Ray Allen Billington (New York, 1977), 20.

20. David Riesman, *The Lonely Crowd: A Study of the Changing American Character* (New Haven, 1961), 18. First edition 1950.

21. Ibid., 21.

22. Aldous Huxley, *Brave New World* (New York, 1974), xxiii.

23. David Potter, *People of Plenty: Economic Abundance and the American Character* (Chicago, 1954), 188.

24. John F. Kennedy, "The New Frontier," July 15, 1960, 5, JFKL, Gerald Bush Papers, box 1, "JFK Speeches."

25. William Allen Whyte, *The Organization Man* (New York, 1956), 7.

26. Ibid., 401, 404.

27. Holocaust Museum, Washington, D.C.

28. Potter, *People of Plenty,* 112.

29. Hartz, *Liberal Tradition,* 306.

30. Potter, *People of Plenty,* 128–141; Hartz, *Liberal Tradition,* 306–309.

31. Peace Corps: Fact Book, 1 April 1961, 7, JFKL, President's Office File (hereafter POF), box 85, "Peace Corps, 1/61–6/61."

32. William Lederer and Eugene Burdick, *The Ugly American* (New York, 1965), 12, 30, 33–39.

33. Ibid., 54, 206, 220, 225–227.

34. Ibid., 73, 108, 145, 153.

35. Paul Goodman, *Growing Up Absurd* (New York, 1960), 17–35. Riesman, Whyte, and Goodman all make reference to one another's work. See Riesman on Goodman (lvii), Whyte on Riesman (396), and Goodman on Whyte (102–103).

36. Goodman, *Growing Up Absurd,* xiii–xvi. First edition 1956.

37. Toynbee column clipped from the Charlottesville, Va., *Progress* of March 10, 1962, JFKL, POF, box 85, "Peace Corps, 1/61–3/62."

38. "Remarks of the President at Peace Corps Meeting in Chamber of Commerce Auditorium," Press Release, June 14, 1962, JFKL, POF, box 86, "Peace Corps, 4/62–6/62."

39. Sargent Shriver, "The Best Job in Washington," draft, May 2, 1963, 15, JFKL, POF, box 86, "Peace Corps, 5/63."

40. Sargent Shriver, *Point of the Lance* (New York, 1964), 40.

41. Bill McWhinney and Dave Godfrey, eds., *Man Deserves Man: CUSO in Developing Countries* (Toronto, 1968), 3.

42. Reinhold Niebuhr, *The Children of Light and the Children of Darkness* (New York, 1945), 159.

43. Ibid., 40.
44. William Sloane Coffin, Jr., *Once to Every Man: A Memoir* (New York, 1977), 88.
45. Robert Dallek, *Franklin D. Roosevelt and American Foreign Policy, 1932–1945* (New York, 1979), 479, 536.
46. David A. Hollinger, "How Wide the Circle of the "We"? American Intellectuals and the Problem of the Ethnos since World War II," *American Historical Review* (April 1993), 317–337.
47. Pierre Ceresole in Anet, *Pierre Ceresole*, 62.
48. Press Release, University of Michigan, "Transcript of remarks made by John F. Kennedy about 2 a.m. October 14, 1960, on the steps of the Michigan Union," courtesy of PCL. Quote by Alberto Lleras Camargo, president of Colombia, from Goodwin, *Remembering America*, 149.
49. Lawrence H. Fuchs, *"Those Peculiar Americans": The Peace Corps and American National Character* (New York, 1967), 5; Sargent Shriver, "Two Years of the Peace Corps," *Foreign Affairs*, July 1963, 706.
50. Shriver, "Two Years," 707.
51. W. E. B. DuBois, *The Souls of Black Folk* (New York, 1982), 54.
52. T. O. Lloyd, *The British Empire, 1558–1983* (Oxford, 1984), 344.
53. For purposes of identifying the American-led bloc in the cold war, I use the terms "Western" and "free world" alliance. However, this is only for convenience, since it was neither entirely Western nor entirely free, as the inclusion of Japan and South Africa attest.
54. Quoted in Cowan, *The Making of an Un-American*, 29.
55. Lederer and Burdick, *The Ugly American*, 14, 215.
56. Coffin, *Once to Every Man*, 143–144.
57. Mary Dudziak, "Desegregation as a Cold War Imperative," *Stanford Law Review*, 41 (1988).
58. Dean Rusk to Robert Kennedy, January 31, 1961, and J. C. Satterthwaite to Loy Henderson, January 5, 1961, JFKL, White House Staff Files (hereafter WHSF), Harris Wofford, box 2, Civil Rights Miscellaneous, 1960–1/62.
59. Memorandum for the President from Harris Wofford, January 20, 1962, JFKL, White House Central Staff Files (hereafter WHCSF), box 670, PC5, Peace Corps Program, 8/16/61–4/8/62.
60. Kennedy in Rice, *Bold Experiment*, 14–15.
61. Lederer and Burdick, *The Ugly American*, 57.
62. Douglas C. Rossinow, "Breakthrough: White Youth Radicalism in Austin, Texas, 1956–1973" (diss., Johns Hopkins University, 1994), 102.
63. Albert Camus, *The Plague* (New York, 1972), 236. First edition 1947.
64. Kennedy, "Remarks to a Group of Peace Corps Volunteers," August 28, 1961, JFKL, POF, box 35.
65. Martin Buber, *I and Thou*, trans. Ronald G. Smith (Edinburgh, 1937), 8.
66. *The Nation*, December 3, 1960, 432.

67. Paul Tillich, *The Courage to Be* (New Haven, 1952), 138–140.
68. Shriver, "Two Years," 707.
69. William Chafe, *The Unfinished Journey: America since World War II* (New York, 1986), 136.
70. John Osborne, *Look Back in Anger* (New York, 1957), 15, 84–85.
71. Albert Camus, *The Rebel: An Essay on Man in Revolt* (New York, 1991), 304. First edition 1956.
72. Interview with Keith Spicer, Hull, Canada, May 18, 1993.
73. Rossinow, 96, 97, 101.
74. Camus, *The Plague*, 211, 287.
75. Camus, *The Rebel*, 304.
76. Norman Cousins, *Saturday Review*, 22, in JFKL, WHCSF, box 670.
77. McWhinney and Godfrey, *Man Deserves Man*, 31. Emphasis added.
78. Fuchs, *Those Peculiar Americans*, 37.
79. Interview with Bill Moyers, December 3, 1993, New York.
80. Quotes from Henri Roser (preface) and John Ferguson (introduction) in Anet, *Pierre Ceresole*, v, x.
81. Irene Pinkau, *Service for Development: An Evaluation of Development Services and Their Cooperative Relationships* (Chicago, 1975), 2:234.
82. McWhinney and Godfrey, *Man Deserves Man*, 31.
83. Cowan, *The Making of an Un-American*, 33.
84. James Baldwin, *Go Tell It on the Mountain, Giovanni's Room, and The Fire Next Time* (New York, 1988), 22–25. *The Fire Next Time*, first edition 1962.
85. *Look*, 14 June 1966, 46.
86. Lowther and Lucas, *Keeping Kennedy's Promise*, 13.
87. Che Guevara in Goodwin, *Remembering America*, 208.
88. Madeleine L'Engle, *A Wrinkle in Time* (New York, 1990), 135.
89. Ibid., 85, 200.
90. Theodore H. White, *The Making of the President: 1960* (New York, 1980), 331.
91. Goodman, *Growing Up Absurd*, 135.
92. Mora Dickson, *A Chance to Serve* (London, 1976), 123.
93. Goodman, *Growing Up Absurd*, 240.
94. Interview, Mora Dickson, May 11, 1994, London.
95. Hapgood and Bennett, *Agents of Change*, 155–156.

2. Shriver Hits the Ground Running

1. Rockefeller Brothers Fund, Prospect for America (Garden City, N.Y., 1961), 391. Kennedy quote from March 20, 1963, University of Costa Rica, San Jose, *Public Papers of the Presidents*, vol. 1963 (Washington, D.C., 1964), 271.

2. John F. Kennedy, "The New Frontier," Democratic National Convention, July 15, 1960, 5–6, JFKL, Bush, box 1, "JFK Speeches."
3. Kennedy quoted in Rice, *Bold Experiment*, 15–16.
4. Shriver, *Point of the Lance*, 11, 70.
5. Letters to Kennedy from Jackie M. Cipiti (February 4, 1961), Bill Copelin (February 2, 1961), and William J. Collins (February 22, 1961), JFKL, WHCSF, box 126, "FG 105–13 Peace Corps, 1-1-61 to 3-15-61." See also Harris Wofford, *Of Kennedys and Kings: Making Sense of the Sixties* (Pittsburgh, 1992), 250.
6. Interview, Warren Wiggins, November 1, 1993, Arlington, Va. See also "A Towering Task," February 1, 1961. Copy provided by Warren Wiggins.
7. Samuel P. Hayes, "Promise and Problems of a Peace Corps," in Madow, *The Peace Corps*, 39.
8. Much of the following information is drawn from the many memoirs and histories of the Peace Corps. In general, I am most indebted to the following books: Rice, *Bold Experiment*; Brent Ashabranner, *A Moment in History: The First Ten Years of the Peace Corps* (New York, 1971); Redmon, *Come as You Are*; Lowther and Lucas, *Keeping Kennedy's Promise*; Schwarz, *What You Can Do*; Wofford, *Of Kennedys*; and Shriver, *Point of the Lance*.
9. Sargent Shriver, "Report to the President on the Peace Corps," February 22, 1961, 4, 11–12, JFKL, POF, box 85, "Peace Corps Shriver Report and Recommendations (A), 1961." Alec Dickson in Mora Dickson, *A Chance to Serve*, 108.
10. Shriver in Rice, *Bold Experiment*, 43. This passage owes much to Rice, especially 39–44. See also Willy Brandt, *People and Politics: The Years 1960–1975* (Boston, 1976), 24.
11. William Josephson, oral history interview conducted by JFKL, 8.
12. Goodwin, *Remembering America*, 4.
13. Redmon, *Come as You Are*, 47–98.
14. Wofford, *Of Kennedys*, 264.
15. Interview, Bill Moyers, New York, December 3, 1993.
16. Ashabranner, *Moment in History*, 42. See also Rice, *Bold Experiment*, 54.
17. "Report to the President," 11, JFKL, POF, box 85, "Peace Corps Shriver Report and Recommendations (A), 1961."
18. "Organizational Status of the Peace Corps," 1, Henry Labouisse to Sargent Shriver, April 20, 1961, PCL, "Peace Corps—History, 1960–1961."
19. Johnson in Wofford, *Of Kennedys*, 265.
20. Ibid., 262–266.
21. Eunice Shriver in ibid., 266.
22. Johnson quote from author's interview with Bill Moyers.
23. Bill Moyers interview.
24. Unidentified congressman quoted in Wofford, *Of Kennedys*, 267.
25. Shriver in ibid., 267.

26. Director's Staff Meeting, March 22, 1961, 1, JFKL, Peace Corps (PC) Microfilm, box 1, 3/3/61–3/29/61.
27. Rice, *Bold Experiment,* 66.
28. Sargent Shriver to Lyndon Johnson, undated letter (c. July 1961), and thank-you note, July 31, 1961, both in LBJL, VP Subject File, 1961–63, box 82.
29. Shriver and Kennedy in Rice, *Bold Experiment,* 84.
30. Goldwater in "Statement of the Month," February 8, 1962, JFKL, POF, box 85, "Peace Corps, 1/62–3/62"; and "Will the Peace Corps Lead to Idealism or Disaster?" Daughters of the American Revolution, August 16, 1961, PCL, "Peace Corps—History, 1960–1961."
31. "Interim Report for Coordinator and Peace Corps, Peace Corps Recruiting Campaign," April 9, 1962, the Advertising Council, JFKL, WHCSF, box 670, PC5, Peace Corps Program, 4/9/62; Warren Wiggins interview; Eric Sevareid, "Pure Intentions Backed by Pure Publicity," *Washington Star,* December 25, 1962. See also Ashabranner, *Moment in History,* 144.
32. Sargent Shriver to John F. Kennedy, March 8 and March 27, 1962, JFKL, POF, box 85, "Peace Corps, 1/62–3/62."
33. David J. Garrow, *Bearing the Cross: Martin Luther King, Jr., and the Southern Christian Leadership Conference* (New York, 1988), 132–133.
34. Shriver, *Point of the Lance,* 44.
35. Director's Staff Meeting, March 29, 1961, JFKL, PC Microfilm, box 1, 3/3/61–3/29/61; Project Development Report, 9/15/61, PCL, "Peace Corps—History, 1960–61."
36. Lowther and Lucas, *Keeping Kennedy's Promise,* 42.
37. Report of the Visit of the Associate Secretary to Jamaica, September 1–9, 1964, 6, CNA, CUSO, vol. 96, "Board Meetings, 1964."
38. Interview, Charles Peters, December 17, 1993, Washington, D.C. See also Peters, *Tilting at Windmills: An Autobiography* (Reading, Mass., 1988) and Rice, *Bold Experiment,* 110–112.
39. Rice, *Bold Experiment,* 106.
40. Larry Radley to family, June 25 and July 25, 1961. From LRP (in the possession of Meryl Radley Katz, La Jolla, Calif.).
41. Rice, *Bold Experiment,* 94.
42. Shriver in Conference Report, March 5–7, 1965, 54, JFKL, Bush, box 7, "Citizen in a Time of Change: The Returned Peace Corps Volunteer."
43. Rice, *Bold Experiment,* 98, 113–115. See William Josephson's justification of the rule to Joseph Califano, Jr., October 7, 1965, 2, LBJL, WHCH, Subject File, box 145, FG 106–6, 10/7/65–3/10/66.
44. Shriver, *Point of the Lance,* 45; Mora Dickson interview.
45. From Tom Scanlon, *Waiting for the Snow: The Peace Corps Papers of a Charter Volunteer* (Chevy Chase, Md., 1997), vii.
46. Director's Staff Meeting, April 13, 1962, JFKL, PC Microfilm, box 1, 3/2/62–4/30/62; "Overseas Evaluation-Brazil," August 17, 1965, 15,

USNA, RG 490, Country Program Evaluations, 1961–1967, box 1, Brazil 1965.

47. Wofford, *Of Kennedys,* 310.

48. Interview, Sargent Shriver, December 10, 1993, Washington, D.C.

49. Lowther and Lucas, *Keeping Kennedy's Promise,* 6.

50. Director's Staff Meeting, November 29, 1961, JFKL, PC Microfilm, box 1, 11/1/61–12/23/61.

51. Gary D. Bergthold and David C. McClelland, *The Impact of Peace Corps Teachers on Students in Ethiopia* (Human Development Foundation, 1968), 140–141.

52. Director's Staff Meeting, July 19 and June 13 (respectively), 1962, JFKL, PC Microfilm, box 1, 6/1/62–7/30/62.

53. Director's Staff Meeting, December 8 and 12 (respectively), 1961, JFKL, PC Microfilm, box 1, 11/1/62–12/23/61. See also Jonathan Zimmerman, "Beyond Double Consciousness: Black Peace Corps Volunteers in Africa," *Journal of American History,* 82, no. 3 (December 1995), 1010.

54. Director's Staff Meeting, July 11, 1962, JFKL, PC Microfilm, box 1, 6/1/62–7/30/62.

55. Colorado State University Final Report, May 1961, 10, JFKL, WHSF, Harris Wofford, box 6, "Peace Corps-General. Colorado State University Final Report."

56. Ibid., 10, and "Executive Responsibility in Intergroup Relations," April 1961, 12, JFKL, WHSF, Harris Wofford, box 5, National Association of Intergroup Relations Officials.

57. Memorandum for the President from Harris Wofford, January 20, 1962, JFKL, WHCSF, box 670, PC5, Peace Corps Program, 8/16/61–4/8/62. See also Julius Amin, *The Peace Corps in Cameroon* (Kent, 1992), 174.

58. Shriver, *Point of the Lance,* 49; Fletcher Knebel, *The Zinzin Road* (New York, 1966), 33.

59. Goodwin, *Remembering America,* 148.

60. Kennedy in Walter LaFeber, *Inevitable Revolutions: The United States in Central America* (New York, 1983), 148, 154.

61. John F. Kennedy to Sargent Shriver, August 29, 1962, JFKL, POF, box 86, Peace Corps, 7/62–12/62.

62. Glenn F. Sheffield, "Peru and the Peace Corps, 1962–1968" (diss., Univ. of Connecticut, 1991), 263; Director's Staff Meeting, November 20, 1961 and February 15, 1962, JFKL, PC Microfilm, box 1, 11/1/61–12/23/61 and 1/3/62–2/27/62.

63. Director's Staff Meeting, April 19, 1962 and May 2, 1962, JFKL, PC Microfilm, box 1, 3/2/62–4/30/62 and 15/1/62–5/29/62.

64. Sheffield, "Peru and the Peace Corps," 130, 259.

65. Interview, Frank Mankiewicz, November 17, 1993, Washington, D.C.

66. Ibid. See also Cowan, *The Making of an Un-American,* 82; Rice, *Bold Experiment,* 172.
67. Hapgood and Bennett, *Agents of Change,* 129.
68. Cowan, *The Making of an Un-American,* 95.
69. Pat M. Holt to Richard Nolte, April 10, 1962, Bourke Hickenlooper Papers, Herbert Hoover Presidential Library, Foreign Relations Committee: Country Series, box 120, ARA Subcommittee, Holt, Pat, 1961–62.
70. Peters, *Tilting at Windmills,* 123.
71. Goodwin, *Remembering America,* 208; Frank Mankiewicz interview.
72. See Eldon Kenworthy, *America/Américas: Myth in the Making of U.S. Policy Toward Latin America* (University Park, Pa., 1995), 31–37.
73. Quote of Lynda Edwards in Schwarz, *What You Can Do,* 79; see also 82–83. Johnson in Rice, *Bold Experiment,* 142. Oral history interview, Frank Mankiewicz, LBJL, vol. 1, 4.
74. Lowther and Lucas, *Keeping Kennedy's Promise,* 57.
75. "The Position of the Students of the National School of Anthropology and History before Problems of Social Change" (undated, c. Oct. 1968), CNA, CUSO, vol. 26, "CUSO: Library and Research Department 1969–71."

3. Peace Corps Cousins

1. James Morris, *Farewell the Trumpets: An Imperial Retreat* (London, 1978), 497.
2. Minutes of the First Annual Meeting, Canadian University Service Overseas, June 9, 1962, 3, in SP (in the possession of Ian Smillie), file: "The New Jerusalem."
3. Donald K. Faris, *To Plow with Hope* (New York, 1958), 163.
4. Ivan Southall, *Indonesia Face to Face* (Singapore, 1965), 28; see also Betty Feith, "An Episode in Education for International Understanding, The Volunteer Graduate Scheme in Indonesia, 1950–1963" (master's thesis, Monash University, 1984), 1–2.
5. Southall, *Indonesia,* 31.
6. Interview with Jim Webb, *Five Stories from the Overseas Service Bureau,* 3, courtesy of the Overseas Service Bureau, Fitzroy, Australia.
7. Southall, *Indonesia,* 34.
8. Quoted from "Newsletter from Herb Feith, August–September 1951," in Feith, "An Episode in Education," 9.
9. Quoted in Feith, "An Episode in Education," 10, 14–16.
10. McMichael in Feith, "An Episode in Education," 5–6, 50.
11. Marjorie Barnard, *A History of Australia* (New York, 1963), 450, 467. See also Stuart Macintyre, *The Oxford History of Australia,* vol. 4: *The Succeeding Age, 1901–1942* (Oxford, 1986), 123–124, 178.

12. John Rickard, *Australia: A Cultural History* (London, 1988), 235; Barnard, *History of Australia*, 577; Feith, "An Episode in Education," 44b, 45, 60.
13. Quoted in Feith, "An Episode in Education," 7, 16, 24.
14. Mora Dickson interview. Also see Dickson, *A Chance to Serve*, 80. This biography of Alec Dickson, with its extensive use of long quotations linked by a thread of narrative, approaches autobiography.
15. Dickson, *A Chance to Serve*, 99, 103–104.
16. Osborne, *Look Back in Anger*, 15, 84–85.
17. Mora Dickson in Michael Adams, *Voluntary Service Overseas: The Story of the First Ten Years* (London, 1968), 46.
18. Dickson, *A Chance to Serve*, 83, 92.
19. Ibid., 84.
20. Copy of letter provided by Mora Dickson. "Service in Sarawak—1958-9," undated.
21. See the stories of Martin Garner and Christopher Tipple in *Arriving Where We Started: 25 Years of Voluntary Service Overseas* (London, 1983), 10–12, 18.
22. Copy of letter provided by Mora Dickson. "Voluntary Service Overseas," June 1959.
23. Arthur Koestler, *Thieves in the Night: Chronicle of An Experiment* (New York, 1965), 137, 140.
24. John Seely to Alec Dickson, September 6 (no year, c. 1960), "A Year of Voluntary Service Overseas," 1. Copy of letter provided by Mora Dickson.
25. Lewis Perinbam, "Report of a Tour of Southeast Asian Countries," July–August 1961, 11, SP, "The New Jerusalem."
26. Lewis Perinbam, "Canadian Volunteer Graduate Program," June 1, 1959, 1 and 5, CNA, vol. 92, CUSO Papers, "CUSO/SUCO History, 1959–64." See also Lewis Perinbam, "The Origins and Founding of CUSO," 2, SP.
27. Interview with David Beer (undated, c. November 1963), courtesy of Ian Smillie.
28. Smillie interviews with David Beer and Guy Arnold (November 11, 1983). Also see Smillie, *Land of Lost Content*, 28.
29. Guy Arnold, Proposal for a "Canadian Voluntary Commonwealth Service," c. Fall 1962, 2, SP, "The New Jerusalem."
30. Guy Arnold, "Canadian Voluntary Commonwealth Service," 6, SP, "The New Jerusalem."
31. Faris, *To Plow with Hope*, 203.
32. Spicer in Smillie, *Land of Lost Content*, 10. Information also taken from author's interview with Keith Spicer, Hull, Quebec, May 18, 1993.
33. Spicer interview in *Toronto Daily Star*, January 23, 1961, 25.
34. See "Submission to the Government of Canada on a Scheme for Commonwealth Graduate Volunteers," December 1960, Keith Spicer, CNA, vol. 92, CUSO Papers, "CUSO/SUCO History 1959–64."

35. Smillie, *Land of Lost Content*, 16.
36. Spicer in ibid., 13.
37. Quotes from "Report of a Meeting of Representatives of Universities and Organizations Interested in Canadian University Service Overseas," June 6, 1961, Montreal, 3–4, SP, "The New Jerusalem."
38. Smillie, *Land of Lost Content*, 18–19.
39. See "The Origins and Founding of CUSO," by Lewis Perinbam, 5, and "The Origins of CUSO," by J. F. Leddy, May 16, 1981, 16, SP, "The New Jerusalem."
40. CVCS Committee Meeting, October 17, 1963, SP, "The New Jerusalem." Letter (unsigned) from Bill McWhinney to COV volunteers, October 22, 1962, CNA, CUSO Papers, vol. 92, "CUSO/SUCO History 1959–64; and handwritten summary of international voluntary schemes, undated, in same file.
41. J. Duncan Edmonds, commencement address, United College, Winnipeg, May 10, 1966, SP, "The New Jerusalem." See also Smillie, *Land of Lost Content*, 254.
42. Interview, Ton Nijzink, May 19, 1994, The Hague.
43. Rossinow, "Breakthrough: White Youth Radicalism," 99.

4. The Cold War versus Decolonization

This chapter was first published, in part, as an article entitled "Decolonization, the Cold War, and the Foreign Policy of the Peace Corps," in *Diplomatic History*, 20, no. 1 (Winter 1996): 79–105.

1. Marshall in Shriver, *Point of the Lance*, 9; Gandhi in James Morris, *Farewell the Trumpets*, 495; George F. Kennan quote from "Long Telegram" of 1946, in *Major Problems in American Foreign Policy*, vol. 2, 4th ed., ed. Thomas G. Paterson (Lexington, Mass., 1995), 246.
2. Mahoney, *JFK: Ordeal in Africa*, 14–19.
3. Eisenhower in ibid., 20; Kennedy in Rice, *Bold Experiment*, 23.
4. Harris Wofford, oral history interview, 2, JFKL.
5. Walter L. Hixson, *Parting the Curtain: Propaganda, Culture, and the Cold War, 1945–1961* (New York, 1997), xii, xiii.
6. For a critique of Kennedy's inattention to the Peace Corps, see Gary May, "Passing the Torch and Lighting Fires: The Peace Corps," in Paterson, *Kennedy's Quest*, 285.
7. See letter of Eugene Harrington, January 15, 1965; Sharry Simerl to her family, December 26, 1963; John C. Schafer to his parents, November 25, 1963; and Susan Stapleton to her parents, undated (c. November 1963). JFKL, Peace Corps Collection (PCC), box 2, "Letters on the Death of John F. Kennedy," files 1 and 2. Kennan quote from Stephen E. Ambrose, *Rise to Globalism: American Foreign Policy since 1938* (New York, 1983), 147.

8. Sargent Shriver to John Kennedy, "Summary of Next Steps," February 22, 1961, JFKL, Bush, box 5, "Report to the President"; Director's Staff Meeting, 5 April 1961, Bush, box 1, "Decision Records, 3/9/61–5/26/61."

9. Sargent Shriver, "Summary of Report to the President on the Peace Corps," March 4, 1961, 9, JFKL, WHSF, Carmine Bellino, box 1, "Peace Corps, General, 1961." Kennedy in "Some Points for the U.S. Presentation to the U.N. on the Peace Corps," April 7, 1961, USNA, RG 59, 800.00 PC/4–161. Also see Sargent Shriver to John Kennedy, "Summary of Next Steps," February 22, 1961, JFKL, Bush, box 5, "Report to the President."

10. Harlan Cleveland to Secretary of State Dean Rusk through George Ball, April 14, 1961, USNA, RG 59, 800.00 PC/4–161.

11. "Hearings before the Committee on Foreign Relations on S. 2000," U.S. Senate, 87th Congress, 1st session, June 22–23, 1961 (Washington, D.C., 1961), 115, 154.

12. Confidential report of the Chair of the U.S. delegation to the 32nd Session of the United Nations Economic and Social Council (5 July–4 August 1961), JFKL, PC Microfilm, box 1, 7/6/61–8/29/61.

13. Interview, Jack Hogan, December 20, 1993, Washington, D.C.

14. Grogan in Rice, *Bold Experiment*, 133.

15. JFKL, Presidential Recordings, "Kennedy and Shriver on Peace Corps, April 2, 1963." Warmongering by the CIA helped cause the Bay of Pigs disaster and, even before Kennedy's inauguration, the assassination of Patrice Lumumba, leader of the Congo. See Mahoney, *JFK: Ordeal in Africa*, 69–71.

16. Dean Rusk to embassies, March 25, 1963, JFKL, NSF, box 285, Peace Corps, 4/63–12/63.

17. Interview, William A. Delano, May 1, 1996, Washington, D.C.; Castro in Rice, *Bold Experiment*, 135.

18. P. David Searles, *The Peace Corps Experience: Challenge and Change, 1969–1976* (Lexington, Ky., 1997), 99; Shriver, "Two Years," 698.

19. Director's Staff Meeting, May 25, 1962, JFKL, PC Microfilm, box 1, 5/1/62–5/29/62; Ed Smith, *Where to, Black Man?* (Chicago, 1967), 24.

20. John H. Morrow to the Department of State, 21 August 1961, USNA, RG 59, 800.00 PC/8–161.

21. Dean Rusk, March 1, 1961, Circular, USNA, RG 59, 800.00 PC/11–460; Belgrade Embassy/Rankin to Secretary of State, March 9, 1961, RG 59, 800.00 PC/3–961; Moscow Embassy/Thompson to Secretary of State, March 16, 1961, USNA, RG 59, 800.00 PC/3–961.

22. Director's Staff Meeting, February 16, 1962, JFKL, PC Microfilm, box 1, 1/3/62–2/27/62.

23. Research and Reference Service, "Western European Attitudes toward Economic Aid and the Peace Corps," i–ii, 2–3, December, 1961, USNA, RG 306, Records of the USIA Office of Research; Public Opinion Barometer

Reports, 1955–62; box 5, WE-4(II) (hereafter "Western European Attitudes").

24. Ibid.; Warren Wiggins interview.

25. Interview with Jim Webb, *Five Stories from the Overseas Service Bureau*, 12 and 16, courtesy of the Overseas Service Bureau, Fitzroy, Australia.

26. Figures from Gerard Rice, *Twenty Years of Peace Corps* (Washington, D.C., 1982), 17 (fiscal year 1962); Smillie, *Land of Lost Content*, 23.

27. W. J. Smith to P. Rogers, February 7, 1962, PRO, Records of the Office of Overseas Development, OD/10/4. See also J. Michael Lee, "No Peace Corps for the Commonwealth?" *The Round Table*, vol. 336 (1995), 455–467.

28. Lewis Perinbam, acting executive secretary of CUSO, "Report of a Tour of Southeast Asian Countries," July–August 1961, SP.

29. Addis Ababa Embassy/Richards to Secretary of State, January 14, 1961, USNA, RG 59, 800.00 PC/11–460; Hal (last name unidentified, initials HHS) to McGeorge Bundy, January 18, 1963, JFKL, NSF, box 284, Peace Corps, 1/63–3/63. Also see *Foreign Relations of the United States, Vietnam,* vol. 1, 1964 (Washington, D.C., 1992), 261; and USNA, RG 490, box 6, India, 1963, evaluation by Kevin Delany, December 30, 1963, 94.

30. "Scope Paper," attached to memo from Florence Kirlin to George McGhee, May 28, 1962, USNA, RG 59, 800.00 PC/1–162; memo from Daniel A. Sharp to Harris Wofford, January 2, 1962, JFKL, WHSF, Harris Wofford, box 7, "Peace Corps—Countries, United Nations, January 2–12, 1962."

31. Dean Rusk to embassies, March 25, 1963, JFKL, NSF, box 285, "Peace Corps, 4/63–12/63"; on the policy of "disassociation" see Memorandum of Meeting, George McGhee, May 15, 1962, JFKL, PC Microfilm, box 1, 5/1/62–5/29/62, Director's Staff Meeting.

32. Warren Wiggins interview.

33. Telegram from Dean Rusk to all embassies, August 3, 1962, 1–2, LBJL, VP Security File, box 1, "V.P. Trips—General."

34. French Ministry of Foreign Affairs to American Embassy/Paris, April 17, 1963, USNA, RG 59, box 3290, "AID, 14, Peace Corps, 4/1/63."

35. Sydney Meller, Rome Embassy to Secretary of State, 31 August 1963, USNA, RG 59, box 3290, "AID, 14, Peace Corps, 7/1/63"; William Haddad to McGeorge Bundy, November 15, 1962, JFKL, POF, box 86, "Peace Corps, 7/62–12/62"; Tokyo Embassy to Secretary of State, December 6, 1963, USNA, RG 59, box 3290, "AID, 14–1, Peace Corps Volunteers"; *International Volunteer* (Washington, D.C.), 1, no. 3 (May–June 1963), copy from the collection of Elizabeth Badon Ghijben, Foreign Ministry, The Netherlands.

36. Rockefeller Brothers Fund, *Prospect for America*, 170. This report combined the expertise of foreign policy luminaries from both political parties, includ-

ing Henry Kissinger, Dean Rusk, Chester Bowles, Henry Luce, General Lucius Clay, Max Millikan, Walt Rostow, and Adolf Berle.

37. William H. Chafe, *Never Stop Running: Allard Lowenstein and the Struggle to Save American Liberalism* (New York, 1993), 104–105.

38. Dean Rusk to American Embassy/Bogota, Caracas, La Paz, Tegucigalpa, February 2, 1963, USNA, RG 59, box 3290, "AID, 14, Peace Corps, 2/1/63."

39. Dean Rusk to American Embassy/Bogota, Caracas, La Paz, Tegucigalpa, February 2, 1963, USNA, RG 59, box 3290, "AID, 14, Peace Corps, 2/1/63"; Khartoum Embassy to Secretary of State, August 18, 1963, "AID, 14, Peace Corps, 7/1/63." See also *International Volunteer*, 1, no. 6 (December 1963), from collection of Elizabeth Badon Ghijben.

40. Interview with Ton Nijzink.

41. Harry Truman in Ambrose, *Rise to Globalism*, 115.

42. David M. Kennedy, *Over Here: The First World War and American Society* (New York, 1980), 62.

43. Nelson Rockefeller to George Marshall, August 28, 1942, USNA, RG 229, OIAA Department of Information, Content Planning Division, box 1459, "Content Liaison"; U.S. Congress, House Committee on Foreign Affairs, *International Cooperation Act of 1949 (Point Four Program)* (Washington, D.C., 1950), 84.

44. Mora Dickson interview. See also Dickson, *A Chance to Serve*, 27–28.

45. Truman quoted in Allan A. Needell, "'Truth Is Our Weapon': Project TROY, Political Warfare, and Government-Academic Relations in the National Security State," *Diplomatic History*, 17 (Summer 1993), 404.

46. Morison in ibid., 412.

47. Eisenhower in Stephen G. Rabe, *Eisenhower and Latin America: The Foreign Policy of Anticommunism* (Chapel Hill, 1988), 90.

48. Kennedy in Rice, *Bold Experiment*, 15; Lederer, *A Nation of Sheep*, 154.

49. Sargent Shriver to John F. Kennedy (undated, c. September 1961), JFKL, POF, box 85, Peace Corps, 1/61–6/61; Shriver to "Darling" (presumably Eunice Shriver; undated, c. Fall 1962), JFKL, POF, box 86, Peace Corps, 7/62–12/62; Shriver to Carter, December 20, 1962, USNA, RG 59, 800.00 PC/9–162.

50. Sheffield, "Peru and the Peace Corps," 16.

51. Keith Spicer interview; McMichael in Feith, "An Episode in Education," 5–6, 50; "Origins of CUSO," personal recollections of Francis J. Leddy, 5/16/81, 23, SP.

52. Hapgood and Bennett, *Agents of Change*, 6–7. See also Geir Lundestad, "Empire by Invitation? The United States and Western Europe, 1945–1952," *SHAFR Newsletter*, 15 (September 1984), 1–21; Michael J. Hogan, *The Marshall Plan: America, Britain, and the Reconstruction of Western*

Europe, 1947–1952 (Cambridge, 1987); and Richard N. Gardner, *Sterling-Dollar Diplomacy,* 2nd ed. (New York, 1969).

53. Ton Nijzink interview; Robert Kennedy in Brandt, *People and Politics,* 87.

54. American Embassy Stockholm/Bonbright to Secretary of State, March 17, 1961, USNA, RG 59, 800.00 PC/3-961; PRO, OD 10/35, Parliamentary Debate on Voluntary Service, December 12, 1962; W. J. Smith, "Service Overseas by Volunteers," 2 March 1962, PRO, OD/10/36.

55. Allard Lowenstein, *Brutal Mandate: A Journey to Southwest Africa* (New York: Macmillan, 1962), 28.

56. Bernard Porter, *The Lion's Share: A Short History of British Imperialism, 1850–1970* (London, 1975), 309.

57. Stimson in David Green, *The Containment of Latin America: A History of the Myths and Realities of the Good Neighbor Policy* (Chicago, 1971), 230.

58. Roosevelt in Dallek, *Franklin D. Roosevelt and American Foreign Policy,* 360; Walter LaFeber, *The American Age: United States Foreign Policy at Home and Abroad since 1750* (New York, 1989), 415, 494.

59. LaFeber, *The American Age,* 531–532.

60. Yaw Agyeman-Badu, "The Attitude of African Nations Toward American Aid: The Case of Ghana and Nigeria" (diss., University of South Carolina, 1980), 72.

61. Ibid., 107, 112. See also Mahoney, *JFK: Ordeal in Africa,* 22–23.

62. Miles Kahler, *Decolonization in Britain and France: The Domestic Consequences of International Relations* (Princeton, 1984), 134–136, 141.

63. Interview, Benôit Chadanet, French Committee for International Solidarity, May 16, 1994, Paris.

64. Mahoney, *JFK: Ordeal in Africa,* 36.

65. *International Volunteer,* 2, no. 1 (March 1964), 2, courtesy of Elizabeth Badon Ghijben. Interview, Catherine de Loeper (Association Française des Volontaires du Progrès), May 17, 1994, Paris.

66. Porter, *The Lion's Share,* 187; Morris, *Farewell the Trumpets,* 507–508.

67. T. O. Lloyd, *The British Empire, 1558–1983* (Oxford, 1984), 332–333; Kahler, *Decolonization,* 130, 134–136, 144.

68. Commonwealth Relations Office to Secretary of State, September 14, 1961, PRO, OD/10/3; also see Lee, "No Peace Corps?" 460.

69. Mora Dickson interview; ARC to Secretary, May 10, 1963, PRO, OD 10/5; see also *The Times,* March 23, 1958, September 11, 1959, and November 2, 1960; *Birmingham Post and Birmingham Gazette,* May 12, 1959; *Scottish Educational Journal,* June 5, 1959; *Daily Express,* April 15, 1961.

70. Sargent Shriver to John F. Kennedy, Weekly Report, August 7, 1962, LBJL, VP Security File, box 12, "Peace Corps Reports."

71. Keith Spicer, "Canada: Values in Search of a Vision," in *Identities in North America,* ed. Robert L. Earle and John D. Wirth (Palo Alto, 1995), 13, 17, 21.

72. Interview, Bert Barten, May 20, 1994, Zuid-Scharwoude, Netherlands; interview, P. B. M. Knoope, May 19, 1994, The Hague; government policy quote and cartoon from Ton Nijzink, *Dag Vrijwilliger: Twintig Jaar SNV* (The Hague, 1985), 11.

73. Open letter from Harris Wofford, January 7, 1964, LBJL, Moyers Papers, box 14, "Peace Corps, 3 of 3."

74. Seymour Martin Lipset, *Continental Divide: The Values and Institutions of the United States and Canada* (New York, 1990).

75. Grant McConnell, "The Public Values of the Private Association," in J. Roland Pennock, *Voluntary Associations,* (New York, 1969), 147.

76. Tocqueville in Benjamin DeMott, "Objective: Local Democratic Action," in Madow, *The Peace Corps,* 125; Shriver, *Point of the Lance,* 45. See also Richard Eells, *Corporation Giving in a Free Society* (New York, 1956).

77. Fuchs, *Those Peculiar Americans,* 171. George F. Kennan, "Long Telegram, 1946," reprinted in *Major Problems in American Foreign Policy,* 3rd ed., ed. Thomas G. Paterson (Lexington, Mass., 1989), 288.

78. Joseph McCarthy, "The Internal Communist Menace," in *A History of Our Time,* ed. William Chafe and Harvard Sitkoff (New York, 1995), 63; Stuart Kennedy, Foreign Affairs Oral History Program, Georgetown University, e-mail communication, May 13, 1996.

79. Remarks of the president at Peace Corps meeting in Chamber of Commerce Auditorium, Washington, D.C., June 14, 1962, JFKL, POF, box 86, "Peace Corps, 4/62–6/62"; JFKL, Presidential Recordings, "Kennedy and Shriver on Peace Corps, 4/2/63"; Sargent Shriver to JFK, June 21, 1963, JFKL, POF, box 85, "Peace Corps, 6/63–11/63."

80. American Embassy/The Hague to Secretary of State, March 15, 1961, USNA, RG 59, 800.00 PC/3–961. Figures derived from McWhinney and Godfrey, *Man Deserves Man,* 449, app. 2, and Rice, *Twenty Years of Peace Corps,* 4, 5, 7.

81. Of the 132 countries that the Peace Corps had served by 1997, 16 asked the organization to leave at some point. They were, in addition to the ones named in the text, Iran, Burkina Faso, Peru, South Korea, and Malaysia. Information from Jack Hogan, associate director, Peace Corps. See also Amin, *The Peace Corps in Cameroon,* 184–185; Ashabranner, *A Moment in History,* 344–345; and Schwarz, *What You Can Do,* 159.

82. Shriver, *Point of the Lance,* 8–9; Susan Stapleton to parents, undated (c. November 1963), JFKL, PCC, box 2, "Letters on the Death of John F. Kennedy."

5. The Hero's Adventure

1. Larry Radley, LRP, letters home, July 25, 1961, 4; November 29, 1961, 2.
2. Interview, Meryl Radley Katz, December 19, 1995, La Jolla, California.

3. Fritz Fischer, quoting the volunteer Michael Parrish, "Americans in the Third World: Peace Corps Volunteers in the 1960s" (diss., Northwestern University, 1994), 121.

4. Larry Radley, LRP, September 6, 1961, 1; December 22, 1961, 1–2; December 29, 1961, 2; February 27, 1962, 2; March 12, 1962, 1.

5. Rice, *Bold Experiment*, 147–149.

6. Ibid., 149–150; *New York Times,* April 7, 1964.

7. Amin, *The Peace Corps in Cameroon,* 69; William Leuchtenburg, *A Troubled Feast: American Society since 1945* (New York, 1983), 59.

8. Amin, *The Peace Corps in Cameroon,* 69; Rice, *Bold Experiment,* 169; telephone conversation with John Demos, June 7, 1996.

9. "Why Do People Join CUSO," February 12, 1971, CNA, CUSO, vol. 26, "CUSO: Library and Research Department, 1969–71." Also see McWhinney and Godfrey, *Man Deserves Man,* 6.

10. Interview, Charles Peters, December 17, 1993, Washington, D.C. Quote of Mrs. Rufus Crozier, *New York Post,* April 25, 1962.

11. It is hard to determine how many blacks served in the Peace Corps because in the 1960s the agency declined to categorize volunteers by race. Brent Ashabranner estimated their presence at 5 percent to start, declining to 2 percent by the late 1960s. See also Jonathan Zimmerman, "Beyond Double Consciousness: Black Peace Corps Volunteers in Africa, 1961–1971," *Journal of American History,* 82, no. 3 (December 1995), 1000–1004; and Rice, *Twenty Years of Peace Corps,* 27. Shriver, "Two Years," 699.

12. Kennedy in Zimmerman, "Beyond Double Consciousness," 1006. Volunteer quote of Ed Smith from *Where to, Black Man,* 15.

13. Alec Dickson in Dickson, *A Chance to Serve,* 107; Amin, *The Peace Corps in Cameroon* 174; memorandum for the President from Harris Wofford, January 20, 1962, JFKL, WHCSF, box 670, "PC5, Peace Corps Program, 8/16/61–4/8/62.

14. Larry Radley, LRP, July 9, 1961, 1. David Crozier to parents, July 27, 1961, 1, copy provided by Nancy Crozier Brown, Bolivar, Missouri.

15. First quote from Colorado State University Final Report, May 1961, 7, JFKL, WHSF, Harris Wofford, box 6, "Peace Corps-General." Also see CUSO Executive Committee, November 14 and 15, 1965, 23, and Minutes from January 22 and 23, 1966, 13, SP.

16. Larry Radley, LRP, June 25, 1961, 2; trick questions and other quote from Moritz Thomsen, *Living Poor: A Peace Corps Chronicle* (Seattle, 1969), 7.

17. "Notes of a Peace Corps Reject," *Esquire,* 65, no. 1 (January 1966), 90, 122–123; Letter to John Kennedy, February 14, 1961, JFKL, WHCSF, box 126, "FG 105-13 PC, 1/1/61–3/15/61."

18. Fairfield in Amin, *The Peace Corps in Cameroon,* 84.

19. Telephone conversations with Adele Davidson and Theodore L. McEvoy, June 12, 1996. Also see Betty Friedan, *The Feminine Mystique* (New York,

1984), 25; UCLA Syllabi for Ecuador (1964), Nigeria (1963), Togo (1964), and Sierra Leone (1964), sections on "Assessment and Selection," copies in possession of Adele Davidson, Palm Springs, California.

20. Cowan, *The Making of an Un-American*, 87–88; Amin, *The Peace Corps in Cameroon*, 87.

21. Sargent Shriver quote from Director's Staff Meeting, May 9, 1962, 2, JFKL, PC Microfilm, box 1, "5/1/62–5/29/62"; LRP, letters home, July 16, 1961, 2.

22. Coffin in Rice, *Bold Experiment*, 153.

23. Rice, *Bold Experiment*, 158.

24. Amin, *The Peace Corps in Cameroon*, 82.

25. See UCLA Syllabi for Ecuador (1964), Nigeria (1963), Togo (1964), and Sierra Leone (1964), sections on "American Institutions and International Relations," copies in possession of Adele Davidson, Palm Springs, California.

26. Rice, *Bold Experiment*, 177.

27. Ibid., 172; "Peace Corps Fact Sheet," Peace Corps Press Office, Washington, D.C., January 20, 1996.

28. Larry Radley, LRP, December 29, 1961, 1; Rice, *Bold Experiment*, 204.

29. Cowan, *The Making of an Un-American*, 197.

30. Larry Radley, LRP, December 6, 1961, 5.

31. Larry Radley, LRP, February 20, March 12, and April "?" 1962, 1; see also "Report on Armenia, Antioquia" by Larry Radley, PCV, c. April 1, 1962.

32. Interview, Harriet Lancaster, January 20, 1995, Accra, Ghana; Cowan, *The Making of an Un-American*, 227. For statistics from the first three years see Ashabranner, *A Moment in History*, 156, 208–209.

33. *To Touch the World: The Peace Corps Experience* (Washington, D.C., 1995), selections by Jacqueline Francis, "'H' Is for Hopsi," 98, Roz Wollmering, "Cross Cultural Dialogue," 21, Abigail Calkins, "Development Is down This Road," 40, and Tina Martin, "Under the Tongan Sun," 96.

34. Quotes taken from Zimmerman, "Beyond Double Consciousness," 1016–1017.

35. Quotes from Ashabranner, *A Moment in History*, 261–262.

36. George Packer, *The Village of Waiting* (New York, 1988), 10, 84–84.

37. Larry Radley, LRP, April 10, 1962, 1; Packer, 38; Paul Theroux, *My Secret History* (New York, 1989), 176; Barnett Chessin, May 8, 1962 to Pat Kennedy, 6, Smithsonian Institution, National Museum of Natural History, Anthropology Archives Peace Corps Collection, (hereafter NMNH), box 31, "Ghana Volunteer Information."

38. Marian Zeitlin, letter no. 7, 3, NMNH, box 31, "Ghana Volunteer Information. Also see Jeanna Baty in Smillie, *Land of Lost Content*, 41.

39. Susan Rich, "Niger 1984–85," 1, and *Di News De*, July 1990, both in JFKL, RPCV, box 8 and 27, respectively.

40. Thomsen, *Living Poor*, 74.

41. Kinney Thiele, "An Inconvenience Is an Adventure, Rightly Viewed," in *To Touch the World*, 28; Rachel Cowan in Cowan, *The Making of an Un-American*, 173.
42. Victoria Derr, "Reasons for Joy," 109, in *To Touch the World*.
43. Ron Arias, "Life on the Death Beat," 75, in *To Touch the World*; Department of State Telegram, Kuala Lumpur to Secretary of State, JFKL, RFK Attorney General Papers, box 45, "Peace Corps, 5/1962–12/1962."
44. Open letter from Harris Wofford, January 7, 1964, LBJL, Bill Moyers, box 14, "Peace Corps, 3 of 3."
45. *Di News De*, October 1989, April 1990, and July 1990, JFKL, RPCV, boxes 12, 26, and 27.
46. Searles, *The Peace Corps Experience*, 134.
47. Mike Tidwell, "I Had a Hero," in *To Touch the World*, 82.
48. "Overseas Evaluation, Brazil," August 17, 1965, 46, USNA, RG 490, 1961–67, box 1, "Brazil, 1965." For snake story, see Ashabranner, 110.
49. Diana Louise Stahl, "Historical Narrative," Description of Service, 1973–77 (written May 1989), JFKL, RPCV, box 11.
50. John Coyne, "But No Postcards," 158–159, and Tom Hebert, "Shakespeare in Calabar," in *To Touch the World*.
51. According to the Peace Corps press office, this gave volunteers a death rate lower than that of their age cohort at home.
52. Betsy Long Bucks to Mrs. and Mr. Earl Hall, February 4, 1966, 1, NMNH, box 20, "Betsy Long Bucks, Colombia 1965–1966."
53. Ashabranner, *A Moment in History*, 156.
54. Smillie, *The Land of Lost Content*, 36.
55. Cowan, *The Making of an Un-American*, 218.
56. Ibid., 222, 229.
57. Ibid., 205; Betsy Long Bucks to family, April 28, 1966, NMNH, box 20, "Betsy Long Bucks, Colombia 1965–1966." Also see Rice, *Twenty Years of Peace Corps*, 42, on poverty in Latin America.
58. Lowther and Lucas, *Keeping Kennedy's Promise*, 61.
59. Larry Radley quoted by Gordon Radley, speech at the Arlington Cemetery Memorial Amphitheater, 25th Anniversary of the Peace Corps, September 21, 1986, copy courtesy of Merle Radley Katz.
60. "Excerpt from the Inaugural Address of Guillermo Leon Valencia," Bogotá, August 7, 1962, 1, LRP.

6. Ghana

Portions of this chapter appeared in "Diplomatic History and the Meaning of Life," *Diplomatic History*, 21, no. 4 (Fall 1997).
1. Epigraph from author's interview with K. B. Asante, Accra, January 19, 1995.

2. "Adinkra Symbolism," poster prepared by Ablade Glover, College of Art, University of Science and Technology, Kumasi, 3rd ed., 1992.

3. Brochure, "The Work of Aktion Sühnezeichen Friedensdienste," Berlin.

4. Address by A. J. Dowouna-Hammond, minister of education, at a meeting of principals of teacher training colleges, December 29, 1960, 1–2, NAG, RG 3/1/456.

5. E. K. Okoh to the principal secretary, Ministry of Education, regarding "Free and Compulsory Education," December 15, 1960, NAG, RG 3/1/456.

6. B. W. A. T. Knight, principal secretary of the Ministry of Justice to the principal secretary of the Ministry of Education, regarding "Compulsory Primary Education," December 15, 1960, NAG, RG 3/1/456.

7. J. S. Kaleem, regional education officer, Northern Region, to principal secretary, Ministry of Education, March 4, 1961, NAG, RG 3/1/456.

8. Warren Wiggins interview.

9. American Embassy/Rio de Janeiro to Department of State, March 28, 1961, USNA, RG 59, 800.00 PC/3–961.

10. American Embassy/Accra to Department of State, April 19, 1961, USNA, RG 59, 800.00 PC/4–161.

11. Wofford, *Of Kennedys,* 268.

12. Ibid., 269.

13. Interview, Samuel George Ayi-Bonte, Accra, January 14, 1995.

14. Interview, Kojo Botsio, Accra, January 13, 1995. Kojo Botsio served as minister of education and welfare in Kwame Nkrumah's first cabinet and later as foreign minister.

15. Francis N. Nkrumah, "Education and Nationalism in Africa," Educational Outlook, November 1943, NAG, Kwame Nkrumah Papers, SC 21/4/6. Nkrumah later dropped the first name "Francis."

16. Mimi Stein, *A Special Difference: A History of Kaiser Aluminum and Chemical Corporation* (Oakland). 116–117. Also based on conversation with K. A. Gbedemah, 19 January 1995, Accra.

17. K. B. Asante interview.

18. American Embassy/Accra to Department of State, April 22, 1961, USNA, RG 59, 800.00 PC/4–161.

19. "It was for Nkrumah, in my opinion, number one," according to K. B. Asante. Author's interview.

20. *Progress in Education in the Gold Coast,* foreword by Kojo Botsio (1953), NAG, RG 3/1/55. See also, same file, "A Plan in Action," March 1955.

21. NAG, Records of the Ministry of Education, RG 3/1/55. Also see Alex Newton, *West Africa: A Travel Survival Kit* (Hawthorn, Australia: Lonely Planet Publications, 1992), 290.

22. Gold Coast Education Department Report, 1937–38, NAG, RG 3/1/154.

23. Report on Tamale Government School, attached to note from Gerald Power, director of education, February 14, 1941. NAG, RG 3/1/55.

24. Statistics from Simon Baynham, *The Military and Politics in Nkrumah's Ghana* (Boulder, 1988), 56.

25. Kojo Botsio interview.

26. American Embassy/Accra (Russell) to Department of State, April 22, 1961, USNA, RG 59, 800.00 PC/4-161.

27. Wofford, *Of Kennedys*, 269; interviews with Kojo Botsio and K. B. Asante.

28. American Embassy/Accra (Russell) to Department of State, April 25, 1961, USNA, RG 59, 800.00 PC/4-161.

29. American Embassy/Lagos (Palmer) to Department of State, April 25, 1961, USNA, RG 59, 800.00 PC/4-161.

30. Wofford, *Of Kennedys*, 271.

31. Dennis Merrill, *Bread and the Ballot: The United States and India's Economic Development, 1947–1963* (Chapel Hill, 1990), 170.

32. Nehru in Wofford, *Of Kennedys and Kings*, 272.

33. Frank Ninkovich, "Culture, Power, and Civilization: The Place of Culture in International Relations," in *On Cultural Ground*, ed. Robert David Johnson (Chicago, 1994), 16–17.

34. Kojo Botsio interview.

35. K. B. Asante interview.

36. August 1962 article, "The Peace Corps Wins Its Way," reprinted in Madow, *The Peace Corps*, 135.

37. "Memorandum for Secretary of State," undated, JFKL, POF, box 85, "Peace Corps, 1/61–6/61."

38. Karen Schwarz's book, *What You Can Do for Your Country*, exemplifies this attitude; see pages 31–32.

39. Samuel George Ayi-Bonte, *Thirty Years of the Peace Corps in Ghana* (Accra, 1991), 4.

40. Packer, *The Village of Waiting*, 99.

41. Eric Sevareid, "Pure Intentions Backed by Pure Publicity," *Washington Star*, December 25, 1962.

42. Imoru Egala, minister of foreign affairs, to Francis Russell, American ambassador, Exchange of Notes, reprinted in Ayi-Bonte, *Thirty Years*, 4.

43. Wofford, *Of Kennedys*, 269.

44. Ashabranner, *A Moment in History*, 62.

45. Author's telephone conversation with John Demos, June 7, 1996; Nkrumah quoted in *Ghanaian Times*, January 2, 1962, George Padmore Library, Accra, Kwame Nkrumah Papers, Major Policy Files, box 409–442, "Office of the Advisor to the Prime Minister on African Affairs, New Years Messages."

46. Country Report, Ghana, November 15, 1963, USNA, RG 490, box: "Ghana-Guiana, 1962–66."

47. Quoted in Madow, *The Peace Corps,* 66.
48. Yaw Agyeman-Badu, "The Attitude of African Nations," 226, 228.
49. Tina Thuemer, "Raid on Entebbe, or My Three Days as a Mercenary," in *To Touch the World,* 78.
50. K. B. Asante, Kojo Botsio, and George Ayi-Bonte all believed that the CIA never planted agents as Peace Corps volunteers in Ghana.
51. Interview, George Carter, March 14, 1995, New York, by telephone.
52. Director's Staff Meeting, May 15, 1962, JFKL, PC Microfilm, box 1, "5/1/62–5/29/62."
53. George Carter interview; Steve Bosworth to friends, October 15, 1963, NMNH, box 31, "Ghana Volunteer Information."
54. Report of January 6, 1965, 32, USNA, RG 490, box: Ghana-Guiana, 1962– 66, "Ghana 1965, Report by Richard Richter."
55. Ibid. See also report by Ruth Olson, December 23, 1963, regarding comments of the Peace Corps volunteer Lorna Fitz, USNA, RG 490, box: Ghana-Guiana, 1962–66, "Office of the Inspector General, Country File, 1963–64, Ghana."
56. Country Report, Ghana, November 15, 1963, USNA, RG 490, box: Ghana-Guiana, 1962–66, "Office of the Inspector General, Country File, 1963–64, Ghana."
57. Report of January 6, 1965, 32, USNA, RG 490, box: Ghana-Guiana, 1962– 66, "Ghana 1965, Report by Richard Richter."
58. Report by Joseph C. Kennedy, February 17, 1969, 12, USNA, RG 490, box: Ghana-Guiana, 1962–66, "Ghana, 1967."
59. Baynham, *The Military and Politics in Nkrumah's Ghana,* 205–227.
60. *Evening News,* November 4, 1964, 5–6, Central Intelligence Agency, FOIA, Reference number F93–2022; Steve Bosworth to friends, October 15, 1963, NMNH, box 31, "Ghana Volunteer Information."
61. Packer, *Village of Waiting,* 256.
62. Jack Hogan interview.
63. *Peace Corps: A Statistical Profile,* July 1989 (Washington, 1989), 20–22.
64. Kwame Gyekye, *An Essay on African Philosophical Thought: The Akan Conceptual Scheme* (Cambridge, 1987), 132, 20.
65. Peace Corps volunteer Jerry Grondin, letter of April 24, 1981, PCL, collection on Ghana, 1981–1988.
66. Gyekye, *Essay on African Philosophical Thought,* 156, 158.
67. John Seely, "A Year of Voluntary Service Overseas," September 6 (c. 1960), courtesy of Mora Dickson.
68. "Evaluation Report: Ghana VIII (1968), 66–01–06," April 30, 1968, USNA, RG 490, box: Ghana-Guiana, 1962–1966, "Completion of Service Conference."
69. Mike Tidwell, "I Had a Hero," in *To Touch the World,* 87.

70. Harriet Lancaster interview.
71. Peters, *Tilting at Windmills*, 123.
72. For an account of the imagery that served as most Americans' introduction to the Third World, see Catherine Lutz and Jane Collins, *Reading National Geographic* (Chicago: University of Chicago Press, 1993).
73. George Carter interview. For a list of "weird African maladies" see ex-PCV Alex Newton's *West Africa: A Travel Survival Kit*, 72.
74. Tim Wilkinson Correspondence, Zaire, 1984–85, JFKL, RPCV, box 27, letters 16 and 18.
75. Tom Livingston to "Washington Group," from Dodowa, Ghana, January 10, 1962, NMNH, box 31, "Ghana Volunteer Information."
76. Author's telephone conversation with John Demos, June 7, 1996.
77. George Carter to Padraic Kennedy and John Alexander, July 3, 1962, NMNH, box 31, "Ghana Volunteer Information."
78. Rice, *Bold Experiment*, 182–183.
79. George Carter interview.
80. Evaluation Report, 67-02-06, July 22, 1969, USNA, RG 490, box: Ghana-Guiana, 1962–1966, "Completion of Service Conference Report." See also "Completion of Service Conference Report for Ghana II, 62-01-06, 1964."
81. Evaluation Report, 67-02-06, July 22, 1969, USNA, RG 490, box: Ghana-Guiana, 1962–1966, "Completion of Service Conference Report."
82. Report by Joseph C. Kennedy, February 17, 1967, USNA, RG 490, box: Ghana-Guiana, 1962–1966, "Ghana, 1967."
83. Completion of Service Conference Report for Ghana II, 62-01-06, 1964, USNA, RG 490, box: Ghana-Guiana, 1962–1966.
84. Evaluation Report, 66-01-06, April 30, 1968, USNA, RG 490, box: Ghana-Guiana, 1962–1966, "Completion of Service Conference Report: Ghana VIII."
85. Evaluation Report, 67-02-06, July 22, 1969, USNA, RG 490, box: Ghana-Guiana, 1962–1966, "Completion of Service Conference Report."
86. Dickson, *A Chance to Serve*, 95.
87. Completion of Service Conference Report: Ghana II, 62-01-06, 1964, USNA, RG 490, box: Ghana-Guiana, 1962–1966.
88. "Ghana," by John Demos (undated, c. 1962), NMNH, box 31, "Ghana Volunteer Information."
89. Evaluation Report, 67-02-06, July 22, 1969, USNA, RG 490, box: Ghana-Guiana, 1962–1966, "Completion of Service Conference Report."
90. Tom Hebert, "Shakespeare in Calabar," in *To Touch the World*, 62; Georgi Shine to Padraic Kennedy, May 8, 1962, NMNH, box 31, "Ghana Volunteer Information."
91. Newton, *West Africa*, 291–292.
92. Opon quoted in Ayi-Bonte, *Thirty Years*, 6–7.

93. Numbers drawn from Ayi-Bonte, *Thirty Years,* 14–15, 39, and "United States Peace Corps Ghana Briefing Paper," October 21, 1994, courtesy of Harriet Lancaster.

94. Interview with Patricia Garvey, January 19, 1995, Accra.

95. Interview, Frank Essien, deputy director for secondary teaching, 20 January 1995, Accra.

96. "Address of Alex Tettey-Enyo at the Opening of an In-service Training Workshop for U.S. Peace Corps," January 9, 1995, copy courtesy of Harriet Lancaster.

97. May, "Passing the Torch," 290–291.

98. Confidential Report of William McWhinney to the Executive Committee of the Board, May 30, 1963, CNA, vol. 96, "Board Meetings, 1963."

99. Schwarz, *What You Can Do,* 31.

100. Report by Joseph C. Kennedy, February 17, 1967, USNA, RG 490, box: Ghana-Guiana, 1962–1966, "Ghana, 1967."

101. "VSO-Ghana Orientation Course, January 15–24, 1995," provided by VSO Ghana office, Accra.

102. Thomsen, *Living Poor,* 6.

103. Report by Alan Cranston, February 18, 1966, USNA, RG 490, box: Ghana-Guiana, 1962–1966, "Ghana, 1966."

104. *Canadian Geographical Journal,* 73 no. 4 (October 1966), 139.

105. Smillie, *Land of Lost Content,* 36, 297. Information on CUSO T-shirts provided by Ian Smillie, who wore one. Interview, Ian Smillie, May 21, 1993, Ottawa.

106. McWhinney and Godfrey, *Man Deserves Man,* 22.

107. Personal recollections of J. F. Leddy, May 16, 1981, 8–10, SP, "The New Jerusalem."

108. Godfrey in McWhinney and Godfrey, *Man Deserves Man,* 415.

109. Address by Alex Tettey-Enyo to U.S. Peace Corps volunteers, January 9, 1995, text courtesy of Harriet Lancaster.

110. Amin, *The Peace Corps in Cameroon,* 111, 121–123.

111. Cameroonian quoted in ibid., 160.

112. Interview, Alex Tettey-Enyo, Ministry of Education, January 20, 1995, Accra.

113. K. B. Asante interview.

114. Kojo Botsio interview.

115. Quote from K. B. Asante interview.

116. Agyeman-Badu, "The Attitude of African Nations," 182, 226.

7. Slippery Slopes

1. Lyndon Johnson's letter to Congress transmitting the Sixth Annual Report of the Peace Corps, LBJL, WHCF, Subject file, box 146, FG 105–6,

3/1/68—. Johnson resignation quote from *Public Papers of the Presidents of the United States: Lyndon B. Johnson,* 1968–69, book 1 (Washington, D.C., 1970), 476. Ad copy courtesy of Young & Rubicam, Inc.

2. Jonathan Shay, *Achilles in Vietnam: Combat Trauma and the Undoing of Character* (New York, 1995), 127, 168, and all of chap. 1, "Betrayal of 'What's Right.'"

3. Lyndon Johnson to Sargent Shriver, November 21, 1963, and November 29, 1963, LBJL, WHCF, Subject File, box 144, FG105–6, Peace Corps, 11/22/63–1/4/64.

4. Paul Conkin, *Big Daddy from the Pedernales: Lyndon Baines Johnson* (Boston, 1986), 51–53.

5. Wofford, *Of Kennedys,* 332; see also 288.

6. Lyndon Johnson, letter to Congress transmitting the Fourth Annual Report of the Peace Corps, March 14, 1966, LBJL, WHCF, Subject File, box 145, FG105–6, Peace Corps, 3/1/66–3/31/67, 2 of 2 files.

7. Oral history, Richard Nelson, vol. 1, 4, LBJL.

8. Bill Moyers interview.

9. Lyndon Johnson to Sargent Shriver, December 2, 1963, LBJL, WHCF, Subject File, box 144, FG105–6, Peace Corps, 11/22/63–1/4/64.

10. Johnson to all Peace Corps volunteers, Department of State telegram, December 3, 1963, LBJL, WHCF, Subject File, box 144, FG105–6, Peace Corps, 11/22/63–1/4/64.

11. Lyndon Johnson to Speaker of the House John McCormack, January 1, 1964, LBJL, WHCF, Subject File, box 144, FG105–6, Peace Corps, 1/5/64–8/19/64.

12. Bill Moyers to the President, December 11, 1963, and Lyndon Johnson to the Speaker of the House of Representatives, May 18, 1964, LBJL, WHCF, Subject File, box 144, FG105–6, Peace Corps, files for 11/22/63–1/4/64 and 1/5/64–8/19/64.

13. Lyndon Johnson to Heads of all Executive Departments and Agencies," May 16, 1964, and Padraic Kennedy to Peace Corps Volunteers, May 1964, LBJL, WHCF, Subject File, box 144, FG105–6, Peace Corps, 1/5/64–8/19/64. Also see Wofford, *Of Kennedys,* 300.

14. Statistics from Memo for the President from John Macy, U.S. Civil Service Commission, August 9, 1965, LBJL, WHCF, Subject File, box 145, FG105–6, Peace Corps, 12/17/64–10/6/65.

15. T. Zane Reeves, *The Politics of the Peace Corps and VISTA* (Tuscaloosa, 1988), 27.

16. Tom Cronin to Bill Moyers, November 7, 1966, LBJL, WHCF, Subject File, box 8, Peace Corps 5, 8/27/66–9/30/67.

17. Benjamin Pearse, "Volunteers to America," *American Education* (July–August 1968), 22–25.

18. Shriver, *Point of the Lance,* 49.

19. Wofford, *Of Kennedys,* 299.
20. General Staff Meeting, comments of John Kenneth Galbraith, January 18, 1965, LBJL, Papers of Richard Goodwin, box 27, "Peace Corps miscellania."
21. Hugh Heclo, "The Sixties' False Dawn: Awakenings, Movements, and Postmodern Policy-making," *Journal of Policy History,* 8, no. 1 (1996), 50.
22. Sargent Shriver to Lyndon Johnson, November 12, 1965, LBJL, WHCF, Subject File, box 145, FG105–6, Peace Corps, 10/7/65–3/10/66.
23. Warren Wiggins interview; "A Question of Values," speech at Hanover College, April 4, 1966, copy courtesy of Warren Wiggins.
24. "The Peace Corps: A Revolutionary Force," Frank Mankiewicz, Peace Corps Discussion Paper, copy courtesy of Frank Mankiewicz. Also see Cowan, *The Making of an Un-American,* 82–83.
25. Cowan, *The Making of an Un-American,* 80; Sargent Shriver to Lyndon Johnson, November 12, 1965, LBJL, WHCF, Subject File, box 145, FG105–6, Peace Corps, 10/7/65–3/10/66.
26. Ashabranner, *A Moment in History,* 217–224.
27. Ibid., 196; Report on the Peace Corps by the Planning Commission of India, July 28, 1965, 8–9, LBJL, Papers of Brent Ashabranner, box 1, "Correspondence, Peace Corps, 1965–69."
28. Weekly Report of Sargent Shriver to Lyndon Johnson, June 8, 1964, regarding Nigeria, LBJL, WHCF, Confidential File, Peace Corps 1963–64; Peace Corps Sixth Annual Report to Congress, 29, regarding Colombia, LBJL, WHCF, Subject File, box 145, FG 105–6, 4/1/67–2/29/68; and "The Peace Corps—How Minorities View It," quote from Minister of Botswana on back cover, in LBJL, Ashabranner Papers, box 2, "The Peace Corps Color Problem."
29. "Overseas Evaluation—Brazil," August 17, 1965, 63, USNA, RG 490, box 1, "Brazil, 1965."
30. Cowan, *The Making of an Un-American,* 71; Bill Moyers interview; Thomas Page to Bill Moyers, October 15, 1965, LBJL, WHCF, Subject File, box 145, FG 105–6, 10/7/65–3/10/66.
31. Andrew Kopkind, *The New Statesman,* February 11, 1966, 185; Dickson, *A Chance to Serve,* 133.
32. Kennedy and Johnson in Leuchtenburg, *A Troubled Feast,* 137.
33. Frank Mankiewicz interview; Wofford, *Of Kennedys,* 293–294; interview, Richard Boone, February 6, 1997, Santa Barbara, California.
34. Daniel Patrick Moynihan, *Maximum Feasible Misunderstanding: Community Action in the War on Poverty* (New York, 1969), 87; Richard Boone interview.
35. Syracuse mayor William Walsh in Allen Matusow, *The Unraveling of America: A History of Liberalism in the 1960s* (New York, 1984), 248.
36. Frank Mankiewicz, oral history, vol. 1, 32, LBJL.
37. Leonard Chazen, *Yale Law Journal,* quoted in Moynihan, *Maximum Feasible Misunderstanding.*

38. Neil Betten and Michael Austin, *The Roots of Community Organizing, 1917–1939* (Philadelphia, 1990), 155.

39. Matusow, *Unraveling*, 125.

40. Frank Mankiewicz, oral history, vol. 1, 30, LBJL.

41. Moynihan, *Maximum Feasible Misunderstanding*, 98.

42. General Staff Meeting, comments of John Kenneth Galbraith, January 18, 1965, LBJL, Papers of Richard Goodwin, box 27, "Peace Corps miscellania."

43. Richard Boone interview.

44. Shriver, *Point of the Lance*, 5 and 6.

45. Wofford, *Of Kennedys*, 320.

46. Ibid., 287.

47. See Moynihan, *Maximum Feasible Misunderstanding*, 99; Matusow, *Unraveling*, 251, 255–262.

48. Bruce Schulman, *Lyndon B. Johnson and American Liberalism* (Boston, 1995), 99–101, 190–191.

49. William Kelly, oral history, vol. 1, 28, 31, LBJL.

50. Moynihan, *Maximum Feasible Misunderstanding*, 141–142.

51. Ashabranner, *A Moment in History*, 216; Lowther and Lucas, *Keeping Kennedy's Promise*, 8–13.

52. Certificate of appreciation for Sargent Shriver, LBJL, WHCF, Subject File, box 145, FG 105–6, 10/7/65–3/10/66.

53. Moynihan quoted in letter to John Erhlichman, April 22, 1969, USNA, NP, WHCF, FG-11–6, box 12, "Peace Corps, 1/6/69–12/25/69, 1 of 2."

54. Frank Mankiewicz, oral history, vol. 1, 45, and vol. 2, 4, LBJL.

55. Kirby Jones quoted by Sargent Shriver in report to Lyndon Johnson, June 1, 1965, LBJL, WHCF, CF, box 129, Peace Corps, 1965.

56. Memo from Brent Ashabranner to all India PC volunteers, November 16, 1965, LBJL, Ashabranner Papers, box 1, "Correspondence, PC, 1965–69."

57. See Kirby Jones interview in Schwarz, *What You Can Do*, 104, and the "Letter from 800 Returned PCVs to Lyndon Johnson," March 6, 1967, LBJL, WHCF, box 147, FG 105–6, 10/1/65–2/29/68.

58. Bruce Murray and Jack Vaughn in Schwarz, *What You Can Do*, 106, 108.

59. Schwarz, *What You Can Do*, 109.

60. Ibid., 110–111.

61. Rice, *Twenty Years of Peace Corps*, 27, 41.

62. "Background Briefing" by Jack Vaughn, November 26, 1968, Off the Record, LBJL, Cabinet Papers, box 17, "Cabinet Review: The Peace Corps, Department of State."

63. Quote from James Jouppi, "A Journey to Nakorn Panome," 26, JFKL, RPCV, box 12. Also see Joseph Blatchford to Peter Flanigan, March 25, 1970, USNA, NP, WHCF, PC 5, box 3, "Peace Corps Program, 1/20/69–12/31/70.

64. Tom McGinley in Schwarz, *What You Can Do*, 113.

65. "Memorandum for the Record," Joseph Blatchford to Henry Kissinger, Janu-

ary 7, 1970, USNA, NP, WHCF, PC 5, box 3, "Peace Corps Program, 1/20/69–12/31/70."

66. Song from author's conversation with Jonathan Coulter (British Overseas Development Administration), Accra, Ghana, January 19, 1995; James Jouppi, "A Journey to Nakorn Panome," 26, JFKL, RPCV, box 12.

67. Quotes taken from Schwarz, *What You Can Do*, 113, 118.

68. Ibid., 123.

69. Robert Amey to Lyndon Johnson, March 21, 1968, LBJL, WHCF, Subject File, box 8, PC 5, 5/27/66—; Bob Anderson to Richard Nixon, October 27, 1970, USNA, NP, WHCF, FG 11-6, box 12, "Peace Corps, 1/7/69–12/31/70."

70. Louis Harris Poll, "A Summary of College Seniors and the Peace Corps, 1969," in USNA, NP, WHSF, John Ehrlichman, box 33, 269 (Peace Corps, 1 of 2).

71. Robert Greenway to Brent Ashabranner, February 21, 1968, 2, LBJL, Ashabranner, box 2, "The Shadow of Vietnam."

72. Godfrey in McWhinney and Godfrey, *Man Deserves Man*, 423.

73. Johnson speech in *Major Problems in American Foreign Policy,* vol. 2, 4th ed., ed. Thomas Paterson (Lexington, Mass., 1995), 542.

74. Johnson quoted in *Newsweek,* October 28, 1996, 62.

75. "Position Paper of the Student Non-Violent Coordinating Committee (1966)," in *A History of Our Time,* 3rd ed., ed. William H. Chafe and Harvard Sitkoff (New York, 1991), 200.

76. Bergthold and McClelland, *The Impact of Peace Corps,* 148–149; Smillie, *Land of Lost Content,* 125.

77. Bergthold and McClelland, *The Impact of Peace Corps,* 149.

78. Glyn Roberts, *Questioning Development* (Paris, n.d., c. 1973), 16, 27–28.

79. André Gunder Frank, "The Development of Underdevelopment," in *Promise of Development: Theories of Change in Latin America,* ed. Peter Klarén and Thomas Bossert (Boulder, 1986), 120.

80. CRV quoted in Schwarz, *What You Can Do*, 132.

81. Smillie, *Land of Lost Content,* 111, 113; David Beer to Irving Greenberg, December 16, 1969, CNA, CUSO, vol. 104, "Special Committees—Committee on Aims and Objectives, 1969–70."

82. Arthur Wild, Journal 2, March 11, 1973, 167, NMNH, Arthur Wild Papers; article by Peggy Buckley, February 1973, SP, CUSO Forum.

8. Under Attack

1. Epigraphs from Schwarz, *What You Can Do*, 124, 134. Alexander Butterfield to Harry Flemming, February 25, 1969, USNA, NP, WHCF, FG-11-6, box 12, 1/6/69–12/25/69, 1 of 2.

2. "Position Paper on the Peace Corps," September 15, 1969, LBJL, Ashabranner Papers, box 2, "The Struggle to Keep the PC out of Politics."

3. Schwarz, *What You Can Do,* 127–128.

4. CRV quoted in ibid., 128.

5. Malaysian Volunteers to Richard Nixon, September 15, 1970, USNA, NP, WHCF, PC 5, box 3, 1/20/69–12/31/70.

6. Interview, Joseph Blatchford, December 6, 1993, Washington, D.C.

7. Peter Flanigan to Darrell Trent, October 31, 1969, USNA, NP, WHCF, FG-11-6 box 12, 1/6/69–12/25/69, 1 of 2; and Commentary of the Peace Corps on "Organization of a National Citizen Action Agency," February 2, 1971, USNA, NP, Blatchford Papers, box 1, "National Volunteer Agency, 1969–71 (ACTION)." See Ashabranner, *A Moment in History,* 292, and Searles, *Peace Corps Experience,* 23–25.

8. Joseph Blatchford to John Erhlichman, USNA, NP, WHSF, John Erhlichman, box 33, "Peace Corps in Micronesia."

9. Agnew in *The National Experience,* vol. 2, 5th ed., John Blum et al. (New York, 1981), 859; Joseph Blatchford interview.

10. Joseph Blatchford interview.

11. Schwarz, *What You Can Do,* 160.

12. Background Briefing of the Cabinet by Jack Vaughn, November 26, 1968, LBJL, Cabinet Papers, box 17, file: "Cabinet Review: The Peace Corps, Department of State."

13. Joseph Blatchford to Henry Kissinger, January 2, 1970, USNA, NP, WHCF, PC 5, box 3, "Peace Corps Program, 1/20/69–12/31/70"; Joseph Blatchford to John Erhlichman, May 3, 1969, and Alexander Butterfield to Henry Kissinger, June 2, 1969, USNA, NP, WHCF, FG-11-6, box 12, 1/6/69–12/25/69; Donald Rumsfield to John Erhlichman, November 9, 1970, USNA, NP, Blatchford Papers, box 1, "National Volunteer Agency, 1969–71."

14. Joseph Blatchford interview.

15. Searles, *Peace Corps Experience,* 77–80.

16. Arthur Wild, Journal 1, September 14 and 27, 1971, and October 30, 1971, 19–20, 24, 30; Journal 2, January 22, 1973, 143, NMNH.

17. Arthur Wild, Journal 1, October 30, 1971, 29, and Journal 2, February 8, 1973, 153, NMNH.

18. Joseph Blatchford to Arthur Hartman, undated (c. April 1970), USNA, NP, Blatchford Papers, box 1, "Correspondence, 1969–71"; Nixon quoted in LaFeber, *The American Age,* 605.

19. Joseph Blatchford to All Country Directors, May 19, 1969, USNA, NP, Blatchford Papers, box 1, "Correspondence, 1969–71."

20. Searles, *Peace Corps Experience,* 82 and 85.

21. Blatchford advocated lowering the voting age to eighteen to be more fair

and "change the political process." CBS Morning News, June 4, 1970. Blatchford quote of Camus in letter to Nixon, December 24, 1969, USNA, NP, WHCF, FG-11-6, box 12, 1/6/69–12/25/69.

22. Memorandum for the President's File, September 11, 1969, meeting of Richard Nixon, Joseph Blatchford, John Erhlichman, and Richard Allen, USNA, NP, WHSF, John Erhlichman, box 33, 269 (Peace Corps, 1 of 2).

23. Lamar Alexander to Bryce Harlow, March 26, 1970, USNA, NP, WHCF, FG-11-6, box 12, Peace Corps, 1/1/71—6/30/71.

24. Pat Buchanan to Richard Nixon, February 20, 1970, USNA, NP, WHCF, PC 5, box 3, Peace Corps, 1/20/69–12/31/70.

25. John R. Brown to Ehrlichman and Kissinger, March 19, 1970, in *Richard Nixon's Secret Files,* ed. Bruce Oudes (New York, 1989), 109.

26. Schwarz, *What You Can Do,* 133–134; *Washington Post,* May 9, 1970.

27. Joseph Blatchford interview. See also Schwarz, *What You Can Do,* 134, for Haldeman quote on busting the Peace Corps.

28. H. R. Haldeman, "Talking Paper—Political," July 25, 1970, and "Talking Paper, Re: Peace Corps and VISTA," July 13, 1970, USNA, NP, WHSF, SMOF, H. R. Haldeman, box 152, Talking Papers, 1970.

29. H. R. Haldeman, "Talking Paper, Re: Peace Corps and VISTA," July 13, 1970, USNA, NP, WHSF, SMOF, H. R. Haldeman, box 152, Talking Papers, 1970.

30. H. R. Haldeman, July 12, 1970, *The Haldeman Diaries: Inside the Nixon White House* (New York, 1994), 181.

31. Nixon in Schwarz, *What You Can Do,* 161.

32. Joseph Blatchford to John Ehrlichman, January 28, 1971, USNA, NP, Blatchford, box 1, National Volunteer Agency, 1969–71 (ACTION).

33. Passman in Ashabranner, *A Moment in History,* 305–306, and in the *Boston Globe,* January 8, 1972.

34. Blatchford quote from telephone conversation, November 18, 1996; also see Reeves, *Politics of Peace Corps and Vista,* 55.

35. Otto Passman quoted by William Timmons to Henry Kissinger, January 24, 1972, USNA, NP, WHSF, SMOF, Haldeman, box 91, William Timmons.

36. *Boston Globe,* January 8, 1972. Also see Joseph Blatchford to All ACTION Staff, March 7 and March 10, 1972, USNA, NP, Blatchford, box 1, Joseph Blatchford Memo to All ACTION Staff, March 1972. Passman quote from Joseph Blatchford, telephone conversation, November 21, 1996.

37. Safire and Ambrose quotes from Stephen Ambrose, *Nixon,* vol. 3: *Ruin and Recovery, 1973–1990* (New York, 1991), 586.

38. Richard Nixon to Bob Haldeman, May 13, 1970, regarding the President's visit to the Memorial, reprinted in Oudes, *Nixon's Secret Files,* 132–133.

39. Ambrose, *Nixon,* vol. 3, 581, 589.

9. The Peace Corps Dilemma

1. PCV Margot James in Schwarz, *What You Can Do*, 60. Michael von Schenck quote from inside back cover of *Volunteer, ISVS, 1969*, copy provided courtesy of Mr. von Schenck.

2. Joseph Nocera, "Sam Brown and the Peace Corps: All Talk, No ACTION," *Washington Monthly*, 10 (September 1978), 40.

3. Ibid., 31, 37–38. Country director in Schwarz, *What You Can Do*, 183.

4. Payton in Schwarz, *What You Can Do*, 185.

5. "Allah plants the trees" quote from PCV Julia Earl in ibid., 251.

6. Loret Miller Ruppe in ibid., 198.

7. Ruppe quotes from "The Heiress Who Saved the Peace Corps," *New York Times Magazine* obituary, December 29, 1996; country director quoted in Schwarz, *What You Can Do*, 201.

8. Schwarz, *What You Can Do*, 200.

9. Ruppe in ibid., 203.

10. Memorandum, George Schultz and Loret Ruppe to Ronald Reagan, July 18, 1983, PCL, "Peace Corps and Foreign Policy."

11. Shriver in Searles, *Peace Corps Experience*, 166.

12. Heritage Foundation in Schwarz, *What You Can Do*, 200.

13. Schwarz, *What You Can Do*, 277.

14. "The New Peace Corps Steppes Out—in Kazakhstan," *Smithsonian*, 25, no. 5 (August 1994), 28, 31, 34.

15. Interview, Dick Bird, VSO, May 13, 1994, London.

16. Dick Bird interview; volunteer quoted in Adams, *Voluntary Service Overseas*, 122.

17. Interview, Lucien Cousin, May 17, 1994, Paris.

18. *VSO, Annual Report 1994* (London, 1994), 4.

19. Dick Bird interview; Alec Dickson speech in USNA, NP, Blatchford, box 2, "Reading."

20. Adams, *VSO*, 220.

21. Bill McWhinney in "Minutes of the Annual Meeting, Canadian University Service Overseas," October 22–23, 1964, SP; Paul Martin in Smillie, *Land of Lost Content*, 258.

22. Thomson quote in Smillie, *Land of Lost Content*, 100.

23. Ibid., 106, 111, 114.

24. *Ibid.*, 103, 309.

25. CUSO volunteer in ibid., 361.

26. Minutes, CUSO/SUCO Board of Directors Meeting, January 10, 1976, CNA, CUSO, vol. 10; Heclo, "The Sixties' False Dawn," 41.

27. Interview, Will Erath, May 19, 1994, The Hague.

28. Introductory address by J. P. Pronk at the Fifth Seminar on International Vol-

untary Service, November 5–9, 1973, Strasbourg, copy courtesy of Will Erath.

29. Interview, P. B. M. Knoope, director, SNV, May 19, 1994, The Hague. Also see SNV brochure, "The Many Facets of SNV," 1994.
30. Will Erath interview; see also Bert Barten interview.
31. Quotes from interviews with Ton Nijzink and P. B. M. Knoope.
32. American Embassy/Asunción to Secretary of State, May 1983, attached to Memorandum, George Schultz and Loret Ruppe to Ronald Reagan, July 18, 1983, PCL, Peace Corps and Foreign Policy."
33. *San Diego Union,* March 20, 1997, G-5.
34. Jack Hogan interview. See also *On the Right Track: SNV's Policy in the Nineties* (The Hague, 1993), 9.
35. Catherine de Loeper interview.
36. Ruppe in Schwarz, *What You Can Do,* 203.

10. Balancing Ideals and Self-Interest

1. Goodwin, *Remembering America,* 9. *New York Times* editorial, December 11, 1994, 14.
2. Godfrey Hodgson, "The Ideology of the Liberal Consensus," in Chafe and Sitkoff, *A History of Our Time,* 4th ed., 104.
3. Hunt, *Ideology and U.S. Foreign Policy,* 160, 176.
4. George F. Kennan, *American Diplomacy, 1900–1950* (Chicago, 1951), 87.
5. Niebuhr, *The Children of Light,* 40.
6. Charles Krauthammer, *Time,* May 17, 1993, 68.
7. *San Diego Union,* November 29, 1996, A-13.
8. Hunt, *Ideology and U.S. Foreign Policy,* 161; Robert Packenham, *Liberal America and the Third World: Political Development Ideas in Foreign Aid and Social Science* (Princeton, 1973), 112.
9. Charles F. Brannan to Sargent Shriver, December 10, 1962, JFKL, POF, box 85, "Peace Corps, 1/62–3/62;" *Look,* 30, no. 12 (June 15, 1966), 40; Moyers in Schwarz, *What You Can Do,* 203.
10. David Arnold, "Making a Difference," *Foreign Service Journal* (October 1995), 23. Other statistics provided by the Peace Corps Press Office.
11. Joe Serna, Jr., in *3/1/61,* 3, no. 4 (Winter 1996), 2.
12. Anet, *Pierre Ceresole,* 116.
13. Brandt, *People and Politics,* 93.
14. Camus in McWhinney and Godfrey, *Man Deserves Man,* 31.

Index